The ocean is generous in the giving,
but suffers greatly to be taken advantage of.
Shells removed from the sea;
See how soon their patterns fade.
Fish gasp and pant, as their lives ebb
with the water draining from their gills.
Coral dulls when parted from its liquid lifeline.

But I Shine.

The pressures of existence fall from my shoulders,
Self-conciousness dissipates:
The freedom in my limbs empowers me
With a desire to stretch the boundaries of my mind,
Which extend infinitesimally towards the horizon.
The ocean makes me gifts that I can never hope to repay.

By Scott Vincin.

Published by Liquid Addictions
2 Ibis St, Doncaster, Victoria 3108
www.liquidaddictions.com.au

Sub-edited by Amelia Church.
Designed by Pepper Publishing.
Printed by Shannon Books.
Distributed by Dennis Jones and Associates.
Logo Design by Martin Noakes

Front Cover. Troy Brooks. Pic. Hilton.
Back Cover. Pic. Scott Fisher.
Page 1. Pic. Nick Clark.

ISBN 0 646 35694 1
Index Included.

Introduction

Surfing is an escape, a time when thoughts of external pressures evaporate with the approaching waves. An opportunity to harmonise with forces greater than ourselves. It makes us aware of so many different aspects of our environment. We look to the trees to see which way they are swaying, praying for the offshore. The fullness of the moon reminds us of the approaching king tides. The first storms of Autumn signal the rising swell. Arriving at the carpark and gaping at the sight before you. An ocean alive with power and beauty. You can hardly pause to wax your board as you scramble into the water. Immersed. Alive. Invigorated.

But we become complacent, consumed by the comfortable patterns of urban living. Work, sleep and human realtionships constitute the focus of life. Swells come and go. The wind has no meaning. We lose a sense of coastal existence The memory of surfing recedes. It returns though. The vision. The light offshore breeze, the crisp, clean groundswell and an ocean so vast... The power to restore the soul. Waves are natural energy. An energy that encompasses the true spirit of living.

The reality began on a cold July morning. Heading out of Melbourne, towards the coast for a three month surf odyssey around this mighty land. This book was the focus of the trip, but then again the trip was a focus for the book. It was never going to be a glossy exposé of surfing greats around the country. That's not what I wanted. It's a culmination of talents that represents surfing's core. Photos of locals, stories of real characters that you meet on the road. Most importantly it is a travel guide for surfers, because surfers are travellers by force of circumstance. That is the beauty of surfing. We are all travellers, constantly exposing ourselves to new experiences.

This guide is my first foray into publishing, and hopefully not the last. It was put together with the help of friends and family. There was no big business pulling the strings or paying the bills. It was a passion to which I gave my soul. I hope this guide has fuelled your dream. The dream that sees you waking before sunrise and scampering to the ocean to reveal the magical gift before you. The dream of planning endless surf trips, then finally one day, doing it.

I hope you find the dream.

Chris Rennie

The Contributors

This guide would not have been possible without the help of many people. I hope I didn't forget anyone.

Amelia Church. Sub-Editor, guiding light and linguistics master. Without her guidance, attention to detail and love of language, this book wouldn't have been the same.

Contributing Writers.
Adrian Turner. THE CENTRAL COAST OF NSW. Adrian was just leaving for G-land when I asked him to write this section. Another surfing adventure in a list of so many. His art reflects the marine environment beautifully. A lifetime of experiences in surfing this coast are reflected in his section.

Ben Horvath. THE SOUTHERN BEACHES OF SYDNEY and extending to WOLLONGONG. His 23 years of surfing was invaluable in providing detailed and insightful information in this section. You can see Ben's work in Underground Surf, where he is currently the editor.

Matt Binns. From NEWCASTLE TO COFFS HARBOUR and KIAMA TO ULLADULLA. Matt jumped at the opportunity to get in the car and travel the familiar roads again. Making sure his memories of the waves he has spent years around haven't dulled. They hadn't.

James McIlvena. VICTORIA. Mexico was my first surf with James. We had just come from the bowels of South America, on our way through to Canada for a season of snowboarding. We talked about his years of travelling and exploring the coastline of Victoria. We had many passions in common. He offered to write this section out of a dedication to portray his state accurately and to assist a close friend.

Peter Court. THE SUNSHINE COAST. Having lived around Noosa Heads for 40 years has given him a fantastic knowledge of the waves in the area. Combined with this close associations with the local surfers provided a different perspective.

Sam Upston. TASMANIA. Sam leapt at the opportunity to write about his home State, as he has travelled extensively throughout the region. Sam reached national level in body boarding competitions, but prefers to surf now. His father is a well known identity in Tasmania and regularly writes the surf reports.

Scott Vincin. THE GOLD COAST TO BALLINA and SYDNEY'S NORTHERN BEACHES. I have worked and travelled with Scott for many years now. Firstly with Liquid Addictions then as co-editors of Freesurf Magazine. We have progressed similarly. Our first surfing adventures consisted of short weekend trips to the local breaks. It wasn't long though, before we were exploring the Mexican coastline and planning future travels. Scott followed his dream of becoming a pilot. Constantly flying over the Gold Coast and surrounding beaches as well as regularly surfing the breaks, gave him a unique understanding of the area. His passion for life is inspirational.

Contributing Photographers.

Hilton Dawe. Much of the exceptional water photography came from Hilton's lenses. He has a talent of shooting photos to create evocative images that stay with the reader forever. He also wrote the Angourie section.

Brett Stanley. The classic images of South Australia and some magic Victorian barrels were shot with his talented hands.

Nick Clark. One of the most beautiful shots of Winkipop I have ever seen.

Steve Ryan, Joli, Steve Conti, Glen Saltmarsh, Stroh, John Brumfield, Lynn Chambers, Jon Falconer-Brown, Scott Fisher, Bill Morris, Mark Newsham, Peter Simons, Emma Moroney and Jane Lewis.

Special Projects:

Dave Mitton / Madurah Graphics. Cartoonist and map designer. The unique designs of these maps are an intrinsic part of the guide. They portray a comical, yet deep understanding of surfing culture.

Martin Noakes. The Liquid Addictions logo was drawn, freehand, by Marti. His love of the ocean, surfing and drawing is portrayed in his work. The logo is the cornerstone of the business as it represents what we are trying to achieve.

Marti Carstairs / Rapture Productions. Without the aid of Marti and his machinery there would be blank pages where the photos should have been. A photographer at heart, Marti provided an artistic eye to the images throughout a long scanning process.

Alan Long. For his cyber skills with web design and generally anything technical.

Special Thanks

Jerome Tymms has been a close friend since childhood. Without his support this project would have been dramatically different. Nick Thomson was my travelling companion for the three month trip, providing comic relief. He was a great roadtripping partner and his words in this book are special. The Surfrider Foundation for their continued battle with polluters of the ocean. Tarn Spencer for the medical insight. Andrew Lowe for visualising the point of sale concept, Jan Gyrn for his exceptional deal making powers. Emma Moroney for some special images. My patient housemates and friends who offered their services without question.

Mum & Dad have always provided me with the inspiration to follow my heart and stick with what I believe no matter what. They have supported me unconditionally. The use of Dad's 4wd for three months was extraodianry by anyone's standards. Their patience with the whole project has touched me deeply. Without their support it would not have been possible to produce this guide.

Gratuitous self promotion time. Having edited several snowboarding publications and worked with Deep Magazine I then co-edited Freesurf Magazine. My life is based around a deep love of the coast and the ocean. This guide is my way of combining my passions with financial reality. I wanted to self publish this book as I knew it would test me to the limit.

Contents

Pic. Hilton

This Is Australia

It all began at....

Freshwater Beach will always remember that day in the Southern summer of 1915 when the great aquatic Hawaiian, Duke Kahanamoku, gave an amazing exhibition of wave riding with a solid surfboard modelled on the very type used by him in his native Hawaii. Over a period of time, while he stayed at the Boomerang Camp at Freshwater, the Duke fashioned a solid board from the local timbers, and it was with this board that he first introduced the Australian surfing community to the ancient craft of Hawaiian kings - the art of surfboard riding.

Out through the surf-break "The Duke" paddled, turned around and having paddled onto the face of a breaking wave, caught the wave back into the beach while standing tall on this newly carved timber surfboard. This exhibition of skill and grace captivated the imagination of all those present. If this were not enough, the Duke selected a young lady from the local crowd - one Miss Isabel Letham - to accompany him on his surfboard. While she lay forward on this surfboard, the Duke paddled out through the surf and then returned to the beach riding tandem.

In this event, young Isabel Letham became the first Australian to ride a surfboard in the Australian surf on this type of surfboard. Miss Letham continued to live in Freshwater Beach from those early years of the twentieth century, until recently, when she died during the Autumn of 1995. On this occasion, there was a gathering of the local community and in particular the Freshwater Boardriders Club and the Freshwater Surf Club.

The original newspaper clippings and photographs taken from those historic days in the Southern summer of 1915 are preserved in the newly refurbished Freshwater Surf Club. The first man to be taught the art of surfboard riding was one Claud West of the Freshwater Surf Club who went on in later days to become the very first Australian board riding champion. The surfboard fashioned by the Duke at the Boomerang Camp at Freshwater Beach was given to Claud West, and he later donated this historic board to the Freshwater Surf Life Saving Club where it is still proudly displayed in the north east corner of the club.

These heavy timber surfboards were still very much in use through the late 1930's and until the early 1940's, but were later replaced by the hollow plywood surfboards which were to become the base designs and forerunners of the "Mal's".

The custodians of the Freshwater Surf Life Saving Club have invested a great degree of care, skillful research and presentation concerning the foundational history of the club, they have made all this history accessible by means of old photographs and records which have been gracefully placed around the walls of the refurbished club house at Freshwater Beach.

For those who are interested in the earliest recorded surfing era in the history of Australia, a visit to the historic (and completely functional) Freshwater Surf Club is highly recommended whenever you happen to have a few hours to spare in Sydney.

Calling The Weather
By Scott Vincin

For a surfer, having a thorough knowledge of weather patterns, and the effect they have on your local break, is a handy skill to cultivate. And when you're on the road, that knowledge can mean the difference between blowing cash on petrol for no apparent purpose, and scoring prime waves. Learning to read the weather takes time and attention: the best place to start is at home. Surf one break long enough, and you develop an innate sense of when it's working.

When you're travelling in search of surf, one of the most important things is to have a map of the coastline you intend to cover. Any other information that comes your way, for example, wind or swell direction, can then be plotted onto the map, giving you a reasonably accurate representation of what's going on weatherwise. Synoptic charts are another useful tool, and are published in most daily newspapers. Points of equal atmospheric pressure are joined by lines, known as isobars, which indicate the presence of high and low pressure systems, which in themselves tell us what the wind is doing.

In Australia, the wind flows clockwise around a low, and counter-clockwise around a high, parallel to the isobars. The proximity of each isobar to its neighbour indicates the force of the wind - if the spacing between the isobars is close, the stronger the winds, and the further apart the isobars, the weaker the wind. Around a high pressure system, the air is sinking, and light winds and fine weather usually dominate. Low pressure systems are associated with rising air, cloudy or overcast conditions with the likelihood of showers or rain.

While Australia's southern latitudes score their best waves during the winter months, as the Roaring Forties winds sweep swell lines in unobstructed from Antarctica, the far north coast of NSW, and Queensland especially, fire during summer, due to cyclonic activity. Tropical cyclones form in a narrow latitudinal band, in the southern hemisphere, between approximately 5 degrees south and 15 degrees south, and occur when a highly localised and intense low pressure system moves over a warm ocean surface. Tropical cyclones that track over water provide the best waves, the longer fetch over which the swell travels allowing for cleaner lines to form. Cyclonic swells, coinciding with the right winds, are what Queensland surfers dream of.

While honing your awareness of what's happening in the oceans and atmosphere around you is necessary for predicting where the waves are, surf forecasting is also about utilising all the available sources. To this end, a number of phone, fax lines, and internet sites have been established which will aid you in the quest. The people behind the counter in surf shops are also an invaluable source of advice and information and are usually more than happy to have a yarn, and pass on a bit of local knowledge.

Good hunting

Web Sites.
www.realsurf.com.
www.pipelinz.com.
www.surferinfo.com.
www.geol.utas.edu.au/surf/swell.html

Fax Line.
1 902 935 266. This will give you a prediction of the swell in Australia for the next 36 hours.

Surfrider Foundation

Protecting the seas under the Southern Cross
by John Foss, Chairman- National Board Surfrider Foundation

Australia is the world's largest island with over 7,000 beaches and approximately 12,000 smaller islands in our waters.

Australia has one of the most diverse marine ecosystems in the world which includes over 4000 fish species, 166 shark species and 500 coral species. Our waters have 30 of the world's 59 types of seagrass, which are critical habitats for a diverse range of marine life, from western rock lobsters to green sea turtles and dugongs.

But our beautiful marine environments are under threat from human impact and pollution. In 1995 the Surfrider Foundation coordinated the State of the Surf (SOS) project, an on-going review of the documenting and assessing of human impacts on beaches around Australia. The report of this project titled, HUMAN IMPACT ON AUSTRALIAN BEACHES (Michael Legge-Wilkinson 1996) identified ocean outfalls and stormwater drains as being key sources of pollution threatening our marine and coastal eco-systems. 80% of discharges and emissions into the marine environment enter the seas from land. (Copies of the report can be ordered by contacting SURFRIDER FOUNDATION NATIONAL OFFICE).

Since 1995, in many cases, things have got worse around Australia, not better. Major sewage spills have polluted the waters of many of our most popular coastal towns and beaches. Stormwater pollution is putting more and more people in hospital. Run-off from creeks and rivers in Northern Queensland has severely decimated much of the coral reefs on the coastal fringe of the Great Barrier Reef and many fish species are in danger of becoming extinct due to over-fishing in many parts of Australia.

As Australia's largest community based coastal and marine environmental organisation the Surfrider Foundation is working hard in every State of Australia to fight the threats to our coastal and marine environments. With over twenty branches around the country, our members put in hundreds of hours of un-paid work each week trying to preserve and protect our delicate coastal environments for future generations to enjoy.

Ocean Outfalls - sewers in the surf
Ocean outfalls are a major source of ocean pollution. There are currently 141 public sewage outfalls discharging human effluent and industrial waste into the ocean around Australia.

The 141 outfalls have a combined discharge exceeding three billion litres per day. The largest ocean outfalls are in Sydney (Malabar Outfall - 430 million litres per day/North Head - Manly - 280 million litres per day/Bondi - 130 million litres per day) and Melbourne (Gunnamatta - 250 million litres per day).

Each year around 10,000 tonnes of phosphorus and 100,000 tonnes of nitrogen are discharged through sewage, much of which finds its way into the marine environment. Elevated nutrient levels may cause eutrophication, the excessive growth of algae, which depletes oxygen levels in the water and may suffocate marine organisms.

Nature seems to survive inspite of our actions.
Unless we want to be confronted by images such as these, we need to take action.

Heavy metals in industrial waste can work their way through the food chain and end up in much of the seafood we eat. A number of fisherman in coastal towns have become seriously ill after catching fish near ocean outfalls.

Australia is a desert continent We believe that the only way to treat sewage is to pump it onto the land and treat it through wetlands or high tech tertiary systems. The effluent can then be used for farming/irrigation/on pine plantations,etc. Pumping billions of litres of effluent into the ocean isn't helping anyone.

Stormwater Outlets - discharging dirt and disease into our oceans The HUMAN IMPACT report identified 383 beaches around Australia with stormwater pipes discharging to the beach and/or its lagoon.

54% of these beaches had litter evident in the vicinity of pipe discharge. The most common litter types evident were plastic bags, cigarette butts and food wrappers. Condoms and syringes were found at 10% of the beaches surveyed.

Urban runoff, whether collected or channelled through a stormwater system is not usually treated before discharge. Pollutants that can be inadvertently 'picked up' by urban run-off include:

Oil leakage from car engines and other sources; bacteria and nutrients from animal faeces (FACT: Each year 34,000 tonnes of dog faeces are washed into Port Phillip Bay, Melbourne); litter and debris from footpaths, gutters and roadways; heavy metals leeched from road surfaces and other sources; bacteria and nutrients from sewage overflows.

Recent studies indicate that urban run-off contributes to 37% of the world's ocean oil pollution. Many local councils have started to address many of the issues raised in the HUMAN IMPACTS report. The Surf Coast Shire in Victoria is currently piloting a 'Poop The Scoop' campaign where they encourage dog owners to scoop up their dogs faeces on the beach and take it home. Other councils are getting more actively involved by putting litter traps over stormwater drains to reduce litter going into the ocean.

On the Gold Coast, the Surfrider Foundation has been conducting water testing programs with schools to monitor the impact of stormwater on rivers and creeks which flow into the ocean.

Reserves, Reserves, Reserves, protecting our coast for the future.
Anyone who has ever travelled to Bells Beach in the last few years would have noticed a dramatic improvement in the health and state of the native vegetation. This is due to the hard work of many individuals in the Bells Beach Surfing Reserve, including Surfing Victoria and local environmental group Surfers Appreciating the Natural Environment who, for the last ten years, have worked hard to protect and preserve the delicate coastal heath through the Bells Beach Surfing Reserve.

Surfers and other visitors to the area have seen the benefits gained in the reserve by putting management of the area in the hands of surfers and local community environmental groups with an interest in enhancement and not exploitation.

During 1998 the Surfrider Foundation will be actively promoting throughout the country surfing reserves and marine protected areas as viable models for coastal management with the Bells Beach Surfing Reserve a shining example of what IS possible.

The SURFRIDER FOUNDATION is currently campaigning for marine protected areas at Bells Beach on Victoria's Surf Coast and in Queensland. Surfrider branches are lobbying for surfing reserves on South Stradbroke Island, at Voodoo Point near Cronulla and Crescent Head. Reserves offer the best chance we have to protect our delicate marine and coastal environments from pollution and coastal development.

There are SOLUTIONS to OCEAN POLLUTION
The Surfrider Foundation has been actively campaigning in all states for the phasing out of ocean outfalls. We have also been working in many states to raise public awareness of the impacts of stormwater through our Stormwater Taskforce. One of the positive initiatives of this task force has been the stencilling of drains with the message "DRAINS TO THE BEACH, PLEASE DO NOT LITTER". This helps to raise awareness of the direct link between stormwater drains and litter on our beaches.

In 1997 the Surfrider Foundation launched our KEEPERS OF THE COAST sticker campaign to emphasize the need for community groups and individuals to take an active interest in their stretch of coast. Surfriders 'Keepers of The Coast' campaign has developed a strong sense of 'ownership' with people for the coast. With ownership comes responsibility and with responsibility comes action.

Here are some handy hints on how YOU can help protect and preserve the environment:

- Don't put waste fats and oils down the sink. Collect them in a container and throw them out with the household garbage. Materials put down sinks and drains can end up in the ocean.
- Stick to paths and tracks when going to the beach. Walking over sanddunes or sensitive coastal vegetation adds the to loss of vegetation cover leading to erosion problems and loss of bio diversity,
- Take your rubbish home. Never leave rubbish at the beach and where possible take it home for recycling,
- Scoop the poop. Dog turds on beaches can be a problem at many beaches. If you must take your dog to the beach ensure you clean up afterwards with a shovel and bag,
- Dispose of cigarette butts properly. Each day thousands of cigarette butts get dropped on beaches and washed into the ocean via stormwater drains.
- Take cans rather than glass bottles to the beach. Broken bottles can pose a major health risk for people walking along the beach.
- Pick up litter when you see it. If every surfer picked up one piece of litter every time they left the surf our beaches would be cleaner and greener,
- Join the Surfrider Foundation. When you become a member of the Surfrider Foundation you join a national organisation which is working to educate and inform government, business and the community about our need to protect and preserve the ocean.

If you would like to find out more about the Surfrider Foundation contact the National Office on 0418 855 870 or write to us c/o P.O. Box 1441 - DEE WHY- NSW- 2099.

There is a SURFRIDER FOUNDATION BRANCH near you, so check us up by tapping into the following web-sites for more SURFRIDER INFORMATION. Our United States branches also provide a valuable resource for people wanting to find out more about how to fix up the problem of ocean pollution.

VICTORIA
http://www.melbourne.net/surfriders/

COFFS HARBOUR
http://www.midcoast.com.au/users/surfrider/

GOLD COAST
http: // www.wetpaper.com.au/SFGC/SFGCpage

BYRON BAY
http: // om.corn.au/surfhey/surfriders/home.html

At Surfrider we have a saying: 'RESPECT THE BEACH'. Look after the beach, keep our ocean clean and they will look after you and give you much pleasure and enjoyment in the surf and sun.

I welcome all readers to join Surfrider and become a part of the solution, not the problem.

The Journey

Travelling Companions for extended roadtrips

Avoid Travellers like this
Pic. Emma Moroney

Selecting roadtripping partners is like buying new underpants, you really want to be sure that you know something about them before they get too close. Consider seriously the fact that you will be spending 24 hours a day, seven days a week with these people, with little chance for respite. This could be a great life experience that you will all cherish, or....... understanding everyone's goal is essential as this is always the sticking point. For example: Do you want to go on a wave hunting mission, that will be complete with pre-dawn paddles and sleeping on cold sand, all in the name of scoring epic waves? Or is it more along the lines of, catching a few waves, mixed with daiquiris and tango dancing at the local clubs and spending nights in the luxurious Flag Inns. Of course there are compromises in between. Also it is important that everyone appreciates the same sense of humour. There is nothing worse then having to politely chuckle at crap jokes that you know will drive you slowly insane over the next two thousand kilometres. Of course there are no guarantees, as people tend to show their real colours in heavy situations. It is always advisable to spend time with your proposed companions prior to your departure. A couple of day trips, even a weekender is a help. The other decision to make is whether to take another vehicle. If you are in the unfortunate position of having to provide the mode of transport, make sure your car is of lesser value than your compatriot's. For several reasons. If you have a brand new 4wd, you will undoubtedly be towing some poor blighter out of a bog, or driving into town for spare parts when the old Holden that you are travelling with has just seized the engine. All this while there are waves to be ridden. Also if your 'new' car does have problems, you will be forced to order the parts from major capital cities, taking a week or more. Having said that, there is no finer way to travel the country, than in a new 4wd. The last piece of advice (a sort of get-out clause) to explain to your friends the following; There may be opportunities that arise that might only relate to one member of the group, and (that you think) it's fine to follow separate paths. The group should travel with that in mind. Because you never know what will happen when you start travelling.

Buying the car

This is often your most important purchase as it will provide you with an opportunity to hunt down those elusive waves. Many vehicles also double as temporary accomodation. The following is a guide that may help you out.
- Holdens and Fords are usually a pretty safe bet. Parts are readily available and almost all mechanics have owned one at some stage. The earlier models are still very affordable and are generally reliable. You could expect to pay between $2,000 to $3,000 for this type of car. Of course there are cheaper about, so keep an eye out.
- Pay the $80 odd dollars to have your potential 'new' car checked out by a professional. There are many companies that specialize in on-site inspections. These

handymen have all the latest equipment and will give you an accurate assessment of the car's potential. ie. Will it make it to Perth? Worth doing as it will save you so much in the long run.

- Check the Youth Hostels for 4 sale signs, as these cars often come with heaps of extras. The seller is usually heading back overseas and can't carry all the little utensils, pots and pans etc in their backpack. They are usually in a hurry to sell, which often means a reduced price.
- Check the Motor Trader or the Trading Post for the most comprehensive list of second hand cars.
- There are schemes where a company will buy back a car at a predetermined price. Call Car Connection on (03) 5473 4469.
- The larger universities are also a great place to find bargain cars for sale.

The old Holden, always great value.

You must be realistic regarding what you want your car to do as the crack in a fanbelt can destroy an otherwise amazing experience. Number one rule is: get the car checked out.

Roadkill Alert

There are more than just sharks and giant waves to contend with on your surf odyssey around this country. Driving can be an extreme hazard, especially in open wilderness areas. Australia has a myriad of animals that can appear unexpectedly on the road, threatening to end your trip prematurely or worse...... The following is a rough guide of the road hazards that you will encounter on your travels. There are of course ways to prevent accidents that rely on common sense. Travelling at night greatly increases your chances of hitting an animal. Although it is fine to say, "don't drive at night", the reality is quite different. Many of us have jumped in the car late at night in order to be early in some far off place. This can seem the only way to do it and sometimes is, so we have highlighted the most notorious areas of road along the coast and what you might expect to see. I have devised a five point rating to describe the seriousness of the hazard, as tabled below.

1. Keep your wits about you, but this isn't a serious risk area. Night time is the only real worry in this region.
2. You will start to see more animals in these areas that often like to bask in the glow of oncoming headlights. Be careful at sunrise and sunset.
3. These are fenced areas that provide some protection from the animals but there is often tell tale roadkill.
4. You will see large mobs of kangaroos roaming free, often tempting fate on the roads. There are no fences here but also no cows, which is your only reprieve. If you must drive at night, take a break at sunset.
5. There is no question that you will see numerous animals on the road, ranging from giant kangaroos to cattle. They are attracted by your vehicle and often lunge forward in an attempt to hit your car. They don't often win. It is a serious risk driving at night and extreme caution should be taken. Infact we would recommend that you DO NOT drive at sunrise or sunset. There are no fences to protect the animals from traffic or vice versa.

Victoria.

Cape Howe to Kilcunda / Category 3. High risk areas are Mallacoota to Orbost.
Wilson's Promontory is renowned for wombats which can cause a much damage.
Phillip Island / Category 1.
The Mornington Peninsula. Pretty safe really.
Point Lonsdale to Apollo Bay. No real worry here.
Cape Otway to Portland / Category 1.

South Australia

Port MacDonnell to Adelaide / Category 2
Kangaroo Island / Category 4. The name
says it all.
The Yorke Peninsula / Category 3. There
are so many kangaroos which will gather
around you in the campsites.
The Eyre Peninsula / Category 4. The
high risk areas are between Port Lincoln
and Streaky Bay. From Ceduna to
Esperance (WA) is notorious for
wandering animals. The Nullarbor has
built a reputation for roadkill.

Western Australia.
Esperance to Walpole / Category 3. Be
careful around Hopetown, Albany and Walpole. These places could even go into a
category 4.
Augusta to Perth / Category 1. Around Yallingup can be a little more dangerous.
Perth to Broome / Category 5. The worst areas are from Carnarvon to Exmouth. There
will be times when it is impossible to drive more than 50kms per hour as the
kangaroos are so thick. Cattle start to come into the equation here which requires some
serious negotiation. It is recommended that you don't drive at night!

Queensland
This whole area is very safe as no sane animal would go within hopping distance of
the Sunshine or Gold Coast.

New South Wales.
The northern border to Coffs Harbour / Category 2. Your main areas of concern would
be between Ballina and Grafton.
Coffs Harbour to Sydney / Category 1. The only area that could be of concern is
around Forster. South from here it is a major highway the whole distance.
Sydney to the border / Category 2. From Narooma south is where you are most likely
to encounter animals.

Tasmania

North Coast. You are pretty safe here.

West Coast / Category 2. From the limited access that you have, these roads can be alive with activity. Some of the roads are gravel, so it is difficult to travel quickly, hence the reduction in danger.

South & East Coast / Category 1. Not too much to worry about. Take care around Southport.

Prevention is best!

There are ways to reduce the risk of hitting any animal. A large set of driving lights are always advisable as this gives you far greater vision. You can also buy little whistles that attach on to your car. These whistles emit a high frequency sound that is supposed to repel kangaroos. The best way, of course, is not to drive too fast. I know the temptation of hurrying to get there, to catch the last beers at the pub before the early session in the morning, but.... If you keep your speed down it will increase your chance of stopping safely. Of course the other factor is your energy levels. When you get that 'White Line Fever' it really is time to stop, as nothing is worth risking another day in the surf.

4WD Tips

One of the best ways to see Australia is by car. Although there are a myriad of different ways to trek around the 30,000 odd kms of coastline, there is no comparison to a 4wd. This allows you to explore some of the most pristine beaches in the world. Imagine a three hour drive along the beach, watching classic A frames breaking along the stretch, cormorants and herons racing you to a protected point break. Here you stay a week, surfing long lefthanders, and catching your dinner on the rising tide. Not a soul in sight, the only sounds are natural, with the occasional primal scream of delight when you emerge from another barrel. This is what lies in store for adventurers who are keen for this sort of mission.

Victoria is the only State that doesn't allow vehicles onto its beaches, which is understandable, as so much of the coast is surrounded by towering cliff faces. Although there is limited access in certain parts, not that you read it here!! The only way to drive on these beaches is with a 4wd or in some instances a VW Combi van (see explanation). Having said this, I have done several long trips in old Holdens and other prehistoric cars and know the exhilaration of finding uncrowded waves throughout Australia, but a 4wd is your ultimate accessory.

There are several important factors when preparing your car for the rigours of driving to some of the more remote beaches that Australia has to offer.

- Tyres are your best friend. These rubber shoes for the car will provide the difference between cruising along the beaches with satisfied, calm-looking faces, and the sheer terror of digging your car out before it is grasped by the incoming tide. There is a large range of all terrain tyres which seem to be suitable for the varied terrain that you WILL encounter. If your tyres are, for example, too sand orientated (very wide and deep tread), you will find that driving on rough and rutted tracks will often cause the tyres to puncture on tree roots or sharp rock. Alternatively, if the tyres are too road orientated you won't be able to get out of a sandpit. Don't be fooled into thinking that just because you have a 4wd you can go anywhere. This attitude will surely seal your fate.

- You will need an air-compressor. These are useful when you need to reduce the pressure of your tyres. Normally you can reduce tyre pressure to about 12-15psi, enabling more tyre contact with the sand, and enabling you to get yourself free. The 12 volt compressors are about $25 from most camping or auto shops. Those that plug into the cigarette lighter are generally the cheapest. There are a range of compressors available, with the top end models costing about ten times as much. Really not worth it, unless you plan to live on a beach and will be reinflating tyres daily.

- Shovels become your best friend. When your car abruptly stops in deep sand, THEY ARE ESSENTIAL. Ideally you need two, with wide noses, so you can remove sand quickly and effectively.

- Axes are also very handy as they have many purposes for the adventurer. You may need to cut down a tree to wedge under the tyres for traction, or simply for firewood if you are stranded.

- A bull bar and winch are great accessories, but are also expensive items. Not so applicable for coastal dwellers, as often there are no trees to winch, near your sandy predicament. It is essential that you take a tow rope though, a snap cord being the most effective.

- Power Jacks are probably the best investment if you are thinking about serious sand driving. Basically they plug into the exhaust, and inflate a vinyl tube that lifts the car out of the bog. The great thing is, it doesn't require a hard surface in which to use it, like a conventional jack. The cost is around the $200 mark, but could save your vehicle.

- There are several ways in which to prepare your vehicle, but that is best left to the experts, not someone with limited mechanical knowledge. It is always essential to take a good range of tools with you, even if you don't know how to use them, someone else might!

Driving Tips

This is quite a brief list but will hopefully assist you on some occasions. For a more comprehensive list there are a range of books you can buy. But realistically, most people learn from experience. I can't really imagine a car load of surfers about to ford a river or entering a beach, getting out their 4wd guide and carefully studying the intricacies of sand driving. It is more like

Your ultimate roadtripping accessory

"lets hit it, you pussy, the waves are cranking". It is only in the aftermath that the blame swings to the driver, so the following tips may come in handy.

Sand Driving

1. Don't ever descend a sand dune if you are not completely confident that you can make it back up. This is one of the most common errors, as many surfers lose judgement when the waves are close. Always err on the side of caution, and if you have to, walk in.

2. Try to stick to existing tracks as these will provide better grip.

3. Keep your speed up as this will get you through tight situations.

4. Don't try to turn suddenly as it is near impossible to do this on soft sand. Always be aware of your destination as far in advance as possible, as it will give you more time to correct your vehicle.

5. If you do get bogged, don't keep trying to force your way out as you will often bury yourself deeper. Make sure you dig the car completely free of sand from the underside of the vehicle. If you are continuing to experience problems, you need to cover your exit path with anything solid. Driftwood, seaweed, plastic containers. The best idea is to jam large bits of wood under the tyres, and carefully try to drive out. When you are attempting to get the car out, it is best to start slowly because once the wheel starts to spin, you must start again. If there is no debris about, use clothing, ie towels, wetties etc.

6. The best tip is not to drive into areas where it looks sketchy. But as Murphy's Law would have it, those tracks often lead to the best breaks. If you are not sure, inch your way in, watching the tyres carefully. You will at least be able to avoid disaster, even if you don't get waves.

Mud and River Crossings

1. ALWAYS wade through potential crossings first. This will give you all the information you will need.

2. When approaching the crossing, enter very slowly, so you don't create a wave that will enter the air filter or the electrics. Of course there are variations on this, depending on the depth. But generally speaking, the slower the better.

3. Discretion is the better part of valour, as water can cause far more damage than sand.

There are obviously many more techniques that you will discover on your journey, but this should be a start.

- VW Combi Vans. These vehicles are quite unique, in the sense that the engine sits over the driving wheels, giving them more traction than conventional cars. Also the clearance is far greater than 2wd, in some cases giving better ground clearance than 4wd's. I have travelled extensively in combi's and found them to be the best alternative to 2wd, although most are air cooled, which can be a problem in hot climates.

To avoid all unnecessary risks with your vehicle, you can stay at home and read about roadtripping in magazines. YEAH RIGHT!!

Cooking up a storm

By Bill Rennie

Damit

Hunger will make most of us want to head for the nearest fast food store to fill that inner deep void that suddenly appears when you stagger up the beach after hours at sea! But maybe a juicy hamburger or two is way out of reach and you need to do something pretty quickly before you die of starvation. That's the time when camp cooking skills are a great asset to have, and not difficult to achieve even for the most simple minded.

What do you need? A little basic organisation and planning! Have on hand some useful equipment and utensils that will make it easy for you. A check list for starters: the good old frying pan a billy or two, some tongs, maybe some aluminium foil, a small piece of steel mesh, plastic bags for rubbish, and something to eat with other than your fingers, plus your choice of ingredients, including fresh water and maybe oil to fry with. Have at least some rudimentary ideas for your meals. Don't go for cordon bleu, keep it simple! Scratching around in the cooler after dark with sand flies for company, and finding all you have is a highly aromatic, green piece of meat with a life of its own, is not the way to go!

If you don't have a gas or liquid fuel stove to cook with, then you will need to use fire, which can be a bit tricky depending on the weather conditions and your location. If there's a howling gale and heavy rain then you really have a problem. And the same goes for searing hot weather when a total fire ban may be in force. Don't tempt fate. For such occasions bread and jam may have to suffice.

Given reasonable conditions, prepare a fireplace strictly in accordance with the recommendations of the local fire authority. This means you must have a cleared area of at least three metres around the fireplace which should be set in a shallow trench (did you have a small spade on your list?) no less than thirty centimetres deep, not more than a metre square, and seven and a half metres from any log or stump. Of course on a beach there should be no problems. Just keep a good distance from flammable material. Get your fire going with very light, dry material and gradually add heavier pieces. The last thing you want is a raging inferno with sparks disappearing into the distance like shooting stars, as this can be extremely dangerous. A vigorous fire is the most difficult to cook on, unless you prefer charcoal to succulent, juicy food. Just use enough wood to ensure reasonable flames and nice hot glowing coals to stare into and to engage the imagination! The small piece of steel mesh (remember your check list?!) laid across the trench can make it easy to grill meat or fish and to support a frying pan and billies. Let the fire subside somewhat before demonstrating your very cool culinary skills to an admiring audience.

Cooking requires a degree of co-ordination that comes with practice, so that the cup-a-soup is still hot when you want to drink it, meat is not charred beyond recognition and the vegies a pulpy mess just as you finish your soup. When you have drunk that last mug of coffee or tea, and the fire has all but disappeared, then cover what remains of it with the earth from the trench until you are satisfied that the fire cannot restart under any circumstances. Maybe gas is the go?!

When ravenous don't attempt to eat your best mate but try this simple recipe for size. Warm three or four spoons of oil in a medium sized billy. Stir in two cups of rice for two or three minutes until it looks transparent. Add two and a half litres of boiling water and cook vigorously for ten minutes or so. Drain off the excess water. Having had the foresight to prepare a delicious mix of chopped salami, onions, sultanas, garlic, tomatoes, and pine nuts, lightly fried in oil with some herbs, add this mix to the rice and stir for a minute or two over the coals of the fire before eating. This sustaining meal should comfortably feed four hungry people.

In fact if you took time to buy an outdoorsy cookbook, you would find many straightforward recipes that you could try between the Big Macs and slurpy sundaes that would guarantee a cholesterol free vascular system. No heart attacks on your board while waiting for the next set

Looking after yourself

Medical Chapter

by Dr Tarney Spencer M.B.B.S.

Introduction

I'll start off by introducing myself as Dr Tarn, I've been surfing since I was about 5 years old, and in that time have managed to face most conditions that the Australian surf can throw at me. I've also surfed Indo, Tahiti, New Caledonia and Brazil, all with differing rates of success. I started my medical training at Monash Uni in 1993 and managed to graduate in late 1998, much to my relief. Anyway, my job here is to try to make your surfing journey down that road less travelled as safe and trouble free as possible.

Before you surf - Stretching

Whether you are going on the surfari of a lifetime or just down the coast for a quickie as the sun goes down, you want to be in optimum condition, ready for anything the ocean can throw at you. To get and stay in this peak condition requires a lot of dedication and devotion on your behalf when you're not out there surfing. By this I mean keeping fit and healthy.

There are two types of fitness you want to work on, cardiovascular and general muscle strength. To put it basically, cardiovascular fitness involves getting your heart and lungs ready for extended periods of surfing, ie this gives you the stamina to keep going for hours! General muscular strength is what you want to give you the ability to paddle out the back in as short a time as possible.

Stretching is something you should do before any surf, exercise or weight training. The basic idea behind stretching is to gently stress the muscle fibres, limbering them before you make them work. Stretching has been shown to reduce the incidence of muscle strains, and is associated with a faster recovery following with the exercise. There are a couple of important points to take note of when stretching, they are:
• Breathing should be slow and rhythmical, keep breathing, don't hold your breath, stretch when your muscles are warm, ie before you get the wettie on, stretch slowly, gradually and under control, always hold the stretch for at least 20 seconds and repeat, don't bounce, always stretch before and after exercise and if you feel pain or discomfort, seek medical advice.

Remember that exercise is not safe for everyone, and that it is advisable to get checked out by your local doctor before leaping into any sort of exercise routine.

Natural Hazards around the Australian Coast

We're lucky in one respect in that we don't have any large mammals that are going to rip your head off, but we do have quite a few creepy crawlies which can do a lot of damage. If you do encounter some of these hazards it will be essential that you have a knowledge of CPR and other important medical procedures. You can pick up detailed handbooks on this subject or enrol into one of the many courses that are offered.

Blue-Ringed Octopus

The bite from one of these is normally painless, so the casualty may be unaware of the danger. The symptoms and signs are:
• difficulty swallowing, blurred vision, numbness of the lips and tonguen and no breathing.

Immobilise the limb that was bitten and seek medical aid.

Box Jellyfish

These nasties are normally found in tropical waters, from the Gladstone area in Queensland, north around the coast to Broome in Western Australia, at all times of the year, but particularly between October and May.

There are preventative measures that should be taken, these include wearing protective clothing (thin wetsuits are ideal, as are lycra stinger suits, but they won't stop everything). Always enter the water slowly and if any sting is felt, back out slowly, don't struggle. Carry 4 litres of household vinegar and broad conforming crepe bandages whenever you go to a tropical Australian beach.

The management is:
• don't rub the stung area.
• flood the stung area with vinegar for at least 30 seconds, and apply pressure bandages and immobilise the leg with a splint. If you didn't take the vinegar like I told you to, gently pick off the tentacles with tweezers or your fingers.
• continually monitor breathing and circulation, seek medical aid urgently, apply ice to relieve pain.

Bullrout and Stone Fish

These camouflaged fish are commonly found in tropical inlets, rocky beaches and coral reefs.

This fish sits in shallow water and has extremely sharp and poisonous spines down its back. The symptoms and signs of an injury from this fish are as follows:
• immediate and intense pain at the site of puncture, spread of pain along the limb, occasionally this spine may remain in the wound, swelling and grey blue discolouration of the stung area and casualty may have a change in consciousness or may be irrational.

The management of the casualty is as follows:
• flush the wound with warm liquids, remove any visible spines and seek medical aid immediately.

Cone shell

Cone shell envenomation is normally painless and affects the casualty in much the same way as a blue ringed octopus bite. As a result symptoms, signs and management are as for blue ringed octopus.

Snakes

We are lucky enough to have some of the most poisonous snakes in the world, and chances are, if you are off in search of waves you'll be heading into snake territory. Snakes are cold blooded animals and, being such, need to sit around in sunny places to get their blood warmed up. As a result you will often encounter them sunning themselves on rocks, open grassy areas and on gravel. Unfortunately they can also be found anywhere else imaginable in the bush. If you are lucky enough to encounter one of these reptiles, give it a wide berth, they can strike about 1/3rd of their length and most people getting bitten in Australia do so while trying to kill these snakes. By the way, I should mention that most of the snakes in Australia are protected by law, so don't go putting holes in them, just get out of the way.

If you do somehow manage to get yourself or your mate bitten there are a number of steps you should follow.
1. Don't panic, keep the victim as still as possible.
2. Do not do any of the following: wash cut, manipulate the wound, apply ice or suck the wound or use a tourniquet.
3. Immediately bandage the site firmly (not too tight). A crepe bandage is ideal: it should extend above the bite site for 15 cm, e.g. if bitten around the ankle the bandage should cover the leg to the knee.
4. Splint the limb to immobilise it: a firm stick or slab of wood would be ideal.
5. Transport the patient to a medical facility for definitive treatment. Do not give alcoholic beverages.
6. If possible, the snake should be identified, or if deceased, brought along.

If the snake can't be identified, don't panic because they should have venom detection kits in hospital, which identify venom around the bite site, in urine or blood.

Not all people bitten by snakes become envenomated, and anti-venom usually isn't given unless there is evidence of this. The evidence one looks for indicating envenomation is:
• Nausea and vomiting, abdominal pain, perspiration, severe headache and blurred vision.

If you or your mates experience any of these symptoms, have a good look around for what could be a bite, it may have only felt like a scratch and you may not have seen the snake!

Spiders

There are two species of spider which are of particular importance in Australia. These are the funnel web spider found on the New South Wales coast and south east Queensland, and the red back spider found in most parts of Australia.

The funnel web spider is a large, black or reddish brown spider. They have been

known to bite without provocation, causing the following symptoms and signs:
- initially intense pain at site of bite, nausea and abdominal pain, breathing may become laboured, numbness and muscular weakness, excessive sweating and salivation and cold shivers.

The management of this problem is as follows:
- immobilise the bitten limb using a splint and fully bandage the area, rest and reassure the casualty and seek medical aid urgently.

The red back spider is small, black and with a red stripe down its back. Envenomation is unlikely to be fatal, but can be extremely painful. The symptoms and signs of a bite are:
- a sharp sting may be felt, pain at the site of the bite spreading to involve the whole body, nausea and vomiting, dizziness, muscle weakness or spasm, sweating, which may be localised around the bite and a rapid pulse (greater than 100 beats per minute).

The management of the red back spider bite is:
- Apply a cold pack over the area and seek medical aid.

Sting Ray

Sting rays can vary immensely in size, and can inflict an extremely painful wound with a sting located half-way down the whip like tail.

The symptoms and signs of such a wound are:
- immediate intense burning pain, possible breathing difficulty, numbness around the sting and bleeding from the wound.

The management of such a wound is:
- gently remove the barb if visible and possible, flush the area with warm water, seek medical aid.

Ticks

There are many different types of ticks. However paralysis ticks mainly occur along the coast from Queensland down to northern Tasmania. They are picked up by walking through scrub, where they drop from trees that are brushed against. They are small (less than 1 cm in diameter) oval and flat, and attach and bury their heads under the skin, feeding on the blood of their victims over a period of days. Their bite is usually painless. Ticks may hide in body crevices, and their venom may cause paralysis, particularly in young children.

The symptoms and signs are a weakness of the face and upper eyelids, progressing to the limbs and breathing muscles.

The management is:
- remove the tick by saturating the tick in petrol or kerosene and leaving for three minutes, then slide the open blades of a pair of small sharp scissors or tweezers, one on each side of the tick, and lever the tick outwards, being careful not to leave the mouth parts in the skin.
- if located in a body crevice or ear, seek medical aid.
- always inspect the rest of the body for further ticks, particularly in the hair.
- if any signs or symptoms occur, seek medical aid.

Skin Cancer THE ENEMY

You're out the back of your favourite break, Saturday 'arvo, and it's goin' off. The sun's beating down and by the temperature of the water, you'd say you were in Indo. No need for a wettie here, this is tan time! Unfortunately for you, the largest organ of your body, the skin, is involved in a life and death struggle against its greatest enemy, the sun.

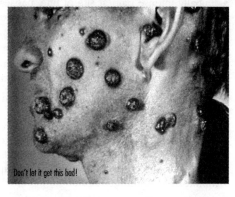

Don't let it get this bad!

That flaming ball up there doesn't just give off heat and light, it's pumping out UV radiation. This UV radiation can't be seen, and remember it's what you can't see that'll hurt you (remember the movie 'Predator'?). UV comes in two forms, UVA and UVB. UVB is the real danger, causing changes in the elastic component of your skin leading to premature aging, wrinkling, dryness and skin pigmentation, but that is just the tip of the iceberg. This radiation also digs into the DNA of your cells, tearing it up in much the same way that Kelly Slater does waves.

The DNA of your cells is responsible for everything that cell does during its lifetime, including reproduce! The big problem is when that UV damages the DNA in such a way that it stuffs up the cells' reproductive centre. The damaged cell loses its ability to know when to multiply, and when to lay chilly, as a result, it starts multiplying and growing with nothing to stop it. Bingo, you just won yourself a very unhealthy dose of CANCER!

THE PREVENTION

As any good doctor will tell you, prevention is better than the cure. Once you've got these cancers, the only chance of a cure is to cut them off, and even then, there is no guarantee they aren't going to grow back, or spread through your blood to any other organ in your body, killing you slowly in the process!

The prevention of these skin cancers is easy, just follow these steps:

Number 1 Stay out of the sun between 11 and 3 o'clock. All the kooks will be out then and shredding them up isn't going to do any good if you die of cancer when you're 30. Let them soak up the UV between these hours when it's strongest, and then you move in for the kill afterwards.

Number 2 Anytime you go out the back, equip yourself with as much protection as possible, wear a rashie, or even better, wear a steamer, slap on a fair whack of sunscreen or zinc to all those exposed bits, and remember to keep it flowing on all day. It'll stop the UV rays getting through to that precious DNA of yours.

Number 3 When you get out of the water to cruise home, do the slip slop slap thing. Put your shirt on, slap on a hat and the sunscreen, and a pair of sunnies. Why the sunnies? Cos UV can do the same nasty things to your eyes.

Just remember, you wouldn't go out without your legrope. Why? Well, to protect your board from ending up on the rocks. Do the same thing, and protect your skin from ending up under the surgeons knife.

Being prepared

A Sample Medical Kit.

It is a good idea to have a first aid kit set up in the boot of your car, because you'll never know when you are going to need it. It all goes according to Murphy's law, that when you need one you don't have one.

Your first aid kit should contain such items as:

Bandages, sterile dressings, scissors, tweezers, safety pins, pocket knife, disinfectant and disposable latex gloves, because many viruses can be caught if handling bodily fluids with bare hands.

Regularly check your kit to ensure that any products that have used are replaced, and that you are familiar with the contents of your kit.

In summary, surfing is an awesome sport that brings you close to nature and the hazards that co-exist. What I have written here is only to be taken as a guide, and if you desire any further information on any aspect, please don't hesitate to speak to your local doctor.

May the surf be with you,

Are you ready?

Does this sound familiar?

Bip bip bip bip bip bip bip bip........ "Thanks for ringing the Surfline for Saturday the 20th, we have perfect conditions on all beaches today with a beautiful 6-8 ft southerly swell being fanned lightly with north westerly wind". You jump in the car with whoever is handy at the time and break every road rule in your quest not to miss one wave. Your first glance of the beach is a surfer disappearing behind a perfectly formed curtain of blue and being spat out of the heaving pit, arms raised in triumph. You stand motionless for a second while your brain processes such beauty, then you must decide if that could be you out there.

Most times you'll go out because the thought of missing such an epic swell would be a burden too big for anyone to carry around, and damn it's fun to surf good waves. But at what point do you say to yourself, "I shouldn't go out in that"? Obviously it's different for everyone, but perhaps there are times when you shouldn't be out there. Why? Well I've been in situations where people have needed to be rescued because they didn't anticipate the force of the rip, or the actual size, power and intensity of the waves. These people are not only jeopardising themselves but often those who come to their aid are also at risk. Sure, everyone makes misjudgements, but there are ways to judge whether you will be able to handle the situation and to prepare yourself for the situation that confronts you.

The most important question that you should ask yourself is, "are you surf-fit?". Think back to the last time you were in the surf. If it was more than a couple of weeks ago, chances are that you will find a dramatic change in your paddling strength and general fitness level. These are two crucial aspects when tackling larger waves. Another important point to consider is whether you are familiar with this particular break. As you'd all know, different waves have different qualities. If you are familiar with the wave and its take off point, it will reduce the chance of you being caught inside. Also knowing what the wave is breaking on is of key importance. If the wave is breaking over three foot of sharp reef, then you definitely want to know about it before you eagerly paddle out! Something that is often overlooked and underestimated when tackling bigger waves is how the ocean works. When the swell picks up, so to do the rips and undercurrents. I have seen young kids swept out over 800 meteres to sea in a matter of a minute or two. This is where it becomes serious. Even if this is your local break, conditions vary vastly and you may be caught unaware.

What can you do?

Preparation is the key to enjoying the benefits of larger waves. It is important that you remain fit at all times if you want to progress. Obviously surfing as much as possible is the ideal, but sometimes Huey just won't play ball. Swimming gives you a great aerobic workout, when it's flat. Even when there are waves, bodysurfing helps build your strength and fitness as well as enhancing your understanding of currents. Try spending an hour bodysurfing. That will give you an idea of your fitness, or lack of it. Another idea is to surf without a legrope for practice. This definitely works you as you're constantly chasing your board. Many of you will understand the subtle changes in the rips and currents that are at work in the ocean. So you should though, this is your key to enjoyable sessions. If you are unsure, take time to observe. Watch where the other surfers paddle out, how much they drift, and where the peaks are breaking. Select a safe spot where you can exit the water, especially on reef breaks. The time spent analysing the situaton could save you many hours of frustrating paddling. Although the temptation is to get onto a wave as quickly as possible, the time spent watching will pay you back ten fold. It is also essential that you respect the rights of other surfers. Everyone knows not to drop in, but this becomes more critical as the wave size increases. Finally, you should always surf with someone else when you are unsure of your abilities.

Only you know your abilities and these will increase with experience, but sometimes it's better to let this swell pass. There will always be another on the way.

Surf Survival.

One of the most important aspects of surfing is understanding your environment. There are so many factors that make up our surfing experience. Wind, swell, sand and reef are just a few of the factors that will lead to your success or frustration. There is nothing worse than watching a surfer sneak into barrels while you flail in the shorebreak wishing that you could share in that majesty. Well you can, if you have the basics. Now I'm certainly not saying that with a sound knowledge of water safety that you will become the barrel maestro, but it will definitely increase your chances.

The key factor before rushing into the waiting surf is to survey your surrounds. This gives you a chance to do three things. Look for the best peak or break, stretch and examine your best point of entry and also your exit. This routine is not obviously a priority when it's two foot and there are a hundred guys in the water, just hit it. This is for the occasions when the swell is up and you need to exercise a certain degree of caution. If you are reading this section, I presume that you have been surfing before but would like to learn more. When studying the beach for suitable exit points you need to look for where the rips occur. These rips will become your best friends over time even if it seems they are the greatest hindrance at the moment. Rips are formed by deep channels that occur on almost all stretches of coastline. Understanding rips takes some time and many thrashings before you stop cursing and start praising. Rips and undercurrents are characterized by a fast flowing section of water. This will happen next to rocks, sand banks, reefs and in channels. The water always has to have an exit point from the beach and this is where you want to be. Of course you must understand how to get in and out of rips before you hurl yourself into the whitewash. Rule 1 is never fight a rip. You will rarely win and it could put you in a dangerous position. Always paddle to the side of the rip and into calm water. Even if you are trying to come in after a long surf and the rip seemingly won't allow you out, there is always a way. If you are having difficulty, remember to paddle at right angles to the rip. This is most important for survival and satisfaction. Rips can be over 100 meters wide, but this is rare. Normally they are a fraction of this size, so with some determination you will make it to the other side. Once there you need to reassess your position. Don't panic, remember that you are a surfer who prides yourself on a love of the ocean, and that this is just a temporary hitch.

Depending on the type of break you are looking at, there are different methods of handling the situation.

The Point Break:

This wave is often characterised by a point or wall leading out to the break. For many surfers it is just a matter of leaping off the rocks at the correct moment. This is often far more difficult than it looks. If you are unsure of the rock option there are other ways. There is always a rip that runs next to the rock wall, although this can feel dangerous, it is normally the safest way. Water rushes out beside the rocks making a perfect aid for you to get out the back. Watch the flow of water just to be sure. In many instances the waves won't break right on the rocks, leaving a clear path from which you can reach the wave.

The Beach Break:

These waves can often be the biggest challenge in terms of getting out the back. Your one weapon against a seemingly impenetrable wall of foam is observation. As you scan along the beach you will notice that there are areas where the water has crept a little further up the beach. This is apparent in the high tide line or simply by watching the incoming waves. These 'high' marks normally indicate the presence of a channel or gutter. This is where the water is deepest, therefore causing a rip or undercurrent. These are normally the exit points for the excess water on the beach and a surfer's best friend. These will aid your attempts of getting 'out the back'. Always try to pick these channels as they become increasingly important as the swell intensifies.

The Reef Break:

This can often be your biggest challenge as you need to find gaps in the reef for your exit point. This is done by careful inspection of the area. Usually the waves will break onto the reef then disperse into the adjoining channels. if you watch a few waves you should be able to pinpoint these areas. It is important to remember that there is not nearly the room for error on this type of break, as the wave can easily wash you over the sharp reef. Keyholes, as they are called, are the best option, as they are breaks in the reef that lead to the beach. If you time it right, it can be like an express train.

Timing is everything

It won't matter how good your rip observation skills are if you make your attempt when there is an approaching set. There is nothing that can save you. Depending on a whole range of factors, it is generally best to wait until the second last wave of the set has broken to begin your assault. If you wait for the complete lull, chances are you will get caught by the approaching set just as you are about to reach safety.

Quick Tips:

One of the best methods employed by surfers when they are caught by a set is to remain calm but also stall paddle. Instead of paddling for your life against the might of the ocean as wave after wave crashes around you, just try to hold your position. Don't exert too much energy as you will want to save it for when there is a break in the sets and you can sprint paddle to safety.

Don't Abandon Ship.

There are times when diving off your board is essential for survival, but not as often as you see people bailing their sticks. This is not in your, nor your board's best interest. It is far better to duck dive as deep as possible then bear hug your board. This means that you come to the surface more quickly and less chance of snapping your board. It is rare that a situation will occur that it is better to ditch the board and swim for cover. You are attached to your board anyhow, so you may as well stay with it.

The Wrap up.

Rips often wash down the length of the takeoff zone, making it extremely difficult to stay in position. What many people fail to realise is that often rips will wash you into shore. Your ultimate goal is to get pulled into position, pick off a wave, then repeat the whole process. If your timing is a little out, then you should wait for the encroaching set, takeoff too late and get washed in. You will then get the rip back out for another try. This will help your timing and late takeoffs immeasurably.

Feeling confident in your water skills is an essential part of every surfer's repertoire. This will come with extended water time and a healthy life. It can be exhilarating to look at a six to eight foot set marching in and realise that this is now what you crave and revel in, instead of it instilling pure terror.

Entertainment

Your essential beer Guide

Acting like a local at any pub is your surest way to find out any secret surf spots that may be lurking around the corner. The first step to acceptability amongst the locals is the purchase of the drink, mainly beer, in style. You would think that ordering a beer would be a simple task, yet, deep within Australian tradition is a ludicrous arrangement of names for differing sizes of beers. Each state has its own separate sizes and accompanying names for their much loved neck oil. I have put this guide together to aid a smooth transition into the pub culture, as beer is as sacred as families, even more so in some cases, in this amber drinking nation. In some instances travellers will order a beer and get a snarled response in return, such as, "Ya wanna Pony or Bobbie Boooyyy". It sounds like some evil, depraved torture rather than a relaxing ale at the end of a hard day's surfing. But fear not my friends, you will be able to slot into the beer swilling antics of the mighty local without a hitch with this information on hand. If your memory evades you at the critical point in the purchase process, simply look for another patron with a beer and mockingly say "I'll have what he's having". Can't be sure that this will work everywhere, so I suggest you memorise at least one correct term in each state.

Victoria

140mls - 5oz. Pony
170mls - 6oz. Small Glass
200mls - 7oz. Glass
285mls - 10oz. Pot *
425mls - 15oz. Schooner

New South Wales

140mls - 5oz. Pony
200mls - 7oz. Seven
285mls - 10oz. Middy *
425mls - 15oz. Schooner
575mls - 20oz. Pint

Queensland

140mls - 5oz. Small beer
200mls - 7oz. Beer
225mls - 8oz. Glass
285mls - 10 oz. Pot *

Northern Territory

200mls - 7oz. Seven
285mls - 10oz. Handle *
425mls - 15oz. Schooner

Western Australia

115mls - 4oz. Shetland Pony
140mls - 5oz. Pony
170mls - 6oz. Bobbie
200mls - 7oz. Glass
285mls - 10oz. Middy *
425mls - 15oz. Schooner
570mls - 20oz. Pot

South Australia

140mls - 5oz. Pony
200mls - 7oz. Butcher
285mls - 10oz. Schooner *
425mls - 15oz. Pint

Tasmania

115mls - 4oz. Small Beer
170mls - 6oz. Six
225mls - 8oz. Eight
285mls - 10oz. Pot *

* Denotes most popular size

As you can see, the list is quite extensive, which is a testament to our love for BEER. There are other considerations as well. There are a few types of beers that are available nation wide, but generally each state has its preferred taste, not that it has that much to do with taste, rather more a sense of state pride. Victoria Bitter is widely available throughout Australia, and it generally accepted as a national beer, so you shouldn't encounter any sideways glances when ordering a VB, as it is fondly known. Western Australia is home to Swan Larger. They are very proud of their own beer and one of its former masters, Alan Bond. There are always countless stories of Bond's legendary status. The fact that the man went to jail doesn't seem to perturb these people. Queenslanders love beer, and they love their XXXX. The climate is just so perfect for a state of beer drinkers. Obsession becomes a religion to many. This was never so perfectly revealed to me as when I recently visited Fraser Island. In amongst huge tent structures that housed 20 or so fishermen and wives, were giant XXXX flags, like some sort of proclamation. There wasn't just one group who did this. Dotted along the some 135kms of east facing coast, there was enormous support for the beer. Fishermen often wore XXXX t-shirts and it was rare to see someone on the Island without them clutching a beer, apart from when the fish were really running. We even came across a group of likely lads who had cracked their first stubbie at 7:00am. When we queried the rotund guys, one burped "itzz ten ferty somewhere in bloody Oz.....uuurrrppp!". Ambassadors for Australia! Tasmanians have their Cascade, which gained more recognition from the release of Bryce Courtenay's 'The Potato Factory'. But there doesn't seem to be the absolute devotion to it, in comparison with their northern neighbours. Emu Bitter is next to deity in SA, and cans are always lovingly handled by hotel patrons. As you can see, there is a strong culture surrounding beer, and it should be known that it is one of the greatest social lubricants. Combine that with your natural wit and charm, and you should be surfing some of the best breaks Australia has to offer.

Guitars, fire and a few beers Pic B Stanley

Triple J Frequencies

Adelaide	105.5 & 95.9FM	Narrabri/Moree (NSW)	99.9FM
Albany WA	92.9FM	Newcastle	102.1FM
Albury/Wodonga	103.3FM	Northam (WA)	98.1FM
Alice Springs	94.9FM	Orange	101.9FM
Armidale (NSW)	101.1FM	Perth	99.3FM
Ballarat	107.1FM	Renmark/Loxton	101.9FM
Bendigo	90.3FM	Rockhampton	104.7FM
Bega/Cooma	100.1FM	Roxby Downs (SA)	101.1FM
Brisbane	107.7FM	Spencer Gulf Nth (SA)	103.5FM
Broken Hill	102.1FM	Sunshine Coast	89.5FM
Bunbury (WA)	94.1FM	Swan Hill (Murray Valley)	105.3FM
Cairns	97.1FM & 107.5FM	Sydney	105.7FM
Canberra	101.5FM	Tamworth	94.7FM
Coffs Harbour	91.5FM	Taree/Port Macquarie	96.3FM
Cootamundra/SW slopes	90.7FM	Toowoomba (QLD)	104.1FM
Darwin	103.3FM	Townsville	105.5FM
Dubbo/Coonabarabran	102.3FM	Townsville (North)	97.5FM
Geraldton	98.9FM	Wagga Wagga/Riverina	101.1FM
Gippsland (Sale)	96.7FM	Warwick/Stanthorpe (QLD)	103.3FM
Gold Coast	97.7FM	Warnambool (Vic)	103FM
Goulburn Valley (Shep)	94.5FM	Wide Bay (Bundaberg)	99.3FM
Goulburn	88.7FM	Yulara (NT)	95.7FM
Griffith/Leeton	96.5FM		
Hamilton Vic	94.9FM		
Hobart	92.9FM		
Illawarra	98.9FM		
Kalgoorlie\Boulder	98.7FM		
Launceston	102.1FM		
Lismore	96.1FM		
Mackay	99.5FM		
Melbourne	107.5FM		
Mildura	101.1FM		
Mt Isa	104.1FM		
Mt Gambier	102.5FM		

If you can't find a frequency give them a call on

Access Triple J- 1900 155 444 60c/min.

AUSTRALIA

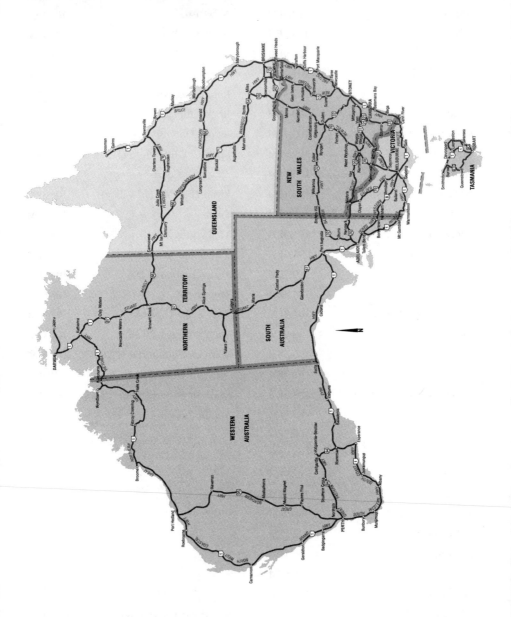

KEY TO MAPS:

Great waves to be found in
this vicinity!

Waves suitable only for beginners.

Crowds tend to be a problem here.
Have fun trying to get a wave
to yourself!

Experienced and/or crazy
surfers only! Heavy waves
and reefs with an appetite
for human flesh!!!

Beware the big mutha, sharp
toothed marine creatures!

Big wave zone!
Big boards required not to
mention big ... er...
plenty of intestinal fortitude!

Never mind the noahs!
Beware the locals here.
Courtesy and patience
are a must!!!

Wayne Such drawing this south coast beast closer than most would ever consider. Pic Steve Ryan

VICTORIA

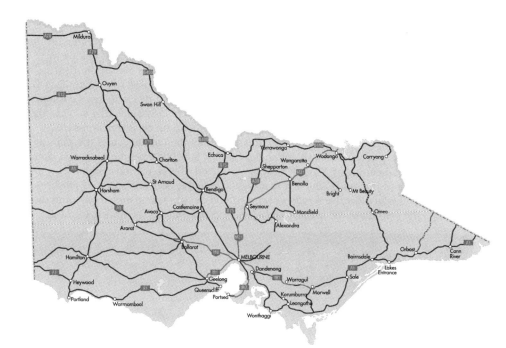

Victoria

Southern Comfort

It was the early '60's when Victoria established itself as an epicentre for surfing in Australia, although the locals had known this for some time. The Bells Beach surf carnival was the beginning of a dynasty that carries on today. Thousands of people flock from everywhere to watch the proceedings that have become so steeped in tradition.

The Mexicans of Australia are lucky people indeed. Blessed with an ocean road that is unparalleled and hundred of kilometres of empty beaches, this state is unique in every way. Unlucky some may say, as the capital is some 100 km away from the closest surf. Lucky is the way most surfers feel, as they are exposed to so many beach options without the problem of overcrowding. Indeed, surfing this state can be a lonely experience. There are stretches of coastline where one would imagine that you are the first inhabitant. Aboriginal caves still remain intact without the crass signatures that often deface their natural beauty. Quaint towns still dot the coastline, and the pubs are full of intriguing patrons who can tell endless stories hunched over their beloved beer. For Victoria is a beer loving State. It is home to Victoria Bitter, the most widely accepted drink in this land. Why is it that they love amber ales and yarns so much? Perhaps it is the fact that the weather seems to find people scampering away from the cold, into the warmth of the taverns and friendly conversation. The trademark of the

Arms back, head down, Cam Lamphard making the drop at Bowon heads. Pic Steve Ryan.

Zane Harrison, completeing the perfect arc at Bells Beach. Pic Steve Ryan.

Vicos: their hospitality. The capital has tried to remain a little antiquated, although this has been altered by the resolute hand of our Premier. A casino is now in place, but for how long, as the inhabitants are keeping away from such a tiresome place. Residents preferring the atmosphere and diversity of the myriad of restaurants and cafés.

For the surfer though, there is much to offer. Torquay, the home of the surf industry, is the starting point for many roadtrips. This is what characterises the coastline. Spectacular ocean views and a diverse landscape that keeps evolving. The variety for the travelling surfer is magnificent. Only South Australia is comparable to the numerous locations that vary so greatly. From the far reaches of the East, where ninety miles of beach link powerful but inconsistent surf to the more populated areas. Places like Phillip Island are still very isolated from the majority of tourists. Then of course there are the popular places such as The Mornington Peninsula with great vineyards and an enduring rural feel, interspersed with powerful ocean breaks. It is the West coast though, that really sparks the imagination. Cold but clean ocean power form endless waves over the numerous point breaks. There are no boundaries on this coast as it keeps going to the west which is the natural progression for surfers in this state. The men and women who regularly surf here are a hardy breed. They stand staunchly in the Bells carpark at the break of day, struggling to see the icy sets peeling around the corner through the early morning mist, the woollen jumpers and beanies wrapped tightly around chiselled faces and bodies. For it takes commitment to surf here year round. The temperature of the water in winter is around the ten degree mark, making for headaches and blue feet in the surf. This is the attraction though. An initiation for a lifetime of surfing for bodies that have been built for stamina. Although you will always hear groaning about the cold, it really is a decoy to keep the pretenders in their cars. There is nothing more treasured than a lonesome session for a Victorian.

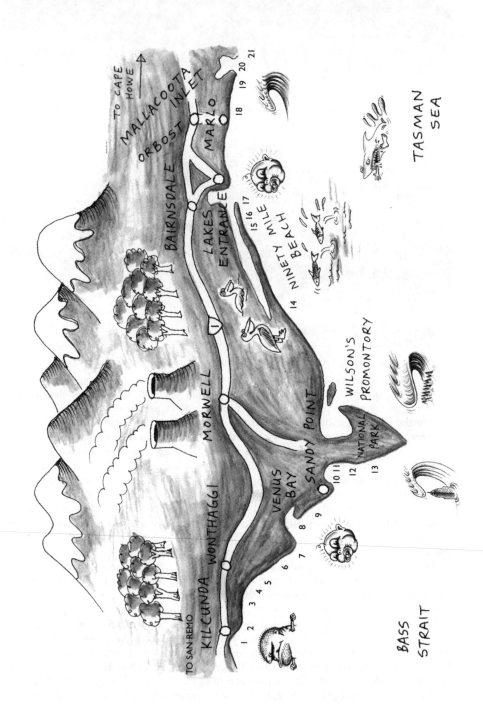

The call of the wild.

The gentle lapping of water on the shore, the crackle of wood burning, gusts of wind that would make trees creak and branches sway. Occasionally there would be a noise that I couldn't decipher, but there was no anxiety.

The all powerful Red Bluff. Pic Steve Ryan.

Gabo Island - Kilcunda

Natures own.

This area is probably the least renowned for quality surf along the expansive stretches of the Victorian coastline. Ninety Mile beach is a barren and dangerous place for surfers, which is unfortunate due to its large coastal frontage, but don't despair. Kilcunda, Cape Patterson, Cape Conran, The Bluff and Mallacoota all have beaches that can produce excellent waves. Giving inspiration to take surfing and fishing adventures through some of Australia's least populated and most beautiful coastal regions.

1.
Break Name: Killers / Kilcunda
Wave Description: A selection of sand banks providing punchy waves that line the beach. Can get a little intimidating on the paddle out if there is a bit of size about, due to the lack of one singular peak. There are plenty of fruits for your labours if you make it out the back.
Sit on a peak, and ride some quality waves.
Best Conditions: SW swell, NE wind, low-mid tide.
Getting There: Follow the main road towards the township away from Phillip Island The best spot for an initial check is from the carpark just beyond Bourne Ck. and the old wooden rail bridge ruins. This area is always well worth a check if the swell is a little too small to be enjoyed at Woolamai on Phillip Island.
Dangers: There is plenty of cause for concern here with powerful waves and strong rips.
Rumours: The lefts from the banks have a history of being better and longer or maybe that's just me because I'm a goofy.
Something Else? I love any place where the pub looks out over the sea.

2.
Break Name: Powlett River
Wave Description: Beach break waves can be found either side of the rivermouth at Powlett River. Although there is a bit of a hike involved and parking is not available right near the break, it can be well worth the mission if the conditions indicate there will be gold at the end of the rainbow.
Best Conditions: SW swell, NE-E wind, variable tides.
Getting There: Take the road that heads out towards the camping area and follow it beyond the river to the parking at the end.
Dangers: Quite a desolate place at times, best surfed with a few friends to watch your back.
Rumours: None that I know of.

Something Else? The camping ground here has a feel to it that not many do. It is one of the few places that you can actually feel like you are really getting away from it all.

3.
Break Name: Wonthaggi / Williamsons
Wave Description: Open and unprotected beach breaks that can be a little wild and woolly.
Best Conditions: SW swell, NE-E wind, low tide.
Getting There: Take a righthand turn off the main road as you enter Wonthaggi and follow the road all the way out to the coastline.
Dangers: This break is at the mercy of the conditions and therefore can be quite a fierce place when gentler conditions do not prevail.
Rumours: Usually one of the windiest beaches around and may well give Warrnambool a run for its money.
Something Else? I have nothing to add here.

4.
Break Name: Seconds / Cape Patterson
Wave Description: Sand covered reefs create some quality waves, even though the ride is usually short-lived.
Best Conditions: SW swell, E wind, high tide.
Getting There: You'll find this break on the western side of Cape Patterson, by taking the road that leads out past the surf club.
Dangers: Needs a huge amount of swell to be working and is therefore rarely surfed enough to be of great concern.
Rumours: The dunes found around Seconds can be a heap of fun for an exploratory mission out to the Cape.
Something Else? Always treat these dunes with respect however much you feel the temptation to climb to the top of the highest one and take the drop.

5.

Break Name: The Channel / Cape Patterson

Wave Description: This righthand reef break can have you stoked on some days and frustrated on others. Seems to be a little fickle but flourishes on the right conditions.

Best Conditions: S swell, N wind, mid-high tide.

Getting There: Head out to the back beach road of Cape Patterson and you will find parking for the Channel near the camping grounds.

Dangers: Can get a little shallow on the lower tides.

Rumours: There is a break as you look out towards the Cape known as Insides. If the swell is big enough to wrap around the point and have this working, it is a wave well worth surfing.

Something Else? It is a worth while weekend getaway.

6.

Break Name: Eagles Nest

Wave Description: A long righthand point break that runs down the bluff leaving good walls with which to work.

Best Conditions: S swell, NW wind, mid-high tide.

Getting There: Well sign posted due to the tourist attraction at the end of the bluff you will be surfing.

Dangers: Getting distracted by the awesome coastal scenery.

Rumours: Outgoing tides here signal that it might be a waste of time to try this location.

Something Else? The historical sight, if you choose to visit the tourist attraction, would warm the patriotic heart in all of us.

7.

Break Name: Suicides

Wave Description: A reef which spurns a worthwhile left and righthand wave, and is a consistent spot when wind conditions are in its favour.

Best Conditions: S swell, NW wind, mid tide.

Getting There: A little further towards Inverloch on the beach road than Eagles Nest. This spot comes complete with valet parking.

Dangers: Can be one of those places you just don't feel easy being out in the water alone with no-one watching over you.

Rumours: It is one of those great summer surfing spots. No wetties required here.

Something Else? A relatively short drive into Inverloch from here to stock up on carbohydrates and vitamin B.

8.

Break Name: Venus Bay

Wave Description: An exposed beach that can provide the greatest challenge in trying to pick a take off spot and stay somewhere near it.

Best Conditions: SW swell, NE-E wind, mid-high tide.

Getting There: Follow the road out to the carpark on the coast through the residential area.

Dangers: Rips, currents, hideous whole wave closedowns onto shallow sand banks. No, I'd say there's no danger, really.

Rumours: Great beach fishing is to be had in this area.

Something Else? It takes good clean conditions to occur for a few days before you develop any real faith in the place.

9.

Break Name: Cape Liptrap

Wave Description: Righthand reef that needs a solid swell to produce its long walling waves.

Best Conditions: S swell, W wind, high tide.

Getting There: Take the Cape Liptrap road out to the lighthouse and you will find it at the base of the steep cliffs under the spectre of the lighthouse.

Dangers: On the lower tides this place can get very rocky, very quickly. Know your tides, or the break well.

Rumours: The track on the way to get to the wave is the first of your worries. Once in the water, don't get to dwelling on the fact that the fishing is awfully good around this area.

Something Else? Its a long way back up those cliffs if you save nothing for the journey home.

10.

Break Name: Dunnyblocks / Walkerville

Wave Description: A righthand reef break that can give you a fun day out if the swell is huge elsewhere.

Best Conditions: SE swell, NW wind, mid-high tide.

Getting There: This break is north of Walkerville, before Cooks Creek.

Dangers: Can get a little shallow at times when there are bigger waves.

Rumours: The most charmingly named break in Victoria.

Something Else? Very protected from the winds that accompany a big swell, so surfable days at this location are not as rare as you'd think.

11.

Break Name: Sandy Point

Wave Description: Beach break waves that can provide a solid grounding for learners. Picks up a reasonable amount of swell and can often be relied upon for some kind of wave in this area.

Best Conditions: SW swell, NE wind, mid-high tide.

Getting There: These waves run along the beach out to the point, and the best bank one day might not necessarily be the one doing it the best the next day.

Dangers: Big dominant fish with several sets of sharpened pearly whites. There has been an attack here.

Rumours: On the positive side the fishing is good.

Something Else? Not many rips or much water movement here, so it is a less strenuous and more enjoyable location to surf than other breaks in the area.

12.

Break Name: Darby Beach / Wilsons Promontory

Wave Description: Beach break waves that will vary in quality according to the sand formations at the time.

Best Conditions: SW swell, NE wind, rising tides.

Getting There: Located north of Tongue Point on the way to the river mouth.

Dangers: Keep a watchful eye out for water movement.

Rumours: This is a fantastic beach, as it is a little removed from the main hustle of the crowd.

Something Else? Check the reef at the northern end of the beach for the righthanders that can peel down the line.

13.

Break Name: Squeaky Beach / Wilsons Promontory

Wave Description: Some classic cruising beach break waves can form at this location on higher tides.

Best Conditions: SW swell, NE wind, rising tides.

Getting There: You'll find it in the bay preceding the Leonard Point picnic area.

Dangers: Can seem like a very exposed and unfriendly beach when heavy weather prevails.

Rumours: A great beach to visit with a clean ocean feel about it. There's good camping available down the road at Tidal River.

Something Else? Country Road should use this location to shoot their next winter wear catalogue. Boat shoes would fare well here.

14.

Break Name: Ninety Mile Beach

Wave Description: Usually dumping beach breaks that are just about unsurfable, unless you are phenomenally keen.

Best Conditions: SE swell, NE wind, variable tides.

Getting There: There is ninety miles of

coastline to be found here. This one would well and truly fit into the idiot test category.

Dangers: Getting stoked at seeing the swell roll in, feathering nicely, only to stroke your way into a hideous closeout.

Rumours: Can get pretty windy along here so if you are even going to consider it you might want to set that alarm clock.

Something Else? Probably more fun as a place to body surf if there is a bit of swell around after a spot of surf fishing off the beach.

15.

Break Name: Lakes Entrance

Wave Description: Probably your best chance of finding a consistent bank is out front of the entrance itself either to the left or right. Although waves can pop up according to bank formations along the length of this beach. Waves here are predominantly small beach breaks that are really probably more useful to learners than more experienced surfers.

Best Conditions: SE swell, N wind, whatever tide will help the banks work.

Getting There: Follow your nose, one of the tourist Mecca's over summer so there is no shortage of metal obstructions telling you how to get there the quickest way possible.

Dangers: Try not to surf in close proximity to the surf fisher-people. Given the quality of fishing compared to the quality of waves, maybe they have more right to hold their favourite position.

Rumours: Good fishing can often mean there are bigger fish in the water, keep an eye out.

Something Else? The banks at the mouth of the entrance can be fickle due to the significant tidal movement in the area, worth a regular check if you are stuck here for family holiday, car breakdown etc.

Adam Robinson, Portland. Pic Steve Ryan.

16.
Break Name: Red Bluff
Wave Description: Power packed lefthand reef break that would be considered the pick of the better known waves in the area. Can provide long peeling waves that are known to give good barrels when the conditions are in its favour.
Best Conditions: SE swell, NW wind, mid-high tide.
Getting There: You'll find this break along the coastal road as you travel towards Lake Tyers area.
Dangers: Can be a hard place to get a good position if it is one of the bigger days. You will often have to make sure your duck diving technique is up to scratch because often there is no easy channel exit out the back.
Rumours: Although the name will set pulses racing, this wave is not quite of the same consistency or quality as its W.A. namesake.
Something Else? Another place in the area where if you feel it might be on, a dawn patrol is a fantastic idea.

17.
Break Name: Sandy Point
Wave Description: A sand spit runs out seawards here that will provide a fun wave on its day. This break has nowhere near the same ability to handle larger conditions as well as Red Bluff and generally has much less power and form.
Best Conditions: SE swell, NW wind, mid-high tide.
Getting There: Approximately half a kilometre further west of the Bluff.
Dangers: Can get taken over by longer boards when it works well, leaving very little in the way of surfable waves for those on the pocket rockets.
Rumours: Well, this is one of those breaks where the name just about summed it all up before you read a word of this.
Something Else? The early bird will defeat the easterly.

18.
Break Name: Cape Conran
Wave Description: The western side of Cape Conran can give rise to some heavy pitching lefthanders that peel down the combination rock/sand base. One of the major selling points of waves at the Cape, is they are some of the few in the area afforded protection from the howling easterly winds that can accompany larger swells.
Best Conditions: S swell, NW wind, incoming tides.
Getting There: You can access Cape Conran by following the signs from the main road into Marlo.
Dangers: These waves are heavier than most in the area with perhaps the exception of the Bluff, so it is a wave that needs to be treated with a degree of respect.
Rumours: Smaller beach breaks are available on the way to the camping grounds for those after a more mellow surfing experience.
Something Else? The camping grounds here are a great place to hang out with a few friends. An area of Victorian surf not generally sought after when thoughts of travel arise.

19.
Break Name: Tip Beach / Mallacoota
Wave Description: This beach houses some shifting sand bank formations that that can give an exciting, albeit short, ride if the swell hits the banks at the right angle.
Best Conditions: SE swell, NW wind, variable tides according to banks.
Getting There: Tip Beach is found below the carpark at the end of the road that takes you past the golf course.
Dangers: Can be a lot of water movement in this area if the swells are bigger and there is the danger of the banks closing out.
Rumours: Check Bekta Rivermouth, as it's known to produce some quality waves on days where the surf doesn't

Summer fun at Cape Conran. Pic Conti.

look that appealing from an initial glance.
Something Else? There is some
unbelievably beautiful native bushland
around this area, which is well worth a
day to walk or drive through.

20.
Break Name: Bastion Point / Mallacoota
Wave Description: Quality righthanders
can be found peeling over the rocks here
with a bit of assistance from good sand
formation.
Best Conditions: S swell, NW wind,
incoming tides.
Getting There: Access via the carpark on
the entrance side of the golf course.
Dangers: There will be a lot of water
movement around this break as well.
Beware of fishing boats coming back into
the entrance and stupidly dropping left
over burley.
Rumours: Further out on the point, there
is a wave that will work just as well as
Bastion on the bigger days. The decision
of where to surf may come down to a
day by day assessment.

Something Else? Stock up here for all
your fruit and vegetable needs, to
smuggle over the border. Only joking!

21.
Break Name: Gabo Island
Wave Description: A very heavy long
lefthand reef break that does not allow
you to relax for a second if it is working
correctly.
Best Conditions: SW swell, N wind,
incoming tides.
Getting There: You need a boat and a
better skipper than Gilligan had on his
side.
Dangers: There is not much about this
place that is not dangerous. If the waves
don't give you a pounding there is always
the chance that the boat will come to
grief crossing the 'Gut'.
Rumours: There are plenty of
shipwrecks in this area which can be a
good indication of the caution required.
Something Else? I don't know why, but
I always tend to feel safer with a
lighthouse watching out for me.

GENERAL INFORMATION

TIDAL RIVER – WILSONS PROMONTORY / CAPE PATTERSON

Where To Stay:

Ring the Parks Victoria office, (03) 5680 9555, or (03) 5690 9500 at Tidal River to arrange your accommodation needs. These may range from a hut, a flat, unit or the ever reliable camping site. Somehow it would seem a shame to visit the beautiful natural setting of Wilsons Promontory and not get out amongst it and camp. It is essential you book though.

Cape Patterson Caravan Park. Ph (03) 5674 4507. Powered sites $17.

Where To Eat:

There ain't none of them fancy linen tabled restaurants out here, boy/girl. It's cook yourself a good old campfire fry up, and even then its usually on the gas stove as fires are banned outside designated areas. This is not the culinary capital of Victoria.

Where To Party:

Make your own fun and remember that a night with a few friends and a couple of drinks can be far more rewarding than a night out at a sleazy nightclub.

Flat Day Fun:

This area is riddled with truly amazing nature walks and plenty of wildlife, so there is no need for a go-carting track, mini golf course or bungy jumping set up. Try the Mt Oberon hike as it gives some great perspectives on the park.

LAKES ENTRANCE / MARLO

Where To Stay:

This is one of those places where there is enough accommodation around that the choice comes down to personal preference. Try the YHA Riviera (03) 5155 2444 or Silver Sands Back Packers Ph (03) 5155 2343, for adequate budget accommodation. Beds from $13.

The Lakes Main Caravan Park, Ph (03) 5155 2365 is worth a go if you want a more secluded place to lay. Sites from $10.

Banksia Bluff Bush Camp at Cape Conran. Ph (03) 5154 8438. This is a great place to stay to getaway from it. You can also camp right on the beach, although winter is a better time for this as the rangers aren't so diligent.

Where To Eat:

The Kalimna Hotel is probably your pick of the counter meal options, and there are a variety of take away options riddling the town. If you want to try something a little different try the fresh seafood in the floating restaurant, Out of the Blue. Try Lake Tyers Water Wheel Tavern for a cheap counter meal.

The Marlo Hotel has a fantastic atmosphere, with excellent counter meals. This is a true fisherman's pub, complete with the stories and characters.

Where To Party:

Not really a party place in the off-season but as with many Victorian coastal town the population explodes in summer giving the whole town a party or holiday-like atmosphere.

Flat Day Fun:

There is plenty to do, but if you are in this area, I say it is a shame if you don't give fishing a go. You can hire boats or simply throw your line into the ocean. Both ways should provide bountiful hauls. Marlo is a fishing Mecca, as is the Ninety Mile Beach.

MALLACOOTA

Where To Stay:

Mallacoota Caravan Park. Ph (03) 5158 0300 has great foreshore sites where you can awaken to the beautiful sight of the ocean. Sites from $8.50.

Beachcomber Caravan Park. Ph (03) 5158 0233 puts you close to the beach breaks

of Tip Beach. Sites from $10.
YHA, The Mallacoota Hotel/Motel. Ph
(03) 5158 0455. Beds from $13. The great
thing about YHA's is that they always
have a heap of info of activities in the
area or how you can get to your next
destination.

Where To Eat:
Check out the veritable array of fast food
places and restaurants that accompany a
typically tourist town.

Where To Party:
Once again this is a town that is fairly
sleepy throughout the year, and just
about the whole place rocks with the
population influx over the warmer
summer months.

Flat Day Fun:
Another place that you expect to find
some first rate fishing but probably the
pick of the bunch is the walking or
relaxing that can be done in the adjoining
Croajingolong National park. The
Wallagaraugh River Wilderness Cruises are
a 5 hour journey through some pretty
interesting areas. Ph (03) 5158 0555. It's
only $40 with lunch included.

Peaky, powerful & down for waves at Mallacoota.
Pic Steve Ryan.

SECTION INFORMATION

Local Shapers
None in the area.

Best Months
April - October

Secret Spot
If you don't mind the hike, you can find
magic waves on the border, but it is a full
mission. You must be prepared for most
eventualities as they will surely present
themselves here.

Quick Tips
Don't expect to get good waves here, as
it is more fluke than anything. That isn't
so much of a concern though, as there
are some magic places to visit.
Unbelievably, there are places that you
don't even need to carry a surfboard,
although I would never recommend this,
as you are bound to find waves if you
don't have your stick with you. Take
plenty of fishing gear as this will
probably be your most used equipment.
The wilderness of this area is its main
feature. Also there have been many
Tasmanian Tiger sightings in the region. It
is believed that the Tiger was transported
here in the early part of the century.
There is a belief that this could be where
we discover our long lost preditor.

Getting There
V/Line is your answer here, as it runs
services as far as Narooma on the
Sapphire coast. From Melbourne it will
cost about $35 to Bairnsdale. From there,
you will need to get a connecting bus.
There is no public transport to
Mallacoota, though. Some of the hostels
have free pick ups. The backpackers'
lodge, Amaroo, takes trips down to the
Prom for about $30. They are pretty
good, I reckon.

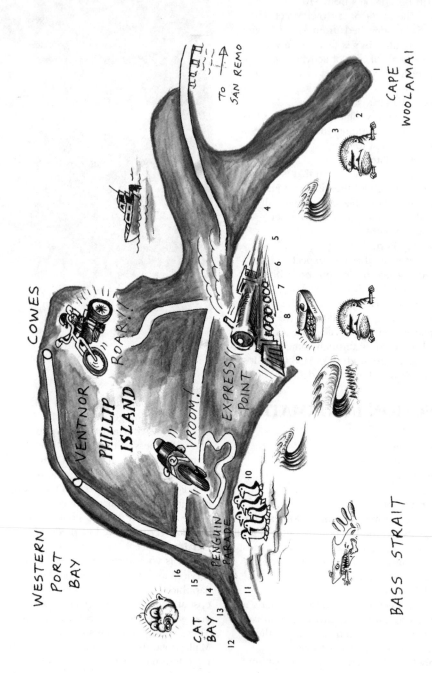

Heavy Sessions

We cracked a beer in celebration of our survival and gazed out to sea wondering what this mighty ocean could have in store for us next.

Darren Watson and E.P doing their thing. Pic Steve Ryan.

Phillip Island

Penguin parades and perfect waves

The Island is known for many things. Most notably the Penguin Parade, which thousands of people flock to every year. Most suburban schools had school camps here at one time or another, but the waves weren't really part of the equation. The sharks were though. As the stark photos in the pub reveal the true size these creatures can grow to. All this, though, cannot detract from the magnificent waves. The beauty of most Islands is their protective nature and the variety of conditions that can make them really pump. For many the catch cry of "It's always offshore at the Island" is no big talk. The stronger reality is the waves here are of a higher class. Catching all available swell makes this place a haven for soul surfers and lovers of the remote. For although it is well serviced, there is a sense of solitude on the Island that is unique in Victoria.

1.

Break Name: Foots / San Remo

Wave Description: Lefthanders break over the rocks here into the entrance of Westernport Bay. On bigger days this break can offer some long rides and a good fun session.

Best Conditions: S swell, NE wind, low-mid tide.

Getting There: Take the beach road out of San Remo until you reach the carpark. The rest of the mission is on foot.

Dangers: Not a dangerous wave but has been known to section and catch a few people by surprise, myself included.

Rumours: Shitty wave that never works.

Something Else? A very rural feel to the area. The Point Leo boys must feel right at home here.

2.

Break Name: Magic Lands / Woolamai

Wave Description: This can provide challenging waves that are quite powerful for sand bank waves. The sand forms over rock here, therefore a degree of stability is enjoyed by the banks. The waves here can give lefts and rights of comparable quality.

Best Conditions: S-SW swell, NE wind, low-mid tide.

Getting There: Take the turnoff to Woolamai and follow the road right out to the surf lifesaving club. Head down towards Cape Woolamai from here.

Dangers: Generally the best protected of the breaks at Woolamai and therefore can be a little safer. You will encounter the odd rip that will move you, and the waves can dish out some punishment on bigger days and lower tides.

Rumours: This end of the beach will provide cleaner waves than elsewhere if there is some southerly direction in the wind.

Something Else? Can be a little less crowded than Carparks, maybe due the laziness of some, or maybe due to the stoke of just wanting to get in the water as quickly as possible if there are waves.

3.

Break Name: Woolamai / Carparks

Wave Description: A quality A-frame beach break that peels off a consistent sand bank. Renowned for providing long rides that will either challenge or be mellow and great for learning, depending on the banks and tide mark.

Best Conditions: S-SW swell, NE wind, most tides.

Getting There: This break you cannot miss, it is right in front of the surf club.

Dangers: Can get incredibly crowded.

Rumours: This break has been taken over as a contest site on more than one occasion when the author has rolled up to get some waves.

Something Else? This break is probably one of the first visited by surfers frequenting the island, as it is a great indicator of what might be happening elsewhere.

4.

Break Name: Surfies Point

Wave Description: A power packed righthand point that will come into use when the swell conditions are big. Can handle conditions up to 2 m. Is usually a good bet if all the other breaks are closing out.

Best Conditions: Big S-SE swell, NW wind, low-mid tide.

Getting There: Follow the signs off the main road and park.

Dangers: If possible wear a helmet, and never take the set waves they are far too big. This break is nowhere near as good as the front beach at Cowes though.

Rumours: It is always worth checking the beachies in the bay here as you never know. The point may be out of bounds but the beach breaks are begging to provide you with a fun day.

Something Else? Can get very crowded when big swell closes out beaches elsewhere. It is well worthwhile to stop and take a look, before blindly paddling out. If the swell direction isn't hitting the reef at the right angle a frustrating time can be had even when the waves look quite good.

5.

Break Name: Express Point
Wave Description: Short, sharp and a punch that Mohammed Ali would have killed for. This is a serious wave and not one to learn on or take less experienced friends to, it is just plain mean. However for those in the know, on its day, some of the best barrel action you'll find in Victoria.
Best Conditions: S swell, NW wind, high tide.
Getting There: It's not that hard to find, but if you don't know, or are not going with someone who does, perhaps it is best left for another day.
Dangers: What could not be dangerous about a wave that will suck dry and buck like a mule.
Rumours: Probably the most photogenic Victorian wave with countless shots of insanely happy guys getting pitted, making sure that crowding is now an issue at this break.
Something Else? Could have been known by another name to this very day, had the nature of the surfing experience here not demanded a more descriptive title.

6.

Break Name: Sunderland Bay
Wave Description: Fun lefthander to be ridden off the eastern point of the bay.
Best Conditions: S swell, NW wind, high tide.
Getting There: At risk of sounding like a broken record, follow the signs. Most of the major breaks and beaches on the island are sign-posted and very easy to find.
Dangers: Surfing here on a low tide is fraught with danger and usually out of the question anyway.
Rumours: Start your own, this is how urban myths are created.
Something Else? The rock pools at the

western end of the beach, a few friends, an esky and no surf about. Not the dire circumstance that the last point suggests.

7.

Break Name: Smiths Beach
Wave Description: Mellow beach breaks will form around a variety of shifting sand banks. Pick the best option on the day and go for it.
Best Conditions: S swell, N wind, mid tide.
Getting There: Take a guess.
Dangers: Not really, quite a good learners' beach, with little to worry the over-anxious parent.
Rumours: It was at this beach approximately 13 years ago that Traci Lords experienced her first kiss by a shy retiring Victorian surfer boy.
Something Else? It is the nature of the gentle drop away in depth that robs this place of the power that other beach breaks on the ocean side of the island enjoy. However, this also means that rips and water movement do not predominate.

8.

Break Name: Y.C.W.
Wave Description: A lefthand point that will provide a classic malibu or learner's wave on its day.
Best Conditions: S swell, N wind, mid-low tide.
Getting There: Signs, signs everywhere the signs, blocking out the scenery, blowing my mind.
Dangers: Not really.
Rumours: Provides some great protection due to the nature of the sheltered bay. If the swell is huge and the winds are all messed up it is beneficial to give Y.C.W. the benefit of the doubt.
Something Else? On big, big days and higher tides it is also worthwhile trying further west. There are breaks along here that although they are blocked by the racetrack for access, have been known to hold a worthy wave.

9.

Break Name: Pyramid Rock / Storm Bay

Wave Description: A relatively set righthand sand bank that although fickle in nature can provide great waves on its day. A fun wave that will break cleanly in the right conditions but can section a little if things aren't perfect.

Best Conditions: SW swell, E-NE wind, mid-low tide.

Getting There: Follow the signs out towards the pyramid rock tourist attraction, access to Storm Bay is gained from this carpark down the hill.

Dangers: If you are enjoying the session and stay out a little too long, you will find you have a battle getting back in over the rocks. Similar to the problems endured by the wary crew at Lennox Head.

Rumours: You have more hope of getting your girlfriend/boyfriend to change a tyre while you sit in the car reading a magazine, than surfing this place on a strong SW wind.

Something Else? Can have a lot of surfers putting booties on their wish list if they catch this place on its day.

10.

Break Name: Kitty Miller Bay

Wave Description: This small enclosed bay is a good bet to find surf under a variety of conditions, probably one of the regular places to check when it isn't working that well at other spots. The quality of the break here can be variable, but on its day, a great wave with challenging sections can be ridden. This place is probably better known for providing a wave when other spots have failed to come up with the goods.

Best Conditions: SW swell, W wind, mid-high tide.

Getting There: The only way you'll get lost is on purpose.

Dangers: Not a treacherous wave by any stretch of the imagination, but the rips can catch you unaware.

Rumours: Picks up a lot of swell, but the best conditions here are found when it is not reforming, after having already broken out the back.

Something Else? One of the few places I've known that can actually work reasonably well in onshore conditions.

11.

Break Name: The Crack / Summerland Bay

Wave Description: A righthand reef that provides a great venue for learning the ropes on the higher tides. Can get a little more challenging on bigger days and lower tides where there can be plenty of action.

Best Conditions: SW swell, NW wind, mid tide.

Getting There: Follow the massive traffic influx to the home of the fairy penguins.

Dangers: Not a dangerous place but can get a little shallow on lower tides.

Rumours: Much more famous for the waddling little birds than the surfing action.

Something Else? Try the point on the higher tides for a more challenging wave than the Crack.

12.

Break Name: Cowrie Beach

Wave Description: This left can provide pulse racing excitement from take-off, with plenty of speed to be derived as the water surges around the point. This wave is often criticised though, as there is a lack of genuine steepness in the walls after the initial rush. This is also a wave that will only really work when the swell is large enough to sweep right around the point almost taking a U-turn.

Best Conditions: W swell, SE wind, high tide.

Getting There: Head out towards Seal Rocks and you will spot the carpark on the Westernport Bay side.

Dangers: I think the fact that Seal Rocks is nearby is enough reason to be aware of sharks.

Rumours: The second largest white

Glyndyn Ringrose guiding his way through this P. I. barrel. Pic Brett Stanley.

pointer was a resident of this area until Vic Hislop caught his prize jewel.

Something Else? Even if the surf is not on, this place is a must see on a blustery winter's day in order to realise the power of the sea and the elements.

13.
Break Name: Left Point
Wave Description: Similar waves to Cowrie beach. Although the wave form on the right tide tends to be a little better and provide a wave with plenty of challenges.
Best Conditions: W swell, SE wind, mid tide.
Getting There: Apply above.
Dangers: Big fishes known in biology circles as Carcaradan Carcarius.
Rumours: This place has the ability to be good but only when conditions are right for it. Read up well on your tides and know the conditions, or alternatively you might just be lucky.

Something Else? Nope.

14.
Break Name: Cat Bay
Wave Description: Probably the best learners' wave that I have encountered, and can also be a bail out option if nothing else, including Kitty Miller Bay, is working. Left and righthanders peel with gentle ease over the shallow banks. This wave will slap you more than punch, if you happen to make the odd mistake or seven.
Best Conditions: W swell, SE wind, incoming tides.
Getting There: Blind Freddy could find it, you can see it from the main road between Cowes and Seal Rocks.
Dangers: Crowds and only crowds, unless one of the big fishes strays a little further afield.
Rumours: Can be a revelation for those learning the sport to spend a day amongst the gentle forgiving waves of Cat

Glyndyn Ringrose & Simon McShane making it pretty clear. Pic Brett Stanley.

Bay. This is a special break as it is offshore when the rest of the Island (south side) is suffering from those terrible onshores.

Something Else? To beat the crowds, pay a younger sibling to swim around wearing a fake shark's fin.

15.
Break Name: Right Point

Wave Description: A surging powerful wave that will challenge the surfer and teach the benefit of keeping a higher line on the wave when the tide is a little low. The point has become known for being bigger and better on a rising tide.

Best Conditions: W swell, SE wind, mid tide.

Getting There: Carpark off the Ventnor Road.

Dangers: Not an ideal place to get pitched or dive off the front of the board on lower tides.

Rumours: Rather cleverly derived its name from being the righthand point of Cat Bay.

Something Else? On the right conditions this wave gives a long memorable ride that will keep you coming back for more.

16.
Break Name: Flynn's Reef

Wave Description: A righthand point with a shallow takeoff point that will take you to the beach via a series of makeable and rewarding sections.

Best Conditions: SW swell, SE wind, mid tide.

Getting There: Turnoff at the roundabout to Flynn's off the Ventnor Road and watch out for the suspension of the car as there is the odd pot hole or two on the way to the beach.

Dangers: Not an incredibly dangerous wave although getting caught inside on the shallow reef can be quite an experience.

Rumours: To this day, one of the best waves I've had the pleasure of riding occurred at this break.

Something Else? Can be incredibly crowded and this problem gets worse if the beaches on the ocean side of the island are not showing much.

GENERAL INFORMATION

COWES

Where To Stay:
Amaroo Park YHA Hostel. Ph (03) 5952
2548 is situated in the middle of Cowes.
It's well known and established as quality
budget accommodation in the area. Beds
start from $13. The great thing here is the
range of activities that can be arranged
including surf lessons. Give them a call.
Kaloha Holiday Resort. Ph (03)5952 2179,
is another central accommodation option
as is the Isle of Wight Hotel.

Where To Eat:
There are a number of viable eateries that
provide for the take-out option along the
main roads of Thompson Ave. and the
Esplanade in Cowes. The hotel will also
provide the famished with a value for
money eating option. For those lucky
enough to have a little bit of money to
splash around The Jetty has some
fantastic seafood on offer. Try the surf
shop on the Islantis as well as it has a
cool little cafe adjoining. You can watch
surf vids while you lap up your banana
smoothie. Clem's Simply Scrumptous, just
near Woolamai, has all home cooked
food and is a great place to charge up on
healthy offerings.

Where To Party:
The Isle of Wight Hotel probably
provides a solution to this question, and
can become really packed over the busy
summer months.

Flat Day Fun:
Phillip Island holds the Australian 500cc
Motorcycle grand prix around October
each year and can provide a hell of a
good weekend for those with an interest
in the bikes. If this is not your scene then
the fairy penguin parade is worth
checking out for a once off, even though
it is so commercial it makes me ill. Also
the fur seals that lounge around at Seal
Rocks are a spectacular site even though

they don't really do the surfers any
favours, by attracting marine life that can
spoil your day.

SECTION INFORMATION

Local Shapers
Islantis - Laurie and Kevin. Ph (03) 5956
7553.
Island - Glyndyn Ringrose and Tom
Tyrell. Ph (03) 5952 3443. Glyndyn has
just made it into the top 44 at the time of
print, making him a pretty unique shaper.
Full Circle - Russell Francis. Ph (03) 5956
7453.

Best Months
The best surfing conditions for the island
are generally found in late summer and
into autumn. Of course winter is king
though, you just need to pick your days.

Secret Spot
Old MacDonald had a .... Near
that...... there was a peeling left, EiEiO.
Near Flynns Reef.

Quick Tips
Always good to check Woolamai first as
this will give you a good indication as to
the size of the swell elsewhere. The other
important factor in a good surf here are
the tides. Due to its position in the bay it
is heavily influenced by the tides.

Getting There
The backpackers runs a free courtesy bus
from its Hostel in North Melbourne. Call
to book this crazy deal on (03) 5952
2548.
Try V/Line as well.
The trip is about 2 and a bit hours from
Melbourne. It is not an easy hitch either
as there are many different routes that
people may take, taking precious surfing
time. I recommend the free service, who
wouldn't?

VIC

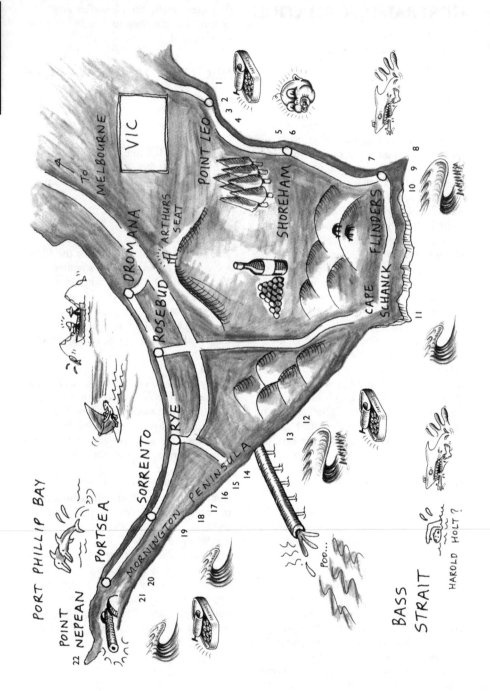

Locals

His quiet demeanour seemed to ooze to coastal life. He dreamily told us of the local beaches, being quietly proud of his surrounding splendour.

Dane Beevor dragging the hand in this peninsula perfection. Pic Brett Stanley.

The Mornington Peninsula

East Coast Magic

The Peninsula boasts some extremely powerful waves and on average has more swell than its westerly neighbour. The beach breaks can be horrendous as the swell has a tendency to destroy banks as soon as they are formed. You can spend excessive amounts of time checking all the different locations without success. On the positive though, there are many rarely surfed peaks here that require some exploring. In an area which houses so many visitors, it's a welcome respite from the overcrowding at the major breaks. When the banks are in place these beaches can turn on complete perfection for the faithful. It also has the advantage of the protected points of Point Leo, a god-send in a coastline dominated by open sandy beaches. The competition can be fierce here as there are few places that are reliable. Keep the faith though as you are bound to find waves.

1.

Break Name: The Point / Point Leo
Wave Description: A quality righthand reef break that will provide long walling waves begging to be enjoyed. The swell generally needs to be breaking reasonably big for this wave to work from the true take off point, but on the positive side, it can often work when conditions are not exactly perfect.
Best Conditions: SW swell, W-NW Wind, and generally bigger and better on the incoming tide.
Getting There: Take Point Leo Rd through the gates and you can park either overlooking the break by taking the first left, or park down near the surf club.
Dangers: Can get a little shallow on lower tides and the paddle out can be a little hairy.
Rumours: If there is too much westerly in the swell direction, the wave tends to section a little.
Something Else? You might have to make a small donation to the rangers of about $3 over the summer months. The money is well spent and a small price to pay for a good session.

2.

Break Name: Suck Rock / Point Leo
Wave Description: Similar to The Point, but the take off is usually a little more vertical. A shorter wave with a great shape. This wave works in smaller conditions and the take-off is just a little further towards the shore and a little to the right.
Best Conditions: SW swell, W-NW wind, and high tide.
Getting There: Same as The Point. Put it this way, you could almost spit downwind between the two.
Dangers: Shallower than the point with a take-off that will have the inexperienced struggling.
Rumours: A.K.A Peak Rock, it assumed the new identity to escape questioning during the rise of Mc Carthyism.
Something Else? Good wave to have short board on.

3.

Break Name: Crunchy Point / Point Leo
Wave Description: Another righthand point that provides quick clean waves that are usually a hell of a lot of fun.

Air-time on the Peninsula Pic Steve Ryan.

Needs a large swell to get going.

Best Conditions: S swell, W wind, mid-low tide.

Getting There: Definitely take the first left after entering the gates, walk left at the bottom of the beach access stairs.

Dangers: Not many a safer wave than The Point, but still requires a little respect.

Rumours: This place is a great indicator when driving in, as to what this and 1st reef might be doing.

Something Else? High tide and small swell is perfect for beginners.

4.

Break Name: 1st Reef / Point Leo

Wave Description: This wave is not overly powerful but can give long fun rides in either direction on its day. The right is generally better on the smaller days as there is a section of reef in the left that closes out unless it gets bigger, or you are really quick.

Best Conditions: S swell, N-W wind, usually better shape on mid tides.

Getting There: Park in the second carpark, down by the surf club.

Dangers: Can get a little shallow on the lower tides, but is generally a very safe and good learners' waves.

Rumours: You might catch the East Coast Surf School here on the smaller days, so give 'em some encouragement!

Something Else? Can get very crowded in summer, so head inland into the dunes for some amber refreshment in the sun. Also, there is a wave known as 2nd Reef but I gotta say it is pretty ordinary. You might see a few sets roll through and you will contemplate the paddle over to the less crowded break. This is usually a waste of time and energy.

5.

Break Name: Honeysuckle / Shoreham

Wave Description: A righthand reef break that can test all with its inconsistent nature. If you do get onto one of the

better waves, usually on days with BIG swell, you can be assured of a wave that you won't forget.

Best Conditions: SW swell, N-NW wind, high tide.

Getting There: This wave breaks out the front of the Shoreham Foreshore camping grounds.

Dangers: The inconsistency of the waves. Rarely do two waves mirror each other at this location.

Rumours: It is worth a look to see if the outer reef here is working, because on its day it can provide great, long rides.

Something Else? Having told about the wave's inconsistency, I have been assured by a local friend, that when it gets the right conditions, it can be true magic.

6.

Break Name: Pines / Shoreham

Wave Description: A righthander that will deliver on swell around or bigger than the 1m mark. However, the swell in the area needs to be quite large for this break to be at its best.

Best Conditions: SW swell, NW-W wind, mid tide.

Getting There: Take the pine lined drive to Shoreham beach, go to the west end of the carpark and if you can't see it you're blind.

Dangers: Can get a little shallow if the tide gets too low.

Rumours: Do you think this place got its name from the abundance of pine trees in the vicinity?

Something Else? Can get extremely crowded on summer days.

7.

Break Name: The Farm / Flinders

Wave Description: A very quick righthander, that requires large swells to get good.

Best Conditions: S swell, NW-W wind, rising tide.

Getting There: This break is found to the south of the Flinders' jetty.

Dangers: Not many, but be careful of the

fact that this wave may close out at a moment's notice.

Rumours: Not a regular performer, occasionally gets a call up from the reserves.

Something Else? Sorry, NO!

8.

Break Name: The Gunnery / Flinders

Wave Description: A short righthand reef break that can often be frustrating, but sometimes produces a fun little wave.

Best Conditions: S swell, N wind, low-mid tide.

Getting There: Take the beach road from the round-a-bout in Flinders, towards West Head, where you will find the carpark just past the golf course.

Dangers: Can be a very infrequent wave and therefore it is possible to get extremely cold in the middle of winter, between sets.

Rumours: If you leave the clubs in the car, there is always a great option to get onto the golf course for a few rounds, of beer that is.

Something Else? The golf course is one of the best public course in Victoria. Very worthwhile having a few rounds, of bee... nah just kidding.

9.

Break Name: Meanos / Flinders

Wave Description: A heavy wave that will break left and right providing plenty of action whilst the ride lasts. The left is generally considered to be the more consistent, and the better, of the two.

Best Conditions: S-SW swell, N-NE wind, high tide.

Getting There: Lives beneath the cliffs of West Head.

Dangers: If you get caught inside during a set, or go over the falls soon after take-off, you will consider taking up an easier sport.

Rumours: If the main wave looks a little intimidating, you can always consider the reform for action with a little less spice.

Something Else? It got its name for a good reason.

10.

Break Name: Cyrils / Flinders

Wave Description: A quality and lengthy righthander breaking down the length of the reef giving a thrill a second. Usually the bigger the better is a rule of thumb.

Best Conditions: S-SW swell. N-NE wind, high tide.

Getting There: Located at the western end of the golf course and accessed along Golf Links Rd.

Dangers: The rock ledge responsible for the quality of the wave always seems to punish the unwary.

Rumours: If you are waiting patiently for Huey to do his thing, take a second for yourself and have a look around. On a good day the scenery is breath-taking.

Something Else? Nope.

11.

Break Name: Lighthouse / Cape Schank

Wave Description: A big lefthander that will provide a long blank canvas for surfers ready to create.

Best Conditions: SE swell, E-SE wind, low tide.

Getting There: Follow Cape Schanck Rd and keep an eye out for a carpark before you reach the lighthouse.

Dangers: Can hold some large waves that are not for the first timers or the unwary.

Rumours: This coast line is absolutely amazing and a walk along the rocks at low tide can teach a lot about reef form as well as beautiful scenery.

Something Else? There are some great views into relatively unsurfed bays from the new golf courses in Cape Schanck.

12.

Break Name: Pumping station / Gunnamatta

Wave Description: A powerful lefthander that barrels down the reef providing a ride that will have your eyes

Clean lines on the open Peninsula beaches. Pic Steve Ryan.

open wide.

Best Conditions: SW swell, NE wind, low tide.

Getting There: Access from the 1st carpark, you'll find it to the right down the beach past the rock pools.

Dangers: Shallow rock landings and ocean outfalls ruining days where the waves are pumping.

Rumours: Write to your local council member and hassle him until he cries about putting an end to ocean outfall.

Something Else? Refer to the Surfrider article at the front to find out how bad Gunnamatta really is.

13.

Break Name: Gunnamatta

Wave Description: Beach break waves that will provide an exciting ride but in order to get it at its best an up to date knowledge of the banks and conditions stand you in good stead. Try calling a surf shop or just keep checking.

Best Conditions: SW swell, NE wind, an incoming tide.

Getting There: Take Truemans Rd into Gunnamatta and surprisingly enough it is

in front of the first carpark you come across.

Dangers: Rips on the outgoing tides or on windy days can cause a hassle.

Rumours: Generally considered the more consistent break when the swell gets bigger and the winds are right.

Something Else? This reserve also charges an entry fee during the summer months. Some of this goes to helping regenerate the sand dunes in the area which is a worthwhile cause. Also, the canteen provides salvation for the starving surfer, but beware, it's only open during certain months of the year.

14.

Break Name: St Andrews

Wave Description: A sand bank break that provides a worthwhile spot to check up on if conditions or crowds are not to your liking at Gunna or Rye.

Best Conditions: SW swell, NE wind, mid-high tide.

Getting There: Take a left at the horseriding school on the way back from checking Gunnamatta, drive along until you see the sign indicating St Andrews.

Easy ! Don't mess around with short cuts in these winding roads, they lead to a waste of valuable water time.

Dangers: The rips can sometimes cause concern but generally a reasonably safe wave.

Rumours: Surfing on a rising tide can lessen the impact of these rips.

Something Else? There are waves in between here and Gunner. Take a walk and you will often find empty peaks.

15.

Break Name: Rye Back Beach

Wave Description: To the right of the carpark the most consistent break can be found. It's a right which breaks off the sand, which forms over the rocks. On its day, this wave can provide waves of similar quality to first carpark at Gunnamatta.

Best Conditions: SW swell, NE wind, low-mid tide.

Getting There: Follow the signs off the back beach road, pick a spot, wax up the board and get into it.

Dangers: Locals run Peninsula Boardriders competitions here, and if they are already setup for the day it could be a long wait for waves.

Rumours: Check the lefts in front of where you enter the carpark as you will often find a good bank breaking.

Something Else? There are generally more surfers here as there is no outfall.

16.

Break Name: Allison Ave / Rye

Wave Description: Generally the best break here will form off the righthand point, looking seaward at the bay. The banks that form here will provide good A-frame waves.

Best Conditions: SW swell, NE wind, mid-low tide.

Getting There: Take the turn off from the back beach road and drive down about 300m. Here you will see a sandy track that will lead you right into the middle of the bay.

Dangers: The break off the lefthand point of the bay can get quite shallow on lower tides. The rips that operate here can also be a cause for concern.

Rumours: This is a much better location on days when the swell is not overly large. On the bigger days the whole bay will close out, providing you with a paddle in that requires expert timing.

Something Else? Don't expect the luxury of the surf check from the car. You gotta walk to this one.

17.

Break Name: Tiber St / Sorrento

Wave Description: Under the right conditions it is a wave that will provide a testing take-off and a good peeling right with plenty of face to work with. If conditions are closing out the sand banks of other beaches, the kelp encrusted reef here may be able to hold the size a little better.

Best Conditions: SW swell, NE wind, high tide.

Getting There: Take the Tiber St. Turnoff from Old Melbourne Rd. and follow it to the carpark at the end. Follow the winding track to the promised land.

Dangers: On lower tides the kelp here has been known to capture more than a few fins belonging to unsuspecting surfers.

Rumours: This break can often be a welcome relief from the hoards of surfers flocking to the better known beaches in the area.

Something Else? Check out the end of St. Johns Wood just a few roads from here. It provides a tower rock, from which the leap into the rock pool, can get the adrenalin flowing if there is no surf action.

18.

Break Name: Central Ave / Sorrento

Wave Description: Again this is a bay location, that houses a variety of breaks that may work. The break from the right point is generally the better regarded and

more surfed, although it can get a little shallow nearer the low tide mark.
Best Conditions: SW swell, NE wind, mid-high tide
Getting There: Follow a similar routine to Tiber St, just take the road down, Central Ave.
Dangers: Again the kelp has been known to claim fins here, the end section near the rip probably the most at fault.
Rumours: The legend of Tim's summer BBQs originates from a location near here.
Something Else? For those in the right state of mind, the sand dunes in this area can provide hours of amusement.

19.
Break Name: Back Beach / Sorrento
Wave Description: Probably only useful for the very occasional shorebreak that might be up when the winds are playing havoc elsewhere. Usually provides an easy wave that may be just what learners are looking for.
Best Conditions: SW swell, N wind, low tide.
Getting There: Take the road straight through from Sorrento shopping centre seawards and you're there.
Dangers: Crowds, otherwise one of the safest waves ever.
Rumours: The outside reef has held waves before but not incredibly good ones.
Something Else? You will pay a toll to get in here over the summer months. There is a great Tea House that has an incredible view, worth checking out.

20.
Break Name: Portsea Back Beach
Wave Description: This is one long expanse of beach, so my advice is take the banks where you can find them. Sand bank generated waves form all along this stretch of beach, but generally the most used and consistent bank lies to the right

An unknown local focussed at a Rye Beachie. Pic Brett Stanley.

Deep inside a secret reef on the Peninsula. Pic Hilton.

the area.

Best Conditions: SW swell, NE wind, the best tide here can vary.

Getting There: Spooks is towards the west end of Portsea and is viewed from the lookout to the London Bridge.

Dangers: This is a challenging wave that does not forgive surfers who have not paid their dues.

Rumours: Watch for the double ups. They can be either heaven or hell.

Something Else? Hit the pub in Portsea afterwards in summer. It's full of action and I mean ACTION!

22.

Break Name: Quarantines

Wave Description: A lefthand bank, that breaks off the Corsair Rock into the bay. Another quality wave that is sure to please those looking for a session away from flatter waves with less power

Best Conditions: SW swell, SE wind, low-mid tide.

Getting There: Access used to be by those lucky enough to get a spot on board a vessel, but where there's a will, there's a way.

Dangers: Not the easiest place to surf and there is always a lot of water movement around the mouth of a bay.

Rumours: You can check out this break as you travel on the ferry from Sorrento pier back across the heads to Queenscliff.

Something Else? One of those places where, if it's all wrong for most beaches in the area, it might be spot on here. The break is bordered by Fort Nepean, which captured a German boat on its way out of the bay. It was the first shot fired in WW1, which was over the bow of the boat as a warning. Apparently the boat had been on a friendly visit when word of the war had broken out. They left in a hurry, only to be stopped by our fellas. The ruins are pretty interesting and it gives you a chance to check out the wave before you commit to the walk or boat ride.

of the luxurious surf club. This bank lurks just beyond the rock pools.

Best Conditions: SW swell, NE wind, mid tide.

Getting There: Follow the back beach road and take the clearly marked signs through the toll booth, the lower carpark, is the better option for that initial surf check.

Dangers: The rips here can be ferocious on an outgoing tide and a windy day. The main bank is a little shallow on the lower tides.

Rumours: An ex-Australian Prime Minister, Harold Holt may either have been taken by a shark or drowned not too far from here.

Something Else? Another of those beaches in the area where you pay a toll to enter in summer. If you are going to be surfing here regularly buy a season pass, or.....

21.

Break Name: Spooks / Portsea

Wave Description: A righthand beach break that is consistent under the right conditions. A challenging wave that will provide plenty of action, and is a class above many of the more fancied waves in

GENERAL INFORMATION

POINT LEO

Where To Stay:
The available options are limited here
with it being either the caravan park or
the camping grounds. It may also be of
benefit to source out the available
accommodation options in either Flinders
or Hastings.

Where To Eat:
If you are surfing at Point Leo the
chances are you will take your luck on
the offerings at the milk bar, next to the
surf shop. Another option is to jump in
the car and drive to Flinders for a counter
meal, fish and chips or the bakery.

Where To Party:
The camping grounds at Point Leo can be
a party within itself if you come well
stocked over the summer months.
Outside these times the Hastings or
Flinders pubs may provide a suitable
venue for a reflective drink.

Flat Day Fun:
If your feeling in the mood to get in
touch with nature you can take the ferry
from Stony Point out to visit with your

favourite koala friends on French Island
(018 553 136), watch out for my little
buddy, I've nicknamed him Bitey. There
is also the Ashcroft Maze closeby, which
can be pretty interesting at times....

SORRENTO

Where To Stay:
Bells Environmental YHA Hostel. Ph (03)
5984 4323. Not only is this great
accommodation, but the owners Ian and
Margaret will put you in touch with some
information on how to get the most out
of your visit to the east coast. Beds from
$12.

Where To Eat:
There are two bakeries in the main strip
of shops in Sorrento, as well as an
adequate pizza house whose devotion to
a team in the A.F.L. is almost as
impressive as the custom made vegetarian
pizza. For those with a heavy wallet,
there is a beautiful little restaurant nestled
in next to the Continental Hotel and a
good counter meal at the historic Sorrento
Hotel.

Where To Party:
There is a trio of historic pubs in which
to party at Sorrento. The Continental

This P.I local is dangerously close to being a kneeboarder,
or an innovator of a classic tube style. Pic Brett Stanley.

being the most popular and probably the place to head. They run a nightclub here over weekends and the summer months that will accommodate your drinking, dancing and chatting up needs.

Flat Day Fun:

If you haven't already seen it, why not take the ferry over to Queenscliff and spend a day taking a look around. This ferry is also a vital link between the east and west coast surfing spots and you are able to take your car, ute, family truckster or whatever along for the ride. Call (03) 5258 3244 for info on departure times. It will cost $36 for your car and one person. The ferries leave Sorrento every even hour.

PORTSEA

Where To Stay:

This is primarily a residential township and has attracted the money of a lot of Melbourne's elite in building their summer getaways. Consequently the options for accommodation here are usually either prohibitively priced or non existent. Probably your best option lies with the Portsea Hotel (03) 5984 2213. B&B starts from $35.

Where To Eat:

There are a few takeaway places opposite the pub, but in general if you want a cheaper option it is worthwhile to drive or bus back to Sorrento. If you have the spare moolah, then the pub offers great up-market counter meals.

Where To Party:

Again the pub remains the central focus, but for the grommets, the foreshore demonstrates some considerable party action around the New Year's period. For those keen to extend a night out, they run buses between the Portsea pub and the nightclub at the Continental over the busy periods.

Flat Day Fun:

Portsea is one of the major places if you would like to try a little scuba diving in the bay. If you have vehicle access, you may want to try some of the horse riding action back towards Rosebud, or visit some of the local craft markets on the weekends. Point Nepean is worthwhile visiting for its interest, and it also gives you the chance to check out the waves in the area. It costs $8 though.

SECTION INFORMATION

Local Shaper

Trigger Bros - Phil and Paul Trigger. Ph (03) 5989 8402

Quarra surfboards - Frank Sambucca. Ph (03) 5988 9459

Best Months

The wind conditions and swell match up to produce the best conditions either just prior to, or after, the busy summer months.

Secret Spot

I live at the end of an avenue and require a little ti-tree adventure walk to be located. My access is marked by the combination of a flammable solid and the Christian name of a dearly departed grunge icon.

Quick Tips

Due to its proximity to Melbourne and the amount of holiday homes in the area this can become really, really busy over the summer months. While this can be a blessing for those looking to head to the region and party on. The better known beaches will become extremely congested. This is one area where owning a decent wettie for the months coming into summer and thinking beyond the square can produce significant rewards for those really interested in surfing.

Getting There

Take the train to Frankston on the suburban line, then transfer to the bus that will take you all the way to Portsea. Ph (03) 5986 5666. The drive would only take about 1.5 hours.

VIC

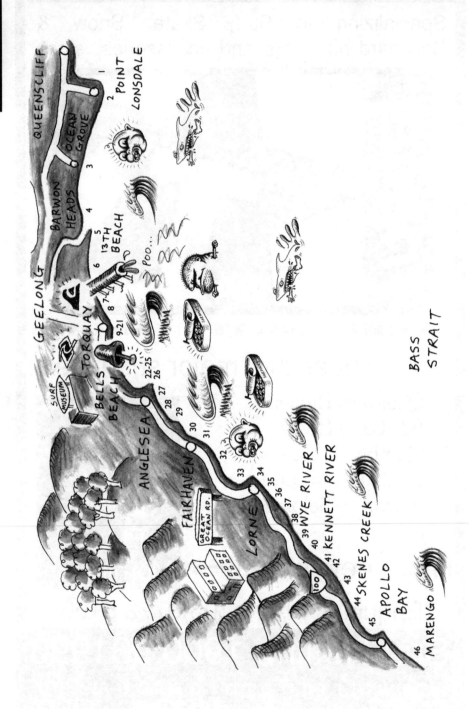

Swell Times

The swell was certainly on the rise, giant plumes surged over the bare rock faces. It looked surfable, just, but the wind was creating some ugly cross-chops that looked certain to cause some weak-limbed surfers imminent grief.

13th Beach perfection. Pic Steve Ryan.

Point Lonsdale - Apollo Bay

The Mighty West Coast

Within this stretch of 300 odd kms of surfable coast, there are some of the best waves in the state. Flanked by the Great Ocean Rd, the endless points and sandy bays play host to a natural paradise. Right point breaks dominate here, dotted around a precariously steep cliff. The road hugs the cliffs for the most part making for an awe inspiring drive.. The area has earned a reputation for raw Southern Ocean surfing. Long walled waves that break ferociously down gnarled reefs are a trademark and dearly loved amongst the inhabitants. It's not all balls to the wall though, as there are places that can have fun waves in even the wildest of swells. The unique aspect to this stretch is the access to the surf. It is generally in full sight of the road, causing excessive drooling among surf hungry hunters. There are still the quieter spots. This is usually when the swell is huge or the few little known nooks that remain relatively untouched. With places like Bells Beach on your side, you can't go too far wrong.

1.
Break Name: Lighthouse
Wave Description: A mellow beach break running along the point that plays home to the lighthouse.
Best Conditions: Large SW swell, NE wind, mid tide.
Getting There: Opposite the shops and cafes at Point Lonsdale. The break is under the shadow of the lighthouse. If you can't find this one there's something wrong.
Dangers: One of the least dangerous waves surfed.
Rumours: Perfect for beginners.
Something Else? The cafés opposite the lighthouse are a perfect way to dream of the perfect surf here.

2.
Break Name: Glenuyes
Wave Description: Pitching lefthand reef break, best surfed between 1 and 2 metres.
Best Conditions: Large SW swell, N wind, mid tide
Getting There: Located at the end of Glenuyes Road. Just beyond the lighthouse in Point Lonsdale.
Dangers: One of the most notorious escalator-like drops operates at this break. Experienced only need apply.
Rumours: The reefs at the front of the lighthouse are a good indicator of the swell for this break.
Something Else? Needs a fairly large swell to perform at its best. Look for that juicy, deep low pressure in Bass Strait

3.
Break Name: Raffs
Wave Description: Right or lefthanded beach breaks. Your choice.
Best Conditions: Huge SW swell, N wind, mid tide.
Getting There: You'll find it at the end of Ocean Grove, a beach break heaven. It's almost as far as the Barwon River mouth, and now has its own carpark to attract further attention.

Dangers: Uncontrolled surf vehicles, you'll get the lot.
Rumours: Occy never fails to surf this break when down for Bells.
Something Else? For those at the beginning of the learning curve, investigate the length of the beach for good wave form and don't just follow the crowd. About 250m either side of the lifesaving club, held a decent bank at the time this was written. EXPLORE!

4.
Break Name: The Hole / 13th Beach
Wave Description: Powerful wave, varied take off points. Generally the rights are the longer, cleaner option.
Best Conditions: SW swell, N-NE wind, mid tide.
Getting There: You'll find this break just west of Point Flinders, Barwon Heads.
Dangers: Shallow on a low tide and, contrary to popular belief, submerged rock is no softer than that which is exposed. If the tide is too low then seek out Band-Aid for a sponsorship. Poor surf ethic is dangerous here as it can test the patience of the locals.
Rumours: Favourite burial site of renowned underworld figure Chopper Read.
Something Else? A very open facing beach which is a good option for waves on a small swell.

5.
Break Name: The Beacon / 13th Beach
Wave Description: Left and righthanders originating from a variety of peaks. This wave has less power than the Hole and is a little safer.
Best Conditions: SW swell, N-NE wind, mid tide.
Getting There: If coming to 13th via the Surfcoast Hwy (B100) then take a left at Lower Duneed Rd and then follow Bluestone School Rd. For this break, look for a shipping marker on the bluff in the dunes.
Dangers: Crowds, especially in summer.

Rumours: To get a peak alone, you need to be early, as numbers are swelling here.
Something Else? Avoid just paddling out with the numbers, take a good look from the dunes and decide whether the most popular take off zone is worth the hassle.

6.
Break Name: Turd Rock / 13th Beach
Wave Description: It is a righthand point break that is considerably smaller than the rest of the breaks on 13th.
Best Conditions: E-SE swell, NE wind, mid-low tide.
Getting There: You'll find it off the road that runs past the sewage pumping plant. Look for the big Westwind propeller. You can't miss it.
Dangers: This becoming your favourite spot.
Rumours: Someone saw a fish out there once.
Something Else? Surfed by those with a bizarre fetish for sewerage or those fishing for some days away from school with a bout of gastro.

7.
Break Name: Bancoora / Breamlea
Wave Description: A righthand reef about 250 m out to sea is where the action is at, however on given days a gentle beach break can form closer to shore.
Best Conditions: SE swell, N-NE wind, mid-low tide.
Getting There: Take Blackgate Rd left off the Surfcoast Hwy. It is another of the signposted breaks and therefore is hard to miss.
Dangers: Tiring yourself out on the paddle to the reef if you've had a particularly big night.
Rumours: This desolate beach once played host to the Australian Lifesaving titles.
Something Else? There are photos that have been taken of this place showing a

solid 2 metre, standup, roaring barrel. I couldn't believe it, but it just proves that everywhere has its day.

8.
Break Name: Insides / Outsides / Point Impossible
Wave Description: Insides is a righthand reef break, and while providing a fun, fairly soft ride, is a little lacking in excitement. Outsides only really differs in the fact that it is usually a little bigger and a little less crowded.
Best Conditions: SW swell, NW wind, mid-low tide.
Getting There: Take the turn to Bremlea off the Surfcoast Hwy, about 7kms south of Torquay. Turn right after the Tiger Moth school.
Dangers: The crazy array of surfcraft can be a serious hazard as there are often plenty of Mals out here.
Rumours: On the rare occasion, this place can get huge with breaks extending east over the rivermouth.
Something Else? It is a great learning wave, as the crowds are very friendly and generally full of beginners.

9.
Break Name: Fishos / Torquay
Wave Description: Breaks over a sand covered reef. Small punchy rights that might surprise.
Best Conditions: Huge SW swell, NE wind, rising tide.
Getting There: You'll find it at the bottom of the boat launching ramp, at Fisherman's Beach. Just east of the Torquay front beach.
Dangers: Including this beach in your surf check ritual, unless the swell is huge.
Rumours: This place gets surfed quite often, more of a malibu wave though.
Something Else? Watch for the presence of petrol stench in the water due to the frequency of outgoing tinnies and ski boats.

VIC

10.
Break Name: Point Danger
Wave Description: A rideable but usually fairly flat righthander can be known to break off the reef.
Best Conditions: SE swell, N-NW wind, mid-high tide.
Getting There: When you find the personal strength to cruise straight through the shopping Mecca that is Surfcoast Plaza without slowing to peruse. Take a left-hand turn at the big roundabout and follow Bell St., past the caravan park, right to its end, or just find the most easterly end of Torquay Back Beach.
Dangers: If the wind is up this break can be considered unsurfable. Not so much because it will make the waves messy, but because the wave jumpers are usually out in force.
Rumours: Jason Polakow KA111, made his start towards dominating the sport of wavejumping, by tuning his skills at this particular location.
Something Else? If you see the windsurfers are in force, think of when

Homer looks at Bart for an anchor to stop the monorail. THINK HARDER. Don't paddle out here and get in their way. There are plenty of better locations for surfers in this area.

11.
Break Name: Drainoes
Wave Description: Usually forms as an A-Frame beak break, but don't be surprised if you find a submerged rock or seven in the vicinity.
Best Conditions: S swell, N wind, mid-low tide.
Getting There: It is almost exactly half way between Point Danger and the Torquay Life Saving club, you'll notice it by the rocks that will pop up in the shore break.
Dangers: Stubbing your toe on a rock on the way in. Alternatively, catching a fin on one of the aforementioned rocks, if you don't walk your board in when it gets shallow.
Rumours: The drain that looms large on the cliff is the source of the break name.
Something Else? This is probably a

Bird Rock, home to the flying spray of Troy Brooks. Pic Steve Ryan

wave that is a little more complex when conditions are right than the one in front of the surf club. However, this always depends on the nature of the sandbanks at the time.

12.
Break Name: Torquay Back Beach
Wave Description: There are a variety of beach breaks that will form here depending on the swell direction and sandbank formation. The best bet is to study conditions before you paddle out. Traditionally the best option here is the bank that forms directly out in front of the hill, and generally the rights are longer.
Best Conditions: S swell, N wind, mid-low tide.
Getting There: This area has had an access road put in over recent years to stop people accessing this beach through the caravan park. You can't miss it because its signposted and only about 100m from the main roundabout.
Dangers: Angry surf life-savers and crowding. This is probably the most crowded beach along the west coast in summer, full of surf skis and Malibus.
Rumours: That one of their own famous Ironwomen was taken out by a surfboat at this beach, causing her considerable injuries.
Something Else? A great place to check in S or SE winds as it does provide considerable protection. Also check the renovations to this beach around the toilet block, SWANKY. The dunes up above this break are a maze of little tracks and alcoves, it used to be a favourite haunt for those seeking out a free camping site before authorities cottoned on and cracked down.

13.
Break Name: Jan Juc
Wave Description: A collection of beach breaks that form according to sandbank movement in the area. The quality of these waveforms are variable and it is

often best to scan the length of this beach in summer to avoid some of the crowding that occurs in front of the carparks.
Best Conditions: SW swell, NW wind, mid-low tide.
Getting There: Turn off the highway just after the golf course, Hoylake Rd. Follow this down to the bottom of the golf course and take a left to find the carparks.
Dangers: This break killed Kenny, the bastard. (If you watch or watched SouthPark you'll understand.)
Rumours: That the break in front of the carparks is the only bank worth surfing. This is UNTRUE.
Something Else? This is a great beach, with protection from the offshores by the cliffs. A beautiful beach in its own right.

14.
Break Name: Bird Rock
Wave Description: One of the more challenging waves in this region as it breaks over a submerged rock point. On the lower tides it can go close to sucking dry on bigger days and therefore remains the domain of the advanced. This wave is a short but crazy righthander with action aplenty.
Best Conditions: SW swell, NW wind, mid-low tide.
Getting There: Take Ocean Bvld., until you see the famous Bird Rock Café. Turn into the newly asphalted carpark and take a peak from the lookouts at what you might expect.
Dangers: Heavy local presence, nosediving on the takeoff.
Rumours: There are many rumours flying about telling of send-ins and threats to those not respecting the locals or surf etiquette. If in doubt, believe them.
Something Else? We all know that nature is the essence of why we get to surf, but what she gives to us can also be taken away. In the last couple of years the nature of the wave at Bird Rock has changed due to the departure of Ziggy, the end section of the reef. Only those

who have surfed the spot over the years can accurately describe the old wave. Take it from me, Ziggy made things a little more interesting at the Rock.

15.
Break Name: Sparrows
Wave Description: Another righthand reef break that runs along a submerged rock ledge.
Best Conditions: SW swell, N wind, mid-high tide.
Getting There: It is the next break west of Bird Rock and can be seen from the same look-out. You may also might want to use the same carpark.
Dangers: Getting greedy and trying to hold on to this wave until the end section closes out, which may result in parting with some of your hard earned cash for a ding repair kit.
Rumours: About three years ago, just after Christmas, this place was picture perfect and looked like the pitching, spitting barrels we all hope to luck into someday.
Something Else? A good option when Bird Rock is crowded.

16.
Break Name: Steps
Wave Description: Righthand reef breaks that can provide heart in the mouth takeoffs followed by a walling wave. On its day this wave is well worth the mission to get there. If there is a northerly blowing and the waves hold up and hollow out, you'll know what surfing is all about.
Best Conditions: SW swell, N wind, mid-full tide.
Getting There: Take Ocean Blvd, up past the Jan-Juc shopping center, to the top of the hill, where, if you are lucky, you'll see the car-park that accesses both Evos's and Steps.
Dangers: This wave is one to check when the conditions are in its favour, otherwise it can turn into a flat dribbling little wave.

Rumours: Uh, uh.
Something Else? Watch out for the walk back to the carpark after a winter session. Remember that numb feet and steep stairs do not go hand in hand. However think yourself lucky because about five years ago it used to be SO much worse.

17.
Break Name: Evos
Wave Description: A fangio like righthand wave that gives you as much speed as you'd like to draw out of it. Probably one of the shallowest waves in the area and if you have decent booties then paddling would be obsolete.
Best Conditions: SW swell, N/NE wind, mid-high.
Getting There: Shift your gaze about 10 degrees west, once you have located Steps.
Dangers: Dings, cuts, scratches, bruises and headaches. All those pleasantries associated with shallow reef surfing.
Rumours: The left is a lot of fun and makeable on every takeoff.
Something Else? Lie as flat as you can when you come off here, as a classic swan dive could end at the Torquay medical centre.

18.
Break Name: Boobs
Wave Description: A reef break catering for both the natural and the goofy footers amongst us, a great spot for an inter-footed surf party. The right is generally better but clean conditions make the left the place to be when it's on.
Best Conditions: Straight SW swell, NW wind, mid-high tide.
Getting There: Take a walk west under the cliff line towards Winkipop and this wave will introduce itself if it's happening.
Dangers: It's a reasonably shallow reef, the rest is fairly inconsequential.
Rumours: A fun walk on a lower tide around the cliff-line used to get you into the Easter Classic for free.

Something Else? There is another break to be found in this area that pumps out the barrels on the good days but the last section is almost unmakeable.

19.

Break Name: Winkipop

Wave Description: One of the longest rides in the area. A roaring righthand point, that breaks over a relatively shallow reef. On smaller days this wave has three distinct take-offs, but when the swell is on (usually around the 2m mark), this wave can link up from Uppers all the way through to Lowers. This gives rise for huge floaters or perfect barrelling sections.

Best Conditions: SW swell, NW wind, mid-high tide.

Getting There: Take the turn off to Bells from the Hwy. Utilise the first carpark, that way you can run straight down into the action.

Dangers: Shallow reef and hot local surfers making sure that the wave is not finished until you see them fall or pull off. It will surprise you some of the sections that these guys will be able to make. Also the paddle here can be exhausting as you are usually running against the current. Getting caught inside can ruin an otherwise enjoyable day. On the big days discretion may need to be exercised and to paddle out off Bells around the button may save you a serious pounding.

Rumours: Check out the action here over the Bells Classic as it is a renowned warm up area for professionals looking to get in a little last minute practice.

Something Else? Also known as the Studio, due to the number of first class surfers that frequent the break as well as the excellent vantage points on offer to view the action.

20.

Break Name: Bells Beach

Wave Description: Another long righthand point break over a submerged reef known affectionately as the tombstone. The wave is so long that is defined into three sections, from the point (Rincon) through the infamous Bells bowl to the shore break.

Best Conditions: SW swell, NW wind, mid-high tide.

Getting There: Continue to the lower carparks if you have decided to surf Bells as it makes access easier.

Kolani Robb fanning the Winkipop wave. Pic Brett Stanley.

Dangers: This break is not the best place to take waves with unmakeable sections and get caught inside. However if this cannot be avoided head straight for the bowl and take a wide line on the paddle back out to catch your breath.

Rumours: Bells beach got its name because when surfers could first access the break by vehicle it was Martha Bell's property through which they had to pass.

Something Else? In the late 1940's, Dick Garrard and a few of his buddies would paddle around from Jan Juc and surf what we now know as Bells beach and Winkipop. The break has come a long way since these times and is the most renowned Victorian surfing venue thanks to the Bells Beach Easter Classic held there. (This statement is a little contentious, as Peter Troy was also a Pioneer here and surfed it in the early days as well. There was a club of around 30 passionate souls that got together to put the road in. They all chipped in for the hire of a tractor. Once the road was in though, everyone started using it, which changed the face of Bells forever.) It is one of the classic waves of the world and has to be surfed, even in the most appalling conditions. You know why. For that surfer pilgrimage thing!

21.
Break Name: Centerside
Wave Description: This wave is a punchy right, breaking on the reef south of the headland.
Best Conditions: SE swell, N wind, mid-full tide.
Getting There: The most convenient access to Centerside involves entering the water from the Bells headland, and paddling south across to the break.
Dangers: Can be relatively dangerous due to the closeness of the reef on a low tide, though one of the safer waves of those described, over the last kilometre or so.
Rumours: Always less crowded than the surrounding breaks. Admittedly because of the drop in quality.
Something Else? Centreside does not link up with Rincon because there is actually a gap in the reef between the two. Whilst this might be disappointing for an extension on the Bells experience, it allows a somewhat safer paddle out if you are to chance your luck from the headland.

The search is on. Near Anglesea. Pic Steve Ryan.

22.
Break Name: Southside
Wave Description: One of the rare quality lefthanders, on the west coast. A quick wave that breaks over another very shallow reef. Works best on swell between 1m and 1.5m. This wave offers great protection if there is too much easterly in the wind direction for the other breaks.
Best Conditions: S-SE swell, N wind, mid-high tide.
Getting There: The best route involves heading on a little further south than the main Bells carparks and taking the turnoff up the hill to the carpark on top of the headland. From here take the track down to the beach and BINGO.
Dangers: Try this break on a mid to high tide unless you've been plagued by taunts of pretty boy and want to add some rugged scars.
Rumours: Long walk up the hill back to the car after a draining session.
Something Else? This carpark is a favourite haven for those looking for a quiet spot to show one's date the wonder of nature when the stars are out (or even if they aren't).

23.
Break Name: Point Addis
Wave Description: Both a left and right can break in front of the point, the left being the better option as it has a little more shape to it as it forms over the rocks.
Best Conditions: S-SE swell, N-NW wind mid-low tide.
Getting There: Point Addis lies at the western most end of the bay that is home to Centreside etc.
Dangers: If you delve deep enough you might just find the rocks responsible for the wave action here.
Rumours: If the swell is big enough for Winki to be going off, check here as the crowds won't be nearly as bad.
Something Else? This spot can give some protection from the south-easters

that chop up the other breaks along this stretch.

24.
Break Name: Grinders / Anglesea
Wave Description: A short but powerful barrelling wave that gives you a classical wave formation under the right conditions.
Best Conditions: SW swell, N-E wind, mid-high tide.
Getting There: Considered as a somewhat secret spot for years as there is no direct sign posting for this break. However, if you take the road down past the scout camp and successfully negotiate the trek down to the beach you've found it.
Dangers: This wave can often turn out to be considerably heavier than it looks and can be a trap for the inexperienced. The track down to the beach can be a trap in itself for those in too much of a hurry to hit the water.
Rumours: The track down can be extremely confusing, with deviations everywhere. Follow your nose.
Something Else? There is still heavy local action when this place is really working, show as much respect as you would anywhere else.

25.
Break Name: Anglesea
Wave Description: A mellow beach break that provides sanctuary for those learning the basics of surfing.
Best Conditions: S-SE swell, N wind, mid tide.
Getting There: Follow the highway through the main township of Anglesea and when you reach a harsh turn in the road with a surf shop on the corner you're getting boiling hot.
Dangers: The waves being ordinary and plenty of drop ins
Rumours: A great place to learn, with a great atmosphere in the water.
Something Else? This beach is a favourite haunt of the west coast learn-to-

surf school, enough said about its credentials as a basis for a grounding knowledge of the sport.

26.

Break Name: Point Roadknight
Wave Description: A relatively flat uninteresting wave that is more popular with the malibu riders, it is a righthand break off the point. The swell needs to be huge for this place to even register. However there is a positive in the fact that this wave will handle westerly winds when others in the area will be blown out.
Best Conditions: SE swell, N/NW wind, mid-low tide.
Getting There: There is a clearly marked entrance off the Ocean Road, so just follow the signs.
Dangers: Expect a lengthy ride if you paddle out on a short board.
Rumours: Two of the contributors for this book met at a house in Point Roadknight for a weekend of debauchery. Only to awaken the next morning at the crack of noon and watch a wind affected four foot wave roll in. The morning had been perfection. Always the way hey.
Something Else? Don't write this place off, it's as fickle as Merimbula Bar, but can get incredibly good.

27.

Break Name: Guvvos
Wave Description: Left and right beach breaks depending on sandbank formation. A good wave shape that is challenging for both beginner and intermediate surfers.
Best Conditions: Straight S swell, N wind, low-mid tide.
Getting There: This break is located about 2 kms past Point Roadknight, you will recognise the carpark as it is marked on the coast highway by a sign. You can see waves breaking directly in front of the carpark but the best and most consistent bank is about 200m left down the beach.

Dangers: There is no definite sign marking this break other than the sign telling you of the carpark. Don't worry if you think you haven't found exactly the break described above, because there are several carparks along this stretch with decent breaks awaiting you, directly in front.
Rumours: Catches a fair amount of swell.
Something Else? The author of this section once lost a Rip Curl time and tide watch at this break, if you find it please contact Liquid Addictions and arrange to forward the watch. I'll be expecting your call. ....Yeah right.

28.

Break Name: Urquart's Bluff
Wave Description: A righthander breaking over rock bottom. Not an incredibly challenging wave usually quite flat. Offshore winds are north to northwest, however this beach is probably more populated when the wind is from the opposite direction.
Best Conditions: S-SE swell, N-NW winds and mid to high tide.
Getting There: Clearly marked carpark entrance off the coast highway.
Dangers: There can be a hell of a rip operating here when the wind is from the south-east, much better to be gliding over the top of the water than in it when this happens.
Rumours: This break is better known by windsurfers than surfers.
Something Else? Long time home of Victorian wild man and legendary surfer Wayne Lynch who still kicks on, busy balancing his shaping with time spent in the water.

29.

Break Name: Fairhaven
Wave Description: Beach break A-frames that will pop up in a variety of locations according to sand movement in the area. This is a great learner's wave as it has enough power behind it to give you a ride but not enough to get you into trouble.

Best Conditions: S swell, N wind, mid-high tide.

Getting There: If you can't find your way to this break don't even bother looking for the nose on your face.

Dangers: This beach is well patrolled over the summer months, therefore the dangers at this beach are well monitored. The only real danger at this break seems to be the occasional strong rip.

Rumours: You may be lucky enough to catch some of the talented locals from the Howard Hughes stable surfing out here when the conditions are good.

Something Else? This is one of the swell magnets on the coast. Second only to Bells and Cathedral Rock.

30.

Break Name: Towerblocks

Wave Description: Similar to Fairhaven, although the banks seem to be a little more stable here creating more consistency in the peaks that form.

Best Conditions: S swell, N winds and mid-high tide.

Getting There: This break has an indicator to its location that is a piece of architectural wizardry. You'll find the break out in front of the house with a room supported by a huge concrete pylon.

Dangers: Running off the road by marvelling at the afore mentioned residence.

Rumours: This is another break with the luxury of its own carpark and can be located about a kilometre past Moggs Creek

Something Else? There are some excellent camping grounds for the budget traveller if you take the roads inland around this area.

31.

Break Name: Spout Creek

Wave Description: Beach break waves that can go either way, on surf up to about 1.5m. It is a good fun wave on its day without the ever present danger of

long hold downs. This wave is well protected from westerly winds and is therefore one of those spots worth a look when many other breaks are blown out.

Best Conditions: S-SE swell, N wind, mid tide

Getting There: This break is located just past the Spout Creek river mouth and the large archway declaring the beginning to the Great Ocean Road.

Dangers: Undetectable undercurrents.

Rumours: Nup.

Something Else? From here you are lucky to be travelling on a road that will take all the twists and turns along this beautiful coastline. Although there are no real acknowledged surf locations from here through to Cathedral Rock, I know that I always keep my eyes peeled just in case.

32.

Break Name: Cathedral Rock

Wave Description: This wave is probably the lost brother of Winkipop. It's hall-marked by the same testing takeoffs, challenging sections and long walling shape that offers surfers a chance to experience real speed. Primarily your concern for great wave opportunities at Cathedral is large swell. The place only really gets going when waves of 1.5m plus, are pounding the point. This is one of those waves with headland protection and can work quite well on variable winds if they are not too strong.

Best Conditions: SW swell, NW wind, low tides.

Getting There: There is parking above this break on the point and it is rare for there to be no cars parked here if there are waves to be surfed. The break is approximately 4.5km north of the township of Lorne.

Dangers: Like most quality waves in this vein, it can be quite on ordeal to get caught inside on the reef here, as escape requires some strenuous paddling. One danger to be very aware of, is picking off the smaller waves and coming precariously close to a reef awaiting the unwary surfer.

Rumours: This wave has long been a favourite of the most talented surfers in the area, so be aware that competition at this break may well be stiff.

Something Else? If you are looking for that super long ride to take you to the beach. Waves that will break a little wider from the point can help you reach your goal.

33.

Break Name: Lorne Point

Wave Description: This is a relatively inconsistent wave but if you get it on its day you will be back here consistently just trying to catch the place working again. Long righthanders will peel off the point taking you 500m plus, from near the pier in towards the beach breaks. In short, if the waves are huge and the wind is getting up, all roads head to Lorne Point. It might just be your saviour.

Best Conditions: E-SE Swell, W-SW wind, low tide.

Getting There: You'll be able to see this break from the beer garden at the hotel or from the penthouse suite of that pink monstrosity, otherwise known as the Cumberland.

Dangers: A relatively safe wave as it is not very heavy. However, one can get into trouble surfing smaller waves too close to the rocks.

Rumours: Check a few of the local surf shops to see photos of epic days at Lorne point.

Something Else? Towards the end of summer every year the annual Pier to Pub swim is conducted and the town erupts. This is usually a great weekend for all concerned, so if you have the means I highly recommend it.

34.

Break Name: Barrels / Lorne

Wave Description: A short righthand reef break that will give plenty of action upon the drop in, but turns into a flat

and fat shoulder very quickly.

Best Conditions: S swell, N-W wind, mid-low tide.

Getting There: This wave is located in the second bay south of Lorne, you will find a carpark there, so it's not an easy place to miss.

Dangers: Never making the takeoff.

Rumours: This can be the end section of an epic ride through this bay on huge days if you make the take-off at Weeds and keep that speed going.

Something Else? There is a great Café on the pier that you can check out the wave from. Great food as well.

35.

Break Name: Weeds / Lorne

Wave Description: Very heavy powerful righthander.

Best Conditions: Large SE swell, NW-W wind, mid tide.

Getting There: Same directions as to find Barrels, only this wave is further south in the same bay.

Dangers: Steep take-offs and a lot of water movement, so keep your wits about you.

Rumours: This place is very fickle and often overlooked.

Something Else? This wave used to be a real favourite amongst those residing in this area, however the quality of the wave and popularity of the break have waned over recent years.

36.

Break Name: Cumberland River

Wave Description: Small beach break waves generally without much punch behind them. Rare wind conditions will suit this wave. Unlike most beaks around the Lorne area, a westerly wind will blow these waves out.

Best Conditions: SE swell, N wind, mid-low tide.

Getting There: South of Lorne on the Great Ocean Road this river is clearly marked both by signs and the fact that there is a beautiful caravan park straddling the river.

Dangers: Having a surf-less holiday in the caravan park, as there can be little action here without one of those infrequent easterly wind swells.

Rumours: When the banks are good, it can produce hollow and fun beachies

Something Else? Those with the option of being mobile might want to check out the caravan park here as a base for their south coast surfing adventure, it is quite picturesque.

37.

Break Name: Bog Alley

Wave Description: A righthander that usually has some power, due to the fact it only works on big swells. Swell needs to be pushing through Bells at around the 3m mark for this break to be working.

Best Conditions: S swell, N wind, most tides.

Getting There: You'll find this break just south beyond Artillery Rocks

Dangers: The same you face every time you paddle out in the water.

Rumours: The author has seen a dark grey shape while out surfing this particular break, though no complete verification of its nature was gained.

Something Else? On the classic days of the big swells, there will always be better waves than this.

38.

Break Name: Wye River

Wave Description: Beach break peaks can provide a thrill or simply a fun ride.

Best Conditions: S swell, N-NW wind, high tide.

Getting There: Cannot miss it, the best beachies are usually to be had to the right of the rivermouth if you are looking seaward.

Dangers: None.

Rumours: The pub is one of the classics on the West coast. A great view, with excellent meals, worth a stop.

Something Else? If I ever have children this would be where I will take them to

Pull over, stop awhile. Summer beachies, Great Ocean Road. Pic Brett Stanley.

learn to surf. You could leave the nippers to practice on their foamies in a reasonably safe environment whilst enjoying a quiet amber refreshment and keeping an eye on them from the Rookery Nook Hotel.

39.
Break Name: Baldy Rock / Wye River
Wave Description: Peeling righthanders on a sand covered reef bottom.
Best Conditions: S-SW swell, N-NW wind, rising tide.
Getting There: Follow the road a little further south from Wye River and you will see a carpark as you approach the point.
Dangers: Believing the legends of the quality of this wave in years gone by. These days it will occasionally work and give a fantastic day's surfing but generally the wave form is far too flat to consider it a top line surfing location.
Rumours: This area is the home of a reasonably friendly shark that has been sighted several times but has never left an impression on anyone.
Something Else? A great place to stay as there is a really friendly vibe here, and the waves are definitely fun. Good for a first experience in surfing.

40.
Break Name: Sawmills
Wave Description: Long, down-the-line righthand reef break, that will handle the bigger swells pushing through the area. One of the best places on the entire coast to surf when a big swell is being ruined by south-westerly winds.
Best Conditions: S swell, N-NW wind, mid-high tide.
Getting There: This wave is located just north east of Kennett River mouth running into the neighbouring bay.
Dangers: The only critical danger is losing your board onto the exposed rocks from riding the wave out too long on the smaller days.
Rumours: A favourite haunt for

knowledgable locals when the swell is up and the wind is fickle.
Something Else? Always worth checking, but rarely surfed.

41.
Break Name: Kennett Rivermouth
Wave Description: Good fun beach breaks form here at the rivermouth. They come in the shape of A frames but the banks formed here generally favour a racy right that will break right along the beach on its day.
Best Conditions: S-SE swell, N-NW wind, mid-low tide.
Getting There: You'll find these waves breaking directly in front of the rivermouth opposite the camping grounds.
Dangers: If the sand banks are not well formed here, the wave will consist of nothing more than a drop-in and a large close out section.
Rumours: Well, actually, no.
Something Else? The camping grounds here are a great place for a few days spent by the beach as there is plenty of beauty to be seen just inland and some great walks to be had, as well as being a quick dash across the Ocean Road to the beach.

42.
Break Name: Kennett Point
Wave Description: A long fun righthander will often be found breaking off the point here. This is a very consistent wave that works when there is not enough swell for a lot of other breaks in the area. The point gives a great amount of shelter from the dreaded south-westerly winds even though off-shores are more westerly in direction.
Best Conditions: S-SE swell, NW wind, mid-low tide.
Getting There: You will see this wave easily from the camping ground as it breaks off the point out in front.
Dangers: On smaller days you will find yourself surfing very close to a shallow

Adam Bell in a south coast beast. Pic Steve Ryan.

rock base on a low tide. Be very cautious and watch for the larger rocks that might become exposed or otherwise a crash course in fin replacement might well be necessary.

Rumours: Not many people let on about the rumours around here, so I'd have to say no.

Something Else? This place tends to work best when the waves are breaking up to 1.5m, if conditions are larger than this the waves will either break wider of the point and take you right into the bay or not work at all. If the second scenario is the case you might be better off heading back up the road to Sawmills.

43.
Break Name: Boneyards
Wave Description: An exceptionally reliable spot providing a righthand, hollow, pitching, reef break. Swell conditions need to be in excess of 1.2 m however. This place picks up a lot more swell than other breaks in the area.

Works better on bigger days as it breaks consistently along the reef and will provide a ride on all tides.

Best Conditions: S swell, N wind, variable tides.

Getting There: Just over a kilometre down the road from Kennett river this spot is marked by a carpark elevated above the break.

Dangers: On a lower tide this place can get quite shallow and the kelp may become a problem.

Rumours: Take the walk down from the carpark and paddle out from the channel to make life easy for yourself.

Something Else? This wave has a horrid takeoff and is definitely only for the experienced. When you actually see it, you'll know what I mean. If there are short punchy hollow barrels coming through this break, the photo opportunity from the rock ledge is excellent. That is, if you can get someone to stay out of the water.

Shane Bevan at mysterious spot x. Pic Steve Ryan.

44.
Break Name: Smythes Creek
Wave Description: Good peeling righthand waves breaking over a sand base at this location.
Best Conditions: Large S swell, N-NW wind, mid-high tide.
Getting There: This wave is positioned just to the right of the camping ground before Skene's Creek.
Dangers: There is a rock ledge that will ruin the end of an otherwise enjoyable ride if you do not keep a look out.
Rumours: A place of little crowds.
Something Else? The landscape here is beautiful, changing quite dramatically from the steep cliffs before Lorne.

45.
Break Name: Harbour Wall / Apollo Bay
Wave Description: A fun righthand wave will peel off along the rock groyne that forms the boat harbour.
Best Conditions: Big S-SE swell, W wind, low tide.
Getting There: Take the Ocean Rd into the township of Apollo Bay and you will find the boat harbour at the western end of the beach.
Dangers: It can get big, but usually it is a great summer spot for fun waves.
Rumours: Check the beach breaks further east along the beach as often a great learners wave might be doing its thing.
Something Else? The huge cypress trees make this one of the most scenic shorelines along the coast.

46.
Break Name: Marengo
Wave Description: Exposed beach breaks
Best Conditions: SW swell, NW-NE wind, mid-low tide.
Getting There: This area is the foreshore to the Marengo township.
Dangers: This wave is messy and will close out unless the conditions are good.
Rumours: Like anywhere, it does have its day, which at best is a fast, fun wave.
Something Else? There is plenty to see in these historic townships, but they are not really regarded as pinnacles of surf action on the coast.

GENERAL INFORMATION

POINT LONSDALE

Where To Stay:
Golightly Caravan Park. Ph (03) 5252 1765. Powered sites from $14.
There is also the guest houses and a motel.

Where To Eat:
Both the cafes near the lighthouse (Pasquini's Dell and Cafe Angelina) are reasonable although a little more expensive than the trustworthy bakery.

Where To Party:
It really doesn't happen here, unless you are 16 and staying in the Caravan Park.

Flat Day Fun:
You can go horesriding, check out the lighthouse, rent a boat, or just kick back. Personally I reckon you head further west.

BARWON HEADS

Where To Stay:
The Caravan Park is pretty cool, with great access to the beaches. Ph (03) 5254 2572. Sites from $8.
You can stay in the Pub but it is pretty expensive. Ph (03) 5254 2201.

Where To Eat:
Threre are some little Café's on the main street but the pub is your best bet.

Where To Party:
One of the all time locations to bring in the New Year. It has had some troubled years, but is generally a hell of a lot of fun. If it is one of the 364 nights of the year that is not New Year's, then try the hotel overlooking the bridge.

Flat Day Fun:
Golf course, or try fishing off the bridge. Far cheaper than the golf course which is private and expensive.

TORQUAY

Where To Stay:
Torquay Public Reserve. Ph (03) 5261 2496, better known as the caravan park, has affordable camping sites and caravans to hire. Early bookings are essential over the Easter period and the summer months.
Zeally Bay Caravan Park. Ph (03) 5261 2400, may be another option and although it is a little further from the surf and the action, it can have sites when the public reserve was booked out long ago.
Nomad Bells Beach Hostel. Ph (03) 5261 7070 is a newer option that resides near the surf coast sales Mecca. Rooms are available here for $20 a person.

Where To Eat:
Most will end up eating at the fish and chip shops on Bell St or sourcing what is on offer in the milk bar. However take the walk or drive to Gilbert St. (main shopping centre) and visit either the bakery next to the supermarket or Yummy Yoghurt further towards the front beach for a meal with a little more substance.

Where To Party:
Torquay Hotel is pretty much the most popular of options and is packed to the eye teeth over Easter and the summer months. If this is the case and you want to escape the crowds a little, it can be useful to try Pabs pub. Here you will find a few more locals that are generally accommodating, unless you want to make an idiot of yourself.

Flat Day Fun:
You can waste hours strolling through the surf retailers' centre trying to convince yourself that you desperately need that new board, shirt, wettie or whatever. However, if you have change left over go and see the Surfworld museum as you will definitely learn about our great heritage. Jack is your man here.
Tiger Moth World is also a treat for those with spare cash and a sense of adventure.

VIC

ANGLESEA

Where To Stay:

Anglesea Family Caravan Park. Ph (03) 5263 1583 has tent sites and cabins available on the foreshore for reasonable rates, but this will get very busy over the hotter months.

Anglesea Backpackers.

Ph (03) 5263 2664 is a fantastic place to stay and you are an even chance to glean a little bit of local knowledge of the good spots to go from the friendly Manager. Tony Evans is your man here.

Where To Eat:

Anglesea Bakery has always been a favourite of mine and usually damn good value. The pies are great. The Anglesea Pub can be relied upon for a good square counter meal.

Where To Party:

The Anglesea Pub is again your answer here with a lot of fun to be had over summer months when a nightclub area is run adjacent to the pub.

Flat Day Fun:

Try the golf course where frequent stops to hit a frustrating little white ball ruin an otherwise lovely nature walk.

One of the many classic righthanders on the West coast. Pic Steve Ryan.

LORNE

Where To Stay:
Try the Lorne Foreshore Committee. Ph (03) 5289 1382 and speak to them about fulfilling all your camp site needs.
Great Ocean Road Backpackers. Ph (03) 5289 1809 has a variety of accommodation options and is a great place to stay in the area.
You can stay at a number of places past Lorne, which often gets you a little away from it all. The first is at Cumberland river. Ph (03) 5289 1382. Sites from $10. Wye River is a killer place to stay, with a cool camp ground and a great pub. The town is tiny, so don't expect anything much. Ph (03) 5289 0240 for the Rookery Nook Hotel as they have motel units from $40 if you want a bit of comfort.

Where To Eat:
Kafe Kaos provides a varied and interesting selection but will be a little pricey if minimum chips and a dimmy is your normal diet when you're not in the water. The Arab cafe is a place your father might tell you a story about coming to and worth a visit. Also, the reliable pub again, chips with the counter meal option.

Where To Party:
The Lorne Hotel is probably the Mecca for entertainment in the area and is a must for a perve over the summer months. The Grand Pacific Hotel is probably a little more low key, but boasts some good bands in their line up, as well as the most incredible view.

Flat Day Fun:
There are some great walks in the area. Angahook-Lorne State Park. You can also go to Erskine falls which are pretty good. A great drive though. There is also the standard array of amusements in the town, nothing exceptional though.

SECTION INFORMATION

Local Shaper
Gash Surfboards - Greg Brown, Mark Phipps (Torquay). Ph (03) 5261 3292
Hughes Surfcraft - Howard Hughes (Fairhaven). Ph (03) 5289 7153
Mocean - Gavin Carroll (Lorne). Ph (03) 5289 1011
Rip Curl - Michael Anthony (Torquay). Ph (03) 5261 3375
Rastas - Ross Eiji Ph (03) 5254 3255
Strapper - Robbo (Torquay). Ph (03) 5261 2312
Evolution - Wayne Lynch (Urquharts Bluff). Ph (03) 5263 2722

Best Months
April to October

Secret Spot
If your vehicle is feeling limber and you feel conditions are right for you to make the trip, then a jaunt down a dirt road to an unmarked beach could have you claiming that X marks the spot.

Quick Tips
This area gets flooded with tourists and people from Melbourne over the peak summer months. The swell is much smaller, but there are still fun waves to be had, but be smart. You don't have to drive all the way to Apollo Bay to find there is no surf. Check places like 13th and Bells for accurate swell appraisals. There are some areas that you can just crash in your car right on the ocean, away from the road. It would be irresponsible to mention the exact location, but if you head past Anglesea, before Lorne you should find it. Another point to know is that there are a few places that receive more swell. These are 13th, Bells, Fairhaven, Cathedral Rock and Kennett. On marginal days these are your best bet.

Getting There
You can take a V-Line train from Spencer St. Station in Melbourne to Geelong and catch the Apollo Bay bus to access most locations along the Great Ocean Road. Ph 13 22 32. You can catch a bus all the way if you like. The full fare is $26. You can also try McHarry's Bus Lines on (03) 5223 2111 for a competitive deal.

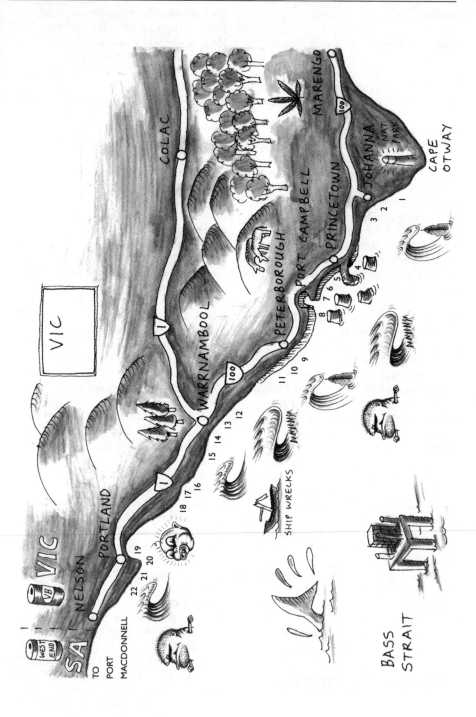

Southern Juice

The Ocean was alive once more. The wind hurled thirty foot sea-sprays, while the ground rumbled with the raw force.

Jeff Sweeney lining up this south coast outer-reef. Pic Steve Ryan.

Apollo Bay - Portland

Appetite for Destruction

There is a dramatic change once you are out of the boundaries of Apollo Bay. The ocean exerts its true force onto the coastline, producing power that is hard to match elsewhere. The landscape is a mix of rainforest, lush dairy country, and flat, inhospitable semi-arid land. It is the sheer power that is overwhelming when you experience places like Johanna and the surrounds. The waves explode onto the shoreline, the jagged cliff faces bearing the scars of constant abuse from the almighty mistress of the sea. This is the roaming territory of sightseers and madmen. From an outsider's perspective, this coastline is good for surveying and tightening the top button of the jacket. For some though, it provides the ultimate challenge of what is possible. Many of the waves are viewed from high upon cliff faces, which don't accurately portray the sheer force at which these waves break. For those who experience it, it can be a life altering event one I highly recommend.

1.

Break Name: Castle Cove

Wave Description: There are two predominant waves here. The righthander is a quick drop into a hollow section, and gets very good. Breaks over sand and reef. The lefthander is at the eastern side of the bay and is generally a longer wave, although the free-fall takeoff is the same as the right.

Best Conditions: S swell, NE winds, low-mid tide.

Getting There: Once through the Otway forest on the Great Ocean Rd, it is signposted with a carpark.

Dangers: Extreme caution needs to be taken when bigger swells hit as there is a lot of water movement within the bay and some strong rips can form. The wave is always SO much bigger when you get in, as the carpark is so high. Don't be fooled!

Rumours: This cove is an important site for history lovers, as there have been fossilised dinosaur remains found here. There is actually a little story board at the carpark, so, in fact, this is not a rumour. Oh well!

A long, long, paddle at Johanna Beach. Pic Nick Clark

Something Else? The heavy sand here is the reason for the consistency of the banks, however with this consistency comes massive close out sections on big days, as well as the ever present rips.

2.

Break Name: Johanna Beach

Wave Description: There are several options for waves here too. There is a left point break at the eastern end which is the most consistent. There are also a variety of shifting beach breaks that can be perfect for weeks. Then as suddenly as they appear, they vanish. Generally the waves are extremely powerful, showing the pure Southern Ocean in all its glory.....or pain!

Best Conditions: SW swell, NE wind, low-mid tide.

Getting There: Take the Red or Blue Johanna Rd from the Great Ocean Rd. You will see the camp ground, next to the tennis court. The best place to camp is next to the trees, as this place has a habit of changing weather, in a matter of hours.

Dangers: Johanna is a heavy wave, make no mistake about that. The 1 metre beachbreak, if you treat it with contempt, will give you a hold down that you won't easily forget. The most important aspect to success on this beach is knowledge of the rips. They are your best friend here, as you probably won't get out otherwise. Both ends of the beach have defined rips from the reef shelf, which should be used. For the centre breaks, use these exits as well if it is big.

Rumours: Johanna is acknowledged as being one of the best locations to head to if there is an unacceptable lack of swell around the reefs that inhabit the Torquay area. For this reason it can get quite crowded, especially over summer time when the swell is not as plentiful as the winter months. For example, if Torquay is 1 metre, then Johanna will be too big, as with Castle cove. If it is dead flat, then you're in for a show.

Something Else? Many followers of professional surfing will be aware that this beach is the preferred venue to move the Bells Beach Easter Classic when the swell is too small to hold a decent contest further back up the coast. Also, the campground now charges. It is part of the tightening of the State Park laws. Some guy will probably try to sting you for $8. Not in winter though. One last thing, the fishing is magnificent. Good catches of Whiting and Salmon can be expected. Fish in the gutters and at first light for the best results.

3.
Break Name: Moonlight Head
Wave Description: Generally the lefts peeling across the reef are the ridden waves at this location. Can sometimes be a little flat requiring skill to maintain momentum and get yourself a decent ride.
Best Conditions: SW swell, SE wind, low-mid tide.
Getting There: There is a small sign off the highway, then it is a bit of a maze to work out from there. There is a walkway and carpark though, so just follow your nose.
Dangers: The remoteness of this location makes you think twice. The rips are also extremely powerful. You are now starting to get into shark territory as well.
Rumours: Check for the evidence of several shipwrecks, they stand as a testament to the harsh ocean conditions that prevail in this area.
Something Else? Beautiful coastline, caves to explore and surf fishing that might just well blow your mind. There is more than something else here. This place is worth a visit if you can make it, for so many reasons other than the surf.

4.
Break Name: Pt Ronald / Princetown
Wave Description: Beach break waves occur in front of the river mouth here, make no mistake, this is one of the biggest locations to pick up all available swell on the coast. The waves here have an incredible amount of power on larger swells and are DEFINITELY not for the inexperienced.
Best Conditions: S swell, NE wind, mid tide.
Getting There: Head out to Point Ronald from the hamlet of Princetown, stand on the cliffs, survey the might of the Southern ocean and decide whether you are up to the task ahead of you. It is a bit of a walk in unless you have a 4wd.
Dangers: Rips, rips and more rips. The water around here has the habit of moving like a freight train. So if you are not sure how to read them or are not confident about taking them on, don't paddle out.
Rumours: There is an old water gate that used to control the height of the river. Well, in theory anyway. Apparently they dug a tunnel through the cliff face to let the overflow from the river, into the ocean. Problem was they did it in summer, but they misjudged the height of the winter high tides (considerably bigger). The whole deal was a fiasco and it now stands as a bizarre human act trying to control nature. Nature kicked our ass this time. Good onya, I reckon!
Something Else? This is no small river at the mouth, it is usually quite wide which of course is perfect for those damned Sharks. I wouldn't recommend surfing in the twilight here.

5.
Break Name: Princetown Peak
Wave Description: A combination of reef and sand base provides similarly powerful, predominantly righthand waves.
Best Conditions: S swell, NE wind, mid tide.
Getting There: You'll find it north west of Point Ronald, take the walking track that can be seen from the road to Port Campbell.

Dangers: Is any break around here truly safe?

Rumours: Not on your life.

Something Else? There are some great 4WD tracks and superb surf fishing to the east of the rivermouth.

6.

Break Name: Gibson's Steps

Wave Description: One of the most famous breaks in the region and rightly so. This place will give you the ride of a lifetime, holding some huge and heavy A frame waves.

Best Conditions: S-SW swell, NE wind, mid tide.

Getting There: You can see the carpark from the Great Ocean Road, but it is the trek down to the beach (or lack of it on high tides) where the challenge presents itself. Some 90 steps actually.

Dangers: The steps, the power, the rips. Any one of these is enough to cause serious injury.

Rumours: There is another location near here with an even more radical access to the surf.

Something Else? Location of some of the great big wave photos taken on this coastline.

7.

Break Name: Harbour Point / Port Campbell

Wave Description: Lefthand reef break creating long horseshoe shaped waves breaking in towards the headland. Works best when the waves are 1.5m or bigger, but generally the swell direction needs to be straight for this wave to work properly.

Best Conditions: S swell, N wind, mid-tide.

Getting There: Out on the headland past the pier within the township of Port Campbell.

Dangers: Shallow reef.

Rumours: This area onwards is generally for the more hard core surfers. Take care not to mouth off about that great 5 foot wave you rode to the rocks. For one, it is rarely impressive, and secondly, could result in a knuckle sandwich.

Something Else? This area becomes one of the busiest tourist towns in Victoria over the summer months as people flock to see the natural wonders of the area and the impressive rock formations that dot this rugged coast line. On top of all the surrounding breaks, the actual harbour can play host to an incredible lefthander. When the swell is huge and from the right direction, a wave breaks across the harbour. A little out from the pier is the takeoff. Hard to believe, when 9 times out of 10 it is quiet and tranquil. When you see it though, it is a magical sight. The tide has a huge effect too. If the swell is out of control on the open beaches, Port Campbell is really your only chance for a wave.

8.

Break Name: Easter Reef

Wave Description: Probably the biggest wave on the coast. It is a ridiculously powerful righthander, that will crush you in an instant.

Best Conditions: S swell, N wind, mid-tide.

Getting There: You could consider paddling from the west side of the harbour, but a boat is the best option. You can see the reef from Port Campbell

Dangers: There is no worthwhile advice if you are competent to take this wave on.

Rumours: The wave has been surfed in the 25 foot category.

Something Else? There is so much to see when the swell isn't great. Take a walk around the headland, as you get into some pretty interesting spots. The diving can be mad, with hidden caves in the cliff face. If you follow the headland west, you will come across a place called Trumpeters Steps. A complete peak, as it looks like the stairs disappear into the ocean below. There are also heaps more breaks than just Easter Reef here. There

Opposites attract at Castle Cove. Perfect lefts & rights. Pic Nick Clark

are several bombies that have some incredible power, but also some crazy shore breaks at the base of the cliffs. Realistically though, if you don't know the area, it will require some exploring. If you are up to it, take every turn to the ocean after Port Campbell for the next couple of kms and you will see a treasure trove of breaks.

9.
Break Name: The Well / Flyhole
Wave Description: A heavy and challenging righthand reef, giving powerful top to bottom wave action. This wave can often be reasonably sectioning in nature, particularly on smaller swells. However, this can work in your favour under the right conditions as there are long, hollow, cover-ups to be had.
Best Conditions: SW swell, NE wind, mid-low tide.
Getting There: You'll find it north-west of the township of Peterborough. It is at the end of a row of houses, look for the large house with huge windows.

Dangers: Entering the water is an ordeal in itself requiring one to jump onto the back of the outgoing waves from a rock ledge. Getting back in, well..... you don't want to know. Go there with someone who knows the tricks or otherwise take the long paddle option and come and go via the adjacent bay.
Rumours: The entry point is a 15 foot leap into water. To get out, you really need someone's assistance, unless you want to completely trash your board.
Something Else? Several people have died in this area clambering around the rocks. They are super slippery and there is an 8 metre fall awaiting your flesh.

10.
Break Name: Elevators / Peterborough
Wave Description: Can hold up to 5m waves, and is known as one of the premier big wave locations in Victoria. It is a righthand reef that is quite a distance offshore. Totally exposed, so it is hard to get this place on a good day, but a north or north east wind and huge straight

swell lines are a great help. The best waves are on a rising tide as a full tide can produce flat waves with shoulder like takeoffs, rather than heart in the mouth excitement.

Best Conditions: S swell, N-NE wind, rising tide.

Getting There: You may paddle out to this location but it is usual these days for the softer and smarter option of boat access to be utilised. It is fairly obvious where the wave is if you take a drive to the beach.

Dangers: What exactly wouldn't be dangerous about surfing waves of this size, apart from eating pies in the warmth of the car watching the beasts roll in?

Rumours: If the swell gets too big for the Well to hold with clean conditions, then there is always the chance that this place just might be on.

Something Else? Responsible for many of the miscellaneously titled photos labelled under the guise of 'southern juice' etc.

11.

Break Name: Bay of Martyrs

Wave Description: Lefthand reef break with plenty of grunt.

Best Conditions: S swell, N wind, mid tide.

Getting There: You'll find it just out of Peterborough, to the west.

Dangers: Extremely long paddles over deep dark channels, with very few surfers to give comfort.

Rumours: There are breaks in this bay which can give protection from huge swells, but they are constantly changing, so you will need to look for yourself.

Something Else? Both here and the Bay of Islands next door, have some of the most amazing rock formations and sunsets in the area. Take a look even if the surf here is a little out of your league. From here to Warrnambool, the road swings inland and surf tracking is difficult. There are plenty of waves but it is a matter of exploring for yourself. If the spots were revealed here, it is likely that I would be hunted down and shot for the dog I had been.

12.

Break Name: Logan's Beach / Japs

Wave Description: Various sand banks form here, and depending on sand movement at the time a variety waves will pop up here. The most consistent of

Fun waves at Portland. Pic Brett Stanley.

these is a lefthander to the right of the carpark looking seaward. This wave needs swell between the 1 to 1.5 m mark to work well.

Best Conditions: S-SW swell, N wind, low-mid tide.

Getting There: Logan's Beach is well signposted if you take the Hopkins Point Rd out of town.

Dangers: Expecting consistent surf here over the generally flat summer months.

Rumours: A Japanese bomber is lying on the ocean floor here.

Something Else? If you visit this beach between January and April it is considered a prime viewing point to perhaps catch a glimpse of a Southern Right Whale.

13.
Break Name: The Flume
Wave Description: Ideal learners' beach break waves without a great deal of power behind them.

Best Conditions: Large S swell, N wind, mid-low tide.

Getting There: This is probably the main beach location in Warrnambool located at the western end of Lady Bay.

Dangers: Crowding, especially in summer where water vehicles of all kinds belt into each other for the rolling waves.

Rumours: Apart from a smutty tale of lust told at the local pub, that has nothing to do with surfing, there is nothing to report.

Something Else? The bay that houses the Flume (Lady Bay), is also the name of the place to head after the Whalers shuts, to party hard and get rid of excess finances.

14.
Break Name: The Cutting / Warrnambool
Wave Description: A quality lefthand beach break wave that peels over a well formed sand bank. This break can competently hold waves from 1m to 1.5m as anything larger has a tendency to close out and anything smaller will not break

consistently along the bank.

Best Conditions: S swell, N wind, mid-low tide.

Getting There: This wave is situated approximately half way between Warrnambool and Port Fairy.

Dangers: This wave is a fairly speedy ride and on smaller days can present the surfer with long close out sections.

Rumours: This wave is located almost directly south from Tower Hill, a site of historical significance. It is believed that the infamous Mahogany ship is buried deep beneath sand dunes in the area.

Something Else? On its day this break is a goofy footer's delight and is well worth a check if the conditions are right.

15.
Break Name: Pelicans
Wave Description: Huge righthand reef break, renowned as a big wave location. It takes huge swells between the 3 to 5m mark before any real action is experienced here.

Best Conditions: S swell, N wind, mid tide.

Getting There: This wave is located directly out to sea from the Cutting on the reef bombie.

Dangers: Is there any wave you've surfed between 3 to 5 m without there being considerable dangers involved ?

Rumours: One of the rare locations that holds swell of this size and offers a rideable wave.

Something Else? It was named Pelicans after a several birds died of a rare disease here.

16.
Break Name: Oigles / East Beach
Wave Description: Oigles is the most popular spot on East Beach and consists of a left and right that break over the top of a ship wreck site. The rest of East Beach has a variety of beach breaks that pop up along its length with differing quality. You will need a huge swell to wrap around the headland into a bay

usually devoid of waves

Best Conditions: S swell, NW wind, mid-low tide.

Getting There: This is the main protected beach for the Port Fairy township, and Oigles can be found just to the west of the surf club.

Dangers: Not likely.

Rumours: The township is really beautiful, with grandiose buildings and some classic pubs.

Something Else? Every year the town has a Folk Festival during the long weekend in March, which is sensational. You will need to book way in advance as it is always sold out. Call (03) 5568 2682

17.

Break Name: The Passage / Port Fairy

Wave Description: This wave is a heavy righthand point break that rates with the best of the waves on offer along this coastline. It can handle waves up to 2.5m as well as providing a place to surf when the swell is struggling a little bit. A quality wave with reasonable consistency.

Best Conditions: Straight S swell, NW wind, mid tide.

Getting There: You'll find it right out front of the carpark as you drive down the back beach road as far towards Griffith's Island as possible.

Dangers: Apart from the murky water and reported sharp toothed sea creatures that hang around the island, the local boys can almost be the worse hazard if your water knowledge and etiquette are not up to scratch.

Rumours: Other than those about the bitty creatures, I think that most people who have surfed the area have a story to tell about this place.

Something Else? When the Folk Festival hits Port Fairy cancel all other commitments and get here, IT GOES OFF!!

18.

Break Name: Gabbos / Port Fairy

Wave Description: Lefthand reef break with the power required to take flight.

The end section of the wave here is superb and there is plenty of time to set up for it.

Best Conditions: S swell, NW wind, mid tide.

Getting There: About 1 km down the road from the Passage.

Dangers: The lip on the end section here would give Mick Jagger a run for his money.

Rumours: Can often be considerably less crowded than the Passage even though the two breaks are in view of each other.

Something Else? Did I mention the FOLK FESTIVAL!?

19.

Break Name: Blacknose / Portland

Wave Description: A very long peeling righthand point break. This place requires a HUGE amount of swell to be around. For example, Bells Beach will need to be running around the 3m mark.

Best Conditions: SW swell, W wind, mid-high tide.

Getting There: Blacknose lies in the middle of a trio of righthand points that are just out of town beyond the smelter. You need to take a dirt track after you have passed under the pipes of the smelter. Ask at the local surf shop if you are unsure. Again employ tactics here. Don't ask straight out, but act as if you have been there before but can't remember exactly. If you ask which track under the pipes, they will probably tell you.

Dangers: Extremely cold and murky winter waters and the rock bottom at low tide.

Rumours: On the days where this place really works, a walk back to the point may be preferable to an arm burning paddle.

Something Else? The break to the west here is normally a little bigger.

20.

Break Name: Yellow Rock / Portland

Wave Description: Good shapely sand

bank breaks that are riddled with rips.
Best Conditions: S swell, N wind, mid-high tide.
Getting There: You'll find it as you are heading south towards Cape Nelson.
Dangers: Unless you're experienced at using rips like escalators to get where you want to go, it may be worthwhile checking the gentler, safer, beach breaks of Narrawong beach.
Rumours: This area has a history of Aboriginal heritage and therefore should be respected at all times by surfers accessing this area.
Something Else? There is NO yellow rock.

21.
Break Name: Murrells Beach / Portland
Wave Description: This is a consistent lefthand reef break that sucks over a treacherously shallow rock bottom.
Best Conditions: S swell, NW wind, mid-high tide.
Getting There: I can't tell you where it is, as my life is at stake.
Dangers: The usual when surfing around

incredibly shallow rock bases.
Rumours: Known to be a bit of a favourite for those in the know.
Something Else? NUP.

22.
Break Name: White's Beach / Discovery Bay
Wave Description: White's is a lefthand reef break amongst the variety of beach breaks found in the bay.
Best Conditions: Big SW swells, N wind, mid-high tide.
Getting There: You'll find it north of Cape Bridgewater.
Dangers: Exposed rocks are known to pop up before you in the wave face Exercise both caution and control.
Rumours: I can liken this wave to the Bird Rock of past years with a carefully negotiated ride through the rocks giving basis to stories of great days had, and regular returns to the location.
Something Else? The bay itself is huge, with potential for other waves. Seek and ye shall find.

A closer look at how picture perfect Gibson's Steps is.....occasionally. Pic Brett Stanley.

GENERAL INFORMATION

JOHANNA/PORT CAMPBELL/PETERBOROUGH

Where To Stay:
The campgrounds at Johanna charge an $8 fee over summer, but is always free in the winter months. It is a magic place to stay, not bad facilities as well.
Port Campbell Caravan Park. Ph (03) 5598 6492. Sites from $10.
YHA Port Campbell. Ph (03) 5598 6305. Beds from $12.
Shomberg Inn Hotel, Peterborough. Ph (03) 5598 5285.
Where To Eat:
Lavers Hill has a general store which can have great snacks and supplies to take back to the camp at Johanna.
The Pub at Port Campbell has great, cheap, counter meals.
Where To Party:
The Peterborough pub can get a bit rowdy, but it really isn't anything spectacular.
Flat Day Fun:
The Glow Worms can be an amazing sight and well worth checking out. Melba Gully State Park is where you'll find them. There are signs clearly marking where it is.

WARRNAMBOOL

Where To Stay:
Surfside Holiday Park. Ph (03) 55612611 is right on the beach and close to the happening Lady Bay Hotel. It's only about a 1 km walk into town.
Great Ocean Road Backpackers. Ph (03) 5562 4874. A great place, with plenty of inhabitants and good prices. Beds from $15.
Where To Eat:
Fishtales Café is one of the best budget restaurants I've had the pleasure to visit

while travelling, great variety and value. If you're on a really tight budget, hit the bakeries or perhaps a counter meal down at the Lady Bay Hotel.
Where To Party:
The Whalers is a great place to conduct a warm up with a few beers in a good atmosphere. If the night looks like going late, there is a fair chance you will end up at the Lady Bay trying your luck.
Flat Day Fun:
It is well worth while checking out the Tower Hill State Game Reserve. This is an amazing place in which to marvel at nature's formations and wild life.
Southern Right Whales frequent Logans Beach from June to October, which is worthwhile looking out for. There are plenty of other places where you can see the whales too, without the hustle and bustle. Try Johanna.

PORT FAIRY

Where To Stay:
Gardens Caravan park. Ph (03) 5568 1060. Sites from $12, with great access to the beach.
EMOH/YHA Hostel. Ph (03) 5568 2468 provides grand accommodation at their usual reasonable prices. Beds from $13.
Star of the West Hotel will also provide worthwhile budget accommodation. Ph (03) 5568 1715. B&B for $20, pretty good actually.
Where To Eat:
Lunch is a deli well worth seeing some of your dollars in exchange for a good feed. There is also that dynamic duo of the bakeries and the counter meals on offer.
Where To Party:
Head to the pubs, but the party time here is over the Labour Day weekend where the town is overrun by the Folk Festival which continues to be a fantastic weekend away, year after year.
Flat Day Fun:
Take a trip via the causeway out to Griffith's Island, where the spectacular

VIC

scenery and Mutton birds are worth checking out.

PORTLAND

Where To Stay:
Centenary Caravan Park. Ph (03) 5523 1487 offers value accommodation within walking distance of the ocean. Sites from $12 (four people)
Gorden Hotel. Ph (03) 5523 1121 is closer to the heart of town and has reasonable pub style accommodation. Beds from $20 and meals are $5.

Where To Eat:
If you're staying at the Gorden why not sample a reasonably priced pub meal, otherwise take away will be the answer.

Where To Party:
Any of the hotels in town will provide a nice atmosphere for some amber refreshment.

Flat Day Fun:
Take a trip just out of town to Cape Nelson State Park where the walking and coastal views will have you hugging trees and praising nature.

SECTION DESCRIPTION

Local Shapers
Southern Guns - Glenn Fairweather (Warrnambool). Ph (03) 5562 0928.

Best Months
Summer here is connected with favourable wind conditions for surf in the area, lots of sun and surfing without the spine chilling cold. Winter of course is when the real power is unleashed. Make sure you are ready for it though.

Secret Spot
Rivermouths are always a good bet for consistent waves and this is no exception. Out of the Otways and before Port Campbell you will find some fresh aire.

Quick Tips
The key to successful surfing here is understanding nature's forces and

working with them. I have watched in anguish as a guy, no more than 20 feet away was getting constantly slotted while I struggled against the rip. I could see the glee in his eye every time I got pounded by another set. These waves are a great opportunity to study the beach carefully, watching for any rogue sets. The rips must be your best friends if you want to surf here.

Getting There
V-Line have buses running through here, so call them. It is about five hours to Portland from Melbourne. Hitching is impossible along a lot of these roads as they are so narrow. Better to hire a car from the city.

Peaceful, perfect, a rare day indeed for Gibsons' Steps. Pic Brett Stanley.

SURFING YARNS.

Fuelling the Fire
Much of the talk was about sharks. There had been an attack only the previous day at Port Lincoln which fuelled much speculation as to the number of sharks in the area. Photos of one and half tonne monsters were pinned to most roadhouses. There were fridge magnets with the largest shark catches. You could buy mugs, caps, T's, just about everything that depicts these fearsome creatures. Every local perpetuated the myth of these fierce predators, by dragging up some town folk story that sent shivers into the hearts of everyone. There were a couple of seemingly brave groms who were heard saying "well when your number's up, your number's up" True enough, but there are ways to reduce the risks.

Stockists – area code 03:

This is a list of your local surf shops. They can help you with pretty much everything to do with surfing. They are also proud to be stockists of The Surfer's Travel Guide.

Anglesea Surf Centre
111 Ocean Rd
Anglesea 3230
5263 1530

Box Hill Ski & Surf
693 Station St
Box Hill 3128
9897 4200

Bumps Ski & Surf
465 Glenhuntley Rd
Elsternwick 3185
9528 2701

Gash Boards
Shop 2 Surfcoast Plaza
Toquay 3228
5261 3292

Hughes Surfcraft
3 Great Ocean Rd
Airey's Inlet 3221
5289 7153

Invert Surf 'n' Skate
61 Church St
Brighton 3186
9593 1765

Island Surfbords
147 Thompson Ave,
Cowes
Phillip Island 3922
5952 2578

Islantis Surfshop
10-12 Phillip Island Rd
Newhaven 3925
5956 7553

Jetty Surf
The Glen Shopping Centre
Glen Waverly 3150
9802 6359

Lorne Surf Shop
130 Mountjoy Pde
Lorne 3232
5289 6713

Mordy Surf & Sail
628 Main Rd
Mordialloc 3195
9580 1716

Ozmosis Surfboards
2/10 Clyde St
Frankston 3199
9781 2930

Peninsula Surf Centre
7A Station St
Frankston 3199
9783 3811

Portalnd Surfin
98a Perry Street
Portalnd, 3305
5523 5804

Port Campbell Trading Company
27 Lord St
Port Campbell, 3269
5598 6444

Quiksilver Boardriders
27 Baines Cres
Torquay 3228
5261 4768

Rastas Surfwear
55 Hitchcock Ave
Barwon Heads 3227
5254 3255

Repeat Performance
87 Ormond Rd
Elwood 3184
9525 6475

Ringwood Surf & Sail
134 Maroondah Hwy
Ringwood 3134
9870 6378

Rip Curl
101 Surcoast Hwy
Torquay 3228
5261 0000

Sea Level Surf Shop
411 Hampton St
Hampton 3188
9598 0716

Southern Guns
176 Liebig St
Warrnambool, 3281
5562 0928

Speakys Surf Shop
114 Market Square Mall
Geelong 3220
5229 2500

Strapper Surfboards
106 Surfcoast Hwy
Torquay 3228
5261 2312

Surf Dive 'n' Ski
211-215 Bourke St
Melbourne 3000
9650 1039

Surf Dive 'n' Ski
Melbourne Central
Shopping Centre
Melbourne 3000
9662 3815

Surf Dive 'n' Ski
500 Chapel St
South Yarra 3141
9826 4071

Surf Dive 'n' Ski
Southland Shopping
Centre
Cheltenham 3192
9583 8200

Surf Dive 'n' Ski
Doncaster Shopping
Centre
Doncaster 3108
9840 2991

Surf Dive 'n' Ski
Knox City Shopping
Centre
Wantirna South 3152
9800 4444

Surfworld Surfing Museum
Beach Rd
Torquay 3228
5261 4606

Thunder Brothers
4/6 Moorabool St
Geelong 3220
5222 6622

Trigger Brothers
484 Nepean Hwy
Chelsea 3196
9772 5100

Warrnambool Surf Centre
100 Liebig St
Warrnambool, 3280
5562 1981

Zee Surf Shop
118 Surfcoast Hwy
Torquay 3228
5261 2288

Trigger Brothers
43 Church St
Brighton 3186
9593 2211

Trigger Brothers
7 Rossmith Ave
Frankston 3199
9770 2223

Trigger Brothers
3297 Nepean Hwy
Sorrento 3943
5984 4401

Trigger Brothers
Pt Leo Rd
Pt Leo 3916
5989 8402

Trigger Brothers
104 Main St
Mornington 3931
5975 9400

The Bombie, Cactus. Pic Brett Stanley

SOUTH AUSTRALIA

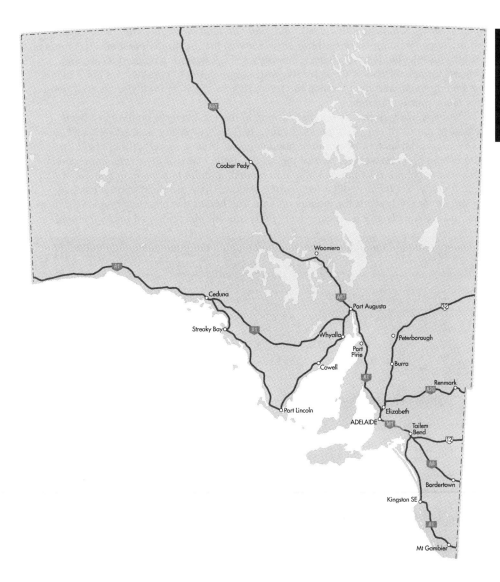

South Australia.

S.A.

Secrets & Lies

Adventuring through the heart of South Australia feels like being inside an Indiana Jones movie, complete with crazed tribesman and narrow escapes from sea beasts, all in the hope of riding some of those elusive waves that haunt the coastline. The myth of South Australia lends to its character. ferocious shark attacks, hardened locals, and rugged terrain. Of course there are the world class waves to consider. It's just a matter of finding them, and then battling the forces that so often confront you on your quest for those precious barrels.

Perhaps many of the stories that abound in the local taverns would have been closer to the mark ten years ago. Certainly, there are still many sharks brooding below the surface, but quite a few of their hunting grounds have moved farther afield due to the fishing ports being well bled of their fish supply. Many of the roads, impassable five years ago, are now paved, or at least graded, and the locals are, in general, warm and friendly. Yet there is still a feeling of isolation. There are many coastal camping zones devoid of humans for months on end. The breaks are often surrounded by deep and dark channels giving an eerie feel. There are still plenty of 4wd tracks that will test

The inside right is 3 foot, the middle rights are 6 foot, the outside left is 8 foot and no-one out. This is South Oz. Pic Chubbs.

Racing a Pondalowie pit, Yorke Peninsula. Pic courtesy Rhino's Tavern.

the will of all adventurers, and the locals can be daunting. However, the rewards by far outweigh the negatives. Endless sandy beaches stretch towards towering dunes that resemble snow fields. Cornices dangle, whipped into perfection by relentless winds. Hundreds of bird and animal species roam the rugged wilderness. Huge salt pans that reflect the searing sun. Lush green hillsides where cattle and sheep stand nervously. There is so much to see, yet so few to see it. There lies the key to anyone who wants to experience adventure. During the months of June and November, great Southern Whales come to calve in a cove at the head of the bight. On one blustery Tuesday, with not a soul in sight, we watched as eight whales calved and played with their young a mere 100 meters offshore. We dived at Piccaninie Ponds where the sea bed suddenly drops to a depth of 500 ft, merely metres from the reedy bank, alone. We also surfed some of the best waves we had seen, alone. This is how the people in the community want to keep it. Quiet, uninterrupted, peaceful. Small diners sulk at large orders from a healthy group of surfers, preferring the meagre taking from locals. The reason for this difference to the Eastern states is their existence has been an isolated one. Those who disliked it left for the East, the rest remain staunchly tight lipped about their bountiful state. No wonder, as they have witnessed many prized east coast areas become overcrowded by busy tourists, and money chasing developers. They fear for the soul of their State and once you have seen the beauty you can understand the dilemma. Government signs, that may have lead the way to some secret wave, are torn down. Tourist brochures are hidden on shelves by fishing tackle and the odd porn mag. Locals grunt at questions and lose interest in talking to the touro. Scratch the surface, and like the mercurial genie, your pot of gold will appear.

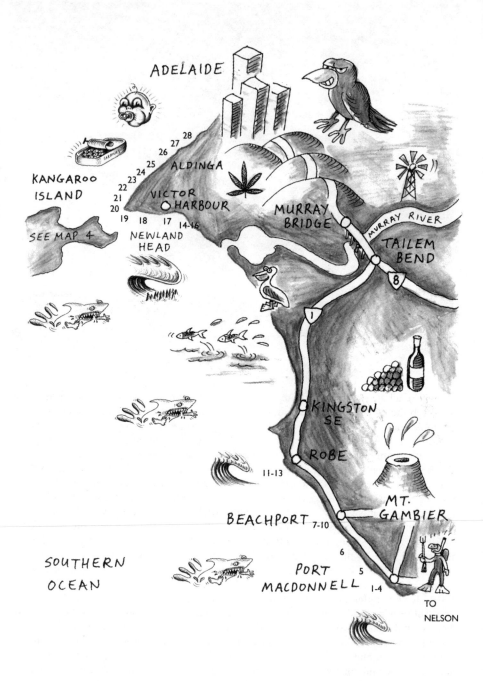

ADELAIDE

KANGAROO
ISLAND

SEE MAP 4

ALDINGA

28
27
26
25
24
23
22
21
20
19 18 17 14-16

VICTOR
○ HARBOUR

NEWLAND
HEAD

MURRAY
BRIDGE

MURRAY RIVER

TAILEM
BEND

8

1

KINGSTON
SE

ROBE

11-13

BEACHPORT 7-10

MT.
GAMBIER

6

5

PORT
MACDONNELL 1-4

TO
NELSON

SOUTHERN
OCEAN

Beach Driving
The birds raced the 4wd along the foreshore, Cormorants and Herons urged their wings along the wave faces to keep abreast of the roaring vehicle.

Two hours stuck in sand-dunes, an hour lost and six hours of wonderment, outside Robe. Pic Nick Clark.

Port MacDonnell - Adelaide

Fishermen, Freaks and 4WD tracks..

Just West of Portland, lies the coastal beginnings of South Australia. This stretch of coast doesn't have the wave reputation that its westerly neighbours share but there is plenty of action for keen adventurers. Uncrowded waves are literally a stones throw from many of the roads, and then you have beach driving. With a well equipped 4wd there is much to explore, but even without this luxury class waves are still easily accessible. The pubs are full of rustic characters who can provide some classic nights of stories and some handy insights to the local spots. This place certainly has its share of power waves, and it provides a good training ground for the more westerly reaches of the state.

1.
Break Name: Yip Yip/Port MacDonnell
Wave Description: Punchy reef breaks which break right and left, the right providing the best option.
Best Conditions: SE-SW swell, NE-NW wind, low-mid tide.
Getting There: Turnoff at Browns Bay, just before you get into town.
Dangers: Sharp reef, and locals that can probably cause worse injuries.
Rumours: The waves here get serious. The swell has been 4 metres on a number of occasions.
Something Else? The fishing can be quite incredible, with large schools of salmon. This region is known to be the largest provider of crays in the world (so the locals say!).

2.
Break Name: Piccaninnie Beach
Wave Description: Hollow beach breaks, mainly A-frames.
Best Conditions: SE-SW swell, NE-NW wind, low-mid tide (works in all tides though).
Getting There: Heading to Port MacDonnell take turnoff just outside Nelson.
Dangers: There tends to be an abundance of marine life, therefore attracting larger fish varieties with sharp teeth.
Rumours: There have been plenty of wrecks on this stretch of coast. Apparently valuable cargo was washed ashore and found by some fortunate surfer.
Something Else? The beach driving is incredible, with endless stretches into Victoria and then into Port MacDonnell. 4WD only.

3.
Break Name: Posties / Port MacDonnell
Wave Description: Powerful righthand reef break, very hollow!
Best Conditions: S-SW swell, NE-NW wind, rising tide.

Getting There: Take the scenic drive to the lighthouse on its eastern side.
Dangers: Can get very big, and the reef is extremely sharp.
Rumours: Nothing worth a mention.
Something Else? Great fishing, especially crays.

4.
Break Name: Cape Northumberland
Wave Description: Left and righthand heavy reef breaks.
Best Conditions: S-SW swell, E-NE wind, low-mid tide.
Getting There: Take the sign to the lighthouse.
Dangers: The breaks are open to huge swells and the reef is hungry for some surfer flesh.
Rumours: If you take this wave on you must be experienced. That is no rumour.
Something Else? Check out Dingley Dell, the home of Adam Linslie Gordon.

5.
Break Name: Carpenters Rocks
Wave Description: Left and righthand reef breaks, outside bombies.
Best Conditions: SE-SW swell, NE wind, rising tide.
Getting There: Take the road to Tantartoola from Port MacDonnell, then follow sign.
Dangers: Long, lonely paddles over deep channels.
Rumours: Take your time to explore this area as there are many hidden treasures.
Something Else? Once again the fishing is very good.

6.
Break Name: Cullens Reef / South End
Wave Description: Lefthand HEAVY reef break.
Best Conditions: SW-S swell, N-NE wind, rising tide.
Getting There: Through South End, then into Conunda National Park.
Dangers: Plenty of crowds in summer, nothing too serious.

This stretch of coast is characterized by the fishermen and lonely waves. Outside Beachport. Pic Chubbs.

Rumours: Plenty of crayfish and secret spots in the area.
Something Else? Set in a beautiful location, worth seeing.

7.
Break Name: Surf Beach / Beachport
Wave Description: Left and right beach breaks, quick and hollow.
Best Conditions: SE-SW swell, NE-NW wind, all tides.
Getting There: Carpark looking onto beach, 2kms before the town.
Dangers: Pretty good all round.
Rumours: Good place in big swells.
Something Else? Ideal place to check swell conditions right along the coast. 4WD coastal tours available. Contact Warren or Michele on (08) 87343029.

8.
Break Name: Kelps / Beach Port
Wave Description: Lefthanders, over a combination of reef and sand, short and punchy rides.
Best Conditions: S-SW swell, N-NE wind, all tides.

Getting There: Follow scenic drive west of town, turnoff at Blowhole.
Dangers: The wave finishes on bare rock. Take your chances.
Rumours: Mozzie the Local knows the break backwards. Show your respect.
Something Else? Great place to watch the local rippers as the wave only breaks 20-30 feet offshore.

9.
Break Name: Suicides / Beachport
Wave Description: Righthand heavy, hollow and fast reef break.
Best Conditions: S-SW swell, N-NE wind, all tides.
Getting There: Follow scenic drive, west of town, turnoff at Blowhole.
Dangers: Board snapping fun.
Rumours: Heavy locals, and sharp reef.
Something Else? Great photo opportunities.

10.
Break Name: Ringwood and Sherbert bombies / Beachport

Lump Forster wasn't so lucky on the next wave. Stony Rise.

Wave Description: Incredibly heavy left and righthander over a, shallow, sharp reef.

Best Conditions: SW Huge swells, NE wind, low tides.

Getting There: Strictly boat.

Dangers: Deep, deep water, and a very unforgiving reef.

Rumours: Couldn't find anyone who had surfed this.

Something Else? Take rods on your journey out there for some game fish.

11.

Break Name: Stoney Rise / Robe

Wave Description: Punchy right and left reef and sand breaks.

Best Conditions: SW-S swell, NE-NW wind, all tides.

Getting There: Turn left at Ampol service station towards Little Dip Conversation Park. Head towards rubbish tip and take right hand fork.

Dangers: The sand dunes can prove a huge obstacle for even the most well equipped vehicles.

Rumours: The fishing is very good, so no doubt those sharp toothed creatures of the sea are prowling around.

Something Else? Great place to camp, if you can get in and out of the dunes.

12.

Break Name: Third Ramp-Long Beach / Robe

Wave Description: Left and righthand beach breaks.

Best Conditions: W-S swell, N-NE wind, all tides.

Getting There: Follow signs from the town.

Dangers: Pretty harmless.

Rumours: Pretty sure this was named after a certain boat ramp!

Something Else? You can drive along the beach to get a peak to yourself.

13.

Break Name: 1st Ramp-Long Beach / Robe

Wave Description: A consistent lefthand reef break, that holds up to 1.5 metres.

Best Conditions: S swell, N wind, most tides(being close to the continental shelf plays havoc with the tides, so you just have to keep checking it).

Getting There: Follow signs from the town.

Dangers: Over reef so take the usual precautions.
Rumours: None that we heard.
Something Else? Great snorkelling spot over summer in the prevailing northerlies.

14.
Break Name: Surfers / Goolwa
Wave Description: Shifting beach breaks over sand, generally protected from larger swells.
Best Conditions: SW swell, NE-NW wind, extremely tidal due to the mouth of the Murray river.
Getting There: Take Turnoff to Goolwa from The Victor - Goolwa Rd.
Dangers: Swells can jump dramatically and the rips can be pretty fierce.
Rumours: Historic Aboriginal land steeped in tradition.
Something Else? An excellent place to catch a feed.

15.
Break Name: The Bay / Middleton
Wave Description: A variety of beach breaks that depend greatly on the sand banks.
Best Conditions: SE-SW swell, NE-N wind, generally on the rising tide.
Getting There: Take the Flagstaff Hill Rd from the Main Rd.
Dangers: Watch the rips.
Rumours: Very fickle!
Something Else? There are some great windsurfing areas around, complemented by a healthy sailboarding population.

16.
Break Name: Bullies / Pt Elliot
Wave Description: A very punchy, and often dangerous righthand reef break. Can get very hollow, giving a hiding if caught inside.
Best Conditions: SW-S swell, NE-N wind, incoming tide.
Getting There: Just off the Port Elliot Rd, opposite the cinema.
Dangers: The locals are nothing to worry about compared to the reef and sharks!

Rumours: With a name like Bullies, you can imagine what the locals are like.
Something Else? The reef breaks that surround this area are all extremely heavy. If it looks too much, just cruise to one of the numerous beachies nearby.

17.
Break Name: Shark Alley / Victor Harbor
Wave Description: This wave is more suited to body boarders as the takeoff is ridiculously steep. You will see what I mean when you get there.
Best Conditions: SE swell, NW wind, lower tides.
Getting There: Head out of town and turn left to Wright Island. It is between the headland and the Island.
Dangers: The name tells a valuable story.
Rumours: This part of the coast has a morbid history of shark attacks.
Something Else? The granite rocks and beautiful beaches make it a killer place to just walk along the coastline. Great fishing as well.

18.
Break Name: Waitpinga / Newland Head Conservation Park
Wave Description: A selection of beach and reef breaks. There is also the possibility of a point break at the west end of the beach.
Best Conditions: S-SW swell, NE-NW wind, all tides.
Getting There: Follow the signs to the Conservation Park, from there on you will find clear directions.
Dangers: The beach is quite remote, and there is a breeding ground for sharks at the west end.
Rumours: There have been a few fatal attacks in this region. You must keep in mind though, that the possibility of a shark attack while you are surfing is small. Just take the normal precautions.
Something Else? There is a very strong aboriginal history in this area.

Mitch Dawkins looking for room to move, outside Robe. Pic Joli

19.
Break Name: Parsons Beach / Newland Head Conservation Park
Wave Description: Punchy reef and sand breaks with a point break in the right swell.
Best Conditions: S-SW swell, NE-NW wind, all tides.
Getting There: Follow the signs, very easy.
Dangers: As above, except it is closer to the shark breeding ground.
Rumours: On its day a very long wave.
Something Else? A beautiful place.

20.
Break Name: Rapid Bay
Wave Description: A combination of shifting beach breaks. Can get quite good on huge swells.
Best Conditions: SW swell, SE wind, most tides.
Getting There: Head towards to Cape Jervis, turn to the west to the turnoff.
Dangers: Just the lively marine population.

Rumours: The name is derived from the speed at which large marine life moves in this area.
Something Else? The Cape itself is quite spectacular.

21.
Break Name: Yankalilla
Wave Description: Several reef and beach opportunities.
Best Conditions: SW swell, SE wind, most tides.
Getting There: The next bay north of Rapid.
Dangers: No swell.
Rumours: Very fickle.
Something Else? The swell has to be huge to make it through to this part of the bay, so check the weather map first. Glacier Rock is 500 million year old Cambrian quartzite, and is 22kms east.

22.
Break Name: Myponga
Wave Description: Reef and beach break combinations.
Best Conditions: S-SW swell, SE-NE wind, most tides.
Getting There: Follow the signs from the esplanade.
Dangers: Nothing out of the ordinary for this area. Did I mention sharks!
Rumours: Steep hillsides and gullies, and western grey kangaroos can be seen throughout Myponga conservation park.
Something Else? If you scour the foreshore you are likely to find Port Jackson eggs. They are identifiable due to the odd formation of the seaweed in which the eggs are housed. The seaweed is in the shape of a sea shell of six inches and up. Don't remove them, but check them out as they look pretty cool.

23.
Break Name: Sellicks
Wave Description: There is quite an array of beach breaks here, as well as reef breaks out the back.
Best Conditions: S-SW swell, SE-NE

wind, most tides.

Getting There: Follow the Esplanade and watch for the sign, very easy to find.

Dangers: Beware the treacherous reefs inundated with deep channels and their local shark inhabitants.

Rumours: Four years ago a young local disappeared whilst diving with his friend. The friend reputedly saw a dark shadow, then he was gone. They never found any remnants of the diver or his gear, even after the most diligent efforts by local authorities.

Something Else? This is one of the few places that you can drive on the beach. In summer they charge around four dollars. There are some incredible fossils on the beach, due to the age of the surrounding hills. Some of the fossilised cockle shells date back one million years.

24.
Break Name: Maslin.
Wave Description: A range of beachies, with a reef to the north.
Best Conditions: S-SW swell, SE-NE wind, rising tides.
Getting There: Follow the Esplanade, then turnoff at the sign.
Dangers: White pointers of the human kind.
Rumours: The swell has to be pretty big to penetrate this peninsula, and generally the waves don't get above 1.2 metres.
Something Else? It was the first legal nude bathing beach, making it worth the check, as this works in all summery conditions.

25.
Break Name: South Moana
Wave Description: Several reef breaks characterize this area, getting quite good when the conditions are just right.
Best Conditions: S-SW swell, SE-NE wind, rising tides.
Getting There: Follow the Esplanade, then the beach is clearly marked.
Dangers: Small fickle waves.
Rumours: Although fickle, it can produce

excellent quality.
Something Else? Definitely worth a check.

26.
Break Name: Triggs1
Wave Description: Like the rest of the reef breaks in the area. Needs large swells.
Best Conditions: SW-S swell, SE-NE winds, best on incoming tides.
Getting There: Off Commercial Rd, turn down Cliff Rd.
Dangers: Often small swell.
Rumours: Prepare for disappointment.
Something Else? Head for the nearest pub.

27.
Break Name: Southport
Wave Description: Combination of differing reef breaks.
Best Conditions: SW-S swell, SE-NE winds, incoming tides.
Getting There: Between the rivermouth and the Hump, or one suburb south of Port Noarlunga.
Dangers: Same as the rest of the coast.
Rumours: Nada.
Something Else? A couple of great surf shops to check out.

28.
Break Name: Christies Reef
Wave Description: A combination of left and right reef breaks. Doesn't get above 1 metre really.
Best Conditions: SW-S swell, SE-NE winds, Low tides.
Getting There: Follow the Esplanade and follow the signs.
Dangers: Like the majority of the mid coast, Sharks, locals, reefs, and Sharks.
Rumours: Sharks are toothless creatures that have never caused any surfer concern.
Something Else? Needs a pretty big swell, and from the right direction, therefore making it quite inconstant.

GENERAL INFORMATION

PORT MACDONNELL

Where To Stay:
Woolwash Caravan Park. Ph (08) 8738 7324. Speak to Ross or Chris Childs. Weekly rates from $50, nightly fee $7. There are 10 cent showers too!
The Victoria Hotel. Ph (08) 8738 2213. Speak to Darren.
Sandunes. There are some killer places to just sleep under the stars. Worthwhile if you want to save some bucks.
Where To Eat:
The Hotel.
The local Bakery.
Where To Party:
Pretty sparse, but on January 6th, the Bayside Festival kicks in and there is plenty of fun to be had.
Flat Day Fun:
Home of the biggest Crayfish in the world, so there is an abundance of fishing in the area.
Piccaninnie Ponds, a definite must see!!!!!
See Eve Carlin at the local tourist Info, she will give you a rundown on the area's attractions. Ph 285 5291.

BEACHPORT

Where To Stay:
Beachport Backpackers. Ph (08) 8735 8197. Speak to Matt, or Annie. It has a killer location right on the beach, rooms for $15 per night with continental breakfast.
Beachport Caravan Park.
Ph (08) 8735 8128.
Where To Eat:
The Green Room. The best Fish and Chips in South Oz, so we're told.
Beachport Hotel.
Where To Party:
Bompas or Beachport Hotel.
Flat Day Fun:
Pool of Siloam - Has the salinity seven

times that of the ocean. Play Jesus if you want.
Salmon Hole - Excellent fishing spot.
Lake George is a Mecca for windsurfers.

ROBE

Where To Stay:
Sea Vu Caravan Park. Ph (08) 8768 2273.
Caledonian Inn. Ph (08) 8768 2029. Old English style, with killer open fire place.
Sand Dunes. Great off track camping with the best view available and a cranking righthander.
Where To Eat:
The Caledonian Inn.
Wild Mulberry Café (licensed).
Where To Party:
Caledonian Inn supports the local surfriders and they normally have presso and piss up nights there. Over summer there is a massive influx of tourists providing fun at the local pub as well.
Surf / Windsurf Carnival over Easter. Contact Pete at Cutloose (Glenelg) Ph (08) 8294 3866.
Flat Day Fun:
Tiger Moth Flights. Ph 018 505 616.
Great fishing and sand driving.
Mountain Bike tours, see Steve's surf shop. They are also proposing a skate ramp.
The Coorong is closeby and is a must to visit.

VICTOR HARBOR

Where To Stay:
The Grosvenor Hotel. Ph (08) 8552 1011. See Pat. They have great backpacker style accommodation as well as some higher end rooms. Great place to eat. There are a couple of caravan parks in the area but try the pub first.
Where To Eat:
The Grosvenor Hotel.
The Crown Hotel, and a load of take away places.

Where To Party:
The Crown Hotel is really the only action. The niteclub upstairs can produce some great nights.

Flat Day Fun:
Take a walk to Granite Island which has amazing views and a large Penguin population.
Take a drive down to Cape Jervis which is the kickoff for Kangaroo Island. Newland Head is quite beautiful as well. The fishing here is also very good, with great catches on most beaches. Check out Encounter Bay.

SECTION INFORMATION

Local Shaper
Fine Cut - Greg Reynolds aka FIN (Beachport). Ph (08) 8735 8206.
NXT Shapes - Mark Benson (shapes for Shane Bevan). (Port Elliot). Ph (08) 85542375.
Cutloose Surfboards. Rod Bedford. (Lonsdale). Ph (08) 8326 0939.
Power Plug - Andy Inxter. (Middleton). Ph (08) 8555 1239.

Best Months
April - August.

Secret Spot
If you follow the heritage of the Aborigines in the area, many hidden treasures will reveal themselves. If you decide to delve into their sea food diet, a monument to the feasting will reveal itself close to the break. Closer to Port MacDonnell than Robe.

Quick Tips
Spend some time exploring this area as there is some amazing coastline. Make sure you take your fishing gear, as there are some killer spots. Be friendly and talk to the locals, as they are your best source of stories and info and are classic characters.

Getting There
Premier Roadlines, will get you most places. Ph (08) 8415 5555.
Hills Transit, part of the government transit system. Ph (08) 8339 1191.
V-line, Adelaide-Mt Gambier. Ph 132 232.
Cut price rentals $15 per day. Ph (08) 8443 7788.
Rent -a-bug., from $17.50 per day. Ph (08) 8234 0911.
Try Wayward Bus tours as they often tour right along the coast and you get to meet heaps of people. Ph 1 800 882 823.

Andrew Joy aka 'Shadow' keeping high on a Bullies beast. Pic courtesy of Southern Surf.

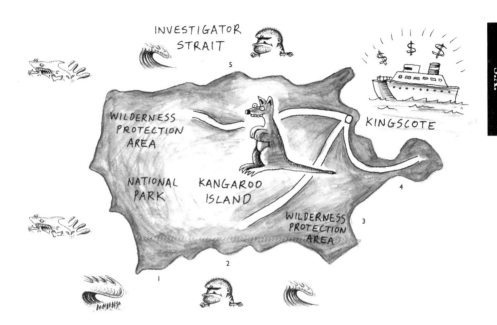

Kangaroo Island

The Lucky Isle.

Open to some of the most powerful ocean swells, Australia's third largest Island (155kms long and 55kms wide) receives more than its fair share of quality waves. Add to this a complete lack of crowds and a temperature that is surprisingly mild, and you have the ideal surf destination....almost. There are always those mitigating factors that add to the adrenalin rush of surf trips. Here, it is the definite loneliness of the breaks which starts the heart racing. There is no question that sharks love the Island and there are countless stories to reinforce this notion. Add to this the often remote locations and deep channels and you have a real challenge on your hands. Isn't that what it is all about, though?

S.A.

1.
Break Name: Hanson Bay
Wave Description: A rocky point break, with shifting sand banks. The point is always far more reliable.
Best Conditions: S-SW swell, N-NE wind, mid tide.
Getting There: Its about 125kms from Penneshaw. If you get onto the South Coast Rd, follow it until you hit South West River Rd.
Dangers: Definitely not for beginners due to its exposure to swell. The rips and undercurrents can be mad too.
Rumours: Surfing the point can be complete bliss, but it can turn within an instant, catching the unaware in vulnerable positions.
Something Else? The diving can be magic off the point if it's completely flat. The fishing is always special here too.

2.
Break Name: Vivonne Bay
Wave Description: A combination of sand breaks which break from rivermouths at both ends of the bay.

Best Conditions: S-SW swell, NE-W wind, mid-low tide.
Getting There: Off the South Coast Rd about 90kms from Penneshaw.
Dangers: Although the rips aren't so bad here, the breaks are in front of rivermouths, which is always a sketchy prospect on the Island.
Rumours: The closer to the western end you are, the smaller the waves.
Something Else? Although this bay is ideal for beginners, it can have some excellent sand banks which can turn it on.

3.
Break Name: D'Estrees Bay
Wave Description: Reef breaks, that are normally best at Cape Gantheaume.
Best Conditions: Huge S-SW swell, NW-W wind, low-mid tide.
Getting There: Follow the D'Estrees Bar Rd from the Hundred Line Rd.
Dangers: All the breaks here are over reef and can be extremely shallow. Be extremely cautious.
Rumours: If you are not 100% confident

Much of your travel on the island will consist of this. Pic. South Oz Tourism Commission.

The massive seal population on the Island is a foreboding sign for surfers. Pic South Oz Tourism Commission.

of your abilities don't even consider it.
Something Else? In winter, the road may only be passable in 4wd. As the break lies within the confines of a wilderness protection area, it is quite remote. Keep this in mind if you are considering paddling out.

4.
Break Name: Pennington Bay
Wave Description: Fun beach breaks that are a welcome relief from the rigours of the rest of the Island.
Best Conditions: S swell, NE wind, most tides.
Getting There: Only 32kms from Penneshaw, off the Hog Bay Rd, you will find this idyllic location.
Dangers: The shallow sand banks can make for some nasty headplants. If the swell is big, this bay tends to close out.
Rumours: Being so close to the main town on the Island, this break is often crowded.
Something Else? There are several good

points here. One being that you can check the surf from the comfort of your car. Also, this break is not so affected by the onshores, due to the surrounding land mass of American River.

5.
Break Name: Stokes Bay
Wave Description: There is a combination of reef and sand breaks here that are often fickle being on the north side of the Island.
Best Conditions: Huge W swell, S wind, most tides.
Getting There: Follow Springs Rd from Hundred Line Rd.
Dangers: When the swell is huge, the reef can give a nasty working, complete with rips and undercurrents.
Rumours: The good waves here are comparable with any south coast perfection.
Something Else? Check out the surrounding bays as they are extremely beautiful and well worth visiting.

GENERAL INFORMATION

Where To Stay:
Kangaroo Island Caravan Park. Ph (08) 8553 2325. Sites from $12, close to town, a good starting point.
Kangaroo Island Central Backpackers Hostel. Ph (08) 8553 2787. Beds from $14. They have a huge range of information about activities.
Penneshaw Youth Hostel. Ph (08) 8553 1284. Beds from $14.
You can also ring the National Parks as they have accommodation at several huts in more secluded places. Ph (08) 8553 2381 for details.
It is best to bring your own camping gear and get amongst it.

Where To Eat:
The Ozone Hotel at Kingscote.
The Queenscliffe Family Hotel.
The bakeries are great in Penneshaw.

Where To Party
The Ozone Hotel.

Flat Day Fun
Fishing. The jetty fishing can be excellent. Try the wharves at Kingscote, Penneshaw and American River. The north coast has some excellent surf fishing opportunities. There are plenty of rivers as well. The Salmon can be legendary on parts of the south-west coast.
There are some beautiful places to scuba dive. Call (08) 8553 1072 for the dive shop in Penneshaw.
Try the Vivonne Bay Golf course for a quick round of nine.

SECTION INFORMATION

Local Shapers
None that would admit to it.

Best Months
The quality of the swell and the direction vary considerably throughout the year. Obviously the prime months are April to October, when the big south-westerly swells roll in accompanied by northerly

winds. The beauty of the Island lies in the fact that it is always offshore....somewhere.

Secret Spots
To give anything away here would be like signing your own death warrant.

Quick Tips
Treat the locals with respect.

Getting There
You can fly to Kingscote with Kendall airlines. Ph 13 13 00. Or Albatross Airlines. Ph (08) 8553 2296.
The other option is to go by ferry which is the only way if you want your car on the Island (preferable). Kangaroo Island Sealink will get you and your vehicle there. Ph 13 13 01. If you just want the passenger ferry call (08) 8261 1111. If you prefer to hire a car when you get there. Call Budget on (08) 8553 3133 or Hertz on (08) 8553 2390.

An essential building on this sea weathered island Pic. South Oz Tourism Commission.

THE NEXT JOURNEY

Check out www.liquidaddictions.com.au for more details

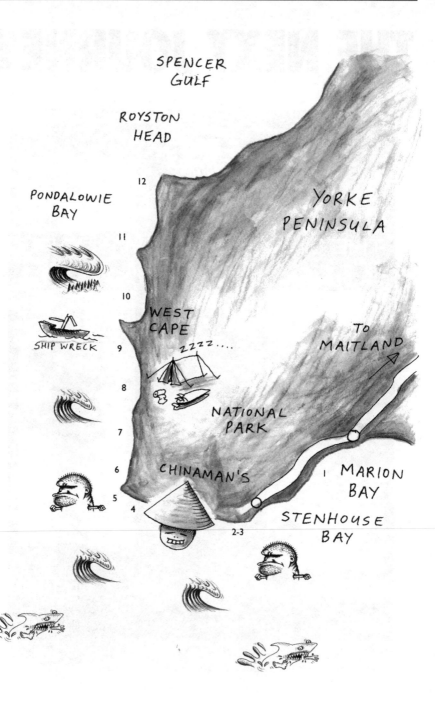

SPENCER
GULF

ROYSTON
HEAD

12

PONDALOWIE
BAY

YORKE
PENINSULA

11

10

SHIP WRECK   9

WEST
CAPE

ZZZZ....

TO
MAITLAND

8

NATIONAL
PARK

7

6   CHINAMAN'S

MARION
BAY

5

4

STENHOUSE
BAY

2-3

Natures Gifts

The transparent sea was rich in colours and a clean four foot swell. The approaching storm, formed a grey ceiling which was broken by sparse pockets where the sun shed its light.

Paul Sikura looking down the line at a lovely chinamans wall. Pic Courtesy of Rhino's Tavern.

S.A.

Yorke Peninsula

Nature walks, National Parks and Killer Waves

In comparison to its meagre surfable coastal zone, Yorke is a giant in the wave department. With so many options in a relatively confined area, and excellent access, there are many wave options. Lonely highways with brutal tracks through empty National Parks used to be characteristic of this stretch of coast The roads have been paved and there is a thriving building business that is erecting more housing every year. In winter, the crowds dissipate and the locals throw back to years gone by, coincidently it is the time for swell. There are so many options in varying conditions, with challenging reef and beach breaks. The locals have their allotted areas, leaving the rest free. This is the second step in completing your very worthy travel in South Oz, another good experience for the wild beast out west.

1.

Break Name: Rhino Head / Innes National Park

Wave Description: An average quality lefthand reef break. Works up to 2 metres, best when all other options are blown out.

Best Conditions: SW-S swell, NW-W wind, mid-high tide.

Getting There: In between Marion Bay and Stenhouse Bay, you can see it from the tavern as well.

Dangers: Although it is over reef, it really doesn't have any hidden dangers.

Rumours: It can get very good, but the locals will deny it.

Something Else? With the pub so close, it is hard not to be drawn in by the allure of the amber ales.

2.

Break Name: Baby Chinamans / Innes National Park

Wave Description: In comparison to its neighbour, a fairly average lefthand reef break. Best for beginners, or those who want some respite from the power of the surrounding breaks. Works best up to 2 metres.

Best Conditions: SW-S swell, NW-W winds, low-mid tide.

Getting There: Just to the east of Chinaman's, which is the first turn past the tavern.

Dangers: The reef can give out some punishment, but is usually pretty tame.

Rumours: Better for fishing than surfing.

Something Else? With the constant action from the neighbouring break, it will be hard for any self respecting surfer to spend much time here.

3.

Break Name: Chinamans / Innes National Park

Wave Description: Extremely hollow, lefthand reef break. The takeoff is horrendous to say the least, with a shallow, sharp reef to greet those who put one bootie wrong. Occasionally it has

a right as well. Don't attempt this wave unless you are 100% sure of your abilities.

Best Conditions: SW-S swell, N-NW winds, low-mid tides.

Getting There: You really can't miss it, as it is the first visible break as you enter the park.

Dangers: Apart from the scary takeoff and the shallow reef, the locals will hand out a pounding if you don't know what you are doing and are getting in their way. It also breaks up to 3 metres, which is pretty much death for anyone.

Rumours: This is where the first Chinese landed in SA.

Something Else? The carpark gives an incredible view of the reef and a great place to take photos. If it is flat, the snorkelling here can be amazing.

4.

Break Name: Ethel Wreck / Innes National Park

Wave Description: A fickle righthander that works best in summer months, can get very powerful on its day.

Best Conditions: SW-W swell, NE wind, low-mid tides.

Getting There: Take the turnoff to the Wreck, about 10 minutes past Chinamans.

Dangers: The scramble down the cliff face can be sketchy. There are also strong rips on bigger days.

Rumours: There are still roughly 40 undiscovered wrecks in the area which are supposed to have valuable cargo on board. A combination of prolific sharks, and the unknown location have halted any further exploratory missions.

Something Else? The remains of the wreck are still clearly visible, and are worth inspecting. If you go to the tavern, they have photos that show the wreck in an almost complete state.

5.

Break Name: West Cape / Innes National Park

Wave Description: A fun left, and

occasional righthand beach break.
Best Conditions: SW-S swell, N-NW wind, low-mid tide.
Getting There: Take the turnoff to West Cape!
Dangers: Pretty harmless.
Rumours: None that the locals wanted to spill.
Something Else? A beautiful beach in its own right, well worth a stroll.

6.
Break Name: Pondalowie Bay / Innes National Park
Wave Description: Good quality left and rights, over a combination of sand and reef. The right generally holds more size,

up to 3 metres
Best Conditions: W-SW swell, SE-E wind, low-mid tide.
Getting There: Clearly marked.
Dangers: Can get very big, and hollow.
Rumours: You can get your 4wd onto the beach, but it really isn't encouraged.
Something Else? The campgrounds are something very special here. Kangaroos will come straight up to you for a feed, there is abundant birdlife, and the amenities are A1. With solar heated showers and clean toilets, you can't go wrong. This place works best in summer as the prevailing winds generally provide offshore conditions.

Yorke local going horizontal. Pic courtesy of Rhino's Tavern.

S.A.

7.
Break Name: Richards / Innes National Park
Wave Description: A quality reef/beach righthander, which can get very hollow and fast. Breaks up to 1.5 metres.
Best Conditions: W-SW swell, E-NE wind, low-mid tide.
Getting There: About 250 metres up the beach from Pondalowie.
Dangers: None that we encountered.
Rumours: Some say this was named after the great MR. Apparently, the crowd was a little overwhelming, so he wandered up the beach a little and found this right. Having completely destroyed every wave that came his way, it became commonly known as Richards.

Something Else? There are heaps of other breaks in the area. Go and explore the options.

8.
Break Name: Trespassers
Wave Description: A very scary takeoff over a shallow reef that will send you spitting on a long righthander... if you make it! It breaks up to 3 metres, so beware.
Best Conditions: S-SW swell, E wind, low-mid tide.
Getting There: Take the Corny Point Rd outside the park area, and head to Little Lizard Bay.

Boardshorts and a sense of style is all you need in Yorke Peninsula, well almost....

Dangers: With a takeoff similar to Chinamans. Not much more needs to be said.
Rumours: Early surfers in the area would have to combat a gun wielding farmer for access to the break.
Something Else? Although outside the Park boundaries, still an excellent place to explore.

9.
Break Name: Baby Lizards
Wave Description: A short righthand reef break, which is not highly rated compared to the other spots in the area.
Best Conditions: SW-W swell, E wind, mid-high tide.
Getting There: Same directions as for trespassers.
Dangers: Same precautions for any reef break: make sure it's not too shallow!
Rumours: There was a proliferation of lizards in the area that escaped from one of the many ships that ran aground on the coast. We encountered zero lizards though.
Something Else? Formby Bay has some great fishing, but try nearby Browns for king size Salmon.

10.
Break Name: Rock Pools
Wave Description: SW swell, N-NW wind, any tide.
Best Conditions: A fickle but heavy right hand reef break that can handle most swell size.
Getting There: At the northern end of Formby Bay, take the Daly Heads turnoff from the Corny Point Rd.
Dangers: When the swell is running, the rips can be extremely hazardous.
Rumours: None about.
Something Else? Snorkelling in the pools can be great if it's dead flat.

11.
Break Name: Salmon Hole
Wave Description: A quick, punchy and extremely hollow, righthand point break.

Best Conditions: SW swell, NW wind, low-mid tides.
Getting There: Around the corner from Daly Heads.
Dangers: Be careful of the suck rock, and the back-breaking reef.
Rumours: The name suggests that there is reasonable fishing around, I think that they're right.
Something Else? There really is some bloody magnificent fishing in the area!

12.
Break Name: Daly Heads.
Wave Description: Heavy left and right reef break, which gets HUGE.
Best Conditions: SW-W swell, SE-E wind, any tide.
Getting There: Take the turnoff to Daly Heads from the Corny Point Rd.
Dangers: There can often be huge swells running here, and the reef can handle most size, so make sure you know what the hell you're doing.
Rumours: Sharks don't seem as prevalent in this part of SA, but there have been sightings here.
Something Else? If the swell is out of control, there are always places close by that will provide something a little more mellow.

13.
Break Name: Spits.
Wave Description: Average lefthand point, which breaks up to 2 metres.
Best Conditions: SW-S swell, SW-SE wind, on most tides.
Getting There: From the Corny Point Rd, take the turnoff to Gleeson's Landing.
Dangers: There can be a vicious rip that runs through, so beware at all times.
Rumours: Named because of the things these waves do!
Something Else? Often there are better breaks in the area if this is working, so make the time to explore.

S.A.

GENERAL INFORMATION

Where To Stay:
There are great camping facilities in the National Park. The rates vary depending on where you want to stay. The prices range from $5 to $15. It is all self registration. Ph (08) 8854 4040.
Marion Bay Caravan Park. Fees start from $10 per night for a tent sight. Ph (08) 8854 4094.
Lodge accommodation within the park which can include self contained miners quarters for 12 people, fully powered, or single roomed cottages with no power. Contact Innes National Park. Ph (08) 8854 4040.
Marion Bay Seaside Apartments. Ph (08) 8854 4066.

Where To Eat:
Rhino's Tavern has great meals, with schnitzel nights and other specials. Call Josh or Julie on Ph (08) 8854 4066.

Where To Party:
Any sort of action happens at the local tavern. There are bands that get down that way. In fact there are three in the area. Generally the biggest parties are to be had at a locals house, so be respectful and friendly and you could find yourself rocking at Bucko's.

Flat Day Fun:
There are no mini golf centres or amusement parks, but the sheer beauty of this place makes up for this. The fishing is first class, with three foot salmon being pulled from the beach. The snorkelling is magic. So are the beach walks. Try Coastline Camel Safaris, from Corny Point. Ph (08) 8855 3400. Also Natty's Fish and Dive Charter. Call Tim on (08) 8852 6338.

Local Shapers
None in the area. Get your sticks in Adelaide.

Best Months
Over the summer months, south-easters are the prevailing wind, so many of the spots are onshore. Generally April to July provide the best swells, although this seems to change every year. To be safe go in Autumn.

Secret Spot
One of Western Australia's best big wave locations has a point named after it. Here you will find uncrowded waves. Keep in mind you only need to get out of your car and walk to find many more hidden secrets around this area.

Quick Tips
Occasionally there is swell outside the areas we have mentioned, but it is very rare, and if there is, there are always better wave options. The roads are in excellent condition as are the camping facilities. So if you are expecting rugged, lonely and untouched beaches this isn't the place for you. It is still very beautiful , but becomes quite populated over summer.

Getting There
From Adelaide the drive will take you three to four hours.
Try Premier Stateliner on Ph (08) 8415 5500.

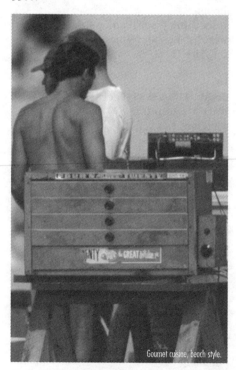
Gourmet cuisine, beach style.

S.A.

Clean and fun at Pondalowie. Pic Courtesy of Rhino's Tavern.

S.A.

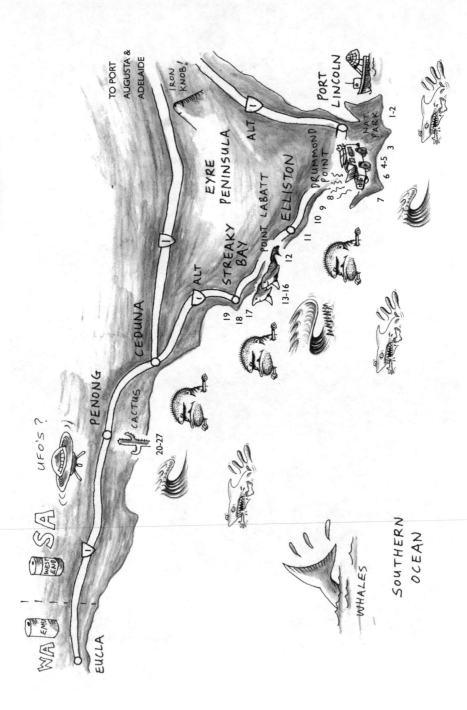

Cactus
We were typically cautious, and started at the inevitable nucleus of this place, (indeed all places), the pub.

S.A.

Vic Hislop and 20 feet of pure terror. Pic Jason Childs.

The Eyre Peninsula
Land of the Long, White, Shark Tooth

This coastal stretch is one of the few remaining expanses of wilderness for surfers. Long, lonely paddle outs, over deep channels characterize much of the surfing. Big bombies breaking in the distance, not even remotely tempting, as sharks patrol many of the outer reefs. Locals that lead a tough existence in the desert, living only for surf and a few of their vices. Ready for confrontations to protect their turf. Miles of saltbush wear the internal workings of most vehicles to the point of destruction. Flash flooding, closed roads. Gigantic swells batter the shores. And then there are the days of perfection. They come often, or once every decade, depending on who you talk to. It is a place of contradictions. Harsh desert, tropical oasis, board snapping reef breaks, mellow beachies. That's the beauty of choice. This place caters to most desires. Just don't rush it, as this has been the downfall of many a travelling surfer.

1.

Break Name: Lone Pine / Sleaford Bay
Wave Description: Fast and hollow
beach - reef breaks that are a variety of
left and rights.
Best Conditions: S swell, NE-NW wind,
low-mid tide.
Getting There: Follow the signs to
Sleaford Bay. It is at the end of the road.
Dangers: This beach is quite safe, which
is rare for this part of the coast.
Rumours: On its day this place will get
the most perfect breaks you are likely to
see.
Something Else? As you near the ocean,
you are confronted by an aqua coloured
lake. It reminded me of Blue Lagoon,
without the chick of course. There are
frequent shark sightings here, but fear
not, only Bronze Walers, which will take
your leg at worst.

2.

Break Name: Barrel Beach.
Wave Description: A combination of left
and righthanders over sand. Can get epic.
Best Conditions: S-SW swell, NE-E wind,
most tides.
Getting There: This is strictly 4wd. As
you hit Sleaford Bay, turn left, and follow
the beach until you find waves!
Dangers: Very easy to get your vehicle
trapped in the deceivingly deep sand.
Rumours: Obviously called Barrel
because it has a strong tendency to do
so.
Something Else? The colour of the water
here is so beautiful. If you do have a well
equipped 4wd, go exploring as there is
much untapped potential here.

3.

Break Name: Jussieu Bay.
Wave Description: A very fickle wave
that is a combination of reef and sand,
giving lefts and rights.
Best Conditions: SW-S swell, NE-E wind,
low-mid tides.
Getting There: Head towards Memory
Cove, strictly 4wd vehicles only.

Dangers: Sand dunes again.
Rumours: There have been several shark
sightings out this way.
Something Else? Cape Catastrophe is very
close by, which is worth checking out.

4.

Break Name: Left Point / Fishery Bay
Wave Description: Strangely enough a
lefthand reef/point break. Breaks even on
the smallest of swells.
Best Conditions: S-SW swell, N-NE
wind, low tide.
Getting There: Take the road to Fishery
Bay.
Dangers: The reef is very shallow, so be
aware. The track in is brutal, even with
the most rugged of 4wd's.
Rumours: This used to be the sight of an
old whaling station and is often
frequented by hungry sharks.
Something Else? Left and Right Point
(see below) face directly opposite each
other, so there is always respite from the
wind, with the exception of a direct east.

5.

Break Name: Right Point / Fishery Bay
Wave Description: Righthand reef/point
break.
Best Conditions: S swell, NW wind, low
tide.
Getting There: Take the road to Fishery
Bay.
Dangers: Same as above.
Rumours: Same as above.
Something Else? Tends to be a better
wave, but I guess that depends on
whether you are goofy or natural.

6.

Break Name: Flatrock
Wave Description: An extremely scary
hollow lefthander, that breaks over very
shallow reef.
Best Conditions: S-SW swell, N-NE
wind, lower tides.
Getting There: Go through Coffin Bay,
and head to Point Avoid, it is directly
below the carpark.

Dangers: The locals refer to this as Pipeline, and having seen this place I understand why. The raw power is terrifying, and only the best should surf it.

Rumours: A local was paralysed after landing in 2 foot of water on an 8 foot day.

Something Else? The surrounding National Park is really beautiful, and worth checking if you have a rugged 4wd.

7.

Break Name: Coffin Bay National Park

Wave Description: There are plenty of reef and sand breaks throughout this National Park. Try the eastern tip.

Best Conditions: W-SW swell, SE-NE wind, all tides.

Getting There: Take the signs to Coffin Bay from Port Lincoln, then the park is clearly marked from the township.

Dangers: It is incredibly isolated out there and any serious injuries would mean at least three to four hours before receiving treatment. The 4wd track is a slow one, challenging even the biggest rigs. So go prepared, knowing that help is quite a distance.

Rumours: There are many options for waves here, and they often provide some real class action. The place is very variable and there will be no one who will give you any pointers to the best breaks, so there is much exploring to do.

Something Else? Coffin Bay was named by Mathew Flinders after his buddy Sir Isaac Coffin. Although this explains the history, you need only look to the shipwrecks, huge swells and shark attacks in this area to think that Coffin is a very appropriate name.

S.A.

Two hours of suspension snapping road will lead you to this oasis outside Port Lincoln. The rides can be 400 metres long. The best thing is there is a righthander on the other headland. Pic Chubbs.

8.
Break Name: Greenly Beach
Wave Description: A variety of shifting beach breaks, which can get very good in big swells.
Best Conditions: W-SW swell, SE-NE wind, most tides.
Getting There: Take the turnoff on the Flinders Hwy, just near Warrow.
Dangers: With such long stretches of beach there is always heavy rip action, so beware.
Rumours: There are several neighbouring waves that provide real quality. Try End Bay, if you can find it.
Something Else? Of course sharks are plentiful here, so you take your chances.

9.
Break Name: Drummond Point
Wave Description: There is a variety of reef and beach breaks here, with some great point breaks.
Best Conditions: W-SW swell, SE-NE wind, low-mid tide.
Getting There: Take the turnoff to the namesake from the Hwy.
Dangers: Plenty of reef action to keep you on your toes.
Rumours: Can provide some very long rides, with several hollow sections.
Something Else? This place is always

worth checking on small wave days, as the headland generates more swell than other alternatives in the area.

10.
Break Name: Sheringa Beach.
Wave Description: Again there are some real quality beach and reef breaks, which require extensive exploring.
Best Conditions: S-W swell, NE-SE wind, all tides.
Getting There: It is signposted to the main area. You will then need to follow the numerous dirt trails to find the break that suits you.
Dangers: This place is also quite isolated, so emergencies will take at least an hour before any assistance. A sobering thought.
Rumours: There is a break closeby called "Hotspot", a roaring lefthander, which is worth discovering.
Something Else? As is the case with most of the areas here, the fishing is magic, with good salmon fishing from the beach.

11.
Break Name: Blackfellows / Elliston
Wave Description: A death defying drop will either put you under the lip for a lefthand barrel of a lifetime, or punish you within an inch of your life. I surfed

The perfect lines of Granites. One of the best places to paddle out, if you love sharks. Pic Brett Stanley.

this at 1-1.5 metres and it felt like a scary 2.5 metres.

Best Conditions: SW swell, E-SE wind and most tides.

Getting There: Take the coastal road from Elliston and follow it out to the point. Alternatively ask where Cape Finiss is. The carpark overlooks the break.

Dangers: The wave throws so far that on a 1 metre swell, you can get a standup barrel if you're good enough. The paddle out is a little hair-raising, as it is over a deep dark channel.

Rumours: Although there are many shark stories, I have been assured there has never been a sighting here. YEE HA!

Something Else? The Elliston locals can get a little protective, but generally there is never too much hassling, as the wave is a great leveller.

12.

Break Name: Venus Bay

Wave Description: A variety of quality reef and beach breaks that generally work on larger swells.

Best Conditions: S-SW swell, N-E wind, most tides.

Getting There: Take the turnoff from the Flinders Hwy, just south of Port Kenny.

Dangers: Generally quite a protected area from the full force of the ocean so it is usually pretty safe.

Rumours: This place can get classic, just a matter of the right day and right spot.

Something Else? A beautiful area that is worth exploring regardless of the swell.

13.

Break Name: Searcy Bay

Wave Description: There are a variety of reef and sand breaks here.

Best Conditions: S-SW swell, NE-SE wind, most tides.

Getting There: Take the dirt road turnoff to Baird Bay then follow the signs.

Dangers: With Australia's only mainland seal colony closeby, there are sure to be a fair number of sharks around.

Rumours: There are plenty of other

marine creatures that can cause serious injury.

Something Else? A cool place to hangout and absorb the remote fishing life for awhile. You are also more likely to be rewarded with tasty wave treats if you show some patience.

14.

Break Name: The Island / Sceale Bay

Wave Description: A very heavy sandunes reef break.

Best Conditions: S-SW swell, NE-SE wind, low-mid tide.

Getting There: There is a fair hike over some sandunes in the bay area. The easiest way is to get to the lookout and scan the coast. The wave is pretty distinctive so you should see the break or the crowd that will be surfing it.

Dangers: The break itself is a very heavy takeoff with a short barrel section. You must be confident in your abilities to surf here.

Rumours: This is very much a locals break and you must pay due respect if you want any waves at all.

Something Else? Although the Island is the prime spot, there are many breaks very closeby that are worth checking if there is a crowd here.

15.

Break Name: Yanerbie

Wave Description: A righthand reef break that needs a lot of swell to work well.

Best Conditions: S-SW swell, N-NE wind, low tide.

Getting There: Follow the signs from Streaky Bay, very easy, on the road to Granites.

Dangers: The reef can be extremely unforgiving, and help is a long way off.

Rumours: Is a very capricious wave and not often surfed.

Something Else? If the swell is huge, with an accompanying easterly or even south-easterly, this place is worth checking.

S.A.

S.A.

16.
Break Name: Smooth Pool
Wave Description: Another scary lefthand reef break, but can give a very long wall, if you can dodge all the semi-submerged rocks.
Best Conditions: SW swell, NE-E wind, mid to high tide.
Getting There: Follow the signs from Streaky Bay to Smooth Pool, on the road to Granites.
Dangers: The shoreline is strewn with large boulders that emerge with the rise and fall of the tide. It isn't often surfed, and you can see why.
Rumours: If you make the paddle out, then the wave is yours for the taking.
Something Else? If solitary, heavy waves are your thing, then this is ideal. There is an excellent shape to the wave that would provide just rewards to the right surfers.

17.
Break Name: Granites
Wave Description: A long lefthand reef break, that has a very steep takeoff.
Best Conditions: SW swell, SE-E swell, low tide.
Getting There: Follow the signs from town. Simple to find as it has camping facilities as well.
Dangers: The break can hold pretty much any size, but the takeoff becomes progressively steeper and shallower.
Rumours: Best not to surf when locals are around as there are likely to be some words spoken. This is not a place you want any distractions.
Something Else? Just to the east lies Indicators. You can see it breaking from Granites. If you can handle the power here, try up the way for some serious barrel action. Be extremely careful as there have been some horrific injuries to surfers at the hands of this wave.

18.
Break Name: Back Beach
Wave Description: There is a constant lefthand reef break, with shifting sand breaks to the east and west.
Best Conditions: S-SW swell, NE-SE wind, mid-low tide.
Getting There: Follow the sign from town.
Dangers: At high tide you could easily be forgiven for thinking this is a beach break, until you head-plant into solid rock. This place can get huge, and the rogue sets have caught many surfer unaware.
Rumours: Again, be deferential to locals.
Something Else? This stretch of beach extends both ways and has good waves all along. If there are people already surfing a peak, look for somewhere else as you are sure to find another closeby.

19.
Break Name: Cape Bauer
Wave Description: Lefthand reef break which can handle all swells.
Best Conditions: SW swell, E-NE wind, low-mid tide.
Getting There: Follow the signs from town.
Dangers: The situation of the cape leaves it open to all swells and an abundance of marine life. This place is not often surfed as a result.
Rumours: The fishing is superb around here.
Something Else? Even if you aren't going to surf here, take a stroll around the Cape as there are some amazing cliffs and you will see some of the most perfect barrels, unfortunately unrideable but beautiful none the less.

20.
Break Name: Witzigs / Cactus
Wave Description: A very punchy lefthand reef break.
Best Conditions: S-SW swell, NE-E wind, lower tides.
Getting There: This is the most southern break at Point Sinclair. Take a look from the carpark and you should be able to identify all the breaks.

Dave Howden charging into a Granite's beast.

Dangers: The break is over an extremely shallow shelf, which can create hideous takeoffs.

Rumours: It is called Witzigs after Paul Witzig who was one of the first surfers in the area, who subsequently bought a huge portion of land here.

Something Else? As is the case with the other breaks, beware of the locals.

21.
Break Name: Backdoors / Cactus
Wave Description: A double peaking, hollow righthand reef break, which can dish out some serious punishment.
Best Conditions: S-SW swell, N-NW wind, low tide.
Getting There: One break north of Witzigs.
Dangers: This wave is extremely hollow, so if your tube skills are a bit rusty, this is not the place to fine tune them!
Rumours: Named after the famous backdoor in Hawaii.
Something Else? Generally a wave that you can get a few sets on as the real

class rights are a little further around.

22.
Break Name: Cunns / Cactus
Wave Description: A good quality lefthand reef break, that needs swell over 2 metres to really perform.
Best Conditions: W-SW swell, SE-E wind, lower tides.
Getting There: The most southerly break in the next bay around from the previous two breaks.
Dangers: Sharp reef and moving closer to the shark breeding ground.
Rumours: This is often the wave that is surfed by the touros as it doesn't interfere with the locals spots.
Something Else? The wave breaks along the cliff face, making entry a little dodgy in big swells.

23.
Break Name: Cactus
Wave Description: A fairly tame lefthand reef break, in comparison to the rest of the wave options.

Best Conditions: S-SW swell, E-NE wind, mid-low tide.

Getting There: It is the break directly infront of the visitors carpark.

Dangers: Again shallow reef and the increasing proliferation of sharks.

Rumours: Probably the most notorious wave in Australia for hardened locals and the like. The wave is actually more suited to beginners as the takeoff is fairly relaxing. Most locals prefer to surf the other breaks, so often you can surf this by yourself.

Something Else? The adjacent camp grounds are well equipped, with nightly wood deliveries and solid shelters make it an ideal desert camp. The cost is $6 per night, plus what the local enforcers will try to extract from you.

24.

Break Name: Castles / Cactus

Wave Description: A punchy lefthander that breaks over several sections which can give you the ride of your life.

Best Conditions: S-SW swell, E-NE wind, mid-low tide.

Getting There: One break to the right of Cactus.

Dangers: All the shark attacks on the point have occurred here, as there is a channel next door that houses some 200 bronze whalers.

Rumours: Sharkbait, who was a very aggressive local, died recently. He had been knocked off his board, and attacked several times by sharks. Ironically, he died closeby in a car accident.

Something Else? The wave is best in swells over 2.5 metres, so it can get very heavy at times.

25.

Break Name: Caves / Cactus

Wave Description: An incredibly hollow, unforgiving righthand reef break.

Best Conditions: S-SW swell, NE wind, low-mid tide.

Getting There: Just north of Castles.

Dangers: This wave is probably the best

in the area so it draws the biggest crowd. There are several locals who will think nothing of trying to fight tourists in the water, simply for being there. Combine this with an incredibly powerful wave and an infested shark channel close by, it really is a matter of how much you want to surf this particular wave.

Rumours: There have been several incidents where a tourist has been punched because he rode a wave without offering it to the locals first.

Something Else? There is one character called Moose who seems to be the local enforcer. Take these warnings seriously, as many years in the desert and constant body abuse tends to send some people crazy.

26.

Break Name: Crushers / Cactus

Wave Description: Another powerful lefthand reef break.

Best Conditions: S-SW swell, NE wind, low tide.

Getting There: Just one cove around from all the other breaks.

Dangers: The same deal as with the other breaks, all though this does not get as crowded.

Rumours: None that compare to the rest.

Something Else? Not a bad place to surf when there are crowds about.

27.

Break Name: Supertubes / Cactus

Wave Description: A powerful righthand reef break.

Best Conditions: S-SW swell, NE wind, low tide.

Getting There: Next door to Crushers.

Dangers: A very fast and hollow wave over extremely shallow reef.

Rumours: The name came from its famous counterpart in South Africa, so it deserves respect and caution.

Something Else? The rocks on the headland are fantastic to fish from if the swell is too small or the crowds to heavy.

GENERAL INFORMATION

PORT LINCOLN

Where To Stay:
Grand Tasman Hotel. Ph (08) 8682 2133.
Port Lincoln Caravan Park. Ph (08) 8684 3512.
Blue Seas Motel. Ph (08) 8682 3022.
Where To Eat:
The Pier Hotel has lunch and dinner specials over the bar.
Country Garden Bistro. Great views and pretty good prices. Ph (08) 8682 1197.
Boston Bakery for your standard pastries.
Where To Party:
The Pier Hotel gets quite a few bands that can provide a decent night. The Boston has a nite club which is the only one in town, and the Grand Tasman is a younger crowd.
Flat Day Fun:
Dangerous Reef Cruises. These boats will take you out to a remote reef which houses the biggest sea lion colonies, which in turn are attacked by white pointers. Great viewing, or it could just

add to the paranoia. Ph (08) 682 2425.
The Port Lincoln Leisure Centre. This is great for a cheap spa and sauna. Rest those aching shoulders. Ph (08) 8682 3883.
Great Australian Bight Safaris. Call Steve or Rosemary on (08) 8682 2750. There is some really beautiful wilderness that surrounds this area. If you don't have a 4wd it is very worthwhile getting on one of these tours.

ELLISTON

Where To Stay:
Elliston Caravan Park. Ph (08) 8687 9061.
Elliston Hotel. Ph (08) 8687 9028.
Where To Eat:
Elliston Hotel.
Elliston Bakery.
Where To Party:
The only option is the Hotel, which has a great beer garden area, complete with outside pool table.
Flat Day Fun:
Lock's Well is world renowned for its salmon fishing. There are tournaments held here during June, July and August.

S.A.

The salubrious abode of the Penong Surf Shop. Pic Chubbs.

The stairs that wind down more than 60 metres were just opened (April '98) and this place is worth checking out. You can also charter planes to go to Flinders Island, which has some excellent surfing spots, although the shark population is enough to deter even the most stupid surfer.

STREAKY BAY

Where To Stay:
Labatt house/ backpackers. check in at the Shell service station, which doubles as a Tourist Info centre. Ph (08) 8626 1126 or (08) 8626 1330 $10 per night.
Streaky Bay Community Hotel. Ph (08) 8626 1008. Rooms start from $40.
Foreshore Caravan Park (08) 8626 1666. Sites from $8.
Where To Eat:
Community Hotel, Sports Club or the local bakeries.
Where To Party:
The only place is the pub, which is actually a very beautiful Hotel. It is owned and run by the people, so all the proceeds go towards the community.
Flat Day Fun:
Point Labatt is Australia's only mainland Sea Lion colony and is therefore definitely worth a visit.
Scenic flights. Ph (08) 626 1385. Good way to check out the potential surf breaks. For a half hour it ranges from $27 (five people) to $68 (two people).

PENONG

Where To Stay:
The Penong Hotel. Average quality for about $35 per room.
Or you could drive down to Cactus and sleep on the beach. Try Fowlers Bay for a sensational place to get into the sandunes and lay out the swag. The 4w driving through these sandunes is quite incredible, as there is such a vast area to explore. The first ascent can be a bit tricky, but the rest is easy. Worth the effort.
Where To Eat:
The hotel or the roadhouse, I suggest you bring your own food.
Where To Party:
The Hotel can get quite crowded, generally with locals, who often don't appreciate outsiders.
Flat Day Fun:
There is a Woolshed Museum, but your best bet is to have a look at the Penong Surf Shop. Classic building and the contents hold some serious history.

SECTION INFORMATION

Local Shaper
Gravelle - Paul Gravelle (Penong). Ph (086) 251 094. One of the most classic surf shops you will ever see.
Geoff White. Port Lincoln.
Best Months
From April to September the waves are the most consistent with the accompanying offshores.
Secret Spot
If you look to the common bird, for another word that means the same, you will find the bay that will give you a magic day. Closer to Cactus than Streaky Bay.
Quick Tips
There are so many breaks in the area that it is unnecessary to try to compete with the locals for the few spots they treasure. Chances are too, that if you stay for awhile you will get uncrowded surf at the prime locations anyway. Make sure you take fishing equipment as it is world class all along the coast. One particularly good spot is at Point Sinclair off the Jetty. Pretty much a guaranteed feed. The camping is extremely cheap with most areas having an honesty box, with a charge of not more than $2 per night. Plenty of firewood to keep you warm. This really is an isolated place with an

incredible array of wave options. From Penong to Eucla (the WA border) there are plenty of waves. Fowlers Bay is definitely worth checking, it is actually much nicer than cactus and has some classic old buildings. There are also some amazing dunes to drive through, and there certainly are waves. Also check Eucla as there is often a wave near the old jetty. The rest of the coast is surrounded by sheer cliffs. Make sure you are prepared for any eventuality and that your surfing skills are up to scratch, as this coast has the most powerful surf in the state.

Getting There

The best way to get there is obviously to drive. The other alternatives are:
Premier Stateline. Ph (08) 8415 5500. This service goes from Adelaide to Port Lincoln, but no further. There is talk of another company setting up tours for the west coast, but there is nothing definite yet. You will have to hitch from Port Lincoln if you don't have your own transport.

By car Port Lincoln is about seven/eight hours. Then it is about an hour and a half to Elliston, and a further three to Cactus. Enjoy.

SURFING YARNS

Lonesome waves

We had been warned about the treacherous tracks around Little Dip Conservation Park, and Stony Rise. Nick, our friend from Torquay, had told of his detaching bull bar when being pulled over one extremely steep dune. This drove our desire. We wasted no time in confirming the locale of the famed Stony Rise. As we wound our way deeper into the scrubbery and surrounding dunes, it became more apparent that this definitely was serious 4w driving. We managed to force our way, aided by sand tyres and a gutsy V8, to a beautiful little haven. I surfed a couple of peaky swells while

Nick scoured the rocks for signs of life. Surfing alone in these waters sends your heart rate skyward. Frantic glimpses into the deep, green below confirmed my thoughts that you can't see a shark coming. Such a comfort! Thoughts of the approaching dune challenge were occupying my mind, and as the third wave unflatteringly dumped me on the shore, I sighed with relief. The dune that we knew would provide the biggest test, was dubbed Denali, after the towering monolith in Alaska. Our third attempt saw the car creeping towards the crest. The real danger was the steep incline to the left, threatening to suck the life out of our prized 4wd, into the awaiting sandy grave. We spent the next 20 minutes crawling the last two metres, providing us with hoots and howls as the vehicle leveled on to a sandy platform. A warm and luxurious abode lay awaiting for us at Victor Harbour, which we couldn't resist.

An unlikely site anywhere in South Oz.
Pic Lynn Chambers.

Stockists – area code 08:

This is a list of your local surf shops. They can help you with pretty much everything to do with surfing. They are also proud to be stockists of The Surfer's Travel Guide.

Cutloose
778 Anzac Hwy
Glenelg 5045
8294 3866

JR's Surf & Ski
121 Greenfell ST
Adelaide, 5000
8223 5505

Ocean Graffix
21 Saltfleet St
Port Noarlunga, 5167
8382 6729

Pt Lincoln Surfing Centre
73 Mortlock Tce,
Port Lincoln, 5606
8682 4428

Southern Surf
36 North Tce
Port Elliot, 5212
8554 2375

Steves Place
Shop 2, 26 Victoria St
Robe, 5276
8768 2094

Surf Power
15 Albert Plc
Victor Harbor, 5211
8552 5466

The Green Room Cafe
18 Railway Tce
Beachport, 5280
8735 8180

The Snow & Surf Company
187 Rundle St
Adelaide, 5000
8223 5277

The deceptively heavy Blackfellows, Elliston. Pic Brett Stanley.

Classic wave at the cove, Streaky Bay. Pic Lynn Chambers.

The virtually unsurfable wave at Cactus, Caves. Not because of the hungry pack of sharks in the channel, not because of the heavy nature of the waves. Just the angry locals. Pic Brett Stanley. (Brett had many parts of his body threatened as well as his camera equipment when he took this photo. Like a true photographer he got the shot. On Ya Mate).

Mick Lowe in the eye of this south west storm. Pic Conti.

WESTERN AUSTRALIA

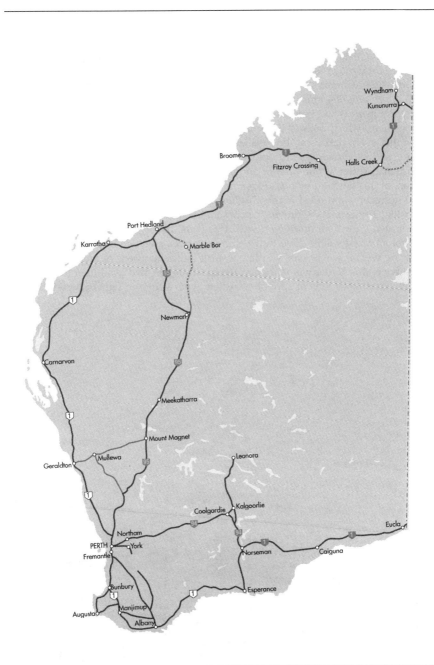

Western Australia

Duels In the Desert

It took the first settlers more than forty years to reach the West, following the colonisation of the much fabled East. This was due to its remoteness and huge area. At a little under half Australia's overall size, Western Australia is certainly the big man of our states. Over 175, 000 kms of road intertwine this vast land, where much of the natural environment is still untouched. Our indigenous population has many of its foundations here, which adds to the spiritual feel, and there is so much diversity in the landscape that every desire can be satisfied. The coastline is spectacular in its appearance and its sparseness of population, although this is changing every year. Every Australian surfer at one time or another has read or seen articles about the adventurers of this land. Surfers who lock themselves in the desert for months on end, to escape normality, and revel in the absolute beauty of their environment.

Places like Tombstones, Grunters, Crazies and Gallows fill most surfers with dread, and a dedicated crew with drooling desire. This is the beauty of such a rugged state, that it is not all Macdonald's drive thru's, and the waves aren't all beach breaks. Hell no. There are reefs that will slice you like a steak knife, hundreds of kms from any medical service. Roads that will tear apart the most rugged 4wd. And then there are the waves. With over 6,000 kms of surfable coastline, you would be right in assuming that

"Whodya reckon mate, is it long enough for us?"
The West Oz boys sport, out west of Esperance. Pic Scott Fisher.

Mick Burke poised in the middle of a NW pit. Pic Hilton

there are some quality waves in this region. In fact some of Australia's premier big wave spots lie within Western Australia's grasp. Most surfs are lonely, long paddles to outer reefs, where spitting beasts dwell, and where the marine life surrounds you. It tests the most adventuring spirits. Howling winds berate the inhabitants, a relentless sun sheds more than its share of uva and b rays. Expensive fuel and redneck attitudes all combine to give a feeling of a separate land, as if the desert is the great barrier between east and west. Technology is slow to infiltrate the sparse ranks of this land. Mobile phones are useless in many areas, and mechanical repairs consist of chewing gum in radiators and stockings for fan belts. A land full of contrast, with the richness and diversity of the south, to the extreme sparseness and hostile environment of the north. The south, with its bountiful wineries, and karri forests stretching hundreds of feet upwards, has received thousands of admirers from the east. Great waves abound this area, with raw power and monolithic sizes being its trademark. In contrast, the North has built its reputation on its tough exterior. Rugged roads, often impassable, gnarled coastlines and mammoth expanses of desert. But weaved in amongst this vastness, is a rare beauty that makes this place magical. The blooming wildflowers, shower their canopy of colours over an otherwise barren landscape. The coastline twists and weaves its way through open facing beaches, to secluded coves and peninsulas, where an incredible array of marine creatures dwell. The reefs are barely touched and haven't been subjected to excessive tourism. Visitors to this area, from the east or further, stand in awe of such majesty. But Western Australia requires more than a cursory glance, since there are secrets hidden amongst its ruggedness that only the most intrepid travellers will find. But search my friends, as you cannot be disappointed in an area that is so rich in every way.

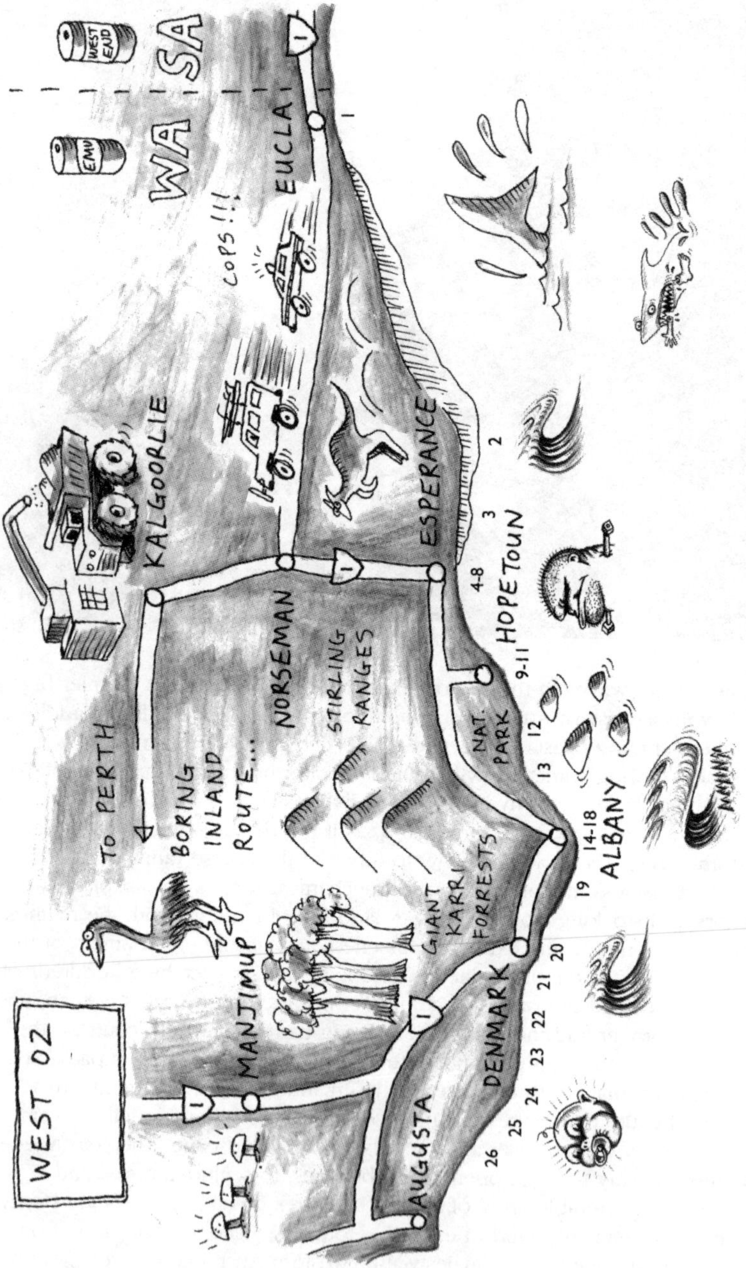
WEST OZ
TO PERTH
BORING INLAND ROUTE...
KALGOORLIE
NORSEMAN
STIRLING RANGES
COPS!!!
EUCLA
EMU
WEST END
WA
SA
ESPERANCE
HOPETOUN
NAT. PARK
GIANT KARRI FORRESTS
MANJIMUP
AUGUSTA
DENMARK
ALBANY
2
3
4-8
9-11
12
13
14-18
19
20
21
22
23
24
25
26
SOUTHERN OCEAN

Secret Spots
Our hosts would often come on our surf hunting mission, just to watch us try to navigate our way through the labyrinth of coves and cliff faces. Ah yes, very funny for them

Cheynes Beach. Pic Scott Fisher.

W.A.

Esperance - Walpole

East Of Eden

This stretch of coastline is the most sparsely populated, by surfers, within the state boundaries. Often the rigours of the pounding Southern Ocean is too great for the myriad of beach and point breaks. Onshore winds and uncontrollable seas are often the telling story of the area, but this is recounted by protective locals who guard their areas like fierce warriors. Look a little harder and you will see that not all the coast faces directly to the roaring ocean. In fact there are spots that offer protection from the fiercest storms, and provide class waves. The huge granite stones reflect a tough existence from this area. The wild seas have bred hardened individuals. They were whalers or worked on the log mills. The whaling operations only ceased in the late 70's and logging is still an important aspect of life. There is no hype to the surfing, only rusted old cars and plain black wetsuits. The surfers are a tight unit, often taking exception to brash tourists. As always, respect everything and your rewards will be great.

W.A.

1.
Break Name: Eucla / Border Town
Wave Description: Shifting peaks, with powerful right, and lefthanders.
Best Conditions: S-SW swell, NE-NW wind, all tides.
Getting There: Get yourself to the SA - WA border, then head to the old pier and you may be lucky enough to find a wave here.
Dangers: The beach is open to the full force of the Southern Ocean which in some cases provides good rides, but here it is often just big and brutal.
Rumours: Apart from the gigantic sharks that patrol these waters, there are a host of other dangers that keeps 99.9% surfers out of the water.
Something Else? It is about the easiest break to find.

2.
Break Name: Cape Arid
Wave Description: There are a selection of reef, beach and point breaks, with some fantastic quality to be found.
Best Conditions: S-SW, N-NE wind, most tides.

Getting There: It is approximately 100kms from Esperance. Take Fisheries Rd to Cape Arid National Park, it is pretty easy.
Dangers: Severe isolation, heavy waves, unchartered territory.
Rumours: If you can find the breaks then you may be surprised at the quality.
Something Else? The tracks are especially brutal on 4wd's, so some sort of idea is helpful.

3.
Break Name: Cape Le Grand
Wave Description: Often small and fickle waves are found here.
Best Conditions: S swell, NE-NW wind, all tides.
Getting There: Follow signs from Esperance, Cape Le Grand road, it's about 60kms from town.
Dangers: A prolific shark school in the area, due to the bustling seal activity on the surrounding archipelago.
Rumours: It needs a huge swell to break, and great for nude sunbaking!
Something Else? Worth visiting just to appreciate the beauty.

The rugged beauty of Cape Arid. Pic Scott Fisher

4.
Break Name: Wylie Bay / Esperance
Wave Description: Heavy shifting peaks, providing hollow and fast waves for those who can handle it.
Best Conditions: S-SW swell, N-NE wind, most tides.
Getting There: Take the turnoff to Bandy Creek, then follow the sign to Wylie Bay. You will need a 4wd to access the beach. It takes about 20 minutes from town.
Dangers: Rips and Currents, and deceptively soft sand that likes to bury cars.
Rumours: At times there are some amazing barrels here.
Something Else? About 800m from shore their is a bombie that looks very inviting and hollow. You can definitely surf it, just make sure you're up to it.

5.
Break Name: West Beach / Esperance
Wave Description: A variety of shifting beach breaks.
Best Conditions: S-SW swell, N-NE wind, mid to low tide.
Getting There: It is the eastern point of the first bay you encounter east from town. Follow the Twilight Beach Rd.
Dangers: Powerful rips and currents, but not too bad.
Rumours: Check this if nowhere else is working.
Something Else? There is a break in the reef a couple of hundred metres west that is worth checking out.

6.
Break Name: Chapmans Point / Esperance
Wave Description: Punchy righthand sand break, that is very close to the point.
Best Conditions: S-SW swell, NE-NW wind, mid to low tides.
Getting There: Follow the Twilight Beach Rd west from town. The first right point that you see will be it.
Dangers: The wave looks deceptively

small and soft from the carpark, don't be fooled.
Rumours: The local crew here can give you the impression that you are an unwelcome touro, but show respect, be friendly, and you may be exposed to the treasures of this coast.
Something Else? The rip action here is incredibly strong. The only way to get out is next to the rocks, either on the beach or off to the middle. Be extremely careful of the black slime, as people have slipped on big swells and lost their lives. The rip will pull you straight out to the lineup. When coming in, you must exit in the same way, as a huge exposed reef thwarts your attempts at an easy escape.

7.
Break Name: Salmon Beach
Wave Description: A short and scary righthand reef/sand break.
Best Conditions: S-SW swell, N-NE wind, low tide.
Getting There: Pull over on the Twilight Beach Road when you see the sign, or alternatively it is around the corner from Chappies.
Dangers: It is an extremely narrow beach, providing for excessive rips and currents. The takeoff is scary, as is the ride.
Rumours: Very few people surf this, as Salmon Holes is notorious for those white toothed hunters of the sea.
Something Else? This place is not suitable for swimming, but the fishing is a treat.

8.
Break Name: Fourth Beach
Wave Description: A variety of shifting beach breaks, that provides real quality in the area.
Best Conditions: S-SW swell, NE-NW wind, low to mid tide.
Getting There: Next beach along from Salmon Beach.
Dangers: Pretty safe unless it is huge.
Rumours: Often less crowded than the

adjacent breaks.
Something Else? This break only works up to 2 metre swells, anything bigger tends to close the beach down.

9.
Break Name: 12 Mile / Hopetoun
Wave Description: Shifting beach breaks, that can get very good, but often very fickle.
Best Conditions: S-SW swell, N-NW wind, mid-low tide.
Getting There: Follow the Southern Ocean East Rd for 12 miles east of Hopetoun.
Dangers: The swell doesn't often get huge here, but watch out for large marine life.
Rumours: There are some real quality beachies around, but they are often blown out by mid morning.
Something Else? Great camping areas, with abundant flora and fauna that is unique to this coastline.

10.
Break Name: Crazies / Hopetoun
Wave Description: A screaming lefthander on a shallow rocky bottom.
Best Conditions: S-SW swell, N-NW wind, mid-low tide.
Getting There: Straight south from the jetty, guarantees you will see it when you get to the waters edge.
Dangers: A deep, dark and long paddle to the break.
Rumours: Very rarely surfed alone, and often would-be surfers only make it as far as the nearby pub.
Something Else? The shape and speed of the waves is what keeps people coming back.

11.
Break Name: West Beach / Hopetoun
Wave Description: Small beach breaks that are constantly shifting.
Best Conditions: S swell, N wind, mid-low tide.

Getting There: Head into the Fitzgerald National Park and check the information board, that will give you the details on road closures and accessibility.
Dangers: The track is strictly 4wd, and even then it is a real mission.
Rumours: The waves aren't worth the drive but the view is.
Something Else? The nature walks are beautiful, a couple of days camping here would be ideal. Great fishing and very peaceful.

12.
Break Name: Mylies / Fitzgerald National Park
Wave Description: A variety of powerful, shifting, beach breaks.
Best Conditions: S swell, N wind, most tides.
Getting There: It is the first beach as you enter Fitzgerald National Park, it's clearly marked.
Dangers: This beach picks up an additional 2 foot of swell than Hopetoun, so it is often too big to surf. Check the town breaks before you venture westward.
Rumours: Alternatively when there is no swell, this often still has a wave.
Something Else? The coastal road is stunning and worth a drive just to admire the surrounds.

13.
Break Name: Cheyne Bay
Wave Description: A very fickle, but excellent righthand barrel.
Best Conditions: S-SE swell, W wind, mid-low tide.
Getting There: Take the turnoff from the South Coast Hwy to Cheynes Beach.
Dangers: Turning up to find howling onshores.
Rumours: To the west of here are some classic breaks.
Something Else? Hassell National Park is worthwhile visiting, yet it is very remote and often blown out.

W.A.

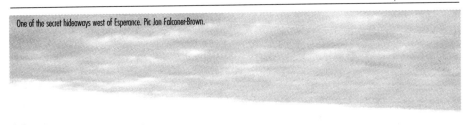

One of the secret hideaways west of Esperance. Pic Jon Falconer-Brown.

14.
Break Name: Nanarup Beach / Albany
Wave Description: Shifting beach breaks that can get excellent barrels at times.
Best Conditions: S-SE swell, NE-NW wind, most tides.
Getting There: Take the Lower King Rd from town, then take the turnoff to Nanarup beach. From there you need a 4wd on the beach, or you can walk in.
Dangers: As with most of the areas here, it is open to the full force of a roaring Southern Ocean, so it does get big and messy, with wild rips.
Rumours: With the opening of an inlet closeby and a fatality in the western corner, sharks are more than just a rumour here.
Something Else? The coastline here is magic as well. Huge cliff faces to the east are worth a visit.

15.
Break Name: Middleton Beach / Albany
Wave Description: Fair quality beach breaks, but needs a huge swell.
Best Conditions: SE swell, NW wind, mid-low tide.
Getting There: Take Middleton Rd to the beach.
Dangers: Lack of waves.
Rumours: The Esplanade Hotel is always worth checking as well.
Something Else? There will always be better waves somewhere closeby.

16.
Break Name: Salmon Holes / Albany
Wave Description: There is a variety of beach and reef breaks in this small bay. The reef is often the best, providing a punchy right and left break. The sand breaks also get good but are quite short.
Best Conditions: S-SE swell, NW wind, mid tide.
Getting There: Take the turn to Frenchman Bay then follow the signs.
Dangers: In bigger swells the reef break can get extremely heavy. The rocks are also incredibly slippery. If you watch the wave for awhile, you will notice that there are rogue sets that break differently, which has caught many a surfer unaware.
Rumours: There have been several lives

Deep, dark and lonely, Albany. Pic Chubbs.

W.A.

lost off these rocks. The swell surges from behind and engulfs the rock. It is very deceptive, which several fisherman have found.

Something Else? The fishing can be excellent and, as the name suggests, there are plenty of salmon.

17.
Break Name: Sandpatch / Albany
Wave Description: Punchy beach breaks, with a variety of left and rights.
Best Conditions: SW swell, NE wind, mid-low tide.
Getting There: Take the Frenchman Bay Rd, then take the Sand Patch Rd. Turn left at the Prison.
Dangers: There is always swell here, often it is unrideable. It is always 3 foot bigger than it looks from the cliff.
Rumours: The roads through here are dangerous. Low hanging branches and exposed tree stumps have caused fatal accidents.
Something Else? If you find this beach, you will see the potential of the

surrounding coast. There are roads that access these areas, it is just a matter of finding them!

18.
Break Name: Mutton Bird Beach / Albany.
Wave Description: Can get excellent beach breaks with long hollow waves, with both lefts and rights.
Best Conditions: S swell, N wind, most tides.
Getting There: Take the Lower Denmark Rd out of town, then follow the signs.
Dangers: It picks up plenty of swell, giving real punch to the waves, and creating strong undertows.
Rumours: None that we were told about.
Something Else? The drive along the beach is a buzz, and worth going for even if there is no swell.

19.
Break Name: Lowlands Beach
Wave Description: Fickle, but fun beach breaks.

Best Conditions: S-SE swell, N-W wind, most tides.
Getting There: Take the Lower Denmark Rd, then turn off on Tennessee South Rd.
Dangers: There are often some extremely strong rips on this beach.
Rumours: The fishing can be excellent, but not as good as the beachies on their day.
Something Else? Can't really think of anything else worthy!

20.
Break Name: Ocean Beach / Denmark
Wave Description: A huge choice of shifting beach breaks and a few reef breaks, which can get excellent. When Wilson Inlet is open, there are hollow and fast righthand barrels to be had.
Best Conditions: SE-SW swell, N-NE wind, mid-high tide.
Getting There: Take the Ocean Beach Rd to the mouth of the inlet, then you can drive along the beach to your desired peak.
Dangers: As always at rivermouths, don't surf at dusk or dawn, and with an open beach it produces strong rips.
Rumours: Some would claim this to be the finest surfing beach in the state.
Something Else? With so many peaks you often don't have trouble with crowds.

21.
Break Name: William Bay
Wave Description: A selection of beach breaks which tend to be a little more consistent than its easterly neighbours.
Best Conditions: SW-S swell, N-NE wind, most tides.
Getting There: Turn off the highway to William Bay Rd (surprise, surprise)
Dangers: There tends to be a few shark sightings in this area.
Rumours: This place is regarded as a secret spot by the Denmark locals.
Something Else? Closeby is Madfish Bay which is perfect for swimming and fishing. It also has a beautiful waterfall, making the trek in worthwhile.

22.
Break Name: Peaceful Bay
Wave Description: A heavy righthand reef break, that can get extremely hollow on its day.
Best Conditions: S-SW swell, NW-N winds, mid to high tide.
Getting There: If you take Ficifolia Rd from the Conspicuous Beach Rd, you'll be there.
Dangers: A rather remote location where emergency help is a fair way off.
Rumours: The 4wd track at Rame Head is still pretty bad, but worth the effort.
Something Else? There are so many nooks and crannies around here that could, on their day, produce excellent waves, but the conditions are very specific.

23.
Break Name: Conspicuous Beach
Wave Description: Can sometimes produce quality beach breaks, but very dependant on the sand build up.
Best Conditions: SW-S swell, N-E wind, mid-high tide.
Getting There: Just past the Valley of the Giants Rd, is Conspicuous Beach Rd, and yes you take this exit.
Dangers: The rips here can be extremely strong, as well as the jaw power of those finned marine creatures.
Rumours: One of the better breaks in the area, as it is protected from much of the prevailing weather conditions.
Something Else? The huge cliffs that surround the beach give you a sense of complete isolation.

24.
Break Name: Hush Hush Beach
Wave Description: Another series of beach breaks, that have to have very specific conditions to turn on a wave.
Best Conditions: W-S swell, NE-NW wind, mid tide.
Getting There: Along Mandalay Beach Rd, turn off to Long Point Track.
Dangers: The isolation and the rips.

W.A.

The long right arm of Chappies, Esperance. Pic Chubbs.

Rumours: The rangers residence lends out surfboards for free!!
Something Else? This particular region is the only declared wilderness area in the state. There is some fantastic fishing throughout the area.

25.
Break Name: Mandaly Beach
Wave Description: Can have excellent beach breaks, due to the number of headlands that retain the sand deposits.
Best Conditions: SE-SW swell, NE-NW wind, low-mid tide.
Getting There: Turn off the South Western Highway at Crystal Springs, where there is a rangers station.
Dangers: One of the most consistent breaks in this stretch.
Rumours: With so many headlands, there is often protection from the prevailing winds, consequently producing quality waves.
Something Else? Definitely take your

fishing rods here, as the deep gutters formed by the strong rips, are excellent for a variety of fish. Fish on the turn of the tide.

26.
Break Name: Windy Harbour
Wave Description: A fickle series of beach breaks, that receive the full brunt of the Southern Ocean power.
Best Conditions: S-SW swell, NE-NW wind, most tides.
Getting There: Head towards Point D'Entrecasteaux, it sits under the shadow of this point.
Dangers: The rips formed by the tumultuous sea are enough of a deterrent usually, if not, the inconsistency is the final straw.
Rumours: A cool place to check out, especially since there is a sealed road all the way there.
Something Else? Couldn't find anything else worthy. Can you?

GENERAL INFORMATION

ESPERANCE

Where To Stay:
Blue Waters Lodge. Ph (08) 9071 1040. This is the local hostel and it is fantastic. The manger, is a classic guy who will start you off on exploring the surfbreaks in the area. He has some classic Bruce Brown surf videos and there is always a really good group of people staying there. Highly recommended. $14 per night.
Esperance Bay Caravan Park. Ph (08) 9071 2237.
The Pier Hotel. Ph (08) 9071 1777. Pretty rough pub but has decent accommodation.

Where To Eat:
West Beach Cafe. See Roger for a selection of tasty pies and foccacias.
Curuso's. Licensed cafe, open for breakfast all day and heaps of other goodies.
Frankies Restaurant. 50's style a-la-carte menu, pretty cool actually.
Esperance Hotel / Motel for $5 meals.

Where To Party:
The Pier Hotel has the only niteclub in town.
Chesters, which has g-string wearing barmen, if you're into that.
Travellers Inn gets some great bands.

Flat Day Fun:
There is a really fun Skate park that is worth putting some turns on.
The Museum is quite fascinating, it is not what you would expect. For $3 definitely worth a visit.
There are plenty of sand dunes to rip up on the right boards. Go to the YHA for details.

ALBANY

Where To Stay:
Albany Bayview YHA. Ph (08) 9842 3388. Mark and Alex are pretty cool. Mark is a

Fun summer waves at Mutton Bird. Pic Scott Fisher.

W.A.

Australia Exposed

COME INSIDE

VICTORIA

Dave Johnstone at that very
critical moment, down south.
Pic: Steve Ryan

Dark, brooding, perfect.
One of the many faces of Win
Pic: Nick Clark.

The men and women who regularly surf here are a hardy breed. They stand staunchly in the Bells carpark at the break of day. **Struggling** to **see the icy** sets peeling around the corner through the early morning mist. The woollen jumpers and beanies wrapped tightly around chiselled faces and bodies. For it takes commitment to surf here year round.

Hawaiian power, Victorian style.
Greg Brown turning hard
at Easter Reef. Pic: Steve Ryan

SOUTH AUSTRALIA

Endless sandy beaches stretch towards towering dunes that resemble snow fields. Cornices dangle, **whipped into perfection** by rentless winds. Hundreds of bird and animal species roam the rugged wilderness. Huge salt pans that reflect the searing sun. Lush green hillsides where cattle and sheep stand nervously. There is so much to see yet so few to see it.

Des's left, Cactus.
Pic: Brett Stanley

Granites, Streaky Bay.
Pic: Brett Stanley

WESTERN AUSTRALIA

....those who chance nothing.
Pic: Hilton

Ben White captured
a desert tube.
Pic:Hilton

Nature rules over this unique environment. Man can only dream about the
freedom of the eagle in such isolation, or
the survival **instincts of the snakes** that
slither around the prickly shrubs. For man
is not king here, we are only just making
do. A special feeling indeed.

Desert simplicity.
Pic: Hilton

The greatest show on earth.
Pic: Simons

QUEENSLAND

Shark buoys and big waves,
Stradbroke Island.
Pic: Joli

Jason Spence in the eye at D-bah
Pic: Jane Lewis

Since the early '60's surfers were juicing up the **Holdens** and **Fords** and **pointing** the car northward in search of the ultimate dream. For many it came true.

The beauty and the beast, Kirra
Pic: Joli

Best tube award to RCJ, Kirra
Pic: Jane Lewis

NEW STH WALES

Justin Allport about to find out why
they call this place Crackneck.
Pic: John Brumfield

Greg Webber in perfect harmon
with a north coast barrel.
Pic:Hilton

Blessed with more accessible surf beaches than any other State, **it's a paradise** for the surf wanderers as many of the places have been documented, yet a large percentage of the natural beauty remains untouched.

The break of day, Angourie.
Pic: Hilton

Indo? Nup, Nth Avoca.
Pic: John Brumfield

TASMANIA

The South West tip, bloody cold.
Pic: Stroh

Secluded, cold and perfect
that's tassie.
Pic: Stroh

Most mainlanders consider the Island navigable in a day or two. Believing that the lack of nightlife and prohibitive water temperature **is enough reason for a short** stay. The true Taswegian would never disagree with this, for they treasure their secret Isle.

Shane Flannigan taking on Bluff Reef and Surviving.
Pic: Glen Saltmarsh

Tara Ryan - age 10

Alex Curasco

Mark Hernage

Paul Groenendyk

Ryan Clarke

Marcus Stocker

Luke Thomas

SURFBOARDS AUSTRALIA

LINE UP SURFBOARDS AUSTRALIA
12b The Strand Dee Why nsw 2099
Tel/Fax: (612) 9971 8624
www.ozemail.com.au/~lineup/
Samoan Surf Camps
JAPAN•NEW ZEALAND•EUROPE•WESTERN SAMO

QUIKSILVER
BOARDRIDERS CLUB

For the largest range of Quiksilver gear in Australia.

*Surf City Plaza, Torquay P.h. (03) 5261 4768

*209 Bourke St, Melbourne P.h. (03) 9654 7636

*88 The Corso, Manly P.h. (02) 9977 8444

surfer so he will let you know some of the spots. The Hostel has a great fire and living area. About $14 per night.

Middleton Beach Caravan Park. Ph 1 800 644 674.

The Esplanade Hotel. Ph (08) 9842 1711.

Where To Eat:

The Harvest Moon Cafe has wonderful continental rolls for $5.

Sonata's.

The Earl of Spencer has pie and pints for $10.

Where To Party:

Legends Bar at the Esplanade Hotel. Happy hour between 5:30 and 6:30.

The George.

1912 Niteclub, which is open Friday and Saturday nights only.

Flat Day Fun:

Whaling Museum, which is a must.

Go-kart racing.

Whale watching on either the Big Day Out or Silverstar.

During summer you can go on twilight sails around the harbour, really beautiful.

DENMARK

Where To Stay:

Wilson Inlet Caravan Park. Ph (08) 9848 1267.

Denmark Tavern and Motel Units. Ph (08) 9848 1044.

Where To Eat:

The local hotel has great, cheap counter meals.

The Bakery is also pretty tasty.

Where To Party:

The hotel is the only place to find some action and even then dog racing is normally the highlight.

Flat Day Fun:

Valley of the Giants is an amazing forest walk through karri and tinglewood trees that stretch up to 47m high.

Greens Pool, which is about 15 kms west of Denmark, in William Bay National Park. The green pool is set in amazing scenery and shouldn't be bypassed.

SECTION INFORMATION

Local Shaper

Paul King based at Emu Point Harbour.

Best Months

The best Surf seems to come from April to July. Certainly less winds and more offshore days.

Secret Spot

In the Whaling capital of this region is a very tasty righthander. The only thing I can say about this area is that the salmon normally reside to the east of this break.

Quick Tips

There is an incredible amount of exploring to be done here, with little assistance of well marked tracks.It requires the most courageous 4wd's to tackle some of these places. So often the waves can be blown out or unable to handle the swell. The locals are typically tight-lipped about their secret spots, understandably. It really is a matter of following your nose. Get as many maps as you can and pick points that you will think will protect the waves from the winds. Many of the roads keep going further and further into the wilderness. Often these are firetrails. Don't make the mistake of following these in the vain hope that they will yield the magic treasure.

Getting There

Westrail services the whole of the southern regions. Give them a call on 13 10 53. There are often rail and bus transfers to all destinations. Hitching can be a long-wait prospect so better to try to organise the hitch from the townships or the Youth Hostels.

Heavy South-West Barrel. Pic Hilton.

W.A.

Jeez I wish I was on that wave. Pic Jon Falconer-Brown.

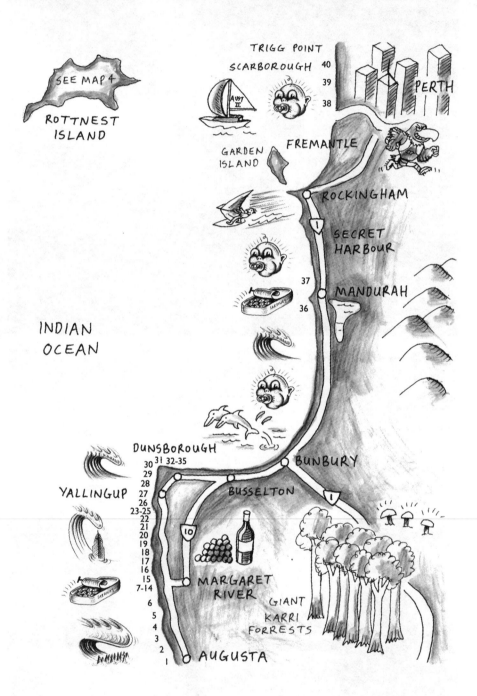

SEE MAP 4

ROTTNEST
ISLAND

TRIGG POINT
SCARBOROUGH   40
                39
                38

PERTH

GARDEN
ISLAND

FREMANTLE

INDIAN
OCEAN

W.A.

ROCKINGHAM

1

SECRET
HARBOUR

37
36

MANDURAH

DUNSBOROUGH
30 31 32-35

BUNBURY

29
28
YALLINGUP   27
             26
             23-25
             22
             21
             20
             19
             18
             17
             16
             15
             7-14

BUSSELTON

1

10

MARGARET
RIVER

GIANT
KARRI
FORRESTS

6
5
4
3
2
1   AUGUSTA

Fooled Appearances

The water here is so clear, almost tropical in appearance, and seemingly so serene. Don't be fooled by appearances though, as the sea is mind numbingly cold and home to Mr & Mrs Big-Ass Whitepointer.

The south west is renowned for reef perfection, this is no exception, Gas Bay. Pic Hilton.

Augusta - Perth
The Jewel In The Crown

This southern region of Western Australia is the most well known area for surfers. From the powerful and often dangerous Margaret River to the relative tranquillity of the city breaks, you would think there are enough waves to satisfy most. Yet surfers in the southern regions display a sense of urgency in their surfing, rivalled only by Queensland's surf starved grommies. There have been many reports and murmurs about the possibility of an artificial reef to relieve the pressure cooker of surfers fighting for waves. Although many surfers would say that the city beaches are so rarely good that they aren't worth mentioning, I found this a little hard to believe. Admittedly, this coast is plagued by the dreaded onshore more than their eastern partners, yet I have still seen five to six second barrels unridden, on suburban beaches. In my book, that makes Perthians a lucky breed. The main attraction of this area, though, is the great south. Margaret River has long held the mantle of the big wave Mecca, and it so often lives up to its reputation. Margaret River is only a small fraction of the choices in the area. Small communities still exist in this thriving centre, and you can definitely test your 4wd skills and find remote places. The waves are world class, but so is the competition, so get hunting as there is much to do.

1.
Break Name: Augusta Rivermouth
Wave Description: A variety of shifting sand breaks, often with a right. Can get good, but it requires heaps of swell.
Best Conditions: S-SE swell, NW-NE wind, most tides.
Getting There: If you can't find it, you should question whether you are a surfer. The clue is that it is at the rivermouth in Augusta!
Dangers: Well it is a rivermouth, and you know the dangers of hungry sharks!
Rumours: Doesn't often get crowded and can have excellent waves.
Something Else? The whole vibe of Augusta is different to the rest of the south-west. It is far more relaxed and there is still heaps to see. The fishing in the Blackwood River can be great and it's not too far from the action at Margarets.

2.
Break Name: Deepdene
Wave Description: Right and lefthand waves over reef, which holds swell up to 2.5 metres.
Best Conditions: S-SW swell, E-NW wind, mid tide.
Getting There: Take the turnoff from Caves Rd to Cosy Corner. From there it is south of the headland. You can walk but really you need a 4wd.
Dangers: The wave can get very heavy and the rocks are very close at hand.
Rumours: Another place that seems to be devoid of crowds.
Something Else? The rock fishing in the nearby areas is of legendary quality.

3.
Break Name: Boranup
Wave Description: A variety of punchy, fast and hollow beach breaks.
Best Conditions: S-W swell, NE -E wind, most tides.
Getting There: Take the turn to Hamelin Bay, then it is a 4wd, on the beach, to the peak of your choice.
Dangers: There is plenty of marine life in the area, but the greater dangers are the massive rips caused by deep gutters. These can also play havoc on your vehicle trying to access the break.
Rumours: It has been said that these are the best beachies on the coast.

"I'm keen if your keen, whadya ya reckon?".
"Lets just watch a little longer". Pic Joli.

Something Else? This stretch of coast doesn't pick up as much swell as Margarets, about half actually.

4.
Break Name: Conto's
Wave Description: A racy lefthander that will test you on the takeoff as well as the end section, mainly over sand.
Best Conditions: S-SW swell, NE-SE wind, most tides.
Getting There: From Caves Rd take the turnoff to Cave Works and follow this about 15kms to the camping area.
Dangers: The end section can get board snappingly hollow.
Rumours: Giant kangaroos feed off small children!
Something Else? The fresh water for the area comes from Conto Springs which is at the end of the beach, pretty cool really.

5.
Break Name: Redgate Beach
Wave Description: Shifting peaks, mainly over sand, gets incredibly hollow, works on smaller swells.
Best Conditions: S-SW swell, S-NE wind, mid tides.
Getting There: Take Redgate Rd from Caves Rd.
Dangers: The power of the waves definitely picks up a notch in this stretch of coast.
Rumours: There is excellent fishing and snorkelling around Isaacs Rock.
Something Else? This is the site of the wreck, Georgette, from 1876.

6.
Break Name: Boodjidup
Wave Description: A myriad of beach breaks that get hollow on both left and right. You can also try the outer reefs here, but be extremely careful.
Best Conditions: S-SW swell, SE-NE wind, mid-high tide.
Getting There: There is no car access anymore, so you have to walk in from

Gas Bay or from Redgate.
Dangers: When the swell gets big, it really is out of the question. It is a heavy wave at the best of times.
Rumours: It is worth the walk in.
Something Else? The walk in gives you a good feel for the surrounding breaks and their power, which is defiantly worthwhile.

7.
Break Name: Gas Bay
Wave Description: Power packed, righthand barrel over sand and reef.
Best Conditions: S-SW swell, SE-NE wind, high tide.
Getting There: Head to Prevally park then south as far as the road goes.
Dangers: With the rides sometimes giving 4-5 second barrels, you can imagine the sort of workings that come with it.
Rumours: Pottz has been known to frequent the hollow tubes.
Something Else? This is where localism starts to make its presence felt. Just make sure you know what you are doing, as the wave looks deceptive from the carpark.

8.
Break Name: Grunters
Wave Description: An extremely heavy righthand, outer reef break, fast and hollow.
Best Conditions: SW-S swell, NE-E wind, mid tide.
Getting There: To the north of Gas Bay.
Dangers: The name says it all. It is a long paddle out, so it always appears smaller, the takeoff is horrendous. There are times where the double up forces you to take the drop for the second time. Gets incredibly hollow as well.
Rumours: It snaps more boards than Margarets.
Something Else? Make sure you are ready for this break, as the hold downs are fearsome.

W.A.

9.
Break Name: Boat Ramp
Wave Description: An excellent lefthand reef break that works up to 5 metres!
Best Conditions: SW-W swell, E-NE wind, mid tide.
Getting There: Take turn to Gnarabup beach from Prevally Park.
Dangers: The long paddle and the fact that it holds 5 metres.
Rumours: If you can't call yourself a big wave rider, don't bother with this.
Something Else? There are several bombies that break through here. Make sure you get the right one.

10.
Break Name: The Bombie
Wave Description: A sickenly big lefthand reef break, with a class right.
Best Conditions: SW-S swell, SE-NE wind, mid-high tide.
Getting There: Just north of Boat Ramp, you won't miss it!
Dangers: The place really gets going at 10 foot, and for anyone who is game to surf it, there are no tips that will save them.
Rumours: There is never a problem with crowds, apart from the viewing platform.
Something Else? For those who will surf it, it will be certainly a wave to remember.

11.
Break Name: South Side
Wave Description: An extremely quick righthand barrel over reef, that works best up to 3 metres.
Best Conditions: S-SW swell, NE-E wind, mid-high tide.
Getting There: Follow Wallcliffe Rd to Prevally Park, it is the break south of the river.
Dangers: Not nearly as brutal as its neighbouring waves, but still manages to pack a punch.
Rumours: Rarely are there hassles with locals as they are surfing better breaks.
Something Else? A good break that

gives you an introduction to, and a look at, the wave potential of the area.

12.
Break Name: Surfers Point / Main Break.
Wave Description: A huge walling left and right over reef.
Best Conditions: SW-S swell, NE-SE wind, most tides.
Getting There: Follow all the other cars, you can't miss it, just near the rivermouth.
Dangers: Where do you begin? The locals, the wave, the wipeouts, it's all there.
Rumours: This is a favoured wave of many surfers like Tom Carroll, Ross Clarke-Jones, Pottz etc.
Something Else? If you make it out here on a big day, all you need to know is: watch out for the humps at the bottom of the wave otherwise the speed will launch you to oblivion. It seems to happen to all first timers to the wave. Take care in your bottom turns.

13.
Break Name: Margaret River Mouth
Wave Description: Small righthand sand breaks.
Best Conditions: S-SW swell, all winds, mid-high tide.
Getting There: Directly in front of the river, can't miss it folks.
Dangers: None that are worth mentioning.
Rumours: Not worth surfing.
Something Else? This is really a last resort wave, as there are so many options around. It is a very protected spot, so great for beginners.

14.
Break Name: The Box
Wave Description: An incredibly powerful righthand break over reef.
Best Conditions: SW-S swell, NE-SE wind, mid-high tide.
Getting There: Same directions for the previous two breaks. It is off the point to the north.

W.A.

Dave Macoulay. Ellensbrook. Pic Tony Asphar

Dangers: The takeoff is virtually over bare rock, and the lip has a tendency to drive surfers into the rocky shelf.

Rumours: It is only the craziest of people who are willing and able to surf here.

Something Else? This spot is worth watching for awhile as you are bound to see some of the best wipeouts you're likely to witness. It doesn't really work over 2 metres though.

15.

Break Name: The Womb and Ellensbrook

Wave Description: A sucky left over a reef bottom.

Best Conditions: SW-S swell, NE-SE wind, mid-high tide.

Getting There: Take the Ellensbrook Rd turnoff from Caves Rd.

Dangers: It is starting to get isolated in this region, and with sharp reef waiting to tear flesh, you should think twice.

Rumours: Often regarded as an uncrowded, yet class wave.

Something Else? The surrounding township is beautiful and in itself worth a visit.

16.

Break Name: Lefthanders

Wave Description: Another sucky and hollow wave over shallow reef, a trademark of this area.

Best Conditions: SW-W swell, NE-SE wind, mid-high tide.

Getting There: Take the turnoff to Gracetown from Caves Rd, then it is a 4wd track south from the township.

Dangers: The takeoff is extremely fast, with plenty of dredging sections. Watch out for the end section, which is usually dry and full of urchins.

Rumours: This is one of the classic lefthanders on the coast.

Something Else? This place often gets crowded with hot locals, so be prepared.

17.

Break Name: Big Rock

Wave Description: A heavy righthander over reef.

Best Conditions: SW-W swell, NE-SE wind, mid-high tide.

Getting There: South of Gracetown through a series of dirt tracks, past the tip. You'll find it.
Dangers: Can get very big, which can cause considerable harm to the unawary.
Rumours: This is a bit of a secret spot, so treat the area with the utmost respect.
Something Else? Excellent fishing prospects on flat days.

18.
Break Name: South Point
Wave Description: A long and wally lefthander over reef.
Best Conditions: SW-W swell, E-SW wind, mid-high tide.
Getting There: Turnoff to Gracetown from Caves Rd.
Dangers: The rocks are always closeby, and the urchins are just below.
Rumours: A great spot when other places are blown out.
Something Else? Gracetown attracts many holidaymakers and this becomes a pretty crowded break.

19.
Break Name: North Point
Wave Description: A hairy and long righthand reef break, with great barrel sections.
Best Conditions: SW-S swell, NE-SE wind, mid-high tide.
Getting There: Just before you get to Gracetown, you will see it.
Dangers: A dredging takeoff, over urchin infested reef.
Rumours: Ian Cairns perfected his snap here over many great sessions.
Something Else? This wave can wrap around for hundreds of metres, making for a sometimes epic ride.

20.
Break Name: Guillotine
Wave Description: A powerful and hollow lefthand reef break.
Best Conditions: SW-S swell, NE-SE wind, mid tide.
Getting There: Well it is now a case of

following instincts, as there is an incredible maze of 4wd tracks that lead to numerous spots. Try taking Cullens Rd off Caves Rd and sniff your way.
Dangers: It is very remote out here, and any serious injuries will be awhile before they are treatable.
Rumours: It was named for a very appropriate reason.
Something Else? If you found this spot, keep exploring and you will be well rewarded.

21.
Break Name: Gallows
Wave Description: A big and peaky lefthand reef break.
Best Conditions: SW-W swell, NE-SE wind, mid-high tide.
Getting There: Just north of Guillotines.
Dangers: Having the quality of breaking off a bombie makes this a fairly critical takeoff.
Rumours: Not often surfed, which is a bonus for hellmen and women.
Something Else? Make sure you take a Salmon rig for your dinner feed.

22.
Break Name: Moses Rock
Wave Description: Lefthand reef break, which can get good.
Best Conditions: SW-W swell, E-NE wind, mid-high tide.
Getting There: Take the Moses Rock Rd turnoff from Caves Rd.
Dangers: The old favourites of shallow reef and sea urchins.
Rumours: There have been several partings of the sea here.
Something Else? Great place to camp and fish.

23.
Break Name: The Window
Wave Description: Right and lefthand reef breaks.
Best Conditions: SW-W swell, NE-SE wind, mid tide.
Getting There: There are several 4wd

W.A.

tracks leading north. Take the one closest to the beach and drive approximately 3kms.
Dangers: Incredibly hollow and heavy.
Rumours: Marijuana plantation closeby.
Something Else? Gun wielding pot heads roam the area protecting crops.

24.
Break Name: Injidup Point
Wave Description: A relatively soft lefthand reef break.
Best Conditions: SW-S swell, E-SW wind, mid tide.
Getting There: Take the Wyadup Rd from Caves Rd, then onto the Cape Clairault Rd.
Dangers: The wave breaks along the rock shoreline, begging you to miss that section.
Rumours: It needs a pretty big swell to get going.
Something Else? There will always be better waves around.

25.
Break Name: Pea Break
Wave Description: Classic hollow righthand reef break.
Best Conditions: SW-W swell, NE-SE wind, mid to high tide.
Getting There: Right in front of the carpark at the point.
Dangers: Breaks over extremely shallow reef.
Rumours: When the swell is small this often gets crowded, so it is worth checking other options.
Something Else? An incredibly classy wave, with long tube rides for those skilled enough.

26.
Break Name: Smiths
Wave Description: A punchy, thick, righthand sand and reef break.
Best Conditions: SW-W swell, NE-SE wind, mid-low tide.
Getting There: Take the Canal Rocks Rd

W.A.

Perfect North Point. Pic Simons.

turnoff from Caves Rd.

Dangers: Pretty placid in comparison to the rest of the coast.

Rumours: None that were startling.

Something Else? Try the beaches north for better action, although a great longboard wave.

27.

Break Name: Supertubes

Wave Description: As the name suggests, fast, hollow and hairy righthand reef break.

Best Conditions: SW-W swell, SE-E wind, mid tide.

Getting There: Take the turnoff to Yallingup then south of the first headland.

Dangers: With such a hollow wave and shallow reef, it is worth taking some care.

Rumours: The drop in here means a termination of ones life.

Something Else? Holds swells of up to 2 metres.

28.

Break Name: Yallingup

Wave Description: A combination of left and rights over reef, which can hold up to 4 metres.

Best Conditions: SW-W swell, SE-NE wind, most tides.

Getting There: Once in Yallingup, just head to the beach.

Dangers: There are severe currents that rip through here, especially when it starts reaching 2 metres.

Rumours: This the home of Taj Burrow, who has learnt to surf on some of Australia's wildest coast line.

Something Else? The town itself has really good vibes, and is very picturesque.

29.

Break Name: Shivery Rock

Wave Description: A punchy lefthand reef break, that works best up to 2.5 metres.

Best Conditions: SW-W swell, E-NE wind, mid-high tide.
Getting There: This is where it becomes difficult. There are tracks leading there, but it is nearly impossible to direct you. The best bet is to ask the locals how the track is, as if you knew the route, but not the day to day conditions. From there proceed to extract information in any way you can. Bribes don't seem to work though.
Dangers: This area is pretty remote and the tracks are viscous on vehicles.
Rumours: If you have come this far, then go to the next break, as the quality is better.
Something Else? The fishing here is excellent. Snapper off the rocks is a possibility.

30.
Break Name: Three Bears
Wave Description: A series of punchy, long lefthand, reef breaks.
Best Conditions: SW-W swell, E-NE wind, incoming tide.
Getting There: Take Sugarloaf Rd off the Cape Naturaliste Rd, from Dunsborough. Then there is a 4wd track, or long walk, south. The set up is very noticeable, you wont drive past.
Dangers: The takeoffs are extremely heavy, and if you don't make it, there is usually a set ready to wash you in on the rocks.
Rumours: The farthest break out is normally the pick, although it can get surprisingly crowded.
Something Else? If you have a tough 4wd, the tracks are worth driving down just to experience some of the country and beaches.

31.
Break Name: Windmills
Wave Description: Small rights and lefts over sand and reef.
Best Conditions: SW -W swell, E-NE wind, mid tide.
Getting There: North of Sugarloaf Rd.

Dangers: If you have surfed the rest of waves in the area, this is no problem.
Rumours: The name gives a pretty easy clue as to its whereabouts.
Something Else? There is a left closeby called 'Other Side of the Moon', which is worth checking out.

32.
Break Name: The Quarries
Wave Description: A variety of beach breaks that can get hollow and big at times.
Best Conditions: SW-W swell, S-SW wind, all tides.
Getting There: Head to Bunker Bay and you will see your choices from there.
Dangers: Really quite safe.
Rumours: One of the few places that is offshore when everything else is blown out.
Something Else? Great fishing off the rocks.

33.
Break Name: The Farm and Boneyards
Wave Description: Mainly righthand beach breaks.
Best Conditions: SW-W swell, S-SW wind, all tides.
Getting There: The eastern side of Bunker Bay, which is accessed from the Cape Naturaliste Rd from Dunsborough.
Dangers: None, apart from crowds on a howling south-westerly.
Rumours: Zip, Zero, Niente, none allright!
Something Else? Needs a really big swell to produce decent waves.

34.
Break Name: Rocky Point
Wave Description: A fun lefthand reef break, that is great for beginners.
Best Conditions: SW-W swell, S-SW swell, incoming tide.
Getting There: Take the Meelup Beach turnoff from the Cape Naturaliste Rd.
Dangers: Plenty of surf-skis in these waters.

W.A.

Rumours: One of the few breaks that surf skiers haven't been shunned from.
Something Else? A perfect family beach, with all the facilities and beauty.

35.
Break Name: Castle Rock
Wave Description: Small right and left reef breaks.
Best Conditions: SW-W swell, S-SW wind, low tide.
Getting There: At Meelup Beach where the cairn stands.
Dangers: Sunstroke from all the lying around.
Rumours: Never has decent waves.
Something Else? One of the best places to learn how to surf.

36.
Break Name: Tims Thickett
Wave Description: Combination of left and righthand, reef breaks.
Best Conditions: W-SW swell, E-SE wind, most tides.
Getting There: This is a bit of a local secret spot, so I'll give you a clue. It is the entrance to a harbour, which is a secret. You'll work it out when you drive past!
Dangers: The wave action here is a little more solid, so beware of the headplant into a shallow reef.
Rumours: The local secret spot.
Something Else? A relatively secluded beach that is worth visiting, regardless of swell, if you are looking for respite from the crowds.

37.
Break Name: Singleton
Wave Description: Shifting left and righthand peaks, a fairly soft wave.
Best Conditions: SW-NW swell, E-NE wind, most tides.
Getting There: Follow the signs to Mandurah, then take the turn to Singleton about 13kms north of Mandurah.
Dangers: As with most of these beaches, it is relatively safe.

Rumours: Try the banks at surf beach, just up the road, often has better banks.
Something Else? The swell needs to be extremely solid to produce anything half decent. If you don't mind travelling, there are always going to be better waves north and south of here.

38.
Break Name: Leighton
Wave Description: Right and lefthand beach breaks, that can get good. Generally doesn't pick up as much swell as Trigg.
Best Conditions: SW-NW wind, E-SE wind, mid-high tide.
Getting There: Heading towards Fremantle, stick close to the coast. When you come through the industrial area, before Freo, you will see it. It also has clearly marked signs.
Dangers: This is a pretty safe beach.
Rumours: This is one of the most unpopulated breaks for surfers and definitely should be tried if there is a decent amount of swell.
Something Else? There are several breaks south of here that are worth checking, if you need to escape the crowds.

39.
Break Name: Cottesloe
Wave Description: A combination of left and righthand beach breaks, with a left running off the groyne.
Best Conditions: SW-NW wind, E-SW wind, mid tide.
Getting There: Directly infront of the Cottesloe Hotel. If you are following the coast, there are several signs that will get you there.
Dangers: Again the crowds are a problem, yet there seems to be a lot of body boarders here, so waves can be had.
Rumours: The left off the groyne, is deceptively good, as you look at it from the overlooking carpark. Definitely take the time to walk down to the waters edge.

The perfect holdup at Trijidup. Pic Joli.

Something Else? Just to the south of the groyne, there are several reef breaks that can get surprisingly good, on the right swell.

40.
Break Name: Trigg
Wave Description: Right and lefthand beach breaks, that can get hollow and fast.
Best Conditions: SW-NW swell, SE-NE wind, most tides.
Getting There: Follow the West Coast Hwy, until you get to Observation City in Scarborough. Ask if you can't find it from here.

Dangers: The crowds are the biggest concern around here, although the hollow waves can be a board snapping experience.
Rumours: There are always better options for waves, which will have less crowds. Although Trigg can handle the larger swells.
Something Else? The area around Scarborough is really "the" place on the city beaches. Some great Cafés and often people watching.

GENERAL INFORMATION

AUGUSTA

Where To Stay:
YHA Baywatch Manor Resort. Ph (08) 9758 1290 This is about as good as they come. We likened it to the fabled Flag Inns. The rooms are from about $14, and it is damn luxurious. Speak to Neville or Jane.
Augusta Hotel Motel. Ph (08) 9758 1944. Good to be near the action, if you can call it that!
Molloy Caravan Park. Ph (08) 9758 4515.
Where To Eat:
The Pub.
The café on the main street, makes great breakfasts, and has a pretty cool balcony.
Where To Party:
The Pub has a "Chase The Ace" competition on Fridays and some good

happy hours, but pretty quiet compared to its northen neighbours.
Flat Day Fun:
The Cape Leeuwin Lighthouse is definitely worth a visit. Having the title of "where two oceans meet", the Indian and Southern, makes this a spectacular place. Jewel Cave, is only 8kms from the town, and is amazing in its structure. An essential visit, worth the entrance fee.

MARGARET RIVER

Where To Stay:
Surf Point Lodge. Ph (08) 9757 1777. The building is in a prime location, and clearly caters for the surfer. With huge posters adorning the wall, this place looks perfect. Unfortunately a spate of robberies have turned the owners a little sour, so be prepared for some quizzing upon arrival. This is the price you pay I suppose.

Prevelly Park Holiday Resort. Ph (08) 9757 2374. Call ahead for here, as it is in the prime location, and gets crowded. Often with young, single people, which makes it interesting.....
Margaret River Inn Town Backpackers. Ph (08) 9757 3698. Beds starting at $14.
Where To Eat:
Settlers Tavern.
The Margaret River Hotel Motel.
Margaret River Tuckshop. A bit of a local hangout and an institution worth visiting.
Where To Party:
The Settlers Tavern has great live music on Fridays and Saturdays. With a large screen TV, and a killer beer garden, it is worth an ale or two.
The other pub can be good on Sunday arvos.
Flat Day Fun:
The wineries are famous in this region, and are worth a look.
Gone are the days of free tastings though, most of the vineyards have tours. Leeuwin Estate is well known in the area, and the wine is pretty good too!
The caves close by are incredible. Mammoth and Lake cave are quite spectacular, and worth the trouble. There are hundreds of caves in the area, yet only four have been developed. So if you're keen, you could find your own cost-free cave.
The fishing is superb along this coast.
YALLINGUP
Where To Stay:
The Yallingup Beach Caravan Park. Ph (08) 9755 2164.
Cape Lodge. Ph (08) 9755 6311.
Where To Eat:
The Yallingup store.
Where To Party:
Wild nightlife isn't a part of this town. Rest well and surf hard.
Flat Day Fun:
More damn caves, but they really are cool. Perhaps just hang out in town, skate a little, talk a little, and wait for the waves to fire.

PERTH / BEACH SUBURBS

There are other places to stay between Yallingup and Perth. Places like Dunsborough, Busselton and Bunbury. These places just don't offer the same quality of waves that you will find north and south. It is always better to spend quality time at premium breaks. Hence the void in details.
Where To Stay:
YHA Northbridge Backpackers Hostel. Ph (08) 9328 7794. A great area, with plenty of pubs and eateries, also close to the city.
Indigo surf-lodge, Scarborough. Ph (08) 9341 6655.
Sunset Coast Backpackers Hostel. Ph (08) 9245 1161.
Where To Eat:
Beachcombers at Mettams baths (just north of Trigg) has great smoothies and burgers, perfect for that post session feed. Uncle Vinney's in Northbridge have huge bowels of Chile Mussels, which are damn fine.
There are numerous cafés near cottesloe, which can have fantastic views, and there are some fine restaurants in town. The best burgers I have tasted were from a caravan that sits on the coast road between Cottesloe and Fremantle. You cant miss it, with burgers and assorted goodies all night long it's a really popular venue for young crew.
Where To Party:
The Cottesloe Beach Hotel has some magnificent Sunday sessions, which need to be seen.The Sail and Anchor in Fremantle, is WA's oldest pub. This place also cranks during the weekends, as does the whole of Fremantle. Steve's Bistro is perched on the waters edge near Pelican Point is also a pretty cool venue during the summer months. The Brass Monkey Bar & Brasserie, has great comedy on Wednesday and Thursday nights. The Aberdeen Hotel is also highly rated. The one place you must visit if you're a visitor to Perth is the hip-e-club. All the

W.A.

backpackers tend to frequent here, and there are great deals on food and drink.

Flat Day Fun:

Just where do you start? Try: Sailing on the Swan River, go-karts at Woodman's Point, stroll through King's park, wakeboard/kneeboard or slingshot yourself at Cables Waterski Park in Spearwood, leap downwards with Bungie West. Then there is Rottnest to consider. Just look around, there are plenty of things to keep you occupied.

SECTION INFORMATION

Local Shapers

MC boards - Maurice Cole. (Margaret River) Ph (097) 579 991.

Yallingup Surf Co - Al Bean. Ph (08) 9755 2109.

SSR surfboards - Dave Lewis/Greg McLauy (North Bridge). Ph (09) 227 5292

Rusty - Mick Button (Osbourne Park). Ph (09) 445 2233.

Clear Water - Steve del Rosso/ Col Ladhams (Rockingham). Ph (09) 592 3636.

Bare Nature - Dave Pillinger (Fremantle). Ph (08) 9336 4400.

Best Months

The best season for swell is between May and August. There are many exceptions to this though, as there are often great waves, down south, during the summer months. Summer can be pretty frustrating as the wind is relentless, and onshores are the go.

Secret Spot

To revel anything that resembled a secret spot on these pages, would spark some sort of witch hunt. What I will suggest is to make the most of the side tracks between Augusta and Margaret River, as there are many untapped areas still left for the adventurous.

Quick Tips

It is really easy to piss surfers off in these parts, as many have claimed the area as their local. With so many blowins spending winters here, and the influx during summer, situations can get tense. So it goes without saying, that respect is of the utmost importance.

Getting There

Westrail. Ph 13 22 32. Buses go daily from Perth to Augusta, for around $30. South-West Coachlines. Ph (08) 9324 2333. Also have a daily service, with numerous stop options. The prices are very close to their competitor. For travel within Perth, Transperth have an excellent public transport system. With free inner city travel and up market vehicles, it is actually a pleasure to ride on the PT. Ph 13 22 13. If you are driving around make sure you know about the rostering system for petrol stations on Sundays. Ph 11573. If you are looking for a rental vehicle, try Bayswater Car Rental. Ph (08) 9325 1000. Fast cars, and cheap prices, it's what you want.

W.A.

Trigg point perfection. Pic Brett Stanley.

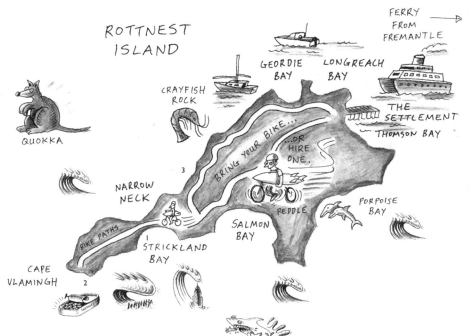

Rottnest Island

Peddle power

A fantastic respite from the extended flat spells and inconsistent reefs of Perth. A cyclists paradise as there are plenty of smoothed tar roads that snake around the Island, devoid of obtrusive traffic. Apart from the annoying Buses it is a very peaceful place. With some of the most incredible reef diving and surfing to be found. The Island has only recently become a popular destination for surfers. The ferry staff are blonde haired surfers who seem to always be gazing at some distant break. There is much exploring to be done here with the use of a pushie and some stamina. The Island is about 20kms long, so a quick check to the surf isn't really an option.

1.
Break Name: Strickland Bay
Wave Description: A combination of lefts and rights with the left being the best option.
Best Conditions: S-SW swell, E-NE wind, mid tide.
Getting There: Follow the incredibly well marked signs on the Island. About a 20 minute ride from the Pub
Dangers: The wave can hold up to 4 metres which is a scary prospect since it breaks over a shallow ledge.
Rumours: There are plenty of breaks west and east of here. You could try salmon point.
Something Else? The best idea to get the most out of this place is take a ride around the Island first without all your gear. It means you can go bush a bit and scope out the possibilities, which there are many of.

2.
Break Name: Bullet Reef
Wave Description: A gruelling set of righthand reef breaks that get huge.
Best Conditions: NW-SW swell, NE wind, mid-high tide.
Getting There: Follow the incredibly well marked signs on the Island. About a 30 minute ride from the Pub
Dangers: This area is open to all swells and hence can get very dangerous. The massive rips and undercurrents are just the tip of the iceberg.
Rumours: The old shack on the hill used to be a surfers abode until he came unstuck at the reef. He was never found, so they locked up the shack. You can still find shelter there though under a little wood storage.
Something Else? Radar reef which is adjacent is also very good, with a quicker takeoff.

3.
Break Name: Stark Bay
Wave Description: One of the most powerful lefthanders on the coast.

Best Conditions: NW-SW swell, NE-SE wind, mid-high tide.
Getting There: Follow the incredibly well marked signs on the Island. About a 20 minute ride from the Pub
Dangers: The wave handles incredible size which can produce lethal barrels.
Rumours: When you see the awesome power of this wave it will make you quiver with fear.
Something Else? To the west at Cape Vlamingh and West end there several other breaks which cop the full force of the Indian Ocean which can be an awesome sight.
Where To Stay:
Rottnest Camping. Ph (08) 9372 9737. Sites from $12.
Kingstown Barrracks Hostel. Ph (08) 9372 9780. Beds from $14. They have a courtesy bus that will take you from the ferry to the Hostel. It used to be an old army Barracks which is pretty errie during the quite winter months.
Where To Eat:
The Rottnest Hotel has nice counter meals.
the bakeries are always good value.
The Rottnest Family Restaurant isn't as tacky as it sounds.
Where To Party:
There really is only the pub, but that can be excellent. Especially watching all the drunk riders trying to cycle home. Very funny indeed.
Flat Day Fun:
The whole Island is extremely interesting. So hiring a bike and taking some snorkelling gear normally takes care of the flat spells.
Local Shaper:
Bring your own boards and repair kit as no-one has the facilities.
Best Months
From March to October there is usually enough swell to set the Island alight. It is the wind that kills it.
Secret Spot
You will have to work this one out for yourselves as it wouldn't be very proper

to expose spots in an already overcrowded place. Needless to say there are many out there. generally just under your nose.

Quick Tips

Plan to stay a few days as it takes a little while to work things out. Most people just come for the day, which is a bit of a waste as there is so much to see. At least three days would give you a good feel for the place.

Getting There

There is quite a bit of competition for passengers now, as there are three carriers. the major ones being. The Rottnest Express on (08) 9335 6406. It leaves from Fremantle and costs $28 return. The Supercat costs $25 call (08) 9430 5127. You will have to hire bikes on the Island unless you bring your own. The Bikes for hire are excellent though.

Getting close now, not long to go. Pic Joli.

SHIRE OF CARNARVON
DANGER
SINGLE LANE TRACK BEYOND THIS POINT IN BAD CONDITION WITH POOR VISIBILITY. *4WD VEHICLES ONLY*

PLEASE RESPECT THIS COASTLINE STRICTLY NO LITTER STAY ON MAIN TRACK NO — CAMPING FIRES SHOOTING

W.A.

Just another tasty barrel!. Pic Brett Stanley

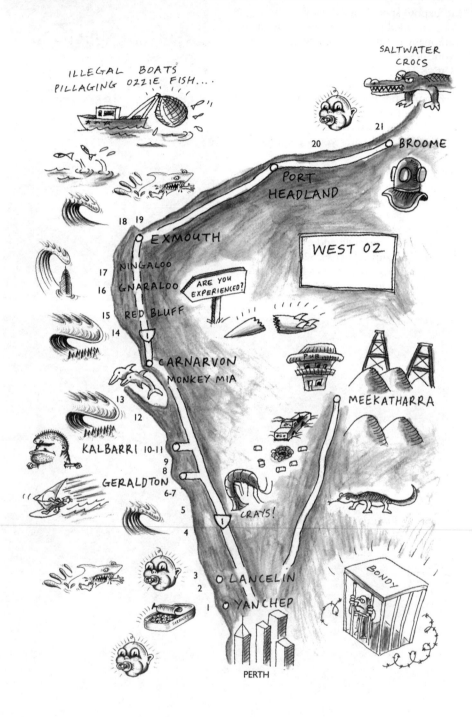

ILLEGAL BOATS
PILLAGING OZZIE FISH....

SALTWATER
CROCS

21

20

BROOME

PORT
HEADLAND

WEST 02

18 19

EXMOUTH

17 NINGALOO

16 GNARALOO

ARE YOU
EXPERIENCED?

15 RED BLUFF

14

CARNARVON
MONKEY MIA

MEEKATHARRA

13

12

PUB

KALBARRI 10-11

9
8
GERALDTON
6-7

5

CRAYS!

4

BONDY

3 O LANCELIN
2 O YANCHEP
1

PERTH

W.A.

River Crossings and a whole lot more...
Having made it, we looked back in admiration, and said "Too easy for the boys". I think at that point we were destined for grief.

The warped tubes of the NW aren't the only danger! Pic Hilton

North - Broome˙

Heart of Stone

The contrast of Western Australia is never more apparent than the road north of Perth. The lushness of the south and the surrounds of Perth give way to a desolate land. Huge eagles feed on dead carcasses that litter the road, while disinterested locals stare blankly at the sky waiting for, well something. The pubs are always full, generally with miners, as this is their only reprise from a land that is extremely harsh. For many, there is little beauty in this part of Australia, yet it is the many moods that make this region so intensely interesting. The blooming of the wildflowers after the monsoonal type rains in the harsh desert environment, and the magnificent, untouched coastal areas. Solitary trees stand steadfast against a relentless wind, giving a home to the many birds of prey. But it is the waves that are of the most incredible beauty for surfers. Endless left-hand barrels spit and peel their way accross jagged reefs. Spanish Mackerel launch and jump their way across the ocean in a desperate attempt to escape their pursuers, and generally nature rules the roost here. That is what is so unique about this environment, that nature is the ruler here. Man can only dream about the freedom of the eagle in such isolation, or the survival instincts of the snakes that slither around the prickly shrubs. For man is not king here, we are only just making do. A special feeling indeed.

1.
Break Name: Yanchep
Wave Description: Lefthand reef break, that can be excellent on its day.
Best Conditions: S-W swell, NE-SE winds, low-mid tide.
Getting There: Take the turnoff from Wannaroo Rd to Yanchep, about half an hour from Perth.
Dangers: The swell holds up to 2-2.5metres, and grinds across reef on good days, so it can give you a hiding.
Rumours: There are other waves in the area, and it could be worth checking out Two Rocks.
Something Else? The much loved larrikin from Fremantle, Alan Bond, invested millions of dollars, not his own of course, into Two Rocks, in the hope of exposing some more of WA's treasures. Good onya Bondy, for wasting more money.

2.
Break Name: Ledge Point
Wave Description: A variety of outer reef breaks, that require some stamina to paddle to.
Best Conditions: S-SW swells, SE-NE wind, most tides depending on the swell.
Getting There: Follow the signs to Lancelin, then take the turnoff to Ledge point.
Dangers: Most of the outer reefs are littered with Mako and Tiger Sharks, so you need to be smart about your surfing hours.
Rumours: There are far better waves in Lancelin.
Something Else? The beach driving can be a blast, but not really in winter, as the tides seem to be too high. A great place to get fresh crays.

3.
Break Name: Hole in the Wall / Lancelin
Wave Description: A punchy righthand reef break, that can get very fast, hollow and powerful at times.
Best Conditions: S-SW swell, SE-NE

winds, most tides, depending on the swell.
Getting There: If you go to the main wharf in Lancelin and follow the buoys out, you can see a break in the distance.
Dangers: Like most 40 minute paddles, you can expect some dangers!!!
Rumours: The best way is to take a dingy out and moor it closeby!
Something Else? There have been many cases of Mako sharks patrolling the area. In one particularly nasty incident, a seal was mauled only metres from the beach. There are some beach breaks in the area. There is one just south of Lancelin which can be accessed by 4wd. The other breaks lie north. You can access them via the 4wd track at the end of town, literally. If you drive far enough north you will enter a naval zone, complete with bombing ranges. That's when the fun starts!!

4.
Break Name: Port Denison
Wave Description: A long lefthander, at times, that breaks over reef.
Best Conditions: S-W swell, NE-S wind, mid tides.
Getting There: Just south of Dongara on the National Highway 1.
Dangers: Pretty safe actually, as most of the real swell action is blocked by reefs.
Rumours: With a tough 4wd there are plenty of options, south of here.
Something Else? The key to these areas is a keen sense of adventure, as there are certain places that have breaks in the reef, allowing swell to push through onto the beaches. Just need to be there on the right day!

5.
Break Name: Flat Rock
Wave Description: A variety of reef and sand peaks that seem to constantly shift.
Best Conditions: S-W swell, NE-SE wind, most tides.
Getting There: What can I tell you other than it is between Dongara and

Geraldton. It is kind of a secret spot.
Dangers: Divulging information about
this area, then publishing it.
Rumours: Can get really good, as there
is a substantial break in the reef.
Something Else? The Houtman Abrolhos
Islands are a long way offshore, some
80kms, so get on a cray boat if you can!

6.
Break Name: Hells Gate / Geraldton
Wave Description: Very powerful
righthander, that breaks over a shallow
reef.
Best Conditions: S-W swell, NE-E wind
and most tides.
Getting There: About one kilometre
offshore from Point Moore.
Dangers: The rips around here are
extremely powerful, so you should
definitely know what you're doing, when
surfing this break.
Rumours: The name has a very definite
meaning.
Something Else? The crays around here

are premium, so get your hands on a
couple if you can.

7.
Break Name: Lighthouse / Geraldton
Wave Description: A fairly soft
lefthander that only breaks in big swells.
Best Conditions: S-SW swell, NE-E wind,
mid-high tide.
Getting There: Directly in front of the
lighthouse.
Dangers: In comparison with the
surrounding breaks, none to speak of.
Rumours: In 1923, the huge frigate
"Lazar" broke up on the outer reefs.
She was carrying food supplies for
the northern reaches of the country,
but also some prize jewels. Apparently,
the ship left England with a stowaway
who had just thieved some of the
Royal Family's stash. The wreck is still
outside the reef, and perhaps the
priceless jewels.
Something Else? A Mecca for
windsurfers.

W.A.

Watching, waiting, for the wind to swing, to make this Kalbarri beast rideable. Pic Chubbs

183

8.
Break Name: Coronation Beach.
Wave Description: A Variety of shifting beach breaks, that work on larger swells.
Best Conditions: S-W swell, NE-E wind, most tides.
Getting There: Take the turnoff, from the number 1, to Coronation Beach.
Dangers: Pretty safe actually.
Rumours: Can get very good at the south end.
Something Else? Check out the caravan park, overlooking Coronation, just off the highway, on top of the hill. There is a private road that hits the beach which can be pretty good. Ask permission first, as you're sure to get busted since the road goes right by the house.

9.
Break Name: Horrocks.
Wave Description: Lefthand reef break down a precarious rock ledge.
Best Conditions: SW swell, E-NE wind, most tides.
Getting There: Take the coast road from Northhampton, about 25kms.
Dangers: There is always the possibility

of sharks around here.
Rumours: This place tends to get a bit more swell than Geraldton.
Something Else? North is Point Gregory, which is worth a look. But who could afford to wait here if you knew what was in store further north?

10.
Break Name: Jakes / Kalbarri
Wave Description: A screaming lefthand reef break, very serious!
Best Conditions: S-SW swell, SE-E wind, mid tides.
Getting There: Follow the coast road around till you are dumbstruck by an incredible left.
Dangers: This place is scary. The takeoff is a freefall at best, then straight into a hollow and angry barrel that spits you onto a huge wall. All the while an incredibly visible rock shelf lies metres from you.
Rumours: If there is no-one surfing it, then there is something seriously wrong. Do not go in! We saw it with no-one out, looking almost makeable, only to be told by the locals that it would have been a

Not perfect, but that is one huge gaping hole isn't it? Pic Chubbs.

W.A.

death mission due to the angle of the swell and the wind. A very precise place at best.

Something Else? This wave is dominated by a heavy local crowd who know this wave intimately, so show more respect here than normal. The wave is heavy enough without additional hassles.

11.

Break Name: Blue Hole / Kalbarri
Wave Description: Hollow righthander that breaks close to the rock ledge.
Best Conditions: S-SW swell, SE-E wind, low-mid tides.
Getting There: Clearly marked off the coast road south of town.
Dangers: Can still get pretty big, and the rocks are always a worry.
Rumours: There are waves everywhere through this region, some just aren't surfable.
Something Else? The rivermouth can be an option too.

12.

Break Name: Steep Point
Wave Description: A very spooky lefthand reef break, that challenges even the most hardened surfers.
Best Conditions: SW-W swell, E-NE wind, mid-high tide.
Getting There: This is a very serious 4wd track, that requires a well equipped vehicle. Turn left at the Overlander Roadhouse, then follow the signs. It is a good three hour mission, at best. There are some pretty heavy going sand dunes.
Dangers: This place is literally teaming with sharks. They love it! The rips are pretty horrendous too.
Rumours: None that will scare you more than the real place itself.
Something Else? This is Australia's most western point, which makes it pretty special.

13.

Break Name: Dirk Hartog Island
Wave Description: Another scary wave,

this time a lefthand reef break.
Best Conditions: SW-W swell, E-NE wind, most tides.
Getting There: There are several tour companies that offer travel adventures to this island. Check out the main street of Denham.
Dangers: Full of sharks, and the rips and currents are extremely fast.
Rumours: Can get some of the best waves on the coast?
Something Else? It really is a mission when just up the road you have...

14.

Break Name: Red Bluff
Wave Description: A huge lefthander, that grinds over a shallow, urchin infested reef. Can hold massive swells and gets extremely hollow.
Best Conditions: S-SW swell, SE wind, mid tides.
Getting There: About 100kms north of Carnarvon. Take the Blow Holes turnoff from the major highway, number 1.
Dangers: This place is for experienced surfers only. The reef is razor sharp, and wounds tend to get infected incredibly quickly. You are a long way from medical assistance too.
Rumours: There have been many claims that this is Australia's best lefthander.
Something Else? Marine life abounds through here. The fishing is magnificent, especially if you have a boat.

15.

Break Name: Turtles
Wave Description: A left and righthand barrel, that breaks over a shallow reef.
Best Conditions: S-SW swell, SE-NE wind, mid tides.
Getting There: Just further north of the bluff camp ground, over the sandunes.
Dangers: This place picks up more swell than Red Bluff, so it can be treacherous.
Rumours: There have been many shipwrecks in this area, and interesting finds by beachcombers on this remote stretch of coast.

Deano very casual in the face of this WA turtle. Pic: Jak

W.A.

Something Else? Never go anywhere around these parts without a fishing rod.

16.

Break Name: Gnarloo / The Point

Wave Description: A long lefthander that can go for over 500 metres, breaks over a shallow reef.

Best Conditions: S-SW swell, SE-NE wind, mid-high tide.

Getting There: Follow the dirt road north from Turtles, and take a turnoff to Three Mile Camp.

Dangers: Again, the reef is razor sharp, and the marine life plentiful. We watched as a 6 foot bronzie was hauled in, right where we were surfing. There were several other larger family members around. Yet, as there is so much marine life to keep them occupied, there has never been an attack here.

Rumours: Even though this place can require sheer determination to get to, there can often be 60 to 70 people in the barren camp. The vibe is great though, and often huge catches of Spanish Mackerel are shared amongst the whole camp.

Something Else? It is worthwhile to take all your supplies with you as stocks are very limited. Although there is a shop that seems to have a better range of basics every year. The camp itself is very exposed and good protection from the sun is essential, so take good tents with annexes. You need to book ahead for a campsite in the winter months as it can often get crowded. Fishing rods are essential, as is snorkelling equipment, but the boat is your ultimate goal. Although there seems to be a very hard edge to the place, people are pretty friendly, always say hi! The showers are hot between 4 and 6 in the evenings, heated by a wood fire.

17.

Break Name: Yardie Creek

Wave Description: A variety of outer reef breaks. All are very powerful and for the experienced only.

Best Conditions: S-SW swell, SE-NE wind, mid-high tide.

Getting There: You can only access this place by boat. There are a few spots where it might be possible to paddle, but be very sure of your abilities.

Dangers: Only attempt to surf this spot if you have a great knowledge of handling small tinnies in big surf, and know how to take 10 foot close outs on the head.
Rumours: We met a group of guys who flipped their tinnie, and paddled it in with their leg ropes attached to the boat. It was a good couple of hours before they reached shore. Not something you really want to deal with.
Something Else? There is a great gorge close by, which was filmed in "Green Iguana". You can jump off the north side cliff, but it can get pretty high. Damn good rush though.

18.
Break Name: The Bombie / Exmouth
Wave Description: A huge lefthand reef break, that is long and hollow.
Best Conditions: S-SW swell, NW-N wind, mid tide.
Getting There: If you drive up to the lighthouse and look down into the bay you will see the break. The lighthouse is about ten minutes from town, just follow your nose to the coast.
Dangers: The paddle is monstrous. The rips can be pretty strong, and it is always bigger than it looks.
Rumours: There are only a few people who will surf this place. Look out for a guy called "Greenie".
Something Else? If the bombie is really cranking and looking too scary, there is a lefthand reef break in front of the caravan park.

19.
Break Name: Dunes / Exmouth
Wave Description: Left and right sand covered reef breaks.
Best Conditions: S-SW swell, NE-NW wind, mid tides.
Getting There: Take the Mildura Wreck Rd from the main coast highway, just east of the lighthouse.
Dangers: The wave can get incredibly hollow, snapping boards with ease. The rips tend to be fierce in big storms.

Rumours: This place is perfect when huge swells batter the outer reefs. It can be perfect, but be prepared to wait.
Something Else? There are some other wave opportunities in the area, it's just a matter of sniffing them out.

20.
Break Name: Eighty Mile Beach.
Wave Description: On really big swells there can be small wave options along here, but it is a pretty vast stretch to explore for limited options
Best Conditions: W-SW swell, E-SE wind, high tides only.
Getting There: North of Port Headland on the number 1 highway, take a turn left to the coast.
Dangers: There are massive tidal influences here, so be careful when leaving your vehicle parked on the beach. The waves are going to be pretty small.
Rumours: Look out for the stingers in summer months.
Something Else? The best wave options will be on the points that are north along the beach.

21.
Break Name: Cable Beach / Broome
Wave Description: Unbelievable as it may seem, this place does get waves during high tide. They are mainly beach breaks, with left and rights. It is worth driving north along the beach if there are waves, as it may surprise you.
Best Conditions: Huge SW-W swell, NE-SE wind, mid-high tide.
Getting There: Follow the signs to the beach from Broome.
Dangers: Make sure you know what the tide is doing as it can trap your vehicle very easily.
Rumours: There are better waves to the north.
Something Else? Don't ever expect waves to be here, as it is extremely fickle to say the least. But what a joyous way to end a Western Australia trek, with fun 2-3 foot beachies.

W.A.

GENERAL INFORMATION

LANCELIN

Where To Stay:
YHA Lancelin Lodge. Ph (08) 9655 2020.
Very comfortable with easy access to the
beach. Beds from $15. They also have a
courtesy bus that runs during the
summer.
Lancelin Caravan Park. Ph (08) 9655 1056.
Lancelin Inn Hotel Motel. Ph (08) 9655
1005.
Where To Eat:
The Pub.
Fish and chip shop.
Café.
Where To Party:
The Pub on New Year's Eve, or summer
Saturdays. Pretty cool at other times as
well. A great beer garden, with stunning
views. In winter the open fireplace is
very inviting.
Flat Day Fun:
Sandboarding.
Monster Truck tours. Ph (08) 9405 3074.
These babies are huge. Similar to the car
munching machines you see in the US.
Five foot high wheels, surround sound
system, the full bogan tour. Not really for
your romantic getaway with a loved one.
Surfsport Adventures. Ph 0417 965 063.
These guys do snorkelling or scuba tours,
with pretty reasonable prices.

GERALDTON

Where To Stay:
YHA Batavia House. Ph (08) 9964 3001.
Beds from $14.
Seperation Point Caravan Park. Ph (08)
9921 2763. Powered sites $9.
The Grantown Guesthouse. Ph (08) 9921
3275. Beds from $22.
Where To Eat:

Jeez, I'm not sure about this! Three Mile camp. Pic Chubbs.

The Cuisine Connection is a food hall, with a variety of choices. Indian, Italian and Chinese meals are all cheap, and good eating. There is also your standard array of takeaway "food".
The Gero has pub meals, but don't expect too much.
Where To Party:
Geraldton Hotel has some pretty appalling theme nights, such as "Money for Nothing". A bit of a laugh though. Frostbites and Circuit are the local niteclubs, which can be fun.
Flat Day Fun:
Touch the Wild Safaris. Ph (08) 9921 8435. This tour gives you a chance to see the local Flora and Fauna of the surrounding area. About $85 per day. Houtman Abrolhos Islands. Plenty of swell 60kms offshore, even on the flattest days. Check at the Tourist Bureau for tour availability. Ph (08) 9921 3999.

KALBARRI

Where To Stay:
YHA Kalbarri. Ph (08) 9937 1430. Beds from $14. This is a popular spot for backpackers, so it's a good idea to ring ahead. The set up has a very communal feel to it. With free snorkelling gear for use and cheap BBQ nights, it is worth the time.
Red Bluff caravan park. Ph (08) 9937 1080. It has onsite vans for $28, and they have BBQ's on Wednesday and Saturday nights, always good value.
Av-Er-Rest. Ph (08) 9937 1101. Beds for $13.
Where To Eat:
Kalbarri Palm Resort has $10 meals with free entrance to the movies, which is the only licensed cinema in Australia.
Seabreeze Coffee Lounge.
Jonah's Fish & Chips.
Where To Party:
Kalbarri Beach Resort / Jake's Bar.
Flat Day Fun:
Kalbarri Coach Tours can take you to

some of the magnificent gorges in the area. You must see the Murchison River Gorge, but there is also other spectacular scenery in the area. Ph Kalbarri Visitors Centre on 1 800 639 468, as they have all the latest info on tours etc.
Abseiling and rock climbing. Ph (08) 9937 1104. Speak to Nick or Gordon.
SHARK BAY / DENHAM / MONKEY MIA
Where To Stay:
The Seaside Caravan Park. Ph (08) 9948 1242. Powered sights from $11.
Bay Lodge. Ph (08) 9948 1278. Beds from $12.
Monkey Mia Dolphin Resort. Ph (08) 9948 1320. You really should visit Monkey Mia as you will see dolphins, and this is the prime spot to camp for an early viewing. Get up at sunrise, and if you're lucky enough, you may get to swim with a dolphin, as opposed to gawking at them with a hundred others. No one seems to like early mornings, so it is a perfect chance for surfers to use their training to get the most out of this place.
Where To Eat:
The Old Pearler Restaurant.
The pub.
Where To Party:
The pub, if you're lucky. Generally full of fishermen and local contract workers.
Flat Day Fun:
Francois Peron National Park, is worth heading into if you want some 4wd excitement. The real action starts on the Islands. Explorer Charters & Cruises, Ph (08) 9948 1246, can take you to Steep Point, where there is some serious wave action.
Shark Bay Discovery 4wd tours, Ph (08) 9948 1320, can also get you out there. You can also get to Dirk Hartog Island which has some interesting wave possibilities. Ph (08) 9948 1253.

CARNARVON

There is really no need to stay in Carnarvon if you are on your way to The

Bluff. Use it as a supply stop. The pubs exude an unfriendly air, and the locals always look suspiciously at you. This was not only our experience as we have heard the same reports from many other travellers.

THE BLUFF

Due to the increasing popularity of this area, the facilities are being upgraded, but with that come changes. You need to book ahead if you want to stay at Gnarloo Station, which is in high demand. Ph (08) 9942 5927. There are other campsites which are not so sought after, such as Red Bluff. Take plenty of supplies in as the facilities are marginal. Also, it kind of adds to the desert feel, when luxuries aren't available.

EXMOUTH

Where To Stay:
Exmouth Cape Tourist Village. Ph (08) 9949 1101. Powered sites from $17
Potshot Hotel Resort. Ph (08) 9949 1200. Even if you don't stay here you must drink a beer beside the pool.
Excape Backpackers. Ph (08) 9949 1201.
Where To Eat:
The Potshot Hotel.
Caper's Fish & Chips.
Whaler's Restaurant.
Where To Party:
The Potshot Hotel has great theme nights, and generally, people go to this Hotel.
Flat Day Fun:
Cape Range National Park is one of the most incredible places you will ever visit. It is surrounded by the Ningaloo Reef, which is teeming with marine life. There are plenty of tours that ferry people to the beaches and back, but..... all you need is some simple snorkelling gear and a car. The pick of the area is Torquoise Bay. There is a drift dive that allows you to view the reef, and its abundant

inhabitants, while being dragged by the current. The dive is probably 300 metres long, but the variety is amazing. Make sure you are there early as there are always tours arriving from 9:00am onwards. There is no camping permitted, but sleeping beside your car......... The fishing is also incredible. Make sure you check before throwing your rod in, as fishing is prohibited is some marine parks. It is worthwhile going to Yardie Creek to see the gorge. This is also the launching spot for reef surfing. During certain times of the year (March to June) you can see Whale Sharks, and in the summer months giant turtles come ashore to lay their eggs. Special stuff! There is a large array of tour operators. Call (08) 9949 1176 for Tourist Information. Some of the better operators are: Ningaloo Safari Tours. Ph (08) 9949 1550, The Ningaloo Coral Explorer. Ph (08) 9949 2424.

BROOME

Where To Stay:
YHA Broome's Last Resort. Ph (08) 9193 5000. Beds from $12. This seems to be the most popular hostel with a great variety of characters.
Cable Beach Backpackers. Ph (08) 9193 5511. Beds from $15. An ideal location, with the beach a stones throw away.
The Roebuck Bay Shire Caravan Park. Ph (08) 9192 1366. Powered sites from $14.
Where To Eat:
Mango Jack's.
The Roebuck Bay Motel Hotel.
Where To Party:
The "Roey".
The Nippon Inn is a pretty cool dance club.
Flat Day Fun:
Sun Pictures is an open air cinema which screens recent releases. Great on hot nights.
It is often flat at Broome, so get used to beachcombing, drinking and relaxing.

SECTION INFORMATION

Local Shapers
BM Surf Designs - Bruce Montgomery (Geraldton). Ph (08) 9964 4966.
Stone - Mick Stone
Slave - Steve Harrison (Geraldton). Ph (08) 9923 9992

Best Months
It is only feasible to travel the north coast in winter, as the surf is particularly inconsistent during the summer months. The onshores are also fierce at this time, with temperatures rising to 44 degrees in the shade. With and a howling wind, it is not a pleasant experience. The insects are extremely prevalent during summer as well. The prime months are June to September, but several months either side should score you swell.

Secret Spot
North of Lancelin there is an Island. Between the Island and the coast there are some quality reef breaks, but more importantly, some beach breaks. Yes, that's right, there are breaks in the reef where the swell pushes into the beach, forming tasty beaches as well. The name is a portion...........

Quick Tips
North of Perth is a harsh environment. The distances are greater and the risks start to mount. It is important to remember this when heading to the region. Understand the dangers that could occur, mainly medical and mechanical woes. Make sure you have a well equipped vehicle, first aid kit and some good maps. Always carry water and insect repellent. A harmonica and guitar can provide relief from the stresses that you so often face. A boat is a worthy investment, even if it is rented for the duration of your trip. You can also buy second hand tinnies that will get you to the surf and some great fishing, for $1200-1500, complete with motor. They are invaluable for really discovering the wilderness in this area. Over half the

W.A.

150 kilometres in nine hours. Yeah the roads are great! PicChubbs.

As good as it gets, Exmouth. Pic Chubbs.

campers at the key spots have some sort of boat. It is the ultimate accessory. Look for good deals in "Boat Trader" or the weekend classifieds.

Getting There

Greyhound Pioneer. Ph 13 20 30, has a service three times a week from Exmouth to Perth, including all the major coastal towns. It runs once a week to Broome. If you want to go to Lancelin, call the YHA as they have a bus service that runs during summer. Car rentals are best done in Perth, and the cheapest is Bayswater. Refer to the Perth "getting there". Hitching is quite difficult, but once you have a ride, it will take you a long way.

SURFING YARNS

Sandy Graves

The 4wd had become our temple, an indestructible pillar of faith. This was about to be shattered

A friend from Melbourne, Emma, had joined the tour for a few days and we were keen to display our improved 4wd driving skills. As it goes when you get two guys and a girl together, the guys are

sure to display their "inimitable cool". With so many beach driving options, it wasn't hard to find suitable terrain. The beach just south of Lancelin would be our base for the next four hours as we scrambled for our pride and vehicle. The entry to the beach seemed harmless enough, although the absence of other vehicle tracks was somewhat of a concern, but the roar of the v8 quashed our fears. As we kept driving to no place in particular, the sand started to soften and the angle of the beach became more acute. Our confidence wouldn't be dampened as we charged on, with the vehicle slowing little by little. We got to the stage where it was obvious that we were headed into a serious situation, so against our male instincts we stopped and conceded that we could go no further. As we sheepishly looked at Emma, she was clearly enjoying the pitiful display that had unfolded before her. It was agreed that we should head back as there seemed no other way. Our only dilemma was how we should return, as there was very little room to turn around and reversing was always a danger. After repeated attempts at a futile three point turn, I was becoming frustrated. The 4wd had never let us down, why would it now? I eyed the soft sand close to the water, and saw the unimpressed faces of my compatriots, I knew what had to be done. Somehow I knew the conse-quences, yet I pushed forward. I slipped into drive and gunned it, hoping the momentum would barge through the soft sand and put me back in control of the situation, which was quickly slipping from my grasp. At that second, control was ripped from my hand as the vehicle sank deep, far too close to the incoming tide. My futile attempts at removing the vehicle from the sandy clutches by pushing the peddle to the floor, saw the vehicle sink up to the doors. I had to push hard to open the door and inspect the dilemma I had created. Emma merely shook her head, as Nick looked on with a sort of disbelieving look. After a frantic half hour of digging, the situation looked hopeless and we sent Emma to the closest town for help, although both of us were dubious of anyone being able to assist us, unless they had a sherman tank. As Emma strolled into the misty distance, Nick and I looked at each other, and I'm sure that both of us sensed that this was different to the numerous other stupid situations we had put ourselves in. The tide was definitely coming closer, and by our tide chart, it still had three hours before it reached its zenith. As we looked down the beach and followed the high tide line back to the car, it was obvious that we HAD to remove the car before the ocean did. I started to feel sick and wanted someone to blame, but there was no hiding from my error. We looked at each other, breathed deeply then screamed until our lungs ached. Then it was time to face reality. I shuffled through the myriad of junk that lay in the boot and retrieved a very small looking spade. I distinctly remember dad saying that we should get a bigger spade, but of course I knew better. The first task was to build a protective wall of sand around the car so there would be some protection from the encroaching tide. Nick went off frantically searching for any type of loose branches that we could shove under the wheels to give some sort of traction. Then the digging began. For a solid three hours we dug. My arms suffered to the point that I could hardly lift a palm full of sand. With the ocean lapping at our heels, we spurred each other on. Finally the car was clear of sand and the foundations had been laid under the tyres. This was a one shot deal. The car lurched forward a couple of inches before coming to rest. My eyes welled and I felt a sense of despair setting in. Nick was clearly exhausted, but managed to roar "let's fucking get this car out, NOW!". Inch by inch we laid out new foundations for the car, until we could make a charge. Our last effort dragged the car clear of the death clutches of the sand. We fell to our knees and wept with joy. As we drove the car towards complete safety we saw the rescue team which comprised of the local mechanic that Em had commandeered with a sweet smile. He looked thankful at our arrival, a grateful glance that could not parallel the sheer joy we felt. We had defiantly earnt our beers at the local tavern that day.

It's going to take more than a six foot log to get out of this. Pic E Moroney

W.A.

Stockists – area code 08:

This is a list of your local surf shops. They can help you with pretty much everything to do with surfing. They are also proud to be stockists of The Surfer's Travel Guide.

Albany Surf Shop
278B York St
Albany, 6330
9841 5544

Bare Nature
185 High St
Fremantle 6160
9336 4400

Beach Life Surf Shop
117 Bussell Hwy
Margaret River, 6285
9757 2888

Big Drop Surf Shop
21 South Coast Hwy
Denmark, 6333
9848 2183

Blue Planet Surf Shop
164 Chapman Rd
Geraldton, 6530
9964 5533

Blue Waters Lodge
299 Goldfields Rd
Esperance, 6450
9071 1040

Fluid Surf
105 High St
Fremantle 6160
9335 1289

Hillzeez Down South Surf Shop
1/65 Queen St
Busselton, 6280
9752 3565

Indiana Surf & Sail
62 Spencer St
Bunbury, 6230
9721 8733

Kalbarri Surf Shop
Shop4 Kalbarri Arcade
Kalbarri, 6536
9937 2076

Lancelin Surfsports
Shop 2&3/ 127 Gingin Rd
Lancelin, 6044
9655 1441

Murray Smith Surf Centre
Shop 14, Beach Shopping Centre
Scarborough 6019
9245 2988

Power Station Surf Shop
Shop1/575 Canning Hwy
Alfred Cove 6154
9330 5535

Salty Dog Surf Shop
Shop 16, South Terrace Plaza
Fremantle, 6160
9430 8808

Sands Surf Shop
Shop 4 Mandurah Tce,
Sands Shopping Centre
Mandurah, 6210
9535 3804

Sessions Surf Shop
4/120 Bussell Hwy
Margaret River, 6285
9757 9080

Star Surf Shop
332 Murray St,
Perth, 6000
9321 6230

Surf Sports Underground
Shop 17A Plaza Arcade
Perth 6000
9221 5840

Surfs Up Surf Shop
12/432 Rockingham Rd
Spearwood 6163
9434 1743

The Surf Boardroom
Shop 22, Ocean Plaza
Scarborough 6019
9341 6843

Vidlers Surf Sports
14 Station St
Cottesloe 6011
9384 2416

Yallingup Surf Shop
2 Valley Rd
Yallingup, 6283
9755 2036

Stange days indeed. Full moon, three foot, Broome! Pic Chubbs.

Another empty wave.

W.A.

Small, tasty, but perfect.

Vetea David stands tall, while this straddie beast tumbles. Pic Joli.

QUEENSLAND

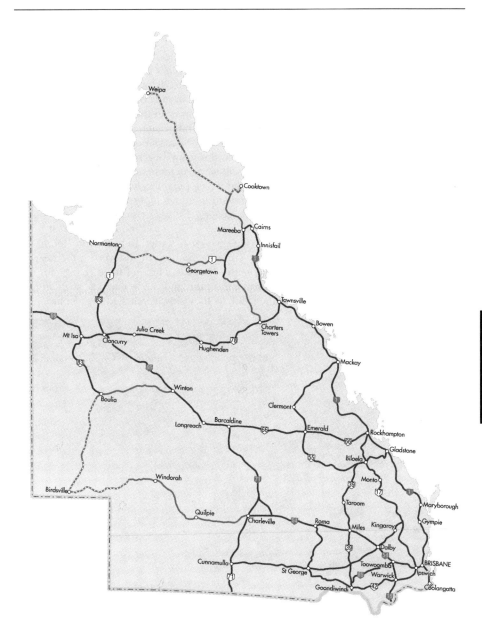

Queensland

Summer Loving

If ever there existed a magical place for surfers it was Queensland. For the majority of surfers who resided in the nations two capital cities, endless hours were spent planning that ultimate roadtrip, 'up north'. We were filled with visions of deliciously warm water, perfect beach and point breaks and, of course, the thousands of women who were desperate to hurl themselves at any surfer who blew in from the south. Since the early '60's surfers were juicing up the Holdens and Fords and pointing the car northward in search of the ultimate dream. For many it came true. Noosa's point breaks were mystical, surrounded by untouched beauty, and the many beach breaks that litter the coastline seemed always to be hollow and hallowed. As more and more people looked towards the semi-tropical climate so to did the developers. Firstly responding to the growing number of tourists, then leaping forward in an attempt to outstrip competitors. High rises sprung from the sandy foreshore, creating a wave of similar developments along the length of one of the more beautiful stretches of coastline in Australia. It wasn't long before the tranquillity of this one time oasis started to turn sour. Heroin worked its way into the ranks of the many surfers who bred themselves on the near perfect conditions of the Gold Coast. The early '70's was a time of huge change for this reason. A sub culture formed, forever ending the calm and peace that was such an intrinsic part of the area. Surfers felt alienated, as they slowly watched their home

Hands up who wants to get barrelled. Dick Bartlett does, at Kirra. Pic Jane Lewis.

Does this give you an idea of how dangerous surfing is here. Fraser Island feeding frenzy. Pic Chubby.

turned into an amusement park that everyone could abuse. There were no longer visions of Bob McTavish dreamily looking towards the pristine beauty of Noosa. It was all go, go, go. Money was to be made and there were people getting rich. The corruption of the Government and the Police Force was unrivalled at the time. Building permits were handed over with a scotch on the rocks and a pat on the shoulder. While this greed was taking hold the soul was slowly slipping out. By the '80's the face of Queensland had changed forever. The magical sand breaks of Surfers Paradise were destroyed by the towering highrises that were perched close to the water. The sandbanks would never again return, neither would the setting sun, as the buildings cast their pale shadows over a slowly dying beach.

Yet Queensland remains firmly entrenched in surfing folklore. There are still many migrating surfers who crave the warmth and perfection of the point breaks. Surfers who feel the draw and take the pilgrimage as so many thousands before have done. The Point Breaks are still perfection, even after the best attempts to destroy them. Kirra is still regarded as one of the most perfect waves anywhere in the world. I mean who would disagree when a wave can produce 12 second barrels? The famous Duranbah is still a classic example of beach break perfection, even after the constant sand dredging. It seems nature had intended something special for this area and nothing will stop it. Severe storms lash the coast ever year, destroying much prime real estate and clawing at the rapidly depleting sandy beaches. Of course this is of major concern to the local government as tourist dollars start to wain. Yet, amongst all this adversity the waves still produce unparalleled quality. Surfers are a hardy breed, and long after the Japanese have declared the beaches unappealing there will still be guys like Occy, Rabbit and Margo who will tear into their home breaks with the same passion that made this place so special. Queensland is still a place of magic, you just need to look a little deeper.

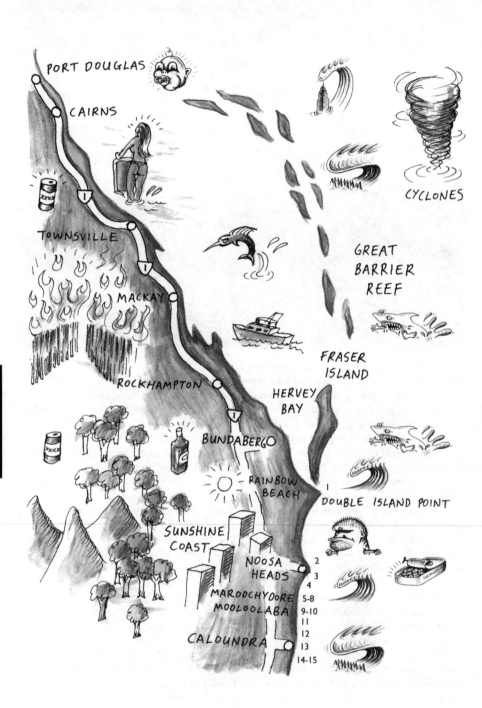

PORT DOUGLAS

CAIRNS

TOWNSVILLE

MACKAY

ROCKHAMPTON

BUNDABERG

CYCLONES

GREAT
BARRIER
REEF

FRASER
ISLAND

HERVEY
BAY

RAINBOW
BEACH

1

DOUBLE ISLAND POINT

SUNSHINE
COAST

NOOSA
HEADS

MAROOCHYDORE
MOOLOOLABA

CALOUNDRA

2
3
4
5-8
9-10
11
12
13
14-15

QLD

The Sunshine Coast

Just never enough.

The Sunshine Coast is situated approximately one and half hours drive north of Brisbane in Queensland. Stretching from Caloundra in the south, to Noosa Heads in the north, with Maroochydore and Coolum in between. The climate can range from energy sapping, consistent 33 degree temps with high humidity in summer and mild 18 - 23 degree days in winter. Along its 60 kms coastline the breaks vary from absolute perfection, such as Noosa's five sand bottom point breaks (which are offshore in south easterly winds), to ruler edged beach breaks and powerful reef setups.

Summer is THE time, with hot sunny days and early surfs, before the prevailing north easterly blows in from the Coral Sea. An afternoon session behind some sheltered headlands can produce down the line, glassy, fun waves if you know where to look. From November to April, cyclones form in the Coral Sea and track down the coast with a ferocity that can produce perfect swell that can last for days, or weeks at a time. These 'tropical storms' vary in size, from one metre to a hell raising five metres. With a water temperature of 25 degrees, and glassy waves, you can revel in your wildest fantasies.

Winter on the sunshine coast is usually short from June to August, with cool, early morning offshore breezes, and mild sunny days. Temperatures in winter can be 20 degrees with dry air, which is a welcome relief from the summer humidity. Westerly offshore winds are prevalent at this time of year with some excellent beach breaks happening.

Many of the breaks can be stacked with local crew, so show some patience and respect, and you will get your share of waves. There are plenty of places to eat out on the coast, like some of Noosa's famous restaurants in the north, and heaps of budget healthy munch places dotted all along the coast. The niteclubs and pubs can be fun, but get pretty crowded at peak holiday times. This is very much a tourist area, being only an hour drive from Brisbane.

Or you can escape the crowds by hiring a 4wd, camping equipment and drive north of Noosa, to Double Island Point. This area is a National Park and Heritage listed land. Huge multi coloured sand hills cascade down to the beach as you drive along the sandy shore. There are some of the most amazing views from the lighthouse on the headland, with Fraser Island in the distance. The waves here can be excellent but are often fickle.

Generally the Sunshine Coast produces excellent waves given the right conditions. Mild to hot weather patterns and warm ocean currents makes it ideal for long surfs and plenty of waves. When the surf is flat, there are endless possibilities for alternate activities. From eating and drinking yourself stupid to roughing it in a National Park. With easy access to some of the best beach and rock fishing spots around, not to mention the wave possibilities, it is paradise.

1.
Break Name: Double Island Point
Wave Description: Sand and rock bottom point break.
Best Conditions: SE-NE Cyclone Swell, SE-S wind, low-mid tide.
Getting There: Vehicle ferry from Noosa Heads, drive north along Teewah Beach, until you get to the point.
Dangers: Strong rips, and some suspect shadows below.
Rumours: The wave can be so long that it is better to walk around the point. You can really feel it in your legs.
Something Else? It is worthwhile staying in the area for more than one session. Being a National Park, it has the sense of solitude from the nearby mayhem. There are also some great wave possibilities. Around at Rainbow beach there are some real quality breaks. Just be respectful of the locals, otherwise you may receive a nasty whipping.

2.
Break Name: Noosa Heads – First Point, Johnsons, National, T-Tree Bay, Granite Bay.
Wave Description: A combination of five, sand and rock bottom right hand, point breaks. They are famous for their ruler edged lines running down wooded headlands.
Best Conditions: SE-NE Cyclone Swell, SE-S wind, low-mid tide.
Getting There: Noosa is about an hour north of Brisbane. Once your in Noosa you'll have no trouble finding the headlands. You'll need to park in the National Park, but when it gets crowded don't even think about it. To get to T-Tree Bay, it is about a 15 minute walk along the cliff face. It is pretty hard not to run as you see set after set pouring in. T-Tree gets the most locals as the wave is a little more top to bottom.
Dangers: The rocks can be just hidden by the tide, but can rear at the worst times, especially when it's small. The crowds can be a problem, as with most

point breaks. With such a narrow takeoff, the pressure can be pretty intense.
Rumours: There are other waves in the area, and these are worth checking. Perhaps you could try the beachies closeby.
Something Else? Unless you're out for a really 'spirited surf', Noosa is best surfed when it's less than perfect. Perhaps a little sideshore and small, but rarely as crowded. You might even have to be the one catching the last wave in near darkness, but it is definitely worth it. You will get the odd one that gives you a hint of all its glory. You can also try exploring the rest of the National Park. There are other coastal areas that can have excellent surf, but you will need to walk in. This is either from Sunshine Beach or from Noosa. Either way it can be a welcome escape from the crazy crowds.

3.
Break Name: Sunshine Beach
Wave Description: A combination of powerful beach breaks, with the northern corner often providing the best option.
Best Conditions: All swell, SW-NW wind, varying tides depending on the banks.
Getting There: Just south of Noosa on the David Low Hwy.
Dangers: Because this beach picks up all available swell, there are often some heavy rips and shallow sand banks. There have been sightings in this area.
Rumours: Just north of here are some great breaks, try Alexandria Bay.
Something Else? When there is no surf on the points, check here as there is often a small wave somewhere.

4.
Break Name: Coolum Beach Breaks
Wave Description: Glassy peaks, in both bays, can get punchy and hollow.
Best Conditions: SE-E swell, W-SW wind, all tides depending on the banks.
Getting There: North of Maroochydore and Caloundra, South of Noosa Heads. If

Double Island Point in all its glory. Pic Peter Court.

you want another option, try at the end of Pita St just north. This place can have great banks. There are plenty of waves in between breaks. Just take the tracks to the ocean, that simple.
Dangers: Can get strong rips on bigger swells, where deep channels form.
Rumours: Goes off in gusty E-SE winds.
Something Else? Excellent waves during winter offshores or glassy summer mornings depending on banks. This place also gets its fair share of swell, worth checking on your way northward.

5.
Break Name: Yaroomba
Wave Description: Combination of rock and sand banks, powerful peaks and a hollow shorebreak.
Best Conditions: SE-E swell, N-NE wind, varying tides, depending on banks.
Getting There: South of Coolum Beach.
Dangers: The rips are dangerous here as well.
Rumours: None.
Something Else? Punchy beach breaks bouncing off coffee rock reefs out back.

6.
Break Name: Mudjimba Island or Old Woman Island
Wave Description: Long winding left point break, with a powerful right on the other side of the Island.
Best Conditions: SE-E Swell, light NE - NW wind, low-mid tide, although conditions vary for both waves, which is the beauty of this place.
Getting There: It is about a 30 minute paddle from the beach, which is always scary in these parts.
Dangers: If you are to make the paddle, don't look down, as you won't be able to do anything anyhow. Best to keep focussed on the job at hand, and that is not getting eaten by the waves.
Rumours: Peter Troy of inimitable surfing folklore rents this Island. It obviously has something going for it. Don't expect to surf it alone if it's good.
Something Else? If you can handle the paddle it is well worth the effort. There are some great Aboriginal Dreamtime stories that go with this break and Island. The Island represents a decapitated head

QLD

in a heated battle between Ninderry and Coolum. It's Coolum's head by the way, unfortunate as Coolum has a certain ring to it, s'pose that's why they have a town named after him!

7.
Break Name: Maroochydore Beach
Wave Description: A combination of beach breaks with long walls.
Best Conditions: SE-swell, SW-NW wind, low-mid tide.
Getting There: Turn off the Bruce Highway north of Brisbane to Maroochydore.
Dangers: Rips on a large swell.
Rumours: None.
Something Else? Great beach breaks when the banks are good, which are littered with a hungry young local crew with plenty of energy.

8.
Break Name: Alexandra Headland
Wave Description: Combination rock, reef and sand bottom breaks.
Best Conditions: SE swell, SW-NW wind, low-mid tide.
Getting There: Turn off the Bruce Highway north of Brisbane to Maroochydore.
Dangers: Rips on a large swell.
Rumours: None.
Something Else? Can tend to closeout and be a very 'full' wave. Lots of mals and beginners.

9.
Break Name: Point Cartwright
Wave Description: Powerful right point break, with a scary ledge break and double-suck pits further out.
Best Conditions: NE-SE swell, SE-W wind, most tides depending on swell angle.
Getting There: At the end of Nicklin Way take the turn to Buddina, just south of Mooloolaba.
Dangers: Shallow sections at low tide.
Rumours: For the most experienced

surfers only.
Something Else? Great point break with some heavy takeoffs out further.

10.
Break Name: Kawana Pocket
Wave Description: Left and right peaks with long walls depending on banks.
Best Conditions: E-SE swell, SW-NE wind, most tides depending on conditions.
Getting There: Just south of Point Cartwright.
Dangers: The banks can be shallow. There can also be strong rips on bigger swells.
Rumours: Good place to go when there are crowds everywhere!
Something Else? Good beach breaks behind rocky outcrops. It's sideshore in the summer north-easterly.

11.
Break Name: Currimundi
Wave Description: Hollow, ruler edged walls from a shifting peak.
Best Conditions: E-SE swell, SW-NW wind, low-mid tide.
Getting There: Just north of Caloundra on Nicklin Way.
Dangers: Anything that is hollow can give you a hiding on the shallow banks.
Rumours: Sorry, none here!
Something Else? Great beach breaks when the banks are good during winter westerlies.

12.
Break Name: Anne Street
Wave Description: Small reef break, right and left breaking down both sides, fun wave.
Best Conditions: SE-E swell, SW-NW wind, varying tides.
Getting There: The name of the break kinda gives it away.
Dangers: Can get really powerful on the bigger swells, catching most unawares.
Rumours: Winter is the time for the flawless waves.

The perfect trio. Man, Board and Ti-Tree bay. Pic Peter Court.

Something Else? It tends to close out over two metres. Check at the reef.

13.
Break Name: The Reef
Wave Description: Solid reef break, powerful peak with a slingshot bottom turn into the barrel, spitting at you as you emerge.
Best Conditions: SE-E swell, SW-N wind, varying tides.
Getting There: The main reef at Caloundra, you won't miss it if it's on.
Dangers: Hitting bottom here can be very dangerous as the reef has more power than it looks. Watch out for the shadows beneath the surface.
Rumours: Take long boards, as you want to get on to these beasts as early as possible! 7'2" or more.
Something Else? Awesome reef break, heavy at low tide, long paddle.

14.
Break Name: Moffats
Wave Description: Reef point break, varying long walls, peaky takeoffs

depending on swell angle.
Best Conditions: S-SE swell, SE-NW wind, mid-high tide.
Getting There: Take the road to Moffat Head from Caloundra.
Dangers: Mal riders, unmakeable sections.
Rumours: Does get good on occasion.
Something Else? Fun point break, few cutback sections.

15.
Break Name: Kings Beach
Wave Description: Combination of coffee rock and sand bottom. Shifting peaks with hollow, closeout shore breaks.
Best Conditions: NE swell, N wind, varying tides.
Getting There: Right in town, you can't miss it.
Dangers: Bodysurfers.
Rumours: Offshore in the summer north-easterly.
Something Else? Fun if you like crowds and small waves, but it is protected. Ahh, whaaddya do?

QLD

GENERAL INFORMATION

NOOSA HEADS

Where To Stay:
YHA, Halse Lodge. Ph 1800 242 567. Beds from $15. The location is excellent and the rooms are clean, but if your looking to party go to....
Koala Beach Resort. Ph (07) 5447 3355. Beds from $14. This is where you can get into some serious beer drinking, with plenty of keen participants.
The Sunrise Holiday Village. Ph (07) 5447 3294. Sites from $12, great location as well.

Where To Eat:
Bay Village food court on Hastings St (main one) has some pretty killer deals. Cafe Le Monde for huge meals from $12.

Eduardo's on the Beach, for that romantic touch! (puke!)

Where To Party:
Koala lodge is the way to go or the Rolling Rock on the Main St. Youth Hostels are always the go in these situations as it is a more natural environment to tell your numerous surf travel stories to the eager, and hopefully adoring crowd. This way your not competing with the locals and it doesn't sound like your big noting yourself.

Flat Day Fun:
Total Adventures. Ph (07) 5474 0177, have some crazy adventure ideas, if you want action.
You can rent out boats from various outlets along with every other water craft available known to mankind. If it were me, I would get in a 4wd and drive north along the beach. You never know what you might find!

Point Cartwright. Yeah wish I was there, instead of writing captions. Pic Peter Court.

CALOUNDRA AND MAROOCHYDORE

Where To Stay:
Hibiscus Holiday Park. Ph (07) 5491 1564.
Sites from $12, very central to Caloundra.
YHA Maroochydore. Ph (07) 5443 3151.
Beds from $16.
Cotton Tree Caravan Park. Ph (07) 5443
1253. Sites from $12, very central to the
waves.

Where To Eat:
The food court at Sunshine Plaza has a
massive range, at reasonable prices.
At the Wharf there are a few more up-
market choices, such as Friday's, or the
Hog's breath cafe.

Where To Party:
The local pubs are always the go. Try
Alexandria headland for live bands.

Flat Day Fun:
If you're not surfing you should be
heading out to the Islands or heading
north looking for surf.

Oooohhhh,
the potential. Noosa
Heads laying dormant....for now! Pic Peter
Court.

SECTION INFORMATION

Local Shapers
Ozmosis - Tony Dempsey (Noosa). Ph
(07) 5474 1222.
Impact Surfboards - Steve Jory (Noosa).
Ph (07) 5474 9198.
Shotgun Surfboards - Mike St John
(Coolum). Ph (07) 5446 4567.
Water Pistols - Stuart Campbell.
Beach Beat - Mick Grace/Paul Pascoe
(Maroochydore). Ph (07) 5443 2777.

Best Months
The summer months produce the
cyclones that everyone so hungrily
awaits, but there is sometimes reprieve in
the 'other months'. Winter can produce
solid swells that are caught by the
northern reaches of this stretch. The
winter is so peaceful compared to the
madness of peak season. The crowds
aren't on every wave and the pubs aren't
overflowing with hoons.

Secret Spot
On your way north from Noosa you will

come across a beautiful rainbow......

Quick Tips
There is no question that the waves are
often crowded in this area, and tempers
can overflow. So your best plan is to be
smart where you surf. Don't go straight to
the points if it's perfect, as there will be
locals everywhere. They will be fiercely
trying to capitalise on the good swell,
which they should. You as the visitor
must look for alternatives. Try the
beaches in the north, shifting peaks
always give you more opportunity for
waves. It's better to have a fun rather
than frustrating surf. Leave the hassling to
the locals, as you're a traveller, and you
will score uncrowded waves wherever
you go (well that's the way it was meant
to be).

Getting There
Greyhound Pioneer and Mc Cafferty's
buses travel the length of this coast. Try
Suncoast Pacific on (07) 3236 1901. It will
cost you about $19 from Brisbane to
Noosa.

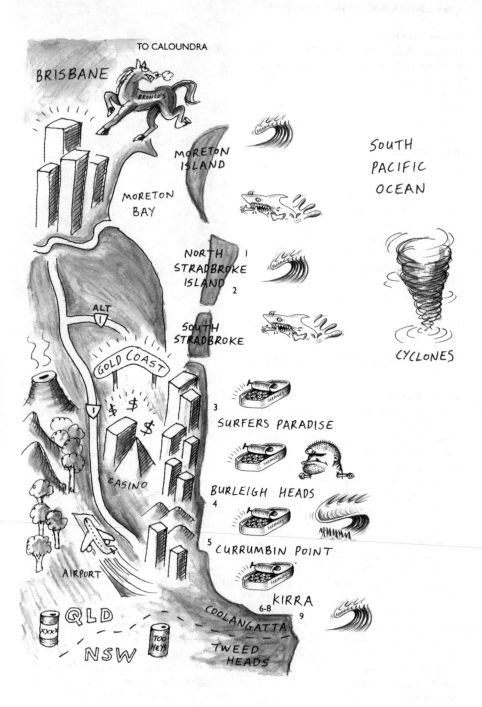

Coincidences make up the fabric of our future

Tackling a South Straddie pearler. Pic Jane Lewis.

The Gold Coast

Fame & Fortune.

Amongst many overseas surfers, this area is the best known region for waves in the country, and many Australian surfers have relocated to the Goldy over the years, especially from the southern regions. Here you can surf in boardshorts most of the year. However, it is without a doubt, the most crowded stretch of coastline in Australia. There are plenty of talented guys and girls that frequent all the breaks, and there is always hot competition. I have been told that you have to drop in to get a wave at Kirra sometimes, I could never condone dropping in, but when you see the crowds....! Fortunately there are still places that can be uncrowded and have quality waves. Options for accommodation, food and entertainment are endless, at all budgets. A smorgasbord for the traveller.

Queensland's Island Surf.
Located offshore of Brisbane, and to the north of the Gold Coast lie a cluster of islands that can offer the roving surf hound some real class action. Access is relatively easy (all islands are ferry-serviced), but moving around varies in difficulty. During the cyclone season (between November to March), the sandbanks which build up off Moreton Island, North and South Stradbroke Islands, are moulded by nature to create crystal clear perfection. This provides relative solitude in comparison to its mainland brother. However, the absence of surfers is not just some dumb luck on your behalf. It is for good reason - sharks. Often seen, and generously-sized, they've been the reason for calling off surf comps on the islands in the past, and attacks on surfers have been recorded out here. However, that said, the true adventurer will find some excellent waves along the deserted golden beaches in this part of the country.

Moreton Island
Travellers to Moreton Island will need to be self-sufficient, and preferably own a 4WD. Bring food, camping gear and water, and you may score some of the many righthanders that lurk at the northern tip of the island, best in Southerly winds, and S to SE swells of considerable size.

South Stradbroke Island
Make a friend who owns a boat, as South Straddie is basically one long beach with no major land features or amenities to speak of.

1.
Break Name: Cylinders / North Stradbroke Island
Wave Description: A thigh-burning righthander, that provides tasty barrels in the right conditions.
Best Conditions: 2m S-SE swell, S-SE wind, most tides.
Getting There: Take the ferry from Cleveland to Dunwich. Call (07) 3286 2666 for Stradbroke Ferries. It costs about $10 return.

Dangers: The sharks here are famous. There are many tales of attacks and sightings, but then again the waves are that good!
Rumours: This is the place to check when all else is flat, it could be just perfect.
Something Else? The two Islands used to be joined until a huge storm in 1896 separated them for life. Apparently the storm raged for a week, completely decimating the entire region, leaving the south alone.

2.
Break Name: Main Beach / North Stradbroke Island
Wave Description: Rights and lefts run the length of the beach.
Best Conditions: S-SW swell, NW-W wind, most tides
Getting There: This is in the middle of the Island and has many wave possibilities.
Dangers: There cannot be enough emphasis put on the dangers of sharks in the area. Although not the White Pointer variety, the resident Tiger sharks can be extremely ferocious.

Kirra Surfs' Paul Jackson, getting some time off in the D-bah pit. Pic Chubbs.

QLD

Rumours: The fishing here is world class and very worthwhile to indulge in.
Something Else? There are several alternatives if the waves aren't happening. Try sandboarding on the nearby dunes. Ph (07) 3409 8082. The boards will cost about $25 for two hours. There are also diving and 4wd tours available.

3.
Break Name: Surfers Paradise
Wave Description: A variety of beachbreaks running the length of coast between Surfers and Broadbeach, with rights and lefts galore. The development has destroyed many of the banks, and it is now rare to find good waves.
Best Conditions: Smaller swells hold up ok on the sandbanks. Anything greater than 2 metres sends the crowds to the points and closes out the beachies. Best in swells from any direction with some east to it, and SW-NW winds.
Getting There: Roads lead right to all the beaches, and sticking out the thumb is an acceptable way of getting around. Plenty of public transport too.
Dangers: Crap and inconsistent waves, shadowed from the afternoon sun by the highrises.
Rumours: Sometimes, just sometimes, this stretch of beach provides the opportunity to score a pleasant little bank all to yourself, free of the crowds hassling each other at the points.
Something Else? A vast array of nightlife in Surfers provides the hormone-charged surfer with opportunities for Vegas-like fun.

4.
Break Name: Burleigh Heads
Wave Description: Burleigh, like it's cousin Kirra further down the road, should appear in the dictionary next to "Perfection." A great righthander, forming off some small boulders next to a protected and picturesque headland, marches around the shoreline over a sand bottom, depositing weary surfers by the main beach, where it's a casual jog back around to the point.
Best Conditions: Up to 2-3 metres, with the swell from the S-SE and winds from the S-W. When these conditions come together, Burleigh makes for an unforgettable and often humbling experience, as the wave can get fairly heavy for the disrespectful.
Getting There: Access is easy, with a carpark at the northern end of the Burleigh headland, and plenty of accommodation nearby.
Dangers: The paddle out can be horrendous when the swell is running, try south at the river mouth. The rocks are also a problem as they can be in your landing area on a big day.
Rumours: Plenty of local and international surf stars frequent Burleigh's barrels, making for entertaining viewing.
Something Else? The shoreys on the inside will often provide some welcome relief from the crowd.

5.
Break Name: Currumbin Alley
Wave Description: A fairly mellow righthander most days of the week. It sometimes turns on barrels, which begin from the point then wind into the more protected waters near the beach. This is where it transforms into a large open wall, demanding aggression be taken out on it's yielding face.
Best Conditions: 2-3m S-SE swell, W-SE winds, mid-high tide.
Getting There: Access is via a short detour from the Gold Coast Highway, and plenty of parking exists.
Rumours: Watch out for the boats coming in and out of the creek mouth, as they try to negotiate the entrance on the bigger days.
Something Else? There are a couple of cool cafés which line the beachfront, and these are an excellent excuse for breaking up a session to appease the hunger cravings, without having to go too far from the action.

6.

Break Name: Kirra

Wave Description: A classic, textbook-style barrelling righthander, breaking in shallow waters off a rock groyne. The sandy bottom creates either a religious experience, a fast track to the emergency room, or a surf shop to replace your board.

Best Conditions: SE-S swells and SW-E winds.

Getting There: Easily accessed by foot from Coolangatta, or make use of the carpark right on the point.

Dangers: The crowds are killer here. When there is a swell running, there could be more than a 100 people in the water. On smaller days you have to watch out for mal riders.

Rumours: One of the classic waves of the world

Something Else? If you're in town during the cyclone season (November - March) you may luck into one of the all-time experiences of your life, as Kirra fires and puts on a show for anyone in town. Look out for the Billabong Pro, held in January or February each year, as it is one of the standout events of the World Tour.

7.

Break Name: Greenmount

Wave Description: A generally cruisey righthander, frequented by all types of surfcraft, and all types of crowds.

Best Conditions: SE swell, SW-W wind, most tides.

Getting There: Located at the southern end of Coolangatta beach.

Dangers: Again the overcrowding has to be taken seriously, as your travels will be over if you are speared in the arm by a rogue surfboard.

Rumours: Look out for the dreaded 'longboardus oldbastardus', a grumpy, snarling creature occasionally seen in these parts. Do not approach under any circumstances.

Something Else? Is protected from

easterlies. which is onshore elsewhere.

8.

Break Name: Snapper Rocks

Wave Description: A fun righthander, which, when the conditions are right, can mean a loonngg ride into Rainbow Bay.

Best Conditions: S-SE swells (surprise), and SW-SE winds (surprise again).

Getting There: Access is around the headland road from Coolangatta, and take the turn off into Rainbow Bay.

Dangers: The crowds are again a problem here, nothing else compares.

Rumours: Dolphins are often sighted in these parts.

Something Else? Try sitting wide as there are always sets that miss the pack.

9.

Break Name: Duranbah.

Wave Description: A multitude of short and punchy right and lefthanders along a short stretch of beach.

Best Conditions: 1-2.5 SE-S swell, NW-SE wind, most tides.

Getting There: Take the Point Danger road from Coolangatta, or continue south from Rainbow Bay.

Dangers: A heavy local crowd and an unforgiving wave.

Rumours: A tricky but rewarding

Getting the most out of what you got is a Gold Coast trait. D-bah getting a whipping. Pic Marty Tulleman

righthander often forms along the breakwall at the southern end of the beach.
Something Else? If there are waves here, there is bound to be swell to the south. From the lookout you can see if the swell is running. Try Fingal way if the crowds are very heavy.

GENERAL INFORMATION

THE GOLD COAST

As everything is so close we have given you a selection of the best.

Where To Stay:
Burleigh Beach Tourist Park - Goodwin Tce, (07) 5581 7755. Campsites cost around $16 to $18 per night for two people, extra bodies cost $5.
Main Beach Caravan Park. Ph (07) 5581 7722. Sites from $16.
Surfers Paradise Backpackers Resort. Ph (07) 5592 4677. Beds from $14, the facilities are amazing, with a gym, sauna, pool room, tennis court and free laundry. That's what we like!
YHA Coolangatta. Ph (07) 5536 7644. Beds from $17, it does have a pool, but not the best of locations.

Where To Eat:
If you want to eat at Surfers, the Mall in Cavill Ave should give you most choices Most of the places around here are very touristy, so lookout for the deep fried junk food.
Montezuma's is a famous Mexican restaurant in Burleigh Heads which has reasonable prices. The many surf lifesaving clubs are a bonus for the budget traveller. They have cheap roast nights and the prices are always reasonable. You can get into some without any affiliations, but it is best to say if you are a member of any other club, as they allow, associated club members.
There are a myriad of other restaurants as

Queenslanders love their beer, no wonder.
Pic Brett Stanley.

well. Best to go to little cafés off the main drag.

Where To Party:
Orchid Ave is where most of the clubs are. Places like Shooters, Cocktails and Dreams, and the Bourbon Bar are probably your likely targets. If you are looking for a band venue, try the Play Room.
The Casino is always another option, but don't bet your new stick on it.

Flat Day Fun:
The Gold Coast is like Australia's version of Disneyland, with an abundance of theme parks such as Wet 'n' Wild (waterslides - pretty cool fun on hot summer, swell-less days), SeaWorld, Warner Brothers Movie World, etc.
Take a drive out to Currumbin Valley, and escape the frantic pace of the Gold Coast in Mt. Cougal National Park, a beautiful primeval rainforest about half an hour from the coast.
Currumbin Rock Pools - on the road out to Currumbin Valley. The Rockpool is a swimming hole with barbeque facilities, and jumps from the rockwalls surrounding the pool can give you a bit of a kick.

QLD

SECTION INFORMATION

Local Shapers

Brothers Neilson - Phil Meyers/Mark Benson. Ph (07) 5572 6412.
Darren Handley Designs - Darren Handley (Kirra). Ph (07) 5599 4566.
Dale Chapman - Dale Chapman (Burleigh). Ph (07) 5576 7622.
Pipedream - Murray Bourton (Coolangatta). Ph (07) 5599 1164.
Skid Star - Dave McDonald (Kirra). Ph (07) 5536 6100.
Stuart Surf Design - Stuart Smith (Mermaid beach). Ph (07) 5572 0098.
Mt Woodgee - Nick Annaostou (Burleigh). Ph (07) 5535 0288.
Nev - Nev Hymen (Mermaid Beach). Ph (07) 5592 4010.

Best Months

The summer period is when you are most likely to see a cyclone storm and this is a truly magnificent sight. There aren't too many problems with crowds when it's eight foot at Burleigh. Many of the beach breaks are empty. Of course the normal ritual is a session on a crowded, small peak. Winter tends to be fairly inconsistent, but if you have enough time you will get waves on this coast.

Secret Spot

If you travel north from burleigh you could count the fingers on your hand and get a sweet bank at the avenue.

Quick Tips

Duranbah picks up most available swell so is worth checking. The crowds are pretty fierce here, with many heated discussions in the water. Play it very cool and you should be able to snag some sweet rides.

Getting There

Surfside Buslines runs a 24 hour service along the coast. Ph (07) 5536 7666. From Brisbane try Greyhound Pioneer on 13 20 30 or McCafferty's on 13 14 99.

Mt. Warning and beyond.

What happens when you find yourself in the vicinity of Byron Bay and the Gold Coast and there's no surf? You either blow (or double) your holiday budget at the Casino at Surfers, or partake in some liquid refreshment found in a glass. However, if the idea of sitting in a beer garden on a sunny afternoon and watching the world go by is wearing a little thin, or you're feeling the need to

"The crowds are just too much, we're heading south!" Pic Joli.

QLD

hurt a little, point the kombi to the west, locate the bold spire of Mt. Warning, pack some water and a decent lunch, and hit the road.

The turnoff for Mt. Warning is on the Murwillumbah - Uki road, approximately an hour from the Goldy, and 45 minutes from Byron. From the carpark, a 4.5 km walk (2.5 hours) along a tranquil and mellow mountain track switchbacks through a splendid rainforest to the summit of the mountain, 1157m above sea level. From the peak, a spectacular 360° view takes in the Macpherson Ranges and Great Dividing Ranges to the west, and Ballina, Byron Bay and the Gold Coast to the east.

If you're motivated enough, it's worth making the pre-dawn trek, as the sun rises first on Mt. Warning before any other point on the Australian mainland. Remember the water though, as you'll need it - especially for the final 200 metres, which ascend almost vertically along a rock face. For those with some interest in the subject, Mt. Warning is the remains of the central magma core of a once giant volcano that existed more than 20 million years ago, and the Nightcap Range and Border Ranges to the south once formed the sides of the massive volcanic bowl - giving you some idea of the magnitude of the volcano. It was identified and named by Captain Cook to provide a suitable landmark for warning sailors from straying too close to the coast.

NORTH OF NOOSA

Beyond the boundaries of the intense development areas, you move to the second tier of Queensland tourism. Low impact, but in reality, very high. Places like Double Island Point, Fraser Island, The Great Barrier Reef, and the Top End all have waves (the Top End being kind of freakish at best!) but it isn't virgin land anymore. Fraser Island, at times, is full of

beer swilling visitors, trying to catch as many fish as possible. I have seen catches of more than three hundred Tailor, for one family. 4WD's roar up and down the 100 odd kms on the east coast of the Island. None the less, it is worth seeing, and there can be some decent waves. Try Indian Head, for the best breaks, but be warned. The beaches around here are seriously alive with sharks. Tigers, Bronzies and Makos all reside here, and have learnt the art of shallow feeding. The fishermen, gut their huge catches of fish on the hightide mark, so the sharks come in close to clean up the remains, and the unwary surfer. We have spoken to many people who live in the area but rarely surf it. Most agree that it has to be absolutely perfect before they would even consider it. It is also very fickle. That doesn't stop people though, and there are guys who surf it fairly often. If you go, which I highly recommend, make sure you take your boards, and balls, because it may just be too good!

The Great Barrier Reef is a plethora of wave possibilities. Heavy, hollow and long reef breaks dot the whole length of the reef, some 1200 kms long. There is obviously some huge potential here, and there are people starting to explore that territory. There is an operation that runs out to the reef from PK's Lodge at Cape Tribulation. Although I couldn't confirm this, as it wasn't running when I visited. There are other ways to get waves on land in the far reaches of Queensland. There are holes in the reef, that allow swell to reach land. This occurs in a few places. Port Douglas is just north of one of these holes. There is a lot of reef close to shore on the road, south, to Cairns. There can be a decent righthand point. Also when there is a monster storm, there can be waves, but you are really starting to get to the desperate stage when you are surfing in tropical storms! Waves abound on this coast, it is just a matter of access, and how desperately you want to surf a reef 60 kms offshore,

QLD

Waddy Point, isolated perfection on Fraser Island. Pic Keith Fizelle.

in shark infested waters. Contact the charter boats in the area, they will quickly steer you in the right direction as to who is running surf charters.

SURFING YARNS

Underground Travels in a Liquid World.

The original scenario would have read something like this. Travelled with Photographer and Two Hot Surfers for one to two weeks, write story for Underground Surf, promote the Book and feature some killer locations, with great surfers. It was more like; missed magazine deadline, four carloads of hungry surfers and one recent fatal shark attack.

As coincidence would have it, I met up with the travelling entourage of surfers on the way back from a day's outing with the Port Lincoln crew. They were frantically searching for surf and had just stopped momentarily to help push start a rusty old Holden. I arranged to meet up with them in Elliston in a couple of hours.

The group consisted of Brett Stanley, photographer, and the only member I

knew personally. Nick Wallace, a hot surfer who had been coveted with the World Junior Grom title in '94, Robbo, shaper from the Torquay area, Tim, Miles, Darren, Scott, Dessmond and MK. I arrived in the sleepy hollow of Elliston to find that the groms had taken a hold of the local pub and were happy as pigs in shit. They weren't quite sure where I was from. I think Brett had told them that I had some local knowledge of the area, which made them look to me as their expert guide. This myth was ingloriously stripped as we all surfed together at Cape Finniss. The standard of these guys was quite remarkable. Late drops, stand up barrels, huge snaps, all which I witnessed as the lip seemed to catch me on every set wave. I picked off a few that missed the pack, as they weren't big enough to break on the actual reef. None the less, each wave I had, I was hooted by at least someone, which made me respect them as surfers. All my experiences with hot groms is they have such an inflated sense of themselves that they forget what surfing is all about. Not these guys though. After being totally inspired and humiliated at the same time, I headed for the mystical Streaky Bay.

Stockists – area code 07:

This is a list of your local surf shops. They can help you with pretty much everything to do with surfing. They are also proud to be stockists of The Surfer's Travel Guide.

Brothers Neilson
Shop 102 & 11b, Paradise
Centre
Surfers Paradise, 4217
5575 3673

Brother Neilson
Shop 17b The Arcade
Pacific Fair Shopping
Centre
Broadbeach, 4218
5572 3522

Brothers Neilson
Shop E160
Wintergarden on the mall.
Brisbane, 4000
3229 3089

Brothers Neilson
Shop 205/5.
Westfield Shoppingtown
Indooroopilly, 4068
3878 2499

Impact Surf
75 Noosa Drive
Noosa Heads, 4567
5474 9198

Inside Edge
14 Memorial Ave
Cotton Tree, 4558
5443 4143

Kirra surf
8 Creek St
Kirra 4225
5536 3922

Mooloolabah Surf Shop
Shop 23, Peninsula Bldg
The Esplanade,
Mooloolabah, 4557
5444 4033

Mt Woodgee P/L
Gold Coast Hwy
Burleigh Heads, 4223
5535 0288

Noosa Lonboards
187 Gympie Terrace
Noosaville, 4566
5474 2722

Noosa Surf World
34 Noosa Junction Rd
Noosa Heads 4567
5447 3538

Ozmosis
Shop2/30 Hastings St
Noosa Heads, 4556
5447 3300

Pipedream Surfboards
Shop1 Showcase on the
beach
Coolangatta 4220
5599 1164

Another empty wave at Kirra, unbelievable! Perhaps there is light at the end of the tunnel. Pic Joli.

QLD

Stanwell Park in all her majesty. Pic Simons

N.S.W.

NEW SOUTH WALES

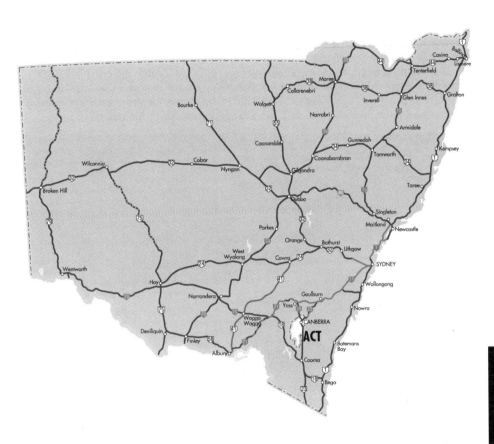

New South Wales

Maximum Density

Blessed with more accessible surf beaches than any other State, NSW has established itself as the Mecca for surf travellers. The coastline boasts an incredible diversity, from the temperate rainforests of the Byron Bay area to the cool, and often inhospitable beaches of Cape Howe. This is a wonderful mix for the wave hungry traveller, as it often represents a choice unparralled anywhere else. NSW is the hub of surfing in this country. It is the most prolific producer of fine surfers and the ever expanding surf industry is deeply entrenched in the nooks and crannies of the northern beaches. No wonder when there are so many possibilities for waves. Although the coast has been thoroughly explored for hidden treasures, this by no means indicates that crowds are prevalent everywhere. Infact just the opposite. It is a dream for surf wanderers as many of the places have been documented, yet a large percentage of the natural beauty

Will Webber tucking into a north coast pipe. Pic Hilton.

N.S.W.

Matty Owens in the heart of the city. How lucky are Sydneysiders? Sth Avalon. Pic John Brumfield.

remains untouched. Certainly in the south, there is still a sense of solitude as many winter swells pound the shore ceaselessly in hollow perfection, without the slightest hint of a surfer's trail. In the north as well, there are many places that can be surfed alone, yet without the total remoteness that often characterises the other States. For many of the non-surfing populous of Australia, places such as Byron Bay characterize everything that surfing represents. Yet this is just the tip of the iceberg. The northern beaches of Sydney were the first place to witness the birth of surfing in the early 1900's and since then, the coast has steeped itself in surfing tradition, with surfing being a regular part of the lifestyle enjoyed by the inhabitants of Australia's busiest capital.

N.S.W.

Travelling was and is, an essential ingredient to every surfer who resides in the heart of NSW, Sydney. It became necessary as the population grew quickly, crowding the once peaceful surf breaks. This led to amazing discoveries that have become a focal point for surfers. Aussie Pipe, Lennox Head and a host of other top class waves are still fondly talked about and passionately surfed. For many of the greatest breaks in Australia lie within the boundaries of this great State. It has bred a hardy group of travellers who are constantly dialling surf reports for the north and south coasts, in the desperate hope that "their' special place will turn it on, and a mad roadtrip dash will yield waves that most dream about. For every surfer in the State's capital must search further and deeper to uncover the beauty that has blessed this region for so long.

Roadtrippin'
It's the unexpected surprises that make you feel alive and living out a dream, of sorts.

Over the river, around the giant gum, down into the valley and this is what you'll get. North coast solitude. Pic Hilton

The North Coast

End of the road.

N.S.W.

Ahh, the joyous exultation of arriving in the warmth and love of the North coast sun after many gruelling hours huddled in the back seat of a dodgy car is unrivalled. It seems to be another land, a place so familiar, yet so removed from everyday reality. The sense of relaxation is overwhelming and that is the magic of this coast. Stretching from Tweed Heads to Coffs Harbour, lie the most famous beaches of Australia, with Byron Bay at the epicentre. For many surfers, this is Nirvana. A place where you can still feel the beauty without the encroaching hands of progress. Although much has changed, more has stayed the same. There are still hippy communities dotted throughout the surrounding hills, and there is a tranquillity that is not often emulated in other regions. It is a must for all surfers, for it is part of what being an Aussie surfer is, as well as being our birthright.

1.
Break Name: Tweed South Wall.
Wave Description: A lefthander running the length of the wall and assorted A-frame peaks.
Best Conditions: NE-E swells, NE-NW winds, mid tide.
Getting There: Turn off from the Pacific Highway (signposted).
Dangers: Not too many, unless you want to attempt the paddle over from Duranbah, in this case watch out for big fish with sharp teeth.
Rumours: Well protected from the summer north-easterlies.
Something Else? The north wall can have waves but is generally not as good as the south.

2.
Break Name: Fingal Beach.
Wave Description: Left and right beach breaks, if the sandbars are working.
Best Conditions: NE-SE swell, SW-NW wind, most tides.
Getting There: Signposted south of Tweed, off the Pacific Highway.

Dangers: The signs in the carpark warning people to lock their cars is a good start.
Rumours: At the northern end there is a sucky left, that is reminiscent of a shorey.
Something Else? Fingal's a peaceful town, a good place for the crowd-flustered surfer to de-stress.

3.
Break Name: Cabarita / Bogangar.
Wave Description: A long righthander forming off a protected point. The odd shorebreak crops up when the banks are on.
Best Conditions: SE swell, SW wind, mid tide.
Getting There: Divert off the Pacific Highway along the coastal (scenic) route (Kingscliff to Pottsville).
Dangers: The occasional shark.
Rumours: Just north of here there is a quality and heavy wave at Kingscliff. Don't surf it at anything other than high tide.
Something Else? There's a really good hostel/motel just between the point and

Another north coast tube. Long and fast. Pic Hilton.

town, on the left-hand side of the road heading north. Very friendly, and good facilities. Chances are high you'll meet other travelling surfers here.

4.
Break Name: Pottsville Beach.
Wave Description: This is really one elongated stretch of beach, from Pottsville to Brunswick Heads, hosting a variety of banks, with some quality lefts and rights which are dependant upon sand and swell.
Best Conditions: NE-SE swell, SW-NW wind, most tides.
Getting There: South of Pottsville, the main road diverges inland from the coast, and you'll either need a 4WD to access the beach to the south, or a good set of legs.
Dangers: Getting bogged on the beach.
Rumours: There are some fantastic fishing options in this stretch and it's definitely worth throwing in the line
Something Else? The northern breakwall at Brunswick Heads turns on a tasty righthander in S-SE swells and NW winds.

5.
Break Name: The Wreck at Byron.
Wave Description: A short and steep righthander, which breaks (surprise!) off an old shipwreck.
Best Conditions: Large SE-E swell, SW wind, high tide.
Getting There: Go to the end of Johnson Street, and look for the crowd.
Dangers: Plenty of people in the water most days, with an interesting variety of surfcraft and skills.
Rumours: You may get offered weed while surfing here, as this is close to the marijuana capital of Australia, Nimbin.
Something Else? Stop by the Beach Hotel for a beer afterwards. As every body probably knows Byron Bay used to have an abattoir right on the beach, where effluent used to run out to the lineup. This of course was perfect for the sharks. They used to patrol the area

regularly and shark sightings were common. Of course that is now shut, and tourism is the clear winner in the monetary stakes here. There are still the odd shark sightings but nothing too serious.

6.
Break Name: The Pass at Byron.
Wave Description: Long righthander over patchy sand/rock bottom, breaking off a lonesome-looking rocky outcrop.
Best Conditions: E-NE swell, SE-SW wind, mid tide.
Getting There: Easily accessed from the township (take road out to the lighthouse).
Dangers: Stubbing your toe on the rocks along the beach while wading out, and of course those bitey marine creatures.
Rumours: Dolphins are often sighted out here. Infact I have met a few people who know a particular pod of dolphins by name and regularly surf with them here. They seem to be very placid and willing to communicate. Probably one of the most reliable dolphin sighting areas on the east coast.
Something Else? The view from the lighthouse gives an interesting perspective on this stretch of coast, and is the most easterly point of mainland Australia. There are also a few breaks closeby that are worth checking out. Main Beach is not nearly as consistent, but can have good breaks if the swell is big enough. Wategos is just slightly outside of The Pass, but is not nearly as consistent and not even close to the perfection that The Pass can achieve. It is also far more open to easterly winds.

7.
Break Name: Tallows.
Wave Description: A combination of power packed beach breaks, that are best in the northern corner.
Best Conditions: S-E swell, W wind, most tides.
Getting There: Tallows is located slightly

N.S.W.

to the south-east of Cape Byron - you'll most likely have to leave your car and take a trek up the beach.

Dangers: What looks like a large fish, is white or grey, and often hungry?

Rumours: This spot is nicely protected from the Summer north-easter.

Something Else? Tallows is really the power packed wave of the area, but it can get very crowded.

8.

Break Name: Broken Head.

Wave Description: A righthander peeling off a rocky point over a sand bottom. The quality of the wave is extremely dependant on the sand banks. At best it is a hollow, howling beast that seems to have barrel after barrel.

Best Conditions: E-NE swells, S-W winds, low-mid tide.

Getting There: Access is via the old coastal highway between Byron Bay and Ballina. Take the Broken Head Reserve turnoff.

Dangers: Plenty of good fishing, which can attract bigger and hungrier creatures.

Rumours: Happily, dolphins are also seen here.

Something Else? This is a worthwhile place to unroll the swag and relax. It has a beautiful campground and a very serene feeling.

9.

Break Name: Lennox Head.

Wave Description: One of Australia's premier righthand point breaks. It can be a long, scary ride, but incredibly fulfilling. Really only for the experienced.

Best Conditions: BIG S-SE swell, SW-S winds, mid tide.

Getting There: Easily accessed, head a few kms north of Ballina. The main carpark overlooks the break.

Dangers: Trying to negotiate the boulder-strewn walk/paddle out on big days.

Rumours: If the rocks don't kill you the locals will. The wave has been surfed up to 5 metres, which would test even the

most courageous surfers.

Something Else? The breakwall in Ballina can sometimes turn on a decent wave. It's fair to assume though, that if Ballina is working, the known spots along the coast will be amping, and are probably the better option.

10.

Break Name: Pippie Beach / Yamba

Wave Description: Punchy beach break, that generally has a good left and right. The left tends to be a lot longer.

Best Conditions: E-NE swell, NE-W wind, low-mid tide.

Getting There: Turn off Pacific Hwy to Yamba, then it's straight to the beach, pretty damn hard to miss.

Dangers: Nup!

Rumours: Our much cherished, Queen of Neighbours, Princess of Pop, Kylie Minogue has just bought property here.

Something Else? The fishing is excellent at Turners Wall, which can also turn on a quality wedge if the sand banks are right. Primarily though, Yamba is a fishing town, but can produce quality waves if the banks are good.

11.

Break Name: Angourie Point

Wave Description: One of the classic right hand points, which wraps around the point to the inside bowl. It breaks over a rock ledge which leaves no room for error.

Best Conditions: SE-NE swell, SW-W wind, low-mid tide.

Getting There: Turn off Pacific Hwy towards Yamba. Just before you get to Yamba, turn right at the round-about and follow the road to the point.

Dangers: It can seem a life or death experience when the swell is over 2 metres, especially jumping off the rocks. The locals here are very tuned in to the wave as well.

Rumours: Honestly, you can't surf the point well on a longboard.

Something Else? This place is home to

legends Nat Young and Baldy Treloar, so show respect to gain respect. There is also great fishing off the rocks, but the tinnie is the way to go.

12.
Break Name: Spookies
Wave Description: A gnarly righthand grinder over a rock bottom, with a hideous take-off
Best Conditions: NE-E swell, SW wind, high tide.
Getting There: Just to the south of the point.
Dangers: Apart from the constant worry about sharks, the wave itself is enough to scare the living bejesus out of most hardened souls.
Rumours: A drop in here could be fatal.
Something Else? If you head south to the National Park you could stumble on some great quality beach breaks. You will need a 4wd and some determination. Try the fishing at Brooms Head.

13.
Break Name: Arrawarra
Wave Description: A long righthand point break, that is relatively soft, that breaks over a rock bottom.
Best Conditions: NE-SE swell, SW-S wind, mid tide.
Getting There: Take the turn from the Pacific Highway when you see Arrawarra Headland Road, head north, you can't miss it.
Dangers: This place can get extremely crowded, and the rocks can be a hazard.
Rumours: When the swell gets big, check the breaks south, as this place tends to closeout in big swells.
Something Else? Great place to sit and relax after a great surf.

14.
Break Name: Mullaway
Wave Description: Has a point break and beach break.
Best Conditions: SE-E swell, NE-SE wind and on a mid-high tide. The swell is best

when it is in the 2-3 metre range, anything bigger begins to close out.
Getting There: Take the turn from the Pacific Highway when you see Arrawarra Headland Road and follow the signs straight to the beach.
Dangers: The wave has a lot of power for a beach break and the unsuspecting surfer can get thrashed on the sand bank.
Rumours: This is the place locals go when the swell is running to get away from the city crowds.
Something Else? Great caravan park nearby that is worth staying in if the swell hangs around.

15.
Break Name: Emerald Beach
Wave Description: An excellent lefthander over sand, which can be very fickle.
Best Conditions: SE-NE swell, NE-NW wind and on a mid-high tide.
Getting There: Just off the Pacific Hwy, south of Woolgoolga.
Dangers: The Sewerage plant.
Rumours: If the sand banks are working, this is one of the best places for goofy footers.
Something Else? Just south is Moonee Creek, which can have some great beach breaks, and is worth checking out anyhow.

Mark Spillane way, way back in this north coast magic. Pic Hilton.

GENERAL INFORMATION

There are so many opportunities for food, entertainment and accommodation that the mind boggles. You generally just wander around like a star-eyed kid at all the choice in Byron. Then it drops off to quite little towns with little or no facilities. So we have given you a selection of the best.

BYRON BAY

Where To Stay:
First Sun Caravan Park. Ph (02) 6685 6544. A tent site costs between $10 -12 a single, and $4-7 per extra person. Cabins cost $38-75 per double, and $5-7 per extra person.
YHA Cape Byron Hostel. Ph (02) 6685 8788. Beds from $13. It has some great features, one being the heated pool.
Aquarius Backpackers Motel. Ph 1800 028 909. Pretty happening place complete with live music, great BBQs and clean rooms.

BROKEN HEAD.

Broken Head Caravan Park, Beach Rd. PH (02) 6685 3245. Double sites are $10-15, $2-6 per extra person. Cabins, sleep up to five people, $35-70.

LENNOX HEAD.

Lake Ainswrth Caravan Park, Pacific Pde (by the beach and lake). Ph (02) 6687 7249. Sites cost $11-14, extra persons are $3-8. Cabins are $28 to $50, $3-8 for extra bodies.

BALLINA.

Shaws Bay Caravan Park, Hill St, by the bridge near the town centre. Ph (02) 6686 2326. Sites cost $11-14, $5 for the extra person. Cabins are $28-50, $8 an extra.
YHA Ballina Lodge. Ph (02) 6686 6737. $15 for a dorm bed.
Where To Eat:
The Beach Cafe in Byron has great views but is pretty expensive.
Fundamental Foods is a groovy place with organically grown fruit and vegies. Try the Railway Hotel for cheap counteries
Where To Party:
Country pubs and hotels are the go around these parts. Byron Bay has a thriving nighlife and entertainment scene, by virtue of the many travellers that pass through here, and the youthfulness of the town's population. Try the Railway Hotel and Beach Hotel for live music, or keep your ear to the street for parties and festivals.
Flat day fun:

Oooohhh the sweet lines of Angourie, it's enough to make you...... Pic Hilton.

Minyon Falls - Located in the Whian Whian State Forest, about 45 minutes from Byron. Minyon Falls plunge 330 feet through a shadowed gorge into a deep rock pool, and are surrounded by walking tracks through the verdant rainforest. An awesome place to escape for a day. Best accessed via the back roads between Mullum and Lismore. Visit Nimbin, to the west of Byron by an hour on the road, for a taste of true alternative culture, and a look at Australia's pot capital. Despite the freaks, there is also plenty of beautiful hiking and cool scenery in and around this town. Take the time to drop into Protesters' Falls while you're here, about 15 minutes along the Terania Creek road from Nimbin. A short walk leads through lush rainforest to a spectacular waterfall, named in respect for the protesters that petitioned for it's salvation from greedy landrapers.

Hand Gliding can also be pretty fun. Call Flight Zone on (02) 6685 8768.

YAMBA/ANGOURIE

Where To Stay:
Nat's Apartments. Ph (02) 6646 1622. Run by the famous Nat Young.
Pacific Hotel. Ph (02) 6646 2466.
Backpacker accommodation from $17.

Where To Eat:
Slow Food General Store, Angourie. The best lentil burgers in the world! Well, there're pretty good anyhow. The Pacific Hotel counteries are great value.
Try the Yamba cake shop as well.

Where To Party:
Pacific Hotel can get some great touring bands, but there is a healthy local scene too.

Flat Day Fun:
Jumping off the green pools, or bushwalking through Yuraygir National Park. Of course there is the standard array of golf courses and tennis courts.

SECTION DETAILS

Local shapers
Bear Surfboards - Tony Squirell (Byron Bay). Ph (02) 6685 6896.
Maddog - Mark Plater, Bob Margets, Neil Cormack. (Byron Bay). Ph (02) 6685 6022.
Dick Hoole Surfboards - Dick Hoole (Byron). Ph (02) 6684 7304.
Local Motion - Gunther Rohn (Ballina). Ph (02) 6686 9879.
Will and Greg Webber-Webber Designs (Angourie).
Albert Fox-Fox Surfboards. (Angourie).

Best Months
February to July

Secret Spot
If you travel through Angourie you may find many hidden treasures. If you take the main route you should be able to find it.

Quick Tips
The biggest problem with travelling this coast is your unlimited surf opportunities over such a large area. A mistake many surfers make is rushing to the well known breaks without realising what they have missed on the way. Often these breaks are quite populated, especially at the key spots. Look elsewhere.

Getting There
It is best to call the Sydney coach terminal on (02) 9281 9366 which deals with most companies and can give you competitive rates. Country Link is the government run network of trains and buses. Ph 13 22 42. Give Aussie Surf Adventures a call on 1800 113 044. Nat & Dan are two classic guys who run surf trips between Sydney and Byron. A really good way to meet like minded people, see some of the best Australian beaches, learn to surf and have heaps of fun. Surfaris is another travel company, Ph 1800 634 951. This is run by father & son Leister & Garth. Ring both companies to find out who suits your needs best.

N.S.W.

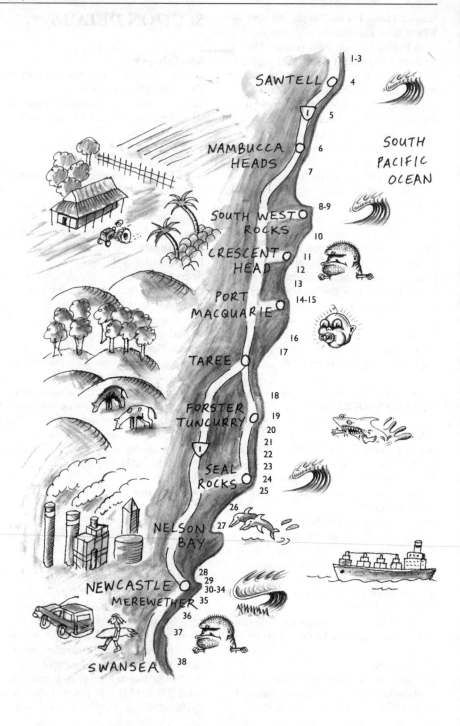

SAWTELL

1-3

4

5

NAMBUCCA
HEADS

6

7

SOUTH
PACIFIC
OCEAN

SOUTH WEST
ROCKS

8-9

10

CRESCENT
HEAD

11

12

13

PORT
MACQUARIE

14-15

16

17

TAREE

18

FORSTER
TUNCURRY

19

20

21

22

23

SEAL
ROCKS

24

25

26

NELSON
BAY

27

28

29

NEWCASTLE
MEREWETHER

30-34

35

36

37

SWANSEA

38

N.S.W.

Timing
Late drops, stand up barrels, huge snaps, all which I witnessed as the lip seemed to catch me on every set wave. I picked off a few that missed the pack, as they weren't big enough to break on the actual reef.

Hurry up son! Michael Barry desperately trying to get high at Newcastle. Pic John Brumfield.

Coffs Harbour - Newcastle
$ave our coast

As progress steps forward, day after day, this is one of the last bastions of solace. Their northern neighbours have accepted fate, and allow the natural progression to flow. Not here though. Signs sprayed on earthmovers and at the edge of the new freeways plead for sanity and mercy. These oases are rare in the north and need to be treasured, yet developers push forward, proclaiming the benefits to small businesses then replacing them with streamlined super stores. Yet all is not lost. Some of the most pristine coastline lies in this stretch from Coffs to Newcastle, and residents are willing to fight. Community groups have formed vigilante movements in order to halt the wholesale destruction of the few reaming outposts. There is sense of camaraderie in the water as most surfers recognise the beauty of this land. People who experience this coastline will realise the importance and will help to preserve it, as it is worth saving for future generations. Experience it you must, as it will leave an impression that fuels your thoughts of perfect waves, as this is where you will find them.

1.
Break Name: Macaulays / Coffs Harbour
Wave Description: A powerful wave
with a lefthand point and sandbank
beach, but you will need a big swell for
the two to connect. On smaller days you
can get a really good righthander that
leads into the point, near the beginning
of the beach.
Best Conditions: SE-E swell, W-NE wind,
mid-high tide.
Getting There: Turn off the Pacific
Highway into Park Beach Road and at the
bottom, turn left into Ocean Parade and
follow this road until you reach the
carpark.
Dangers: A very powerful beach break.
Rumours: Most of the town's good
surfers frequent this place, because of the
quality of the wave, and due to the fact
that it always picks up the most available
swell.
Something Else? There is a righthander
that breaks in the corner on most days.

2.
Break Name: Park Beach / Coffs Harbour
Wave Description: A combination of
peaky left and righthanders, which can
get excellent if the banks are good.
Best Conditions: S-SE swell, NW-SW
wind, mid-high tide.
Getting There: Turn off the Pacific
Highway into Park Beach Road and head
towards the caravan park. The break is
directly in front of the camp sites.
Dangers: A very powerful beach break.
Rumours: Watch for the rogue sets, and
the strong rip.
Something Else? You can usually find
somewhere in this area that is protected
from onshores, just a matter of looking
down the beach.

3.
Break Name: Gallows / Coffs Harbour
Wave Description: One of the most
powerful waves in the area, with a
hideous takeoff.
Best Conditions: SE-E swell, N-NW

wind, mid-high tide.
Getting There: Just south of the Harbour,
you can't miss it, if it is working.
Dangers: This really is a serious wave,
and can catch you unaware if you don't
treat the wave with the utmost respect.
Rumours: There have been shark
sightings in this area, so beware.
Something Else? The fishing can be
excellent off the rockwalls.

4.
Break Name: Sawtell
Wave Description: It has left and rights
that form off a sandbank bottom.
Best Conditions: NE-SE swell that holds
up to 1.5 metres with SE-NW winds.
Getting There: Turn off the Pacific
Highway into Lyons Road. Follow that
until you come to Second Avenue and the
beach is a stone's throw away.
Dangers: A very fast down the line wave
when the swell is big and banks are right.
Rumours: Probably the last of the best
surf beaches in Coffs Harbour. The break
infront of the creek is called 'Trapdoors'
which can handle just about any size. The
takeoff can be scary, as it is over a rock
platform which always makes the takeoff
fast.
Something Else? There are more waves
further south with quality, but a 4WD
drive and tent are highly recommended.

5.
Break Name: Valla Beach
Wave Description: A classic little beach
break, which can have some great waves,
and full of power at times too.
Best Conditions: S-SE swell, S-SW wind,
low-mid tide.
Getting There: Get onto Valla Beach
Road from the Pacific Highway and
follow the signs to the beach.
Dangers: The break can be quite
powerful because the waves break close
to the shore.
Rumours: The clarity of the water alone
is enough to make it a worthwhile stop.
Something Else? The caravan park is

Kirk Day, Coffs Harbour. Pic Brett Stanley.

very closeby and a worthwhile stopover if you are looking for less crowded waves.

6.
Break Name: Nambucca Heads
Wave Description: With the break wall on the river, the beach can produce small quality waves.
Best Conditions: E-SE swell, NW-W wind, mid-high tide.
Getting There: Take the turn off from the Pacific Highway and follow the signs.
Dangers: Nambucca doesn't always produce good waves which can lead to frustration when it gets crowded.
Rumours: Because of the river mouth it is known for the odd shark and great fishing. In fact, count more on the possibility of catching fish than waves here.
Something Else? There is a tourist park on the Nambucca River that is in a very beautiful spot. Ph: (02) 6568 1850.

7.
Break Name: Scotts Head
Wave Description: A long, long righthand point break.
Best Conditions: SE-E swell, S-W wind, low-mid tide.
Getting There: Turn off at Macksville to the name sake.
Dangers: The wave can section when the bank or tide isn't right, which can make it pretty gnarly on big days.
Rumours: When this place gets going, it can give a ride of up to 500m. It is definitely worth checking on your way through. Also, behind the surf club there is a short track that leads to a little beach. A top surf spot that should be treated with caution.
Something Else? When it is big, just getting off the rocks is a challenge, watch out for those large marine creatures up here too. If the surf is flat, Warrell Creek offers good fishing.

N.S.W.

233

Will Webber doing the crab. Pic Hilton.

8.
Break Name: Little Bay
Wave Description: Left point and beach break.
Best Conditions: SE-E swell, W-NW wind, most tides.
Getting There: If you are coming from Horseshoe Bay in South West Rocks you need to get on to Phillip Drive and follow it all the way to the end of Wilson Street, turn right into Gladstone Street and then left into Carri Street.
Dangers: A lot of retirees come up this way.
Rumours: There could be other small little breaks around if all the elements are perfect.
Something Else? The water and outset make it great when waiting for the sets to come in.

9.
Break Name: Smokey Cape / South West Rocks
Wave Description: An open point that leads onto the beach.

Best Conditions: NE-E swell, SW-W wind, mid tide.
Getting There: If coming from Trial Bay Gaol, head down Arakoon Road and then turn left into Lighthouse Road and that will lead you to Smokey Cape.
Dangers: Plenty of closeout waves.
Rumours: Is open to most swell, but doesn't often get very good.
Something Else? South West Rocks got it's name when, in 1800, Captain R J Jamieson, a pilot officer, directed vessels entering Trial Bay, to anchor in deep water 'south west of the rocks'.

10.
Break Name: Hat Head
Wave Description: A righthander that runs along a rocky shelf.
Best Conditions: SE-NE swell and SW-S wind, mid-low tide.
Getting There: Go south from South West Rocks on Rocks Road and then you will come to Hat Head Road.
Dangers: If you get into trouble it's a long way from help.

N.S.W.

Rumours: Hat Head has some extensive bush walks to hike.

Something Else? This wave is often overlooked in the hurry to get to the more 'known' spots, but it is definitely worth while to stop in.

11.
Break Name: Crescent Head
Wave Description: A peeling righthander that starts at the point and wraps around the beach, it can get really long in the right conditions.
Best Conditions: E-SE swell, SW-SE wind, mid-high tide.
Getting There: Follow Pacific Street until you come to a roundabout, turn left and follow it until you see Crescent Head going off.
Dangers: You get a lot of long boarders riding the waves.
Rumours: It is a classic little surf town, with characters who depict the surf scene as it was in the '70's
Something Else? First discovered in the mid 1900's, Crescent has become a famous surf spot. No wonder too, with a such beautiful surroundings and a wave that can produce such quality.

12.
Break Name: Goolawah Beach
Wave Description: A very open beach that has left and right hand points.
Best Conditions: Due to the size of the beach, the left and right hand points are open to any available swell that is running at the time.
Getting There: Turn into Baker Drive and follow that until you see a blue sign that says Beach. Turn left and you will head up an old dusty road, then there will be a sharp right and that will lead you to Goolawah Beach.
Dangers: The beach is unpatrolled and can get very rippy.
Rumours: The rangers are very strict about 4WD's on the beach, so be very careful.
Something Else? A good alternative to

the frequent 'overcrowding' at the more popular spots.

13.
Break Name: Point Plomer
Wave Description: Point break and open beach break which works similarly to Crescent.
Best Conditions: S-SE swell, SW wind, mid-low tide.
Getting There: Either coming or going, the turn off is on Crescent Head Road and then follow the signs along the rugged road for 16 kms.
Dangers: Your only real worry is that if something did happen, say cracking your head on the rocks, then medical help is a little way off. But really, how often does that happen!
Rumours: You might not get many surfers here due to the unforgiving access road. Try the back beach as it can give great protection from the summer north-easterlies. It is also a good wave in its own right.
Something Else? This has to be one of the unspoilt retreats on the North Coast.

14.
Break Name: Flagstaff / Port Macquarie
Wave Description: A righthander that breaks alongside the breakwater. This beach is one of the few that can handle a sizeable wave.
Best Conditions: E-SE swell, SW wind, mid-high tide
Getting There: Go north onto Pacific Drive and you will see a street sign to Flagstaff.
Dangers: As it catches most available swell, this place tends to get overrun with locals. Better waves can be found elsewhere, try south
Rumours: If you have a 4wd, you can access some special breaks.
Something Else? Head out to Sea Acres Rainforest Centre, which is a 30 hectare reserve of coastal rainforest. It also gives you access to some great beaches. There is a fee, but well worth the cost.

N.S.W.

15.
Break Name: Flynns
Wave Description: A rocky point that leads into the beach, but with some unsuspected large rocks on the bottom.
Best Conditions: NE-SE swell, SW-NW wind, mid tides
Getting There: Head south along Pacific Drive from Town Beach and there will a sign directing you down to the beach.
Dangers: Another break that is in the heart of the town, which makes it crowded and aggressive.
Rumours: There are always going to be better waves, closeby.
Something Else? How about a big fat nothing.

16.
Break Name: North Haven
Wave Description: A combination of beach breaks, which can be very good, especially at the northern end.
Best Conditions: 2-4m NE-SE swell, NW-

SW wind, most tides.
Getting There: If you follow the coast road, you can't miss it.
Dangers: Try not to upset any of the older locals, and watch out for those sharks.
Rumours: Can be excellent, at times, try a couple of the breaks south of here.
Something Else? Although this place gets crowded in summer, it is generally not filled with capable surfers, but young kids and bodyboarders.

17.
Break Name: Uggs Reef
Wave Description: A long righthand reef break, that has similar qualities to Crescent Head, not quite as soft though.
Best Conditions: S-E swell, NE-NW wind, mid tides.
Getting There: Just south of Old Bar.
Dangers: Can be quite powerful at times, with the takeoff being another free fall situation. The wave can also section

Not Crescent Head, but very close.... Pic Joli

without warning, so be careful.

Rumours: This break is also known as Saltwater, and can break up to 400 metres long.

Something Else? Surfers flock to this break due to its protection from southerlies, and because it can handle the size.

18.

Break Name: North Wall

Wave Description: A combination of lefts and rights, which can be fast and very challenging, but when a big swell hits, the right is more common.

Best Conditions: Huge NE-E swell, S-W wind, most tides.

Getting There: Get onto Wharf Street, turn right into Beach Street and then turn into Rockpool Road. This will lead you into a massive carpark and there is a lookout to check the surf.

Dangers: Try not to upset any of the older locals.

Rumours: Tuncurry Bar can get quite extreme when the cyclone swells hit.

Something Else? When this place gets good, you will find it difficult to secure waves, as many people will travel hours from either direction to score this place. Don't worry though, if this place is good, there are heaps of other options in this area, head south.

19.

Break Name: Forster Beach

Wave Description: A wave that comes around from the outside point and breaks on a rock shelf.

Best Conditions: NE-E swell and S-SW wind, mid tide.

Getting There: Cross the bridge from Tuncurry, go along Wharf Street, turn left into Beach Street and follow that until you see the beach and carpark.

Dangers: The wipeout can be quite severe.

Rumours: Needs a huge swell, to make it break.

Something Else? Better options south.

20.

Break Name: Janie's Corner.

Wave Description: A rock shelf point that leads into the beach. The lefts are a lot better than the rights.

Best Conditions: SE-E swell, W-NE wind, most tides

Getting There: The northern end of Seven Mile Beach. The entrance is a little tricky, but when you get there it will be worth the effort

Dangers: If the swell is big, the paddle out can be treacherous, especially if you are attempting it off the rocks.

Rumours: A bit of a secret spot, so treat this place with extra care, as the locals will let you know if you are showing any disrespect.

Something Else? At northern end there is a medium size sand hill, so get your hands on a bodyboard, you can do some great sand surfing.

21.

Break Name: Boomerang

Wave Description: A left and right hand point break that can be excellent, and some magnificent beach breaks in between.

Best Conditions: North Boomerang is best in SE-NE swells and NW winds. South Boomerang is best in SW swell, but is more protected in the NE winds.

Getting There: Turn off the Lakes Way into Boomerang Drive, follow that until you see the beach. There is a car park at the northern end and street side parking at the southern end.

Dangers: Be careful when getting in or out at the southern end as the rocks can be just submerged. The wave tends to be more powerful than you think, it also throws unexpectedly. It will give you a solid hiding if you're not aware.

Rumours: There are often Dolphins in the bay chasing the multitude of fish. Try some fishing in the gutters and you should be able to secure a good feed.

Something Else? The headland at the southern end makes for a spectacular viewing platform. During the day you can watch the eagles soaring above their nest, or the waves peeling through. At night it is perfect for star gazing, also a bit of a trip wandering around there under darkness.

22.
Break Name: Blueys Beach
Wave Description: A combination of quality beach breaks, although tends to be blown out early.
Best Conditions: S-SE swell, W-NW wind, most tides.
Getting There: The next beach south of Boomerang.
Dangers: This beach is more open to swell, creating heavy rips and undercurrents.
Rumours: If Boomerang is a little crowded, check this beach.
Something Else? There is some excellent fishing here. Try at the southern end, in the first gutter.

23.
Break Name: Sandbar
Wave Description: A series of beach breaks, with the best being at the northern end. A magnificent wave when it's working.
Best Conditions: SE swell, W-NW wind, mid tide (can take E-NE swells as well).
Getting There: Turnoff when you see the sign to the name sake.
Dangers: Can get very heavy at times, with shallow sand banks. Look out for those pesky sharks.
Rumours: One of the best breaks on the coast. Surfers come from Sydney on the sniff of a barrel here.
Something Else? The surrounding area is a mish mash of beauty and environmental terror. Sandmining has destroyed much of what once was an expansive rainforest. Now, only a small portion remains. Treat this place with care, (pick up rubbish if you see it) as this place is worth preserving.

24.
Break Name: Seal Rocks
Wave Description: A soft, right hand point break, that needs a huge swell for it to break.
Best Conditions: Gigantic SE-NE swell, N-W wind, mid-high tide.
Getting There: Just beyond Bungwahl, on the Lakes Way, you will see a clearly marked sign.
Dangers: With a name like this, it is bound to attract some interest from sharks. The overdevelopment of this area. It was once a tiny fishing oasis, it still remains fairly intact, but the claws of progression are starting to penetrate.
Rumours: One of the few pristine areas on the coast, but not for long. There is a 'super highway' slowly getting closer.
Something Else? The campground here, is a real treat. Most people are overly friendly, which makes an extended stay worthwhile. Make sure you get there soon, as the place is beginning to change quite rapidly.

25.
Break Name: Treachery Head
Wave Description: A combination of beach breaks and a left hand point break..
Best Conditions: SE-E swell, W-N wind, mid-low tide.
Getting There: Once in Seal Rocks, follow the road onto the dirt. If you keep right and follow the signs, you will make it. There's a campground to signal the entrance to the ocean.
Dangers: It is called treachery for good reason. There have been several deaths on this stretch, so be extremely careful.
Rumours: This catches the most swell on the mid coast, generally a couple of foot bigger than Sydney.
Something Else? There are several beaches in the vicinity that provide some excellent options. Try Lighthouse beach, although this is particularly sharkie, it can be worth it. The northern end is excellent fishing, but you'll need a 4wd or a good

set of legs. Check out the lighthouse, pretty much your ultimate beach villa.

26.
Break Name: Hawks Nest
Wave Description: An amazingly fickle, but magnificent, lefthander over sand, that is full of power.
Best Conditions: Giant S-SE swell, NE-NW wind, mid-high tide.
Getting There: Take the turnoff from Pacific Hwy, through Tea Gardens.
Dangers: The rips here are horrendous, and of course with such proximity to deep waters there are bound to be sharks.
Rumours: One of the most perfect, but inconsistent, lefthanders in this country.
Something Else? This stretch has a tropical feel to it. In fact the water temperature is similar to Byron Bay's. There are also some breaks closeby that are worth checking out.

27.
Break Name: Shoal Bay
Wave Description: A variety of protected beach breaks such as Zenith and Box Beach.
Best Conditions: NE-SE swell, W-NW wind, most tides.
Getting There: Just north of Raymond Terrace there is a sign to Nelson Bay, which will get you there.
Dangers: Box Beach is a heavy wave at times, and can catch out the unaware.
Rumours: Closeby in Fingal Bay, when there is a huge SE swell, it can be the spot to surf.
Something Else? The surrounding Port Stephens is actually two and half times the size of Sydney Harbour. Surrounded by two volcanic headlands makes this place very special. It is still relatively unspoilt by the pesky claws of developers.

28.
Break Name: Stockton Beach
Wave Description: A large expanse of

beach breaks that occasionally get good.
Best Conditions: NE-SE swell, W wind, all tides.
Getting There: There is a passenger ferry that you can catch from Queen's Wharf which takes you over to Stockton Beach, or you can drive from Williamtown.
Dangers: Such an open beach can cause a lot of rips and is not always patrolled.
Rumours: The breaks north are the way to go.
Something Else? If you can find Morna Point you will find the best waves available.

29.
Break Name: Newcastle Harbour
Wave Description: A death defying wave which can see you dodging scrap metal and concrete lumps, but can have a great barrel.
Best Conditions: Big NE swell, S-SW wind, any tide if it is big enough.
Getting There: Follow all the signs into town. It will be pretty obvious from there.
Dangers: A crazy takeoff and a hideous barrel.
Rumours: Not often surfed due to its intense position.
Something Else? Only the very experienced tackle this wave.

30.
Break Name: Nobby's Reef
Wave Description: A selection of shifting peaks over a shallow reef.
Best Conditions: S-E swell, NW wind, mid tide.
Getting There: Follow Hunter St (Main St) until the end, where you take a left on Nobby's Rd. You shouldn't have too much problem from there.
Dangers: The shifting peaks and the way they pitch at times can leave you severely out of position. Take the time to watch a few of the locals and how they negotiate the rip.
Rumours: Your best two alternative options for waves are very closeby. Try The Wedge for a power packed

N.S.W.

lefthander or Stratts Spit. The 'Nobby' as it was once known, (as it was a singular rock before the break wall joined it) was originally used to house the wayward women of the area. The sailors would hear the women wailing as they pulled into port. Just an interesting tit bit.

Something Else? You will find the competition pretty hot around here, as this break is a favourite with the locals. If you know anything about the locals of this town, you'll know they are a hardy breed and don't like being messed with.

31.
Break Name: Cowrie Hole
Wave Description: A perfect righthand reef break if all the conditions are in your favour.
Best Conditions: SE swell, NW-W wind, mid tide
Getting There: Just next to the Soldier Baths swimming pool on the Esplanade.
Dangers: A talented crew of local surfers and a sharp, unforgiving reef break.
Rumours: If the southerly is destroying the waves, try at the southern end of Nobbys Beach.
Something Else? There is a left that breaks off the Hole, called Flat Rock, which works in NE swells.

32.
Break Name: Newcastle Beach
Wave Description: A selection of beach breaks, with a left in the north corner that is the most consistent.
Best Conditions: NE-SE swell, NW wind, (protected in NE too) most tides.
Getting There: It is right in the heart of the city. If you can't find this, then God help you and your future surf trips!
Dangers: Being literally only minutes away from the CBD makes it a prime spot for many beach goers, which can cause some carnage in the lineup.
Rumours: This is a great spot for protection from the NE summer wind. This beach is also home to many of the surf contests held in the Newcastle area.

Something Else? You may see some of Newcastle's many legends on the waves around here. Names like Nicky Wood, Luke Egan, Matt Hoy and Mark Richards have made this place a breeding ground for talented surfers.

33.
Break Name: Bar Beach
Wave Description: A selection of breaks that can be extremely powerful and perfect on the right banks.
Best Conditions: SE swell, NW-SW wind, most tides.
Getting There: If you follow Memorial Drive to Dixon Park Beach, it is at the northern end.
Dangers: An aggressive group of hardened locals, who drop in on each other. Also the crowds can be ridiculous.
Rumours: The reforms are the way to go in crowded times. They can actually get very good.
Something Else? You really should check this break out. It is one of the famous surf spots in Australia, hence it holds something special to those who have surfed it. Don't expect to get the waves of your life, as there are many surfers who make it their life to surf every wave possible, but it is worthwhile hitting the water no matter how crowded.

34.
Break Name: Merewether
Wave Description: A classic righthand reef break, that can handle most swell sizes.
Best Conditions: E-SE swell, SW wind, low-mid tide.
Getting There: At the southern end of Dixon Park Beach, directly infront of the Beach Hotel.
Dangers: The wave throws quickly, and with such a talented crew in the lineup, you need to sit so far inside ensuring the wave is unmakeable, or on the outside where a few escape the pack. The reef can give you a good working over.
Rumours: All the great surfers of the

area. Blooded themselves on this powerful break, Which can handle up to a five metre swell.

Something Else? The Beach Hotel is directly opposite, which makes it an excellent viewing station, especially when you have a couple of liquid ambers in hand. If you do want to get waves, make it super early, as there are many dedicated souls here.

35.
Break Name: Redhead
Wave Description: A combination of left and rights on a reef bottom, the left being the best.
Best Conditions: NE swell, NW wind, mid-high tide.
Getting There: Just off Dudley Rd, south of Merewether.
Dangers: Can get quite heavy at times, so watch the pitching lip.
Rumours: During NE winds, it can offer some great protection.
Something Else? These breaks on the outskirts of Newcastle can offer a welcome relief from the overcrowding at the main breaks. Try also Leggy Point, Shallows and Crosses Beach for other options.

36.
Break Name: Blacksmiths
Wave Description: A classic river mouth break, that can be excellent when the sand banks are right.
Best Conditions: SE-NE swell, W-NW wind, mid-high tide.
Getting There: If you follow the Pacific Hwy south, look for the turnoff to the name sake.
Dangers: As with most river mouths, there is always the possibilitie of large marine action, and watch for the rips.
Rumours: There are quite a few breaks north along Nine Mile Beach which can have some fun beach breaks.
Something Else? This place is one to check in southerlies, as it can still have quality waves.

37.
Break Name: Crabbs Creek
Wave Description: A combination of a short left and long, long right.
Best Conditions: S-E swell, W-SW wind, most tides.
Getting There: Just south of Swansea Channel, you will see the turnoff.
Dangers: The right can be one of the most powerful waves on the east coast, so take extra care here. Also the locals regard this as a semi-secret spot, so just be a little careful.
Rumours: The right can break for up to 300 metres, with a hideous bowl section.
Something Else? If the swell is huge along this coast, the left is the place to hit. It is protected by the surrounding headland, giving rise to a very hollow and fast wave.

38.
Break Name: Swansea
Wave Description: A combination of left and rights over sand and rock, depending on where on the beach you are surfing.
Best Conditions: NE-SE swell, NW-SW wind, most tides.
Getting There: Follow the Pacific Hwy south from Newcastle, and look for the turnoff, the same turnoff to Crabbs Creek.
Dangers: There is a healthy population of hungry surfers which makes the session fairly competitive.
Rumours: There are several other breaks in the area, notably Frenchman's and the fickle Caves Beach. Caves needs a huge swell, and is located at the southern end of the beach near the breakwall.
Something Else? The southern corner used to be a consistent place for barrel heaven. Since the construction of the breakwall, the wave has virtually ceased to exist, except for the rarest of days. Another modern engineering feat that has surprisingly had a negative effect on the surrounding beaches!!

N.S.W.

GENERAL INFORMATION

COFFS HARBOUR

Where To Stay
Parkbeach Caravan Park. Ph.(02) 6652 3204. Tent sites, $12, on-site vans from $26. Pillows and blankets are required in all vans.
Aussitel Backpackers Hostel. Ph (02) 6651 1871. Beds from $14, the managers are very cool and will arrange any activities that you might want to do. They also have a courtesy bus, which most hostels have anyway.
YHA Albany Lodge. Ph (02) 6652 6462. Beds from $15, bikes and surfboards are free to use which is pretty cool.
Rest Inn. Ph (02) 6650 9101. Sweet rooms for $39. Good value.

Where To Eat
The Ex-Serviceman's club can have some excellent cheap meals.
Park Beach Bowling Club, great specials nights.
Plantation Hotel has cheap ($5.50) lunches with a free drink.
Try the Tahruah Thai Kitchen for cheap ($7) dishes.

Where To Party
The Plantation Hotel has live bands from Wednesday to Saturday.
The Sawtell RSL gets the pick of the touring bands.
Parkbeach Bowling Club Ocean Parade.
Moonee Tavern (Home of the Elvis Bar), on the Highway.
Green House Tavern on the Highway.
Hoey-Moey Pub has bands most Fridays and Saturdays.

Flat Day Fun
Absolute Adrenalin is what it says. Ph (02) 6651 9100 for a huge range of activities. They represent most of the tour companies in the areas.
Coffs City Centre Cinemas. Ph (02) 6652 2233, bookings (02) 6651 1647.
Endless Summer Adventures. Everything from white water rafting to surf rafting. Ph (02) 6658 0850.
Coffs City Skydivers Ph. (02) 6651 1167.
4WD Discovery Tours. Ph (02) 6651 1223.
Deep Sea Fishing. Ph (02) 6658 4379.

CRESCENT HEAD

Where To Stay
Crescent Head Holiday Park Phone: (02) 6566 0261. Powered sites from $15, and backpacker rates from $8. Prices vary during peak seasons.
Bournes Holiday Units. Ph (02) 6566 0293.

Where To Eat
Crescent Head Country Club.
Crescent Head Tavern.

Where To Party
Due to the isolation of Crescent Head, the main place is the local tavern. The country club can be good value in the summer holidays.

Flat Day Fun
If you are into nature treks there is plenty on offer in Crescent Head, from the Skyline Lookout where you get magnificent 360 degree views.
There is a local golf course along Rankin Street.
There are plenty of places to throw a line and go fishing. If you brought the snorkelling gear, the point makes an interesting dive when Crescent Head is flat. Just be wary of the rip out on the point.
There are some good 4WD areas but be cautious as some parks and beaches need permits and the local rangers will be quick to pull you up.

PORT MACQUARIE

Where To Stay
Sundowner Breakwall Tourist Park. Ph (02) 6583 2755. Sites from $15 and caravans for $38.
YHA Beachside Backpackers. Ph (02)

N.S.W.

6583 5512. Beds from $13, free use of
bikes and surfboards.
Taskers at Flynn's Beach. Ph (02) 6583
1520. Doubles from $45.
There is a large number of places to stay
in Port Macquarie, so to find out more
information you can phone the Port
Macquarie Visitors Centre, Clarence Street
on (02) 6583 1077.

Where To Eat
The Fishermans Co-op sells some
beautiful seafood straight off the boats.
Hog's Breath Café.
Port Macquarie RSL Club.
Pancake Place Restaurant.

Where To Party
Down Under Niteclub.
TC's Nite Spot.
Port Macquarie RSL Club.

Flat Day Fun
Dolphin Spotting Cruises. Ph (02) 6583
3058.

Total Adventures, everything from
abseiling and camel rides to skydiving. Ph
1800 003 648.
Peppermint Park, full of activities from
water slides to pedal supa carts. Ph (02)
6583 6111.

FORSTER-TUNCURRY

Where To Stay
Tuncurry Beach Caravan Park. Ph (02)
6554 6440. Sites from $12.
YHA Dolphin Lodge. Ph (02) 6555 8155.
Beds from $15, with surf at your door
step, it is damn worthwhile.
Forster Beach Caravan Park. Ph (02) 6554
6269. Sites from $12, on-site vans from
$33.
There are cheap rates on Motels in the
winter months, which can be worth
checking out.

The tankers give this place away. Newcastle. Pic John Brumfield.

Moby Dick Caravan Park, Boomerang. Ph (02) 6554 0631. Sites from $15. Onsite vans from $40.

Where To Eat
Make sure you decide early as many of these eateries close quite early.
Happy Inn Chinese Restaurant.
Pelican Pizza.
Pizza & Ribs.

Where To Party
Leagues & Sports Club.

Flat Day Fun
The Big Buzz Fun Park. Ph (02) 6553 6000.
Great Lakes Aquatic & Leisure Centre. Ph (02) 6555 5866.
Curtis Collection (Displays of Vintage Cars and Motorcycles). Ph (02) 6555 4800.
Game/Sport Fishing & Reef Fishing. Ph (02) 6559 2692.

NEWCASTLE

Where To Stay
Backpackers Newcastle. Ph (02) 4969 3436. Beds from $14, it is in nearby Hamilton, but they have a courtesy bus. There are free surfboards to use as well. The owner is a keen surfer who gives lessons also.
Aloha Motor Inn. Ph (02) 4963 1283. Rooms from $58.
Beach Hotel. Ph (02) 4963 1574. Beds from $45. The view is perfect. You can have the complimentary breakfast watching the wave spit and twist infront of your eyes.
Stockton Beach Caravan Park. Ph (02) 4928 1393. Sites from $12, it is a little way out of town though.

Where To Eat
Your cheapest and often best option, is the Hunter Tafe College on Parry St. Main meals can be as cheap as $3.50. Now that's what I call value!
The Beach Hotel is also a great place to eat.
Customs House Hotel.
Giovanni's Deli Café.

Star Hotel.

Where To Party
The Castle is pretty much your dance club in the area. Open until 5am on the weekends it will get you rocking.
Hunter on Hunter is a good live venue and gets some good acts.
The Beach Hotel is the perfect place for Sunday arvo beers.
Cardiff Workers Club.
Kent Hotel, Northern Star Hotel have jazz nights.
Check out the gig guides in Thursdays papers as they will give you the full run down. There are plenty of live bands playing most nights of the week.

Flat Day Fun
Checkout Blackbutt Reserve which is a cool place to wander around. With wildlife enclosures, some funky looking flora and of course a Koala hang out, it is worth seeing.
Fighter World RAAF Base. Ph (02) 4965 1717.
Newcastle Region Maritime Museum. Ph (02) 4929 2588.
Ambition Fishing & Cruises. Ph (02) 4971 3323.
Apollo Yacht Charters Ph (02) 4943 6239.

SECTION INFORMATION

Local Shapers
DS designs - Darren Symes (Port Mac). Ph (02) 6581 2577.
Cornish Designs - Peter Cornish (Crescent Head). Ph (02) 6566 0550.
Red Sun / Flying High - Scott Wylie (Forster). Ph (02) 6554 9878.
Pacific Dreams - Gordon Jackson (Newcastle). Ph (02) 4926 3355.

Best Months
May to October. Although there are many areas on this coast that have great breaks year round. You should be able to get waves somewhere no matter what the month. Coffs Harbour has better waves in summer due to the cyclonic conditions in Queensland. The swells roll down the

N.S.W.

Perfect Merewether. Pic Bosko.

coast making it ideal.
Secret Spot.
Where ever I lay my.......... is my home.
Now that is pretty clear! How about
another one. In the seal rocks region
head towards the light.
Quick Tips
The best way to choose a destination for
maximum swell potential is to look at a
map and pick out the most protruded
areas. You will always find this to be true.
Try this theory and you won't be
disappointed at the results. Seal Rocks is
a magic place to visit if you are looking
for good swell. If you choose to visit
here, however, there are a few rules. It is
essential that you pick up rubbish if you
see it and show the utmost respect for

the land. No boom boxes scaring the
animals and no idiot behaviour which
spoils the experience for everyone else.
This truly is a magic spot which needs
our help.
Getting There
(this is the same info for the 'Border to
Ballina')
It is best to call the Sydney coach
terminal on (02) 9281 9366 which deals
with most companies and can give you
competitive rates. Country Link is the
government run network of trains and
buses. Ph 13 22 42. You could also try Oz
Experience, for backpackers. Ph (02) 9368
1766. They have reasonable rates, but
more importantly it can be fun to travel
in a bus. Yes, that's right, FUN.

N.S.W.

TO SWANSEA

TOUKLEY 1-2
3
4
5

THE
BURBS...

THE
ENTRANCE
6
7
8
9

TERRIGAL
10
11
12
13

UMINA 14

15

HAWKESBURY
RIVER

16 PALM BEACH

NATIONAL
PARK

17 WHALE BEACH

PITTWATER

18 AVALON
19 NEWPORT
20 NEWPORT
21 MONA VALE
22
23 NARRABEEN
24
25-26

SEA
EAGLE

27 DEE WHY
28
29
30
31

MANLY

32

PORT
JACKSON

TO BONDI

BOMBIES

A Place To Stay
The home was flooded with an assortment of loose characters, almost a semi half-way house. Surfing pics adorned the walls, sharing space with the footyclub, the boat and Miss September.

North Shelly, beutiful hey! Pic John Brumfield

The Central Coast & The Northern Beaches of Sydney

Paradise Lost?

N.S.W.

Central Coast

Situated between Newcastle and Sydney, this coast is really a pot of gold. From Umina in the south, to Catherine Hill Bay in the north, this stretch boasts a diversity of waves not often found in other areas of Australia. Endless beach breaks are surrounded by fun point breaks and several quick reef breaks. On the right day, the barrels are plentiful and also powerful, sending you spinning without the slightest warning.

Even with such proximity to the states capital, the Central Coast retains that country feel. With such a talent pool of surfers this is a beautiful place to visit. Surfers like Glen Winton, Ross Clarke-Jones, Bryce Ellis, Paul Green and the late Mark Sainsbury established a stronghold in this area in the early '80's, paving the way for the younger generation. Names such as Shane Powell, Wayne Seacomb, Adam and Nick Leslie and Drew Courtney are the driving force behind this power packed stretch. It is often by-passed by travelling surfers on their way north or south, but that is a great loss as it can provide some of the waves of your life.

Wamberal with its freight train rights. Pic John Brumfield.

Northern Beaches

The northern beaches of Sydney hold an esteemed position in Australian surfing folklore, having nursed many a talented surfer from the smorgasbord of breaks that abound in the area, through to national and international recognition, and a few World Titles to boot.

From Manly in the south, to Palm Beach at the northern tip, this 40-odd kilometre coastline boasts some heavy credentials, and promises enough variety to keep everyone satisfied. Moving north from Manly, the concrete surrounds give way to lush vegetation, and the crowds thin down considerably. The climate is generally user-friendly. Summer means boardshorts, long, hot days, small waves and consequently, afternoons spent lapping up the scenery in any one of a number of fine beer gardens that populate the peninsula. When Autumn rolls around, the southerly swells become more consistent and the weekend packs aren't so large, nor voracious. The rains start in and the air temperature hovers in the low 20's. Rubber rears it's ugly head in the form of spring suits and the odd steamer. The arrival of Winter is usually heralded in by the first big swell in late May or early June, setting the pattern for some fine times over the next few months. Steamers are the go, the days get lighter later and darker earlier, outside temperatures drop below 20, and at some breaks you may only have to share the wave with one or two other surfers. Then Spring breaks, a wonderful time to be alive in Sydney. The odd decent swell still lurks about, the weather and the water start warming and the days get longer. The whole vicious cycle starts gain. There are reef, beach and point breaks that are within easy access, making this whole stretch one of the more user friendly coasts. A regular public transport system is in effect along the length of the northern beaches, and they do carry surfboards at time of print, depending on how crowded the bus is. This place is a dream of sorts, with many kids surfing before and after school, mixed with the committed businessmen who crave their liquid fix before dealing with the corporate world. It can seem surreal, getting barrels and amazing waves, often shared with Dolphins in such a densely populated area. That is the magic though. Once you've experienced it, you can't forget it.

1.
Break Name: Catherine Hill Bay
Wave Description: Often one of the best banks on the coast, with a classic A-frame setup.
Best Conditions: SE swell, NW wind and most tides.
Getting There: The turnoff is from the Pacific Hwy, just south of Swansea.
Dangers: It is actually pretty safe.
Rumours: A good place to check if there is seemingly no swell.
Something Else? If you are seeking a little more solitude, try south, in the adjoining bay. Moonee can often have waves and you have to walk in, which keeps the crowds down.

2.
Break Name: Frazer Park
Wave Description: A combination of beach breaks, which tends to be fickle due to its protected nature.
Best Conditions: Big NE-SE swell, W wind, most tides.
Getting There: There is a road straight off the PacificHwy that leads to the beach.
Dangers: There can be strong rips in the area, so be aware.
Rumours: Not a good place to check if the swell is small.
Something Else? The surrounding area is quite beautiful and worth the visit, even if it is flat. When the swell does hit though, it can be worth exploring a little more deeply as there are a few secrets to discover.

3.
Break Name: Norah Head
Wave Description: A reef break, mainly for competent surfers.
Best Conditions: Big NE-SE swell, W-S wind, mid tide.
Getting There: Head towards Toukley, then to Norahville, it is just south of that.
Dangers: The reef breaks can be horrendous around here, with free fall takeoffs.

Rumours: Those bloody sharks seem to rear their ugly dorsal fins around here.
Something Else? This area seems to pick up the most swell on this stretch of coast.

4.
Break Name: Soldiers Beach
Wave Description: A selection of fun peaks, with a left point break.
Best Conditions: SE swell, NW wind, most tides.
Getting There: Follow Soldiers Point Drive.
Dangers: The break can get heavy, but nothing to worry about really.
Rumours: Check over the hill in southerlies as you might get a pleasant surprise.
Something Else? This is often regarded as the best and most consistent break on the whole coast. It is protected from the summer north-easterlies and it picks up all available swell. A great year-round break.

5.
Break Name: Pelican
Wave Description: A selection of beach breaks that rely on the build up of sand.
Best Conditions: SE swell, NE-NW wind, most tides.
Getting There: Just south of Soldiers Beach.
Dangers: The wave tends to close out over 2 metres and can have some strong under currents.
Rumours: If you are looking for a beach that handles more swell try Blue Bay.
Something Else? A small NE swell is ideal for this place.

6.
Break Name: Shelley Beach
Wave Description: A combination of beach breaks, with the northern end being the best bet. The left at the northern end can hold a very large swell and can be excellent.
Best Conditions: NE-SE swell, W-SW wind, low-mid tide.

N.S.W.

Getting There: The main beach at The Entrance. It is clearly marked.
Dangers: A very safe beach.
Rumours: It is a great summer wave, often providing fun peaks when there is little else on the coast.
Something Else? This place is generally frequented by beginners and mal riders. Although, it can get very good. The water is amazingly clear.

7.
Break Name: Crackneck
Wave Description: A lefthand reef break, that is very fickle but fast.
Best Conditions: NE-E swell, NW-W wind, low-mid tide.
Getting There: Just south of Bateau Bay, you will find Crackneck Point and the lookout. You cant miss it from there.
Dangers: The wave often breaks quite shallow and hence the name.
Rumours: A great place to escape the crowds, if you can find it.
Something Else? Often a very fickle wave that can prove frustrating to even the staunchest of believers.

8.
Break Name: Forresters
Wave Description: A combination of power packed left and right reef breaks, up to 600 metres offshore.
Best Conditions: S-SE swell, W-NW wind, varying tides depending on the break. Leave low tide alone!
Getting There: Turn off The Entrance Rd, up Forresters Beach Rd.
Dangers: The outside reef breaks are only for the most experienced hellmen and women. With a shallow rock ledge on takeoff, and scary rips, this place is to be treated with the utmost respect. The hardened local crew just add to the whole experience. If you are able to surf these waves then the locals won't be a problem
Rumours: This place is the premier big wave spot on the East Coast. (It may be close, but this is just a rumour, right?)

Something Else? Primarily there are three distinct reef breaks, which can hold swell of up to six metres. Banzai is the probably the pick of the breaks, with an incredibly hollow section.

9.
Break Name: Wamberal Beach
Wave Description: A combination of beach breaks that can be be excellent, especially at the northern end.
Best Conditions: SE-E swell, W wind, most tides.
Getting There: Follow Ocean View Dr out of Terrigal.
Dangers: The northern end has quite a few exposed rocks which can give you a nasty working.
Rumours: Don't even reckon there's one for here.
Something Else? It can offer protection from the prevailing summer north-easterlies.

10.
Break Name: Terrigal Haven
Wave Description: A legendary righthander that has become famous for its power and length, some 250 metres.
Best Conditions: E-S swell, SW wind, mid tide.
Getting There: Head towards the name sake, and you can't lose. The break itself is about 500 metres off the beach.
Dangers: The boulders on the takeoff are a nasty treat, as they are often exposed, and can be deadly especially for such a hideous takeoff zone.
Rumours: The wave can warp and throw square at any time, although you should be able to predict it if you surf it enough.
Something Else? Apart from the Queen of England walking on this hallowed turf, grommies flock from everywhere to surf this break. The beachies can be fun and are a great option for beginners.

11.
Break Name: Avoca Beach
Wave Description: One of the most

N.S.W.

consistent breaks on the coast, with a selection of lefts and right beach breaks with a right hand point at the southern end.
Best Conditions: E-S swell, W-S wind, most tides.
Getting There: Come off Terrigal Drive and onto Tramway Road and then turn left into any street that leads to the beach. Follow Avoca Drive from there.
Dangers: The crowd can be quite fierce at times, but when the swell is running that is the least of your worries.
Rumours: On any good day, when the Pro Tour is not on, Shane Powell is seen carving up the local break.
Something Else? There is a huge selection of breaks along this stretch from North Avoca (it is actually separated from the rest of the beach by Avoca Lake, still pretty easy to get to) to the beach itself. It is a great place to check if the swell is really small, as the beach breaks normally have some sort of wave.

12.
Break Name: Copacabana Beach
Wave Description: A lefthand point break over a ledgey rock bottom, that ends up in a fun, wedgy, beach break.

Best Conditions: S swell, NE-NW wind, most tides.
Getting There: At the northern end of MacMasters Beach, which is on The Scenic Road.
Dangers: Well, uhh, errr, nah!
Rumours: There once was a boy called..........
Something Else? Can have excellent waves when the conditions are right, definitely worth a check.

13.
Break Name: MacMasters Point
Wave Description: A fun, but often slow right hand point, breaking over sand and rock.
Best Conditions: S-SE swell, W-SE, high tide.
Getting There: Off Marine Pde, it really shouldn't be that hard.
Dangers: A damn heavy local crew.
Rumours: There are some excellent waves just south, which require a walk, but worth it though.
Something Else? Apart from the surfing, the area is fairly devoid of any other entertainment. A good place to get away from the crowds in summer.

Eddy Blow in the Banzai Slot. Pic John Brumfield.

14.
Break Name: Bouddi National Park
Wave Description: A selection of secluded beach and reef breaks. As they are open to all swell directions they can be very dangerous, especially the remoteness of them.
Best Conditions: SE-NE swell, NW-W wind, varying tides
Getting There: You have to walk to all the breaks, which can mean wasting valuable surf time if it's not working, but then again.......
Dangers: Isolation and some extremely powerful reefs.
Rumours: One of the last 'wilderness' areas of the central coast.
Something Else? Wherever you see a National Park on a wave infested coast, it is worth checking. Perhaps not on your first trip, or second, but at some time your curiosity is going to get the better of you. Often it leads to disappointment, as waves tend to be fickle. On the right day though, Ohh Lordy it is a wave fest.

15.
Break Name: Box Head
Wave Description: One of the longest lefts in Oz, but is probably more fickle than that damn Merimbula Bar.
Best Conditions: S swell, NE wind, low tide.
Getting There: It is generally regarded as a boat trip from the northern beaches, or a long, long walk from the southern tip of the central coast.
Dangers: Never having waves, but when it's on, watch out for the rips, as it sits on the mouth of the Hawksbury. Of course you know by now that rivermouths are the favourite hangout of the dorsal finned demon.
Rumours: The wave can break up to a kilometre, or longer, in length.
Something Else? When this place is working, don't expect to surf it alone. The word gets out pretty quickly and boats appear from everywhere.

16.
Break Name: Palm Beach.
Wave Description: Great beachbreaks of varied styles and intensities.
The jewel in the crown is Barrenjoey, at the far northern end, a relatively isolated, fickle, but beautiful lefthander.
Best Conditions: NE-SE swell, SW-NW wind for the beachies, and NE-E swell and W wind for Barrenjoey. Most tides.
Getting There: Follow Barrenjoey Rd to the most northern point on the coast.
Dangers: The beachies can get pretty heavy, but it has to be a huge swell. Crowds can also be a problem at the southern end.
Rumours: Be warned - Barrenjoey may induce a mind-numbing feeling of tropical solitude due to its location and peacefulness.
Something Else? The walk up to the lighthouse provides inspiring views along Pittwater and north over the Central Coast. Well worth the effort, and a cool place to hang out for a while.

17.
Break Name: Whale Beach.
Wave Description: The Wedge is a fast lefthander at the far northern end and is the highlight of Whale Beach, while left and right hand beachbreaks proliferate along the shoreline.
Best Conditions: Big NE swell, NW-NE wind, low-mid tide.
Getting There: Follow the signs off Barrenjoey Road.
Dangers: When the Wedge is working, don't attempt to go right. The wave can pitch further than you could imagine.
Rumours: This break is home to the famous Martin Potter, often you can see Pottz and his mates taking this wave completely apart.
Something Else? The surrounding hills provide a spectacular backdrop for this break. There are some great cafés too.

18.
Break Name: Avalon
Wave Description: A classic lefthander towards the northern end of the beach which barrels over a sand bottom, and a righthander accessed by jumping off the pool wall at the southern end of the beach. Little Avalon, at the southern end, can be one of the scariest waves around, generally a bodyboarders break.
Best Conditions: North Av is best in big NE-E swells, and South Av works its magic under the influence of NE-S swell, W-S wind, low-mid tide.
Getting There: Directly off Barrenjoey Rd.
Dangers: The takeoff on all the breaks can be brutal, combine this with a talented local crew, makes surfing here frustrating at times.
Rumours: The magical appearance of a formidable posse of top-class locals when the waves are on, including the mercurial Mr Slater.

Something Else? Little Av to the south is a sketchy takeoff over an eager-for-flesh rock bottom, followed by a beautifully deceptive and devious barrel, nursed into existence by E-SE waves and W winds.

19.
Break Name: The Peak / Newport
Wave Description: Directly in front of the carpark, The Peak is a hotly-contested A-frame which breaks suddenly over a patchy rock bottom.
Best Conditions: S-NE swell, W-S wind, mid tide.
Getting There: Right on Barrenjoey Road.
Dangers: The reef at the southern end can be a brutal thrashing. The rest of the waves can be quite powerful but in comparison to the local crew it is nothing.
Rumours: Keep an eye peeled for local hero Tom Carroll.
Something Else? Newport Reef is

Murph in the early morning glow of south Shelly. Pic John Brumfield

at the southern-most end of the beach, in front of the pool, providing an easy takeoff and long, cruisey rides in S-SE swells, and W winds. Watch out for the odd boulder in the shorebreak.

20.
Break Name: Bungan.
Wave Description: A lefthander at the northern end, A-frame beachbreaks, and a menacing, and rare, right at the southern end.
Best Conditions: E-NE swell, W-SW wind, most tides.
Getting There: Pittwater Road turns into Barrenjoey Road in Mona Vale, and Bungan isn't marked on any street signs. Turn right just prior to the top of the hill between Mona Vale and the descent into Newport to the north.
Dangers: The run down the steps can be lethal, especially when you can see the point going off and the run becomes a full blown sprint.
Rumours: No juicy gossip about Bungan, but it's a gem of a spot to surf, tucked away from the main roads and the crowds.
Something Else? If you've got some snorkelling gear handy, head out off the northern point for some cool viewing.

21.
Break Name: Mona Vale.
Wave Description: Located to the north of Warriewood, along the same stretch of beach. Mona Vale offers an array of beachbreaks, plus a lefthander off the rocks at the south end of the swimming pool over a rock/sand floor. The wave can be a hollow grinding beast in the right conditions.
Best Conditions: NE-SE swell, N-W wind, most tides.
Getting There: Right at the traffic lights just to the north of Mona Vale hospital.
Dangers: The shorebreak can be a boardsnapping affair.
Rumours: This stretch catches an enormous amount of swell and is always worth checking when heading north or south.
Something Else? Mona Vale Golf Course is one of the best on the peninsula, and provides a welcome respite from flat day madness.

22.
Break Name: Warriewood.
Wave Description: A righthander which passes around the cliff face.
Best Conditions: E-SE swell, S wind and mid tide.
Getting There: Follow the coastal road from North Narrabeen up. When you're a

couple of kilometres along, and looking down at the break from about 150 feet, you've arrived.

Dangers: The only danger here is being dropped in on.

Rumours: Just south of here are some secluded breaks that can be excellent on big swells.

Something Else? The break is protected by the southerly and south-westerly winds.

23.

Break Name: Narrabeen.

Wave Description: Left and righthand beach breaks aplenty between Collaroy and North Narrabeen. North Narrabeen itself, is comprised of a legendary lefthander, and can also turn on a great A-frame in front of the carpark.

Best Conditions: The beachbreaks work best in E swells and W winds. North Narrabeen is at it's glorious best when the big NE-E swells charge in, sending long, hollow barrels roaring along the sandbanks in front of the lagoon spillway. Carpark Lefts and Rights are best in E-SE swells and NE-NW winds. All the breaks work on most tides, although when you are looking for perfection at 'Northies' you should hit it at low-mid tide

Getting There: Follow that magical Pittwater Road, and turn off at the traffic lights in Narrabeen, then hit the coast road, can't miss it.

Dangers: This break boasts one of the hottest local surfing communities anywhere. From the tour stalwart Damien Hardman, to the new crew of Ozzie Wright, Nathan Hedge and Chris Davidson. These guys dominate the best peaks when they are out. Don't drop in! The wave itself can give a severe hiding, especially when it gets big. The rips can also be out of control. Definitely a place you want to be alert.

Rumours: The sand enema delivered from a mistimed takeoff at Carpark Lefts and Rights is delightful, try it sometime.

Something Else? The southern aspects of

Narrabeen are nowhere near as consistent nor close to the quality, but the crowds are almost zero. If you check at the south end often enough it will produce some classic days, where you will have a chance of pulling the bombs.

24.

Break Name: Collaroy.

Wave Description: A small, slow and long lefthander, popular with longboarders and beginners.

Best Conditions: A large E-SE swell, S-W wind, low-mid tide..

Getting There: Just around the corner from Long Reef.

Dangers: Copping a longboard on the head.

Rumours: A few times a year, this break can be magic, but rest assured if Collaroy is classic, then the rest of the surrounding breaks will be beyond perfect.

Something Else? Slightly south from Collaroy are scattered a variety of breaks, mainly over reef. Access can be had by a walk over the rock, and a well-timed jump - a more challenging destination for the experienced surfer. The waves here, can be magic, especially if the conditions are right. Take a drive down to the golf course, which will give you a prime viewing spot of the action. Look out for the hairy break called White Rock. Very scary!

25.

Break Name: Butterbox.

Wave Description: A great left, and shorter rights over a surreal seagrass-covered rock bottom.

Best Conditions: S-SE swell, NE wind, low-mid tide. The break works best on swells over two metres.

Getting There: Clearly visible from the Long Reef carpark, in the south east corner, but more easily accessed by taking the road through to the Long Reef Golf Club to its end. From there it's a ten minute walk and scramble down a steep incline.

N.S.W.

Dangers: The break is quite powerful and it's not until you go to stand up on one of these beasts that you realise the enormity of the situation. Good to watch a couple roar down the reef first.

Rumours: Time to discover the truth behind those shark stories.

Something Else? Little Makaha, the most outlying tip of the reef off Long Reef point, turns on the goods during huge SE swells and SW winds, and provides the true soulman (or woman) with a challenging and long deep sea paddle.

26.

Break Name: Long Reef.

Wave Description: Northwards from Dee Why, and easily identified by the prominent golf course on the headland, is Long Reef, a series of breaks over a few hundred metres' worth of sand and rock.

Best Conditions: Generally a wave to be had on the inside in most conditions, but works especially well in E-SE swells. As the swells increase in size, the breaks multiply outwards from the Long Reef carpark and surf club, the large waves expending their energy on the offshore reefs, before twisitng on to a shorebreak finish. Long rights and lefts from offshore A-frames merge with the shorebreaks when the swells are large, making for a powerful finish to a great wave. S-W wind, low-mid tide.

Getting There: Follow Pittwater Road along the coast, and you can't miss the Long Reef turnoff.

Dangers: Mixing it with the longboarders that sit outside claiming the best waves for themselves.

Rumours: The oft-repeated shark sightings off the point.

Something Else? Pay parking is the rule along the northern beaches, and you're meant to purchase a ticket anytime you see one of the automatic vending machines. Unfortunately, the parking officers are usually pretty diligent, especially on weekends. In order to save a few bucks, you might have to take a short walk and park a little further away.

27.

Break Name: Dee Why Point

Wave Description: A solid righthand point that wraps down the rock platform at the southern end of the beach.

Best Conditions: BIG S swell, S-SW wind, mid tide.

Getting There: Again it is off Pittwater Rd, and very difficult to miss.

Dangers: The dash across the rocks to get out when the swell's overhead.

Rumours: The takeoff, next to a protruding rock shelf, and proceeding into a whirling vortex of water, is easy.

Something Else? The inside shorebreak, and a righthander in front of the clubhouse, can provide some relief from being starved of waves at the Point by dialled-in locals.

28.

Break Name: Curl Curl Beach

Wave Description: Beach breaks everywhere, and a decent righthander along the rocks at the southern end.

Best Conditions: E-SE swell, W-NW wind, most tides.

Getting There: One bay south of Dee Why.

Dangers: Keep your eyes peeled for flying boards when the crowds are out.

Rumours: "It's always better at Curlie", is often heard in carparks to the north.

Something Else? The northern end provides a welcome respite to the summer nor-easterly winds. Generally speaking, Curlie does get the same size swell as north Narrabeen but the crowds are definitely far heavier.

29.

Break Name: Harbord or Freshwater

Wave Description: Rights and lefts along a small beach.

Best Conditions: E swell, NE-W wind, mid-high tide.
Getting There: One bay north of Manly.
Dangers: The odd influx of bluebottles during summer.
Rumours: Did Hawaiian legend The Duke provide Australians with their first taste of surfing at this spot?
Something Else? A great break in the summer north-easters, as it offers full protection.

30.
Break Name: Queenscliff.
Wave Description: Mostly a righthander on to rocks, with an occasional left by the point.
Best Conditions: E-NE swell, W-SW wind, most tides.
Getting There: Queenscliff is a rivermouth break at the most northern end of Manly beach.
Dangers: Can get crowded.
Rumours: Former ASP Tour vet Barton Lynch appears for the crowds every afternoon at five.
Something Else? There is a bombie that is about one kilometre off shore. It hardly ever breaks, and only when the swell is massive. A pretty awesome sight though.

31.
Break Name: Manly beachbreaks.
Wave Description: Shorebreaks and A-frames litter this wide expanse of beach, offering lefts and rights throughout.
Best Conditions: E-SE swell, W wind, most tides
Getting There: Ferries depart Circular Quay in town and arrive in Manly about 45 minutes later. Plenty of beachfront parking.
Dangers: Stray boards and bodies, and over-zealous clubbies.
Rumours: That you'll ever surf this place alone.
Something Else? This place is a great people watching venue, as it really is a tourist meeca.

32.
Break Name: Winki Pop & Fairy Bower.
Wave Description: Both the breaks can be found at the south end of Manly beach. Fairy Bower wraps around the cliff face, while Winki Pop is located further around the point. These are the most famous point breaks in Sydney and for good reason. The wave is a power packed explosion onto rocks, with a steep takeoff, only for the most experienced surfers.
Best Conditions: Big NE - SE swell, W wind, low tide .
Getting There: Access to Fairy Bower is via the headland carpark, ditto for Winki. The car park is in the southern corner of Manly.
Dangers: Surfers should be aware of the rocks that line the cliff base, making the journey out and back in during large swells great viewing for the crowds.
Rumours: May cause surfers to develop a resemblance to the Toxic Avengers due to sewage outfalls located out to sea.
Something Else? A top place to watch the action during huge swells. The headland is a beautiful spot to check out other reef possibilities as well.

Steve Clements in a mute grab at south Avalon. Pic John Brumfield.

GENERAL INFORMATION

CENTRAL COAST

Where To Stay
Avoca Beach Tourist Park. Ph (02) 4381 1456.
Norah Head Tourist Park. Ph (02) 4396 3935.
Terrigal Beach Backpackers Lodge. Ph (02) 4385 3330. Beds start from $17.
Bellbird Caravan Park Terrigal. Ph (02) 4384 1883. Sites from $12.
Ocean Beach Caravan Park Umina. Ph (02) 4341 1522.

Where To Eat
Avoca Tavern has some great counter meals.
Avoca Cake Shop, some joyous vanilla slices and a mouth watering range of donuts.
Florida Beach Bar.
Galley Beach House, The Haven Terrigal.
Light House Coffee and Takeaway, Norah Head.

Where To Party
Central Coast Leagues Club in Gosford is THE place. If you are looking for the big night out, everyone from the area congregates here.
Ettalong Beach Club.
Beachcomber Hotel.
Gosford Hotel.

Flat Day Fun
The best use of your time when it is flat, is to explore the National Park. It is a beautiful walk and can give you an idea of what the wave possibilities are. Failing that you can go and spend some of that hard earned cash on the following:
Buzzy Boats Watersports Gosford. Ph 0414 431 199.
Central Coast Kayak Tours, Avoca Beach. Ph (02) 4381 0342.
The Paintball, Kulnura. Ph (02) 437 1411.
Hoyts at Erina. Ph (02) 4367 7117.

Local Shapers
Nirvana Surfboards - Bill Cilia

Outer Island - Mitchell Ray

Best Months
May to September are the prime months, but the central coast can have some great fun waves throughout summer.

Quick Tips
There is far more to the Central Coast than most imagine. At first glance it can appear to be an overcrowded hub of many differing places jammed together, but.... Once you begin to explore the region you will soon see the potential of this place. Make sure you take a look at the parks as these can have some fantastic areas.

Getting There
You can catch a ferry from Palm Beach to Patonga, then a bus service. Ph (02) 4368 2277.
There is also a train service from Sydney. Ph 13 22 42.

SYDNEY'S NORTHERN BEACHES.

Where To Stay:
No shortage of accommodation along this stretch of coast, ranging from caravan parks to pitching a tent, through to hotels and pubs. Summer can get a little busy, finding a van or tent site can be tricky.
Lakeside Caravan Park. Ph (02) 9913 7845. Sites from $16 or vans from $67.
Manly Backpackers Beachside. PH (02) 9977 3411. Dorm beds from $15, single rooms $30.
Manly Paradise Motel . PH (02) 9977 5799. Rooms from $90.
Sydney Beachouse at Collaroy is awesome! Ph (02) 9981 1177. Brand new in 1999. It has everything you could want including Rob, the manager, who is a wealth of surfing knowledge.

Where To Eat:
A staggering variety of cafés, bars, restaurants and takeaways.
The Corso in Manly is literally packed with food options, but the best bets are always a little removed from the main tourist areas. Try the Japanese restaurant

just behind the Corso (north side, halfway down), or the cafés along the esplanade. The Aangan curry House in Newport has cheap and tasty meals. The counter meals at the Steyne Hotel are pretty good. Newport Arms for counteries, and The Beach Hut at Whale Beach.

Where To Party:
Plenty of choices here, some of the more well-known:
The Newport Arms, check the beer garden overlooking the Pittwater, huge crowds in Summer, Friday and Saturday nights. Restaurant and bistro provide a filling feed with a view.
The Narrabeen Sands, the foremost venue for bands on the peninsula. Restaurant, bistro, beer garden.
The Mona Vale Hotel, Niteclub runs Thursday, Friday, Saturday and Sunday nights with cover charge.
The big night is a combination of drinks at the 'Newie Arms' then hop on one of the many buses that will take you to the Jet Club in Dee Why. Then it's a scramble to get a taxi at the end of the night. The bus ride can be a blast, as it is much like a party.

Local Shapers
Aloha - Greg Clough (Brookvale) Ph (02) 9905 5816.
Balck Flys - Chad Asser. Ph (02) 9999 4385.
Division - Peter Daniell. Ph (02) 9779 5334.
Hot Buttered - Terry Fitzgerald. Ph (02) 9913 1755.
Warner Surfboards - Brett Warner. Ph (02) 9938 5316.
CHP - Matt Haymes. Ph (02) 9997 3352.
Simon Anderson surfboards - Who do you reckon? Ph (02) 99797414

Best Months
April-October are the prime months with May being the highlight of recent years. Summer flat spells can drive the most sane, INSANE!

Quick Tips
The weekends here are bedlam. Many of the surfers from the western suburbs

Guess Where. Pic Rowan Keegan.

make the trek to these beaches and are intent on getting waves. Then of course you have the 9-5 workers desperate for a few waves and then those grommies, they are everywhere! Best to hit the water just after the school bell, and work whistles ring in the morning. The crowds thin considerably. Don't spend your time driving the whole coast in search of a magic little break. Although this can be the case, assess the conditions and work out where will be best, because there are many speed cameras along the stretch of Pittwater that are funded entirely by surf crazed men and women on the hunt. The conditions may vary from break to break, but not so much as to risk. If you have the technology of the modern world wired, you can hook into the web site www.realsurf.com for up to the minute reports on the northern beaches. Live pictures and swell predictions should cut down your travelling time.

Getting There
The northern beaches are well serviced by a bus system that is generally on time and inexpensive. You can also access the northern reaches of Sydney by way of Ferry from Circular Quay. Ph 13 15 00 for all the details you require on Ferries, Trains and Buses.

N.S.W.

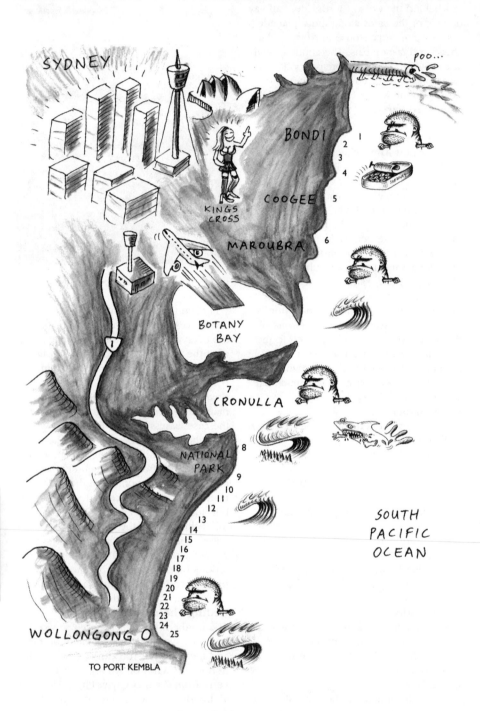

The wind was constantly shifting, contorting the wave into a mangled beast that no sane man could ride.

McKenzies Bay looking very heavy. Pic Bill Morris.

South Sydney - Woollongong
The Better & Badder Side

Having surfed both sides of the Harbour for more than 20 years, I feel confident in saying that south of the bridge scores more quality surf than its more famous brother, The Northern Beaches, and that's a fact.

Let me just expand on that theory and clarify my point, so I don't get written off as a parochial southsider, because I'm not. Both regions have their advantages in different seasons. Fact is though, the Cronulla region, in particular, boasts numerous world class reef breaks that can handle sizeable swells during solid autumn, winter and sometimes even spring southerly groundswells. The northside really only boasts Fairy Bower as a genuine big wave spot, and it's soft in comparison to Cronulla Point, Voodoo or Shark Island, not to mention some of our hidden treasures (yes that's right we actually still have one or two low key jewels less than a 40 minute drive from the city centre). When I say that Fairy Bower is soft, I don't mean 6ft Winki Pop, I'm talking 8ft or bigger Bower. When it's that solid you take off wide of Winki or even outside Winki and charge wide of Surge and Racecourse into the safety of a deep channel and easy paddle out.

N.S.W.

Bronte. Pic Bill Morris.

In comparison, big Cronulla Point, Voodoo, Shark Island or the "Southie" which is the Bombie at Coogee, can handle three metres solid and beyond, sometimes up to five metres! Many of these breaks come into their own as full tilt, pedal to the metal, pit action, at that size. So while the north side of Sydney pumps in small to medium sized north-easterly swells, the whole stretch generally closes out in a lined up quality south swell. Just when the southside really comes into its own.

As a rule of thumb the northern beaches provide great waves in east or north-east swells from January through June. The Cronulla reefbreaks often pump in winter, while the city beaches are fickle. If you can handle the crowds and don't mind jumping in your car every now and then to escape the rat-race, southern Sydney can provide an interesting surfing lifestyle. Most days have some sort of a rideable wave, because you can seek protection from most wind directions. So all in all the south side has more quality waves, more often than its northern neighbours.

The Coal Coast - Stanwell Park through to Wollongong.

The Coal Coast rules. There are enough surfable nooks and crannies in this little stretch of winding road, known as Lawrence Hargrave Drive, to keep both locals and day tripping Sydney crew happy on... most occasions.

Stanwell Tops lies just over an hours drive south of Sydney (just south of the National Park.) The majority of Wollongong's population lives on a pretty narrow flood plain, wedged between the Illawarra ranges and the Tasman Sea. Everyone lives near the beach, so in that sense Wollongong, and its northern suburbs towards Stanwell Park, is kind of a surf city. There is a huge variety of surf spots, beginning at Stanwell Park in the north, through to the city metropolitan breaks. There is generally somewhere surfable in any wind or swell combination. Wollongong began as a rural area and grew up around BHP's vast Port Kembla Steel Works and Coal refinery. In more recent times the steel and coal industries have slowed a little resulting in more unemployment and greater crowds in the surf.

1.
Break Name: Bondi, Australia's most famous beach, only 20 mins from the city centre.
Wave Description: Good beach breaks, generally in the 3 to 4 foot category, with left and right peaks from the middle to southern end.
Best Conditions: 1-1.2 metre S-E swell, NW-NE wind, on mid to high tide in autumn or winter.
Getting There: Train from city to Bondi Junction Station. The number 380 bus down Bondi Road to the Beach. Depart Campbell Parade for beach access.
Dangers: Learners, backpackers, hordes of swimmers in summer, and gorgeous, distracting women. Close out sets over 5 foot. Bondi picks up the most south swell in Sydney.
Rumours: Most good surfers have moved away from the area. Formerly the home of the infamous ITN boardriders club. Crew like: Cheyne Horan, Richard Cram, George Wales, Will and Ben Webber, Dave Davidson, to name a few, have all moved on to greener, less crowded pastures.
Something Else? The council moved the stormwater drain from the southern corner in between 1st and 2nd ramp, to outside the icebergs a few years back and the banks haven't been the same since. (The stormwater drain, as unhygienic as it may sound, used to create stable rips and gutters after the rain.) To make matters worse the council nowadays employs a tractor to clean the beach daily during the summer months which obviously flattens the sand which in turn can lead to closeouts!

2.
Break Name: McKenzies Bay
Wave Description: Can have fun wedgy lefts and smaller rights.
Best Conditions: Small to medium E-S swell(or bigger NE swell), NW-NE wind, low-mid tide.
Getting There: Follow Campbell Parade

around from South Bondi, turn left into Sandridge Street and follow your nose through Mark St and you'll see the Pacific Ocean.
Dangers: Rocks & Closeouts. Macca's is to be avoided in a southerly or big swells as it rapidly turns into a washing machine.
Rumours: MacKenzies can go without waves for a whole year or two. After the infamous '74 storm swell, Macca's didn't break for well over a year due to a lack of sand. It also copped a beating this past winter but hopefully will return in time for summer.
Something Else? Less than one kilometre south of Bondi, lies a semi secretive, rock lined bay that can be guttered for months or super consistent depending on the sand build up. Macca's tends to be guttered after the big winter swells, so basically it's generally best in the summer months when the predominant north-east sea breeze blows side shore off shore into fun little wedging lefthanders.

3.
Break Name: Tamarama
Wave Description: Tamarama is another small little bay kinda similar to MacKenzies in that it serves up peaky wedges, only there is a sandy beach to be enjoyed year round. Tamarama is most renowned for its peaky wedging lefthanders that break outside of the point right across the bay in NE swells.
Best Conditions: Small to medium E-NE swell, N wind, mid-low tide.
Getting There: It's only another 200 M South of MacKenzies. You can catch the 361 Bus from Bondi Junction to Tamarama or MacKenzies, or you can walk, as it's only 5-10 minutes south from Bondi.
Dangers: Tamarama is a small rippy beach at the best of times, so as you can imagine when the swell gets up to 2 metres or larger it can be gnarly. South swells and south winds are a no no. The southern end rocks have been known to

N.S.W.

swallow up many a board.

Rumours: Syringes can be a problem in the sand and I don't recommend hanging around the toilet block.

Something Else? Tama is often referred to as "Glamourama' because it is THE beach for Sydney's "beautiful people" (ie., models, yuppies, tryhards etc). The clubbies restrict surfing between 7am and 6pm during daylight savings, so it's off limits for surfers except for the early or the late. However between Anzac Day, April 25 and the October Long weekend (1st weekend in Oct) the beach is handed back to surfers. Incidentally, this is the best time of the year for surfing at Tama anyways.

4.

Break Name: Bronte

Wave Description: Bronte is a quiet, picturesque little bay just south from Tamarama. The southern end reef break can have its days and there can also be powerful ledging lefts and rights on the beach, but Bronte is fickle!

Best Conditions: Small to medium SE-NE swell, SW-NW wind. The reef is best at high tide on a 1.5 metre E swell with W winds whilst the beach can be good in a medium S swell or even a peaky NE swell with W winds. Occasionally the reef can handle a 2 metre plus south swell if its clean.

Getting There: You can catch the 378 bus from Bondi Junction or even from Central Station or Oxford St in the City. If you're keen you can even walk from Bondi in 20 mins or less.

Dangers: Again Bronte is a relatively small beach so there is a fair bit of rip action. There is generally a strong rip running out from the beach between the reef and the predominant left hand bank on the beach break. There is also generally a strong south to north sweep and the sandbanks drop off dramatically. One of Sydney's most dangerous beaches for swimmers.

Rumours: There is a famous picture of

Bronte reef lining up at a solid 15ft and clean with one or two guys out in the late '70's, which used to hang proudly in Jay Carters old Bronte surf shop. It hadn't been ridden that big until the winter of '97 when Rod (Box) Kerr and friends paddled out and had to be rescued off Ben Buckler headland at North Bondi.

Something Else? The best thing about Bronte is that it offers a little protection from south-west or even southerly winds.

5.

Break Name: Coogee

Wave Description: Coogee doesn't really fit into the category of a surfing beach, however, there is plenty of entertainment in the area so we'll still give you a few tips. Coogee is an ideal safe little beach for swimming or sunbaking if you're into that. Wedding Cake Island which lies less than 1km offshore shelters most of the swell action. However in a big swell Coogee can be fun.

Best Conditions: Coogee requires NW-SW winds to be at its best. There is a small reef at the southern end of the beach that can produce the occasional fun right. The beach breaks, as I mentioned, are rare unless the swell is pretty much out of control at the other more exposed eastern suburbs beaches. "The Southie" is an offshore reef located half way between Wedding Cake Island and the southern end of the beach. It can get interesting in bigger S swells with offshore winds. Wedding Cake island itself can be ridden in medium to bigger swells also.

Getting There: Catch the 314/315/316 from Bondi Junction to Coogee beach.

Dangers: Coogee is generally a deep water beach so the shore break sure does dump. It can snap boards and backs.

Rumours: It used to break so much better before the '74 storm - yeah right!

Something Else? Coogee Bay Hotel is one of Sydney's more infamous live band venues. Check your local gig guides but you could stumble upon anyone from

Midnight Oil, The Angels right through to alternative overseas acts like Sonic Youth, NOFX, Bad Religion or Rage against the Machine, if you get my drift. There are also plenty of nightclubs - the Palace, The Oceanic or restaurants and cafés for your entertainment. Accommodation wise there is no shortage of Backpackers hostels or more upmarket hotel style accommodation but I won't go into too much detail because the surf generally doesn't justify staying here.

6.
Break Name: Maroubra
Wave Description: 5 minutes south from Coogee lies Maroubra beach arguably the eastern suburbs' most consistent surf spot. Maroubra produces some sort of a rideable wave in most conditions whether the swell is from the south or the north. The southern end of the beach provides some sort of protection from SW-S winds

whilst the northern end is quite rideable in N winds.
Best Conditions: Maroubra can be good in a variety of swell and wind combinations. "The Bra" is at its best in a medium or even solid E-NE swell with winds from N-SW. Lefts can wrap right down the beach and there is often a consistent righthander called the dunny bowl that hooks back towards the northern corner. There is a reef break at the southern end that can get good in E-NE swells with SW winds and there can also be some fine beachbreak banks right along the beach even in S swells.
Getting There: Catch the 400 bus from Bondi Junction to Maroubra Junction and then the 395/396 from Maroubra Junction down to the beach.
Dangers: Because access to the beach via public transport is more limited than the other eastern suburbs beaches, and the fact that there is very little

Shark Island, a very shallow grave, for some Pic Tim Vanderloon.

accommodation, Maroubra is way more localised. The local lads, the "Bra Boys" as they are affectionately known, often have the Maroubra post code tattooed to various parts of their anatomy. These guys are very protective of their waves.
Rumours: First surfed by native Aboriginals that settled the La Perouse area.
Something Else? Just north of Maroubra lies a big wave reef break called Lurline Bay. Lurline holds the largest rideable waves in the eastern suburbs. "The Bay" doesn't start breaking until the swell hits 3 metres. It's been ridden up to 5 and 6 metres. There are also a couple of spots just south of the Bra at Malabar (which is pretty much just an average beach break, except for the occasional day off the southern point) and further south still towards Botany Bay. There are one or two sneaky localised reefs and even a big wave Bombie at the entrance to Botany Bay.

7.
Break Name: Cronulla
Wave Description: Cronulla is the southern most beachside suburb of Sydney. "The Nulla" is surrounded by the waterways of Botany Bay in the North and Port Hacking to the south. The sense of isolation provided by the waterways is fading rapidly as urban developers seem hell bent on creating another concrete jungle by the sea. There is a huge variety of surf on offer in the Cronulla region ranging from fair to perfect beach breaks. Cronulla's beaches from the Alley in the south to Greenhills in the north, encompassing The Wall, Elouera, Midway, John Davey and Wanda. These breaks are more consistent than most of Sydney's beach breaks. The reef breaks, which Cronulla is most famous for, are simply world class.
Best Conditions: The beach breaks from Elouera North to Greenhills, are usually best in small or medium size E-SE swells from 3 to 6ft with offshore SW-NW winds.

Occasionally Wanda and Elouera can handle solid swells on the outer banks but they must be peaked up swells, not straight ground swell lines. The Alley and the Wall beach breaks are semi sheltered from S winds.
Getting There: Train access right to the beach from Central Station.
Dangers: The surrounding reef breaks are some of the heaviest on the east coast. Experienced surfers only.
Rumours: The sand mining of the infamous sand dunes at Green Hills in the early 80's led to a deterioration in the quality of Cronulla's beach breaks. They used to be world class, now they still have their days, but are far less consistent. The towering dunes also used to funnel the prevailing NE seabreeze almost straight offshore up at Wanda and Greenhills.
Something Else? Shark Island lies just a couple hundred metres offshore from Cronulla point. The island is for extremely proficient surfers only. This righthander is of extreme consequence. It's best in a straight SE swell with offshore winds from W-SW. Definitely only a mid to high tide break. One of the best tubes in the world. Cronulla Point has many moods. On solid days "The Point" is a serious right hand wave that rapidly detonates across the reef with Hawaiian-like power and class. It's at its best in a solid SE-S swell with S-SW wind. The Point is rideable in any swell direction and is sometimes more hollow in a E-NE swell. However when it's really big, S swells are best. Voodoo is right on the north-eastern tip of Bate Bay. Voodoo is at its best in a solid S swell with NW-NE winds. It is a world class left that can handle up to 15ft easily. There is a whole bunch of lesser known reef breaks and even beachies within the confines of Bate Bay (Cronulla), but we simply haven't got the space to rave on about each and every one of them here. In summary, the Cronulla region has a wave for everyone in just about every wind condition.

Voodoo at Cronulla, empty and perfect. Pic CSP.

8.
Break Name: Royal National Park
Wave Description: Just under an hour's drive south from Sydney's CBD, lies the jewel in every southern Sydney surfer's crown, The Royal National Park. Fifteen thousand hectares of breathtaking native Australian bushland including some 20 kms of surfable coastline lie within the confines of the park. A world of its own, a study of peace and tranquillity and the ultimate escape for the stressed out city dwelling hordes or weekend wave warriors. The Royal National Park has three main breaks Garie, Era and Burning Palms as well as a handful of less accessible semi secret options.
Best Conditions: The peaky sometimes epic, always powerful, shifting beachbreaks at Garie, North Era and Burning Palms all work in similar conditions. W-N winds are required and medium E or NE swells are best. The lefts at North Garie and Nth Era Point can also hold 2 and sometimes even 3 metres of E or NE swell. Solid S swells tend to closeout, however, Garie can get good in small south swells with west or north

west winds. All the beaches in the park are really open and exposed swell magnets which subsequently blow out in S winds.
Getting There: Car or cycle access only, although for bushwalkers or hitchers you can take the train to Waterfall, Sutherland or Otford. By car take the Princess Highway south to Waterfall railway station and then take the only turn off to the left over the railway and you're well on your way to Garie. Its a pleasant 15-20 minute winding drive from the Waterfall entrance to Garie. There are 2 other entrances at Sutherland and Stanwell Tops (but Waterfall offers the quickest route to Garie).
There is a $7.00 entrance fee after 8.00 am on weekends in the warmer months.
Dangers: The winding road in, potential for bush fires, falling rocks on the walk to Era or Burning Palms.
Rumours: The creeks at North Garie and North Era used to flow constantly back in the day, creating even better banks on both beach breaks. There was a time you could surf Garie all to yourself all day, perfect in the middle of summer.

N.S.W.

9.
Break Name: Stanwell Park
Wave Description: Stanwell offers
generally punchy left and right beach
breaks up to 2 metres on a sand bottom.
The lefts at the northern end can get
really long in an E-NE swell.
Best Conditions: Medium E-NE swell or
small S swell, N-W wind, most tides.
Getting There: Take the Princess
Highway to just south of Waterfall, where
you have the option of taking the first
right, the scenic route to Stanwell or
continuing on the Highway to
Wollongong. Otherwise take the train to
Stanwell Park station and walk a few
minutes.
Dangers: Strong south to north current.
Beginners getting in your way.

Rumours: The south end used to pump
when the creek was open.
Something Else? Um, I don't think so.

10.
Break Name: Coalcliff
Wave Description: Coalcliff offers some
protection from S winds and generally
offers punchy shorey type beach breaks,
left and right. The left peeling back
towards the southern end pool seems the
most consistent.
Best Conditions: Small to medium SE-NE
swell, W-S wind, low-mid tide.
Getting There: Heading south along
scenic Lawrence Hargrave Drive, you'll
come across a half horseshoe shaped bay.
Continue along Lawrence Hargrave Drive,
turn left at Coalcliff signpost or a 5

Glen McEwen at Redsands. Pic Steve Conti.

minute walk from Train Station.
Dangers: Water quality can be a bit suss, due to creek outlet and proximity to coal mine. Also watch stray rocks on beachbreak.
Rumours: The point used to go off.
Something Else? There is also a fickle left hand bombie, that requires E-N swell and W winds. The south end reef break is usually a hoax.

11.
Break Name: Scarborough / Wombarra
Wave Description: Scarborough can get pretty good in NE swells when the left runs down the beach, but generally the banks are pretty straight. At the other end of the beach Wombarra can be epic a couple times a year when the sand packs in on the southern end rocks.
Best Conditions: Medium E-NE swell, NW-SW wind for the winding lefts at Scarborough, or E-SE swell with SW-S winds for the fickle rights at Wombarra.
Getting There: Can't miss either, turn left off the main road, Lawrence Hargrave Drive. Walk from train station.
Dangers: Rogue rocks sticking out at both beaches.
Rumours: Shaun Thomson got a 12 second tube at Nombarra in the early '80's when the bank was lined up perfectly.
Something Else? The best months for this break seem to be April and May.

12.
Break Name: Coledale
Wave Description: Coledale often has a peaky, sucky, wedging righthander, just north of the southern end rocks. It's entirely dependant on sand build up (usually best after a solid NE swell has deposited some sand in the corner).
Best Conditions: 1 to 1.6 m E-S swell, W-S winds, low tide.
Getting There: Can't miss it, as you drive straight past it on Lawrence Hargrave Drive.
Dangers: Shallow sucky sand banks, can

snap boards and bones.
Rumours: There was a fatal shark attack here in the post war years.
Something Else? uh uh!

13.
Break Name: Thommo's
Wave Description: Thommo's is a fickle lefthander, bombora/reef break. Breaking over a patchy sand/reef bottom.
Best Conditions: Solid 2 m E-NE swell or bigger, W-NW wind, low tide.
Getting There: Fall out of the car in Sharkie's car park and look 50 yards to the north, or walk from Coledale Station.
Dangers: Jumping off the rock shelf can be hazardous, take care between sets.
Rumours: The rights on the northern side of Thommo's are well worth a look too.
Something Else? Well, no actually.

14.
Break Name: Sharkie's
Wave Description: Sharkie's can be a fat, pregnant, left and right, sand on reef break that occasionally can get really good.
Best Conditions: Medium 1.5-2 m E swell, NW-SW wind, mid tide.
Getting There: Again can't miss it, off Lawrence Hargrave Drive. Walk from Coledale Station.
Dangers: Bits of reef protrude on the low tide, be careful not to get washed in over them.
Rumours: Sharkie's used to handle 8 foot plus swells 10 years ago.
Something Else? The name has some reference to those marine creatures.

15.
Break Name: Headlands
Wave Description: Just south of Sharkie's lies Headlands. It is a tricky, though world class, horseshoeing, right hand reef break.
Best Conditions: N swell, W-SW, mid-high.
Getting There: You drive straight past it

N.S.W.

on LH drive. A 10 minute walk from Coledale train station.

Dangers: Shallow, gnarly reef that can go close to sucking dry on some barrels.

Rumours: My cousin broke his nose there on an epic big day late winter '87. I was unable to assist him as the surf was just too damn good.

Something Else? On S swells, headies can still be a powerful, more performance-orientated wave. But in a NE swell it is a serious, gapping barrel.

16.

Break Name: Austinmer

Wave Description: Austinmer and little Austie just to the north, offer fun, peaky sometimes hollow lefthand beach breaks.

Best Conditions: 1 to 1.8 m E-NE swell, NW-SW wind, mid tide.

Getting There: You drive straight past it, off LH Drive. A 5 min walk from Austinmer train station.

Dangers: Hordes of swimmers and bodyboarders in the summer months.

Rumours: Heavy biker v's surfer fights at the nearby Headlands hotel went down in the '70's.

Something Else? E-NE swells, off the pool at the southern end of Austie, can provide fun rights up to 1.5 metres.

17.

Break Name: Macauleys / Thirroul

Wave Description: Thirroul can offer some pretty interesting peaky beach breaks.

Best Conditions: NE swell, W-NW wind, high tide.

Getting There: Turn left off LH Drive. 10 min walk from Thirroul Station.

Dangers: Clubbies. There is a real surf club culture about this beach. The Mercer Brothers hail from here.

Rumours: Clubbies suck.

Something Else? It can also be fun in clean little S swells as well. The general rule is the lefts are better in N swells, whilst the rights can get good in S swells.

18.

Break Name: Sandon Point

Wave Description: Sandon Point, in my humble opinion, is the most consistent right point break on the NSW coast. Rideable from 1 to 5 metres, Sandon has many moods.

Best Conditions: 1.5-2.5 E swell, W-S wind, low-mid tide.

Getting There: Drive down the highway and descend down the infamous Bulli Pass where you take a left turn at the church into Point Street. Proceed to the end, you can't miss the setup. You could also walk approximately 15mins from Bulli Train station.

Dangers: A very, very protective local crew. You can't blame them!

Rumours: Hardcore localism was prevalent in the '70's, even early to mid '80's. Cars torched, windows smashed, tyres let down, rock throwing and fights were common place.

Something Else? The NE swells can mean freight-train barrels and huge S swells can be fun too. For experienced surfers only.

19.

Break Name: Peggy's

Wave Description: Peggy's is an interesting righthand reef point break. It's unpredictable and weird, but it can and does get classic.

Best Conditions: E-NE swell, S-SW wind, low tide.

Getting There: 2 mins south of Sandon. It's visible from the Sandon Car Park.

Dangers: Sharp and slippery rocks conveniently located at the jump-off spot.

Rumours: Locals only.

Something Else? The wave can actually pack a pretty powerful punch, so it is worth showing some caution instead of the standard reckless abandon.

20.

Break Name: Bulli

Wave Description: Bulli is an uncrowded beach break option that can

N.S.W.

Royal National Park. Pic Stroh.

produce a good righthander at the southern end.
Best Conditions: 1.5m SE-NE swell, W-SW wind, low-mid tide.
Getting There: You take the Woonona turn off from the Highway and look north from Woonona. You can't miss it.
Rumours: Kane Palmer used to live here.
Something Else? Close by is a break called Banzai, which lives up to its heavy reputation.

21.
Break Name: Woonona
Wave Description: Woonona is Wollongong's answer to North Narrabeen. A real swell magnet that often produces long walling lefts and shorter punchy rights.
Best Conditions: 1 to 3m E-NE swell, SW-N wind, low-mid tide.
Getting There: Turn left off the highway at the Woonona sign.
Dangers: Heavy local crowd of rippers.
Rumours: This was the break that shaped the legendary Terry Richardson's style.
Something Else? This is the place to check if the swell is small.

22.
Break Name: Belambi
Wave Description: Belambi really is just a desperate southerly option when the swell and wind are out of control.
Best Conditions: Huge out of control S-NE swell, S wind, low-mid tide.
Getting There: Don't bother.
Dangers: Out of control mal riders and sewerage outlet.
Rumours: Robbie Page grew up here.
Something Else? There is a quality offshore bombie that can get good in big clean swells accompanied by light offshore W winds, if you're keen.

23.
Break Name: Corrimal
Wave Description: Corrimal's beach breaks can be worth a look in any small to medium swell.
Best Conditions: NE swell, NW wind, mid tide.
Getting There: If you take Towradgi Rd off the Princess Hwy, then walk north over the inlet you should be right on the money.

N.S.W.

Dangers: It's pretty safe.
Rumours: East Corrimal has a fickle reef set up that occasionally pumps.
Something Else? Ah, erhum, no!

24.
Break Name: Towradgi
Wave Description: Towradgi has a shifting peaky sand on reef set up, that can link-up with the inside banks.
Best Conditions: 1.6m NE-SE swell, NW-S wind, most tides.
Getting There: If you take the Towradgi Rd from the Princess Hwy, you're there!
Dangers: Exposed rocks.
Rumours: Zilcho.
Something Else? To the south, Fairy Meadow can produce some decent beach breaks. There is also a classic wave off the coast of Port Kembla, called Port Reef (amazingly!) that is worthwhile checking out.

25.
Break Name: Wollongong
Wave Description: Wollongong has 2 main beaches, north and south beach. North Beach can be fun in peaky NE swell or larger S swell.
Best Conditions: North Beach is best in peaky 1-1.5m NE swell, SW wind. South Beach is best again in NE swell, N wind, most tides.
Getting There: The highway takes you straight into Wollongong, then its a matter of heading east to the beach. Follow your nose.
Dangers: Swimmers, flags, clubbies.
Rumours: There used to be heaps of fights over waves, not exactly what you want from a relaxing surf.
Something Else? North beach is protected from S winds. South beach offers great NE wind protection.

Sandon Point. Pic Stroh.

N.S.W.

GENERAL INFORMATION

BONDI

Where To Stay:
There is no shortage of variety here to suit all budgets starting from $15.00 per night per person in dormitory style, Try: Nomads Backpackers (on the beachfront), Bondi Beach. Ph (02) 9130 1366. Thelellan Lodge, Bondi Beach. Ph (02) 9130 5333 located 2 mins walk from the beach. Rooms start at $35.00
The Alice Motel is $65.00 per single per night offering some Ocean views, 5 minutes walk from the beach. Ph (02) 91305231.
For Honeymooners or lovers wanting to splurge, try the Swiss Grand Hotel, formerly the Ramada on the corner of Campbell Parade & Beach Road where a standard suite will cost you $220 per night or $260 with an ocean view. Ph (02) 9365 5666.

Where To Eat:
Bondi is virtually the cosmopolitan café, restaurant, take out and ice-cream centre of Sydney. Here are some tips:
No name restaurants, located next door to the Pavilion in the old Regis Hotel. Cheap pasta, schnitzels and salads are the go here.
Red Kite café located in Campbell parade has cheap vego dishes and fresh juices.
Montezuma's Mexican located in Campbell Parade is always a good bet.
The infamous Lamrock café located on Campbell Parade is the yuppie hangout. Good if you're into people watching but you pay the price, very expensive.

Where To Party:
The Pavilion, Pool Hall upstairs, Bands and Babes 5-6 nights a week. Surf vids most nights.
Bondi Hotel, disco and beer garden on beachfront.
The Icebergs at Sth Bondi, great view, cheap beer.

North Bondi RSL, again cheap drinks and free movies on the big screen.
For more hardcore dance fans, catch the 380 from the beach to the popular nightclub strip on Oxford St and ask for places like: The Q Bar, Byblos and Mr Goodbar.
(Look out for and pick up 3D Magazine, Large, Revolver or the Drum Media in most cool pubs, clubs and street stores for information on what's going down, either band wise, or in the dance underworld.)

Flat Day Fun:
For 24hour surf reports call Dial-a-Wave on 1900 922 323, you never know, there may be a wave somewhere.
Good vert skate ramp and mini ramp on beachfront, movies at Bondi Junction, people watching on the promenade (there are freaks everywhere) or too cool café hanging.

Secret Spot
Right in the corner at north Bondi, when the flags are down for the late in summer, or any time in winter at high tide in a medium swell. There can be a sneaky uncrowded left and right bank if you're lucky.

Best Months
Generally from April to September is least crowded, although Bondi can be good in summer because it's protected from the predominant north-east sea breezes. Crowds are manic though.

CRONULLA

Where To Stay:
Cronulla Caravan Park. Ph (02) 9523 4099. On site vans from $30.
North Cronulla Hotel, cnr Kingsway and Elouera Rd. Ph (02) 9523 6866. Singles from $45 (includes breakfast).
Cronulla Motor Inn, 85 The Kingsway. Ph (02) 9523 6800. Singles from $60
Rydges, Cronulla Beach. Ph (02) 9527 3100. Rooms from $180.

Where To Eat:

N.S.W.

The Wholesome Café, vegetarian with an Italian twist.
Voodoo Lounge, Pasta and Pizza.
Bachus, upmarket pasta.
Nulla Nulla Café, juices, coffee and light foods.
The Haven, burgers and shakes.
Cronulla Pie Shop.
These are all located in, or just off, Cronulla Mall.

Where To Party:
North Cronulla Hotel, Fri,Sat,Sun nights.
Biggles Night Club, disco for 25's and over.
Daves Place in the Tarren Point Hotel, disco for 18 - 25 years.
Carmens Night Club Miranda, disco for 18 - 30 years.
Carringbah Inn Coyotes, disco Thurs, and Sat nights are live band night.
Cronulla RSL or Cronulla Leagues Club for cheap drinks.

Flat Day Fun:
Westfield Miranda Shopping Mall. The so called biggest shopping mall in the southern hemisphere (shops, movies, timezone, people watching).
Cronulla cinema.
Vertx Indoor Skate Park, Tarren Point.
Tarren Point Go Karts or Tarren Point Indoor Soccer and Cricket Centre.
Golf courses in the district.

Secret Spot
Suck Rock near Voodoo or Sandshoes reef, south from Windy Point.
There is a semi secret spot in between Bronte and Coogee called Thompson's Bay. It's a super sucky left and right reef break that requires off shore winds and medium sized swells. High tide only and experienced crew need only investigate. (Bronte is also making a belated charge on the café scene, if you're that way inclined.)

Best Months
Definitely from March through to September.

ROYAL NATIONAL PARK

Beauty and the beast, Port Kembla. Pic Mark Newsham.

Where To Stay:
Free camping permitted in the gully behind North Era beach, tents only, no facilities.
YHA, Garie Beach. Ph (02) 9261 1111. Beds are $7, but bookings are essential, as you need to pick the key up in Sydney.

Where To Eat:
There is only one small kiosk at Garie Beach which is only open weekends or holiday periods. Bring a picnic lunch if you want to surf all day.

Where To Party:
You're limited to small sensible campfires except of course in the instance of a total ban which often occurs in summer (bring your guitar, cards, chess set, ghetto blaster and batteries).

Flat Day Fun:
Great fishing, nature walks, river boats for hire up towards Otford, horse riding at Otford, ferry rides from Bundeena to Cronulla.

Secret Spot
There are a couple of interesting reef breaks north from Garie but south east from Bundeena. There are also one or two other spots in close vicinity to Burning Palms. Enough said!

Best Months
The beach breaks at Garie, Era etc, tend to be best from Christmas through to about June when there is an abundance of north east swells and winds. However Garie can be good all year if the big winter swells don't erode the sandbanks for spring.

WOLLONGONG

Where To Stay:
Corrimal Beach caravan park. Ph (02) 4285 5688.
Bulli Caravan Park. Ph (02) 4285 5677. Both these parks are council run and have sites from $15.
Keiraleagh House. Ph (02) 4228 6765. Dorm beds from $15.

Harp Hotel. Ph (02) 4229 1333. Rooms from $40, but hey, you do get your own TV and a bathroom.

Where To Eat:
Wollongong is a multi-cultural city, there is an abundance of cafés and restaurants on Keira St, in the CBD. Particularly good thai and italian restaurants. For surfer's on Lawrence Hargrave Drive, look out for the Dolphin café on top of the hill at Coalcliff, (great view and a variety of healthy food) or Ruby's at Stanwell Park and Bulli.

Where To Party:
Depending on what your looking for, Wollongong caters for most tastes. The Oxford Hotel in Crown St, Wollongong, showcases local alternative guitar bands. Waves Nightclub is kind of a beer barn/disco on Saturday nights, sometimes big bands play there too. Wollongong Uni bar has alternative bands; The Beach Bistro at the Novotel has a disco on Wed, Fri and Sun nights. There are many other pubs, clubs etc. in town and along the coastline.

Flat Day Fun:
Movies, pinnie parlours, golf courses, hang gliding at Stanwell Tops.

Secret Spot:
Puccky's can be a worthwhile righthand reefbreak, into the creek entrance just to the north of North Beach Wollongong. South Pipe or Shitties, as its more affectionately known, is half way along south beach near the golf course. It ropes in any north-east swell. At Port Kembla/Coal loader there are some sheltered southerly options near the groins.

N.S.W.

SECTION INFORMATION

Local Shapers
Vudu Surfboards - Stuart Darcy (Caringbah). Ph (02) 9527 4627.
Byrne Surboards - Phil Byrne (Wollongong). Ph (02) 4226 9372.
Skipp Surfboards - John Skipp

North beach at Woollongong. Pic Mark Newsham.

(Wollongong). Ph (02) 4228 8878.
Carabine Surf Designs - Mick Carabine
(Wollongong). Ph (02) 4229 9462.
Force 9 - Stuart Patterson (Cronulla). Ph
(02) 9526 1007.

Best Months
Because this is such a large area, we
included the best times to score these
killer places in their own sections, so flip
back a couple of pages and check out
when you should go.

Secret Spot
Same as above.

Quick Tips
This is a huge area in terms of surf
potential. It will take you a long time to
explore these places. Best idea is to target
an area that suits you and work that for
awhile. No point heading into Sydney for
a look at the beaches there, when all you
really want is to kick back in natures
arms and enjoy. Head to Royal National
Park instead. When surfing this whole

area, remember the size of the surfing
population here and how you should
handle this. It will be rare for you to get
waves to yourself, so be prepared to
show a great deal of respect, as this will
make life a little more enjoyable.

Getting There
Call (02) 4226 1022 for details of buses
that will get you most places. The other
option is through the metropolitan train
system. Ph 13 15 00 for all rail, bus and
ferry enquires. To reach The Royal
National Park other than driving catch a
train to Cronulla then a ferry to Bundeena
(in the park boundaries) Ph (02) 9523
2990. The coastal walk is about 26kms,
but it will give you the best idea of the
breaks. It is a really beautiful walk as
well. Probably overnight. Call the visitors
centre on (02) 9542 0648.

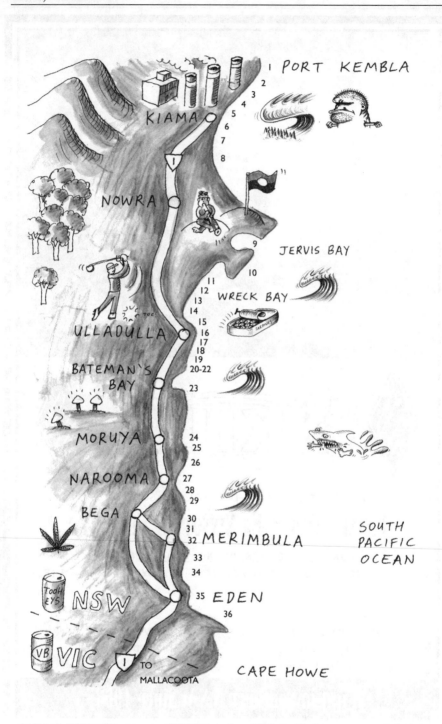

PORT KEMBLA

KIAMA

NOWRA

JERVIS BAY

ULLADULLA

WRECK BAY

BATEMAN'S BAY

MORUYA

NAROOMA

BEGA

MERIMBULA

SOUTH PACIFIC OCEAN

EDEN

NSW

VIC

TO MALLACOOTA

CAPE HOWE

N.S.W.

Tall Tales

As the sun slipped below the distant horizon, we pulled the car into the only local tavern. The bar was alive with fish stories and atmospheric smoke. We nodded knowingly about the size of the Salmon off the rocks and drank our beers.

Shellharbour moments before detonation. Pic Mark Newsham.

The South Coast

The Great Escape

N.S.W.

Traditionally it was the north which was the allure of the suburban surfers of Sydney. South was cold, inhospitable and unknown. Much of this still remains, as does the power of the ocean. Travellers have found heavy reef breaks and perfect beaches in amongst the litany of coves and bays, but that's not all. A different attitude prevails here, as many of the residents distance themselves from the rigours of city living. There is no interest in huge shopping malls, as locals would still search out their favourite stores, shunning the lure of the glitz and glamour. This is their secret though, and although developers want them, they aren't interested. There are still many unexplored areas that will provide a wealth of surfing opportunities for adventurers and this, my friends, is enough.

1.
Break Name: Windang Island.
Wave Description: A serious lefthand wave that spits barrels down the reef.
Best Conditions: NE-SE swell, NE-NW wind, mid-low tide.
Getting There: If you take the road south from Port Kembla you will run straight into it. The break is at the entrance to Lake Illawarra
Dangers: Well, the fact that the wave can handle swells up to 5 metres makes it extremely dangerous. Added to the fact that it is at the entrance to a river. You shouldn't be surfing here at dawn or dusk.
Rumours: There is a break on the northern side of the Island called Sharkie's.
Something Else? Heed the warnings of this place. Power, shallow reef and sharks. Is that enough?

2.
Break Name: Cowries / Shellharbour
Wave Description: A hollow reef break that has some real power.

Best Conditions: E-SE swell, SW wind, mid-high tide.
Getting There: Keep following the road south and you will drive straight in. This break is at the northern end of the bay.
Dangers: It breaks over a shallow rock ledge. This is enough to make the Danger category.
Rumours: The southern end houses a couple of quality breaks, with lefts and rights.
Something Else? The left is called Shatters due to its insatiable appetite for fibreglass.

3.
Break Name: The Farm
Wave Description: Righthand point and beach break.
Best Conditions: SE swell, NW-W wind, mid-high tide.
Getting There: Turn into Buckleys Road off Shellharbour Road and follow it until you see the surf.
Dangers: As the popularity grew of this place so to did the negative aspects. Cars are starting to get broken into and the

Mystics. Pic Steve Conti.

waves are far more populated.
Rumours: The road leading into The
Farm looks deceiving and will give the
appearance that you are not driving to a
beach.
Something Else? This whole area is still
very beautiful, but much has changed
since the early days of its discovery. Jack
Eden has captured some of those magic
moments. The photos are available in
some of the surf shops. If not, most will
have some hanging on the walls so you
can see the differences.

4.
Break Name: Mystics
Wave Description: A lefthand wave that
bounces off the cliff and forms a peaky
takeoff.
Best Conditions: NE swell, NW-W wind,
mid tide.
Getting There: Follow the road that
takes you to The Farm but keep going
south.
Dangers: A shallow reef break that likes
human flesh.
Rumours: Further south still you may
find a wave called Boneyards. Worth the
search.
Something Else? It is worthwhile taking
this road as it gives you a full
appreciation of how many nooks and
crannies can host waves on their day.

5.
Break Name: Bombo
Wave Description: Depending on the
swell you can get good sandbanks at the
north or south ends of the beach.
Best Conditions: Any swell, SW-NW
wind, mid tide.
Getting There: The road overlooks the
break so it is pretty hard to miss.
Dangers: As the beach picks up so much
swell, there are often rips and
undercurrents.
Rumours: The locals can get pretty
heavy, as there are always people here
on good swells, due to its proximity to
the road.

Something Else? It can often offer
protection from the prevailing winds.

6.
Break Name: The Pool
Wave Description: A lefthander off the
rocks.
Best Conditions: NE-SE swell, SW-W
wind, low-mid tide.
Getting There: Right next to the
Blowhole, not hard to find.
Dangers: When the swell gets big, the
takeoffs can get very vertical.
Rumours: There is another grinding
lefthander just south called The Wedge.
Something Else? There is a great pub in
town to sooth those weary arms.

7.
Break Name: Werri Beach
Wave Description: A selection of beachbreaks with a north and south end point.
Best Conditions: NE swell, N-NE wind,
low tide.
Getting There: Turn into Bridge Road off
Fern Street and follow that until you see
the surf.
Dangers: The point breaks should only
be surfed by the experienced.
Rumours: The southern end can have
some classy righthand barrels off the point.
Something Else? This wave has been the
breeding ground for some of Australia's
talented surfers. Todd Prestage is one of
those talents who displays his skills here
as often as possible.

8.
Break Name: Black Point
Wave Description: A lefthand point
break, which can get surprisingly good.
Best Conditions: SE swell, NW-N wind,
mid-high tide.
Getting There: Follow Fern Street until
you come over the hill and see the
beach. There are a number of different
places to access the point.
Dangers: When the swells hit, the rips
can be extremely dangerous, as well as
the hold-downs.

N.S.W.

Rumours: On the northern side of the point there are several other reef breaks that are worth checking out.

Something Else? To the south, Seven Mile Beach has become popular with the windsurfers, but there are also some good waves... very occasionally.

9.
Break Name: Plantation Point / Jervis Bay.

Wave Description: An extremely tasty righthander when the swell is big enough.

Best Conditions: Huge SE-E swell, SW wind, mid-high tide.

Getting There: Head towards Huskisson off the Hwy, then to Vincentia.

Dangers: Not too many around here.

Rumours: This is not the only place to look if the swell is huge. Try Huskisson at the mouth of the Moona Moona Creek. It can have amazing righthanders.

Something Else? There is a great hotel in town that has surprisingly good nightlife.

10.
Break Name: Aussie Pipe / Summercloud Cove

Wave Description: A screaming, hollow and heavy lefthanded tube. The right can get good as well.

Best Conditions: SE-S swell, NW-E wind, mid tide.

Getting There: If you take the signs to Jervis Bay, then The Wreck or Summercloud Cove, you will get to a carpark. From there it is a 10 minute scramble to the point.

Dangers: An extremely heavy wave and patriotic locals.

Rumours: A couple of coves south is a place called Caves Beach which can have some great beach breaks. Try here when Pipe is too packed or not doing its thing

Something Else? The Aboriginal community that live overlooking this special place have a real affiliation with this area. Many of the kids surf now, with a real sense of pride because they live in such a beautiful region. The kids have been encouraged to surf by the youth workers, as they believe, for their people, it is a spiritual place, and for everyone.

11.
Break Name: Sussex Inlet

Wave Description: A variety of beach breaks and a reef closeby.

Best Conditions: S-SE swell, W-N winds, Most tides.

Getting There: Take the turnoff from the Hwy and head for either Bherwerre Beach or Cudmirrah Beach.

Dangers: Pretty safe actually.

Rumours: There is a reef closeby called Conneeley's Reef which can have lefts and rights.

Something Else? This area is a bit of a labyrinth of roads, but keep exploring as there are some great spots.

12.
Break Name: Bendalong Beach

Wave Description: A long beach that has a north and south point.

Best Conditions: E-SE swell, W-N wind, mid tide.

Getting There: Follow Bendalong Road until you see the caravan park and the beach is directly opposite.

Dangers: It can get crowded in the summer holidays and on weekends.

Rumours: This picks up all available swell, so it is a great summer break.

Something Else? There are several other breaks in Bendalong starting with the boat ramp and Flatrock at North Bendalong.

13.
Break Name: Green Island

Wave Description: A long, peeling lefthander over sharp reef.

Best Conditions: NE-SE swell, N-NW wind, mid tide.

Getting There: You need to get onto Cunjurong Street in Manyana and follow that. It is at the mouth of Lake Conjola.

Dale Walker, Werri Inlet. Pic Steve Conti.

Dangers: The sea urchins have cleverly disguised themselves under the green seaweed awaiting the unsuspecting surfer. Luckily that won't be you.
Rumours: When paddling out to the reef at Green Island the first deep area of water is a shark pit.
Something Else? To the left of Green Island there are quality breaks that are worthwhile investigating.

14.
Break Name: Golf Course Reef
Wave Description: A heavy lefthand wave that gets better as it gets bigger. It breaks over a shallow reef.
Best Conditions: SE-NE swell, W wind, mid tide.
Getting There: Turn into Golf Avenue off the Princes Highway and then into the road that runs through the golf course and follow it to the end.
Dangers: Low tide can reveal some rocks that appear suddenly in the wave
Rumours: There is a righthand reef break just south of the main break which can

be as good. It also has a left off it that is extremely fast, but makeable.
Something Else? The paddle can be long and arduous, especially on larger days.

15.
Break Name: Mollymook Beach
Wave Description: A selection of beach breaks that can pack a punch.
Best Conditions: E-SE swell, N-W wind, low-mid tide.
Getting There: Follow Golf Avenue until you see the beach. It is characterised by the Golf Club at the southern end.
Rumours: The best waves can often be found in the middle of the beach as it is the most consistent.
Something Else? There are many breaks that are closeby, it's just a matter of looking. A good tip is to follow the road to the end and all will be revealed.

16.
Break Name: Ulladulla Bommie
Wave Description: A heavy righthand

N.S.W.

reef that is more than willing to give you a hiding. There is sometimes a lefthander as well.

Best Conditions: S swell, NE wind, mid tide.

Getting There: Turn off the Princes Highway onto Warden Head Road, (where the lighthouse is) and there you will find a little car park on the right.

Dangers: The wave twists and warps over boils making it hard for anyone other than the very experienced.

Rumours: This could be the place where the Billabong Challenge is held on June 7, 1999.

Something Else? Ulladulla has been a target for travelling surfers looking for solid power, for many years now. This has made many of the locals jaded and therefore quite aggressive. Just be friendly though, and it will be fine.

17.
Break Name: Rennies Beach.
Wave Description: A selection of beach and reef breaks.
Best Conditions: S-E swell, NW-NE winds, most tides.
Getting There: Just south of the bombie. Follow the sign to the namesake.
Dangers: This beach picks up much of the available swell and is very open. This causes strong rips and undercurrents.
Rumours: The author of this book retains the same surname of this classy wave. Surely a tribute.
Something Else? Just south of here there is a sweet little lefthand barrel called Racecourse. It shouldn't be too hard to find as there is a creek named after it.

18.
Break Name: Dolphin Point
Wave Description: An excellent lefthander that breaks over a shallow reef.
Best Conditions: NE-E swell, W-SW wind, low-mid tide.
Getting There: Take the turnoff after Burrill Lake.
Dangers: The wave is very changeable

and can often warp unexpectadly.

Rumours: There are some worthwhile beach breaks just north of here.

Something Else? Quiksilver have just started running their Boardriderz events here again after there was much unrest with the locals. They keep the contest pretty low key now. Even having the Presso night at the Caravan Park.

19.
Break Name: Bawley Point
Wave Description: A scary, free-fall, righthand point break.
Best Conditions: SE-NE swell, S-SW wind, mid tide.
Getting There: Take the turn at Termeil for the namesake.
Dangers: The takeoff is seriously horrendous, with an equally challenging wave.
Rumours: The takeoff doesn't get any less intense as the size drops. It just doesn't hurt as much.
Something Else? There is a wave that is just inside this break called Guillotines. This has a heavier takeoff even though it is slightly protected from the full brunt of the swell. The wave can handle swell of up to 4 metres.

20.
Break Name: Depot Beach
Wave Description: A selection of beach breaks that can get excellent.
Best Conditions: NE-SE swell, W wind, most tides.
Getting There: Take the Durras North Rd at East Lynne, north of Point Upright.
Dangers: The isolation is not really a danger. Infact the danger is losing this isolation
Rumours: There are plenty of breaks that lie to the south that are worth walking into. The landscape is really spectacular and well worth the time.
Something Else? Plan to spend some time camping here as it is very worthwhile. You will probably get some waves as well.

N.S.W.

21.
Break Name: Durras North
Wave Description: A selection of lefts and rights that provide an excellent ride.
Best Conditions: NE-SE swell, NW-SW wind, mid-high tide.
Getting There: Take the turnoff from the Hwy.
Dangers: There can be some heavy rip action due to the reef that runs directly out from the beach.
Rumours: Look out for Beagle Bay.
Something Else? The actual township of Durras has a host of great waves. You can stay at the cool little Caravan Park there as well.

22.
Break Name: Malua Bay.
Wave Description: A good lefthander at the northern end of the bay.
Best Conditions: E-SE swell, W-SE wind, mid tide.
Getting There: Take the signs from Batemans Bay. It's about 10 minutes.
Dangers: The rocks can be a bit of a hazard, but nothing compared to some of the other breaks.
Rumours: Look for Mackenzies Beach and Rosedale Beach.
Something Else? There are several other little bays to the south which can hold good waves.

23.
Break Name: Broulee Island/Pink Rocks.
Wave Description: A fairly steep take off, but the rest is a cakewalk.
Best Conditions: Massive NE swell, S-SW wind, mid-high tide.
Getting There: You have to paddle to the Island (not far) then head to the NE corner. There you will meet your maker. It is Broulee of course.
Dangers: The jump off spot and take off are your only worries.
Rumours: Excellent spot to check if it is out of control elsewhere.
Something Else? There are several bays just north of here worth checking on BIG days.

The dream lineup. Pic Simons

24.
Break Name: The Wall / Moruya
Wave Description: A great fun righthander that is protected from the prevailing winds.
Best Conditions: NE-SE swell, W-SW wind, mid tide.
Getting There: Take the turnoff to Moruya Heads, then follow your nose.
Dangers: The break can have a strong rip down the breakwall, which is more of a benefit than anything.
Rumours: There is a good lefthander known as the Entrance.
Something Else? You can't imagine that sharks haven't thought of this place. With a rivermouth and great fishing, you just wouldn't surf at dawn or dusk.

25.
Break Name: Congo.
Wave Description: A selection of everything. From beaches to long reef breaks.
Best Conditions: SE swell, SW-W wind, most tides.
Getting There: Take the turnoff from the Hwy, clearly marked.
Dangers: The danger that this place will keep changing.
Rumours: Dolphins are often found on the southern beaches.
Something Else? This is a beautiful spot to stay in the campgrounds. During winter it is almost deserted at the camp, but don't expect the same treatment in summer. It is normally packed. Bring your rod as the campground is flanked by a stream full of fish. Generally a beautiful area. One of my favourites.

26.
Break Name: Kianga
Wave Description: A surprisingly hollow and heavy righthander off a breakwall.
Best Conditions: NE-S swell, SW-W wind, low-mid tide.
Getting There: Take the turnoff just before you hit Narooma.
Dangers: The rip can be quite strong

pulling you out of position. The wave can throw a long way, over extremely shallow banks.
Rumours: There are waves along the beach that can get as good.
Something Else? Check the other side of the point as well, as it could be good.

27.
Break Name: Narooma Breakwall.
Wave Description: Righthanders that can get extremely fun.
Best Conditions: NE-SE swell, NW-SW wind, low-mid tide.
Getting There: If you can't find this, you really don't deserve to be a surfer.
Dangers: Pretty placid.
Rumours: There is a great lookout at the southern end of the town that is worth checking as it gives you a good perspective of the coast.
Something Else? The fishing here is magnificent. You can expect a good feed of Blackfish off nothing more than seaweed on a hook. Try the fluro green stuff first.

28.
Break Name: Mystery Bay
Wave Description: A selection of lefts and rights that break over sand.
Best Conditions: NE-S swell, SW-NW wind, most tides.
Getting There: Take the turnoff from the Hwy, 9kms south of Narooma.
Dangers: That this place will start getting crowded.
Rumours: There are many bays in this area that can have excellent waves, but it requires large swell.
Something Else? The breaks offer great protection from the summer north-easterlies.

29.
Break Name: Camel Rock
Wave Description: A solid lefthand beach break, that can also provide a right as well.
Best Conditions: NE swell, NE-W wind, most tides.

Jeremy Harboc, deep inside Aussie Pipe. Pic Mark Newsham.

Getting There: Opposite Wallaga Lake, 6kms north of Bermagui.
Dangers: Not too many unless you take on the powerful right, in which case watch out for the shallow banks.
Rumours: Another area that is protected from the summer onshores.
Something Else? Bermagui is a fishing Mecca and worth checking to see what you might be missing.

30.
Break Name: Mimosa Rocks National Park
Wave Description: A large variety of reef and beach breaks.
Best Conditions: NE-S swell, SW-NW wind, low-mid tide.
Getting There: There are several access roads that all lead to the ocean. The National Park is clearly marked. It wouldn't be fair to pinpoint you right on the best breaks. Needless to say, if I did, I may never be able to surf these places again. Try your luck, enjoy your adventure.

Dangers: It can get quite powerful here, and you are a fair way from medical help.
Rumours: This place generally picks up a foot and a half more, than the surrounding towns.
Something Else? The area is very beautiful and worth checking out for nature's sake.

31.
Break Name: Tathra
Wave Description: A series of beach breaks, with a lefthand break at the rivermouth.
Best Conditions: NE-S swell, NW-SW wind, low-mid tide.
Getting There: About 20 minutes north of Merimbula, on the coast Hwy.
Dangers: Pretty mellow, except for the rivermouth.
Rumours: If this place is going off, you can be pretty sure that there are other spots that will be better.
Something Else? Nup.

N.S.W.

32.
Break Name: Merimbula Bar.
Wave Description: One of Australia's classic lefthanders, although extremely fickle.
Best Conditions: Giant S-SE swell, NW-NE wind, low-mid tide.
Getting There: For the best view, head to the Aquarium. You will have no trouble finding it, believe me.
Dangers: Just the crowds when it does get good. You also have to contend with surf skis and Mals.
Rumours: When this gets swell, it can break up to 300 metres of perfection.
Something Else? Check on the northern side of the headland as there is often more swell there. It is also a pretty cool place just to chill out.

33.
Break Name: Pambula rivermouth
Wave Description: One of the most hollow righthanders available.
Best Conditions: Huge NE-E swell, S-SW wind, low tide.
Getting There: Just follow the signs to the town, then follow your nose to the beach. Too easy!
Dangers: It is pretty hard to fathom the perfection of this place without seeing it. It is a hollow beast which makes it extremely hard to make the barrel.
Rumours: The wave has been known to hold 10 second tubes which are near impossible to make.
Something Else? Check out the rope swing over the hole just near the rivermouth. The hole is actually a breeding ground for sharks at certain times of the year. At other times it can be a blast.

34.
Break Name: Leonards Island / Ben Boyd National Park (northern end)
Wave Description: A quick and punchy righthand point break.
Best Conditions: NE-E swell, W-S wind, mid tide.

Getting There: Just north of Eden about 5kms.
Dangers: The shallow reef covered by urchins is enough.
Rumours: There are several other breaks in this area that can produce quality waves.
Something Else? There is excellent fishing and diving here on flat days.

35.
Break Name: Eden
Wave Description: A selection of beach breaks, with the southern end being the best.
Best Conditions: SE swell, NW-SW wind, mid tide.
Getting There: Just follow your nose.
Dangers: Pretty safe actually.
Rumours: Not really.
Something Else? The camp ground is a great place to stay, waiting, waiting, for that damn swell.

36.
Break Name: Saltwater / Ben Boyd National Park (southern end)
Wave Description: A classic righthand break, that can handle real swell.
Best Conditions: S-SE swell, NW-SW swell, lower tides.
Getting There: Follow the old logging road south from Eden for about 30kms.
Dangers: This place can handle size up to 4 metres.
Rumours: There is limitless potential in this stretch of coastline, it is just a matter of exploring.
Something Else? South of here is Nadgee Nature Reserve. It is often blown out or doesn't have adequate sand banks, but it is absolutely beautiful. The fishing is magnificent, especially at Little River. This is defiantly worth visiting, as Kangaroos, damn big ones too, bound around, dodging giant Goannas. This place is cool.

N.S.W.

GENERAL INFORMATION

KIAMA / GERRINGONG

Where To Stay

Blowhole Point Holiday Park, Lighthouse Road. Ph (02) 4232 2707. Sites from $12. Fantastic location.

East Van Park, East Beach. Ph (02) 4232 2124. Sites from $12.

YHA Gerringong. Ph (02) 4234 1249. Beds from $13.

Werri Beach Holiday Park, Gerringong. Ph (02) 4234 1285. Sites from $15.

Where To Eat

Stella's Italian Pizza Restaurant, good wholesome pizzas.

Ritzy Gritz New Mexican Grill. Good food, but weird place.

Harbourside Brighton Restaurant, ah for the romantics in us all.

Gerroa Boat Fisherman's Club.

Where To Party

Kiama Leagues Club is usually your best bet.

The local Hotel generally has bands on a Saturday night and can get pretty rowdy.

Gerringong Hotel, Cnr Belinda and Campbell Streets. Ph (02) 4232 1451.

Flat Day Fun

Kiama Blowhole is definitely worth seeing, even if you have seen every damn blowhole on the tourist trail.

The fishing can be good off the beaches, not as fruitful as further south though.

Kiama Aquatic Centre. Ph (02) 4232 1877.

Jamberoo Fun and Recreation Park. Ph (02) 4236 0114. For the kids... in all of us.

ULLADULLA

Where To Stay

South Coast Backpackers. Ph (02) 4454 0500. Beds from $15.

Beach Haven Caravan Park. Ph (02) 4455 2110. Sites from $10.

Mollymook Caravan Park. Ph (02) 4455 1939. Sites from $12.

Durras Lake North Caravan Park. Ph (02) 4478 6072. Has onsite vans for backpackers for $10. It is a lovely spot too.

Where To Eat

The Blue Marlin has reasonably priced counter meals.

Ulladulla Chinese Restaurant, is your very standard oriental cuisine.

Mollymook Golf Club, has a great atmosphere and a stunning view.

Where To Party

The Blue Marlin Hotel has some really good bands. Most people then go to the niteclub across the way.

Mollymook Golf Club, Golf Rd. During summer this place can have a good atmosphere.

Flat Day Fun

There is a fantastic skate park that has so much variation, set in the bush, it's killer.

Ulladulla Boat Charters and Dive Shop. Ph (02) 4455 5303.

The golf course is pretty spectacular, especially if it is followed by a few ambers.

NAROOMA/MERIMBULA/EDEN

Where To Stay:

One of the best campsites is at Congo, just north of Narooma. It is free usually, just don't go in the height of summer.

YHA Blue Water Lodge. Ph (02) 4476 4440. Beds from $15. The staff are really friendly and give you heaps of info on activities etc.

Try the camping in Mimosa Rocks as well. Very spectacular and you definitely feel like you have got away from it all.

YHA, Wandarrah Lodge, Merimbula. Ph (02) 6495 3503. Beds from $15. The location is really close to the surf as well.

Try the camping at Nadgee Nature Reserve, it's free.

There is a great campsite at Eden but try the Australiasia Hotel first. Ph (02) 6496 1600.

N.S.W.

South Coast slot. Pic. Mark Newsham.

Where To Party:
Merimbula is your best for drinking options, with several pubs and a niteclub in summer. Nothing too spectacular, but can be bloody funny. There are of course other pubs in the other towns, but I really wouldn't call them party venues.

SECTION DESCRIPTION

Local Shapers
Southerly Change - Michael Mackie (Ulladulla). See Totally Board for details.
South Coast Lonboards - Brian Kellway (Ulladulla) Ph (02) 4455 3313.
Mogrel Surfboards - Vern Jackson (Ulladulla) Ph (02) 4455 1658.
Wave Creation - Paul Robinson (Gerringong) Ph (02) 4234 1931.

Best Months
The winter months, May to September are your only real chance of scoring these areas. Summer is a heap of fun, but not for the wave hungry traveller.

Secret Spot
North of Mollymook and south of Lake Conjola you can find some satisfying, lonesome breaks.

Where To Eat:
Narooma has one of the best bakeries around. It is on the hill just south of town. Very small, but super friendly staff and killer pastries.

The Hotel on top of the hill at Tathra has one of the best low-key venues for a Pub. Grand views, great priced counter meals and classic characters.

Merimbula has a variety of different pizza and other takeaway type meals. The Pub overlooking the water is a great choice for fresh seafood.

If you want to indulge in the fantastic taste of fresh oysters, you need look no further as this is the hub. You can buy great seafood from the markets. Try Pambula too.

There are some great seafood restaurants in Eden. Try the one on the Wharf for reasonable prices and great seafood.

Quick Tips
South of Ulladulla the swell drops off dramatically. It seems to be far more fickle in the Merimbula region. Narooma seems to get a little more swell than the surrounding areas and has plenty of protection from the wind. Fairly uncrowded as well. Merimbula is a place you need to plan a little if you are thinking of surfing here. Keep checking the weather conditions as it requires large swells to make it worthwhile. It is a beautiful region to camp in but the waves are a little more elusive than scenic campgrounds.

Getting There
Try Greyhound Pioneer on 13 20 30. They have buses running from Sydney. Costs about $50 to Merimbula. The Sapphire Coast Express. Ph (02) 4473 5517 runs services to Melbourne.

Pioneer Motor Service. Ph (02) 4423 5233 has some excellent rates for a service between Eden and Sydney. Worthwhile checking it out.

Hitching is pretty good along this stretch, although there are several State forests that have a morbid history with missing hitchhikers. Like everywhere, though, you need to display the utmost caution if you are hitching. Although that is a little hard to do once you are in a stranger's car.

SURFING YARNS

Coastal Beer Halls

The thick aroma of smoke impacted on our lungs as soon as we pushed the doors aside. A toothless regular snarled while others cocked their heads slightly to see what cretins had entered their domain. Toothless Harry marched straight up to us, telling us that he could beat the shit out of everyone here, if he wanted to. At 5'4" and a beanpole appearance, no one took old Harry too seriously. In fact, the only reason he was in the pub, was courtesy of the new owners, of three months, who had lifted his 15 year ban. It seemed it wouldn't be long before he was just a shadow under the awning of The Victoria Hotel once more.

The Pick Up

We called it a night, though, when Jenette started telling us how she was more guy than girl. I couldn't help but ask what were the things that made her feel like this and why I was having this conversation. I realised the error of my ways when she started describing, in detail, the way she like to fart and burp. As I raised my hand to stop what was clearly a topic I needed to know nothing about, it was already too late, and we were told of things that still wake me in the middle of the night.

Stockists – area code 02:

This is a list of your local surf shops. They can help you with pretty much everything to do with surfing. They are also proud to be stockists of The Surfer's Travel Guide.

Aloha
1119 Pittwater Rd
Collaroy 2097
9971 4824

Aloha Surf
44 Pittwater Rd
Manly, 2095
9977 3777

Australian Surfer HQ
3/49 North Steyne Rd
Manly 2095
9977 7281

Australian Surfer HQ
96 The Esplanade
Terrigal 2260
4384 5472

Bay Action
14 Johnson St
Byron Bay, 2481
6685 7819

Boarderline surf 'n' skate
1/421 The Entrance Rd
Long Jetty 2261
4332 7175

Bombora Surf
Shop 1E Cooper St
Cessnock 2325
4990 7395

Beach Town Surf Centre
Shop 3/605 Ocean Drv
North Haven 2443
6559 8048

Beach Without Sand
1 Nth Avalon Rd
North Avalon 2107
9918 4402

Beachin Surf
262 Main Rd
Toukley 2263
4396 5159

Bondi Surf Co
Shop 2/ 72-76 Campbell Pde
Bondi 2026
9365 0870

Breakaway Surf Co
181 Pacific Hwy
Charlestown 2290
4943 2699

Byrne Surf Ski
115 Princess HWY
Fairy Meadow 2519
4226 1122

Coastal Curves
2/42 Bowra St
Nambucca Heads 2448
6568 6902

Coopers Surf
380 Hight St
Coffs Harbour 2450
6652 1782

Crescent Head Surf Co
Shop 1 Tavern Complex
Main St, Crescent Head 2440
6566 0550

Cronulla Original Surf Co
71-73 Cronulla St
Cronulla 2230
9523 0557

Dripping Wet Surf Co
Shop2/93-95 North Steyne Rd
Manly 2095
9977 3549

East Gosford Surf Shop
58 York St
East Gosford 2250
4324 8942

Emerald surf City
130 Cronulla St
Cronulla 2230
9527 4149

Extreme Surf & Ski
80 Market St
Wollongong 2500
4226 3145

Geffro's
Shop 405, Castle Towers
Shopping Centre
Castle Hill, 2154
9899 9537

Get Wet
Shop 14/Cascade Arcade,
Stockton St
Nelson Bay 2315
4981 4944

Graffiti Surf Designs
47 Donald St
Nelson Bay 2315
4981 3409

Hydro Surf
Shop 4/53 Pacific Drv
Port Macquarie 2444
6584 1477

Iguana Surfwear
195 Victoria St
Taree 2430
6551 3738

Insurf
98 terralong St
Kiama 2533
4233 1177

Jacks Surf
Shop 12/ The Galleria,
William St
Port Macquarie 2444
6584 2999

Kempsey Surf Shed
32 Forth St
Kempsey 2440
6563 1880

Line Up Surf
12B The Strand
Dee Why 2099
9971 8642

Littles Surf Centre
Shop 123 Market Place
Gosford 2250
4323 6600

Long Reef Sailboard & Surf
1012 Pittwater Rd
Collaroy 2097
9971 1212

Low Pressure Surf Co
Beach St
Tuncurry 2428
6555 8556

Merimbula Surf Shop
3 Princess Hwy
Merimbula 2548
6494 9294

Narooma Surf & Skate
30 Princess Hwy
Narooma 2546
4476 1422

Natural Necessity Surf Shop
opp Gerringong Town Hall
Gerringong 2534
4234 1636

Newport Beach Surf House
303 Barenjoey Rd
Newport 2106
9997 8833

Offshore Surf Shop
68 Vulacan St
Moruya 2537
4474 4350

Pacific Dreams
7 Darby St
Newcastle 2300
4926 3355

Pure Sea
108 Cronulla St
Cronulla 2230
9523 8664

Rip Curl
Cnr Gordon & High Streets
Coffs Harbour 2450
6652 6369

N.S.W.

Saltwater Wine
Cnr Manning & Albert
Streets
Taree 2430
6552 3778

Saltwater Wine
Shop5/Central Shopping
Centre
Port Macquarie 2444
6584 1600

Skipp Surf
24 Flinder St
Nth Wollongong 2500
4228 8878

Slimes Surf 'n' Skate
Shop 47T/ Erina Fair
Erina 2250
4365 4411

Southern Man
136 Princess Hwy
Ulladulla 2539
4454 0343

Surf Dive 'n' Ski
Shop 18 Warringah Mall
Brookvale 2100
9905 4119

Surf Dive 'n' Ski
213 Oxford St
Bondi Junction, 2022
9387 2912

Surf Dive 'n' Ski
Shop G4 Chatswood
Chase
Chatswood 2067
9419 8374

Surf Dive 'n' Ski
Shop 127 Darling Harbour
Sydney, 2000
9281 4040

Surf Dive 'n' Ski
Shop 2042 Westfield
Miranda
Miranda 2228
9524 1472

Surf Dive 'n' Ski
Shop 2119 Westfield
Parramatta
Parramatta 2150
9687 1411

Surf Dive 'n' Ski
1st Floor Argyle Centre,
Argyle St
Sydney 2000
9251 5552

Surf Dive 'n' Ski
462-464 George St
Sydney 2000
9267 3408

Surf Dive 'n' Ski
Shop 1120-22 Westfield
Tuggerah
Tuggerah 2259
4352 1466

Surf Dive 'n' Ski
Shop 29-30 Crown Central
Wollongong 2500
4226 9300

Surf Dive 'n' Ski
1st Floor Arvavle Centre
The Rocks 2000
9251 5552

Surfection
94 Pittwater Rd
Manly 2095
9977 4777

Surfection
1729 Pittwater Rd
Mona Vale 2103
9999 3727

Surfection
651 Pittwater Rd
Dee Why 2099
9971 8144

Surfection
74-78 The Corso
Manly 2095
9977 6955

Surfection
308 Oxford St
Wollahra
9387 1413

Surfection
205 Oxford St
Bondi Junction 2022
9386 0400

Surfers Choice
473 The Entrance Rd
Long Jetty 2261
4334 6532

Surfworld
250 Coogee Bay Rd
Cogee 2034
9664 1293

The Surf Shop
Shop 8 / Fountain Plaza
Karalta Rd, Erina 2250
4365 1397

Totally Board
Shop 3 , Pacific Tce
Princess Hwy, Ulladulla
2539
4454 0694

Tripple Bull
57 Elouera Rd
Cronulla 2230
9544 0354

Wave Wear
1/15 Livingstone St
South West Rocks 2431
6566 5177

Wicks
1103 Pittwater Rd
Collaroy 2097
9971 0760

X-Sight Surf Co
33 Wharf St
Forster 2428
6554 7811

Ben Boyd National Park. Pic Mark Newsham.

N.S.W.

Sit back, relax and enjoy the ride. Matt Fisher doing exactly that at Eaglehawk Neck. Pic Sean Davey.

TASMANIA

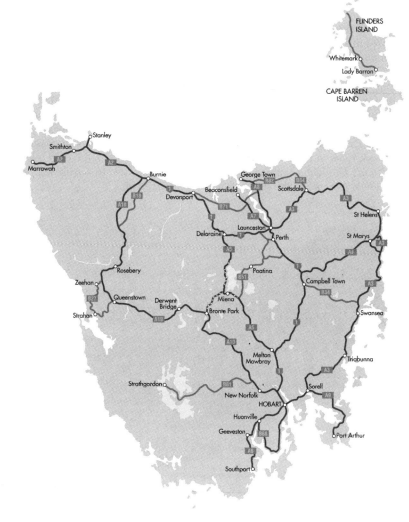

Tasmania

Lost In space

There are many ways to experience this historic land. An old EH Holden, four mates, $150 and a month to burn, is my favourite way. Most mainlanders consider the Island navigable in a day or two. Believing that the lack of nightlife and prohibitive water temperature is enough reason for a short stay. The true Taswegian would never disagree with this, for they treasure their secret Isle. Opting for a life of little change, without the services of the greedy developers.

Besides the major cities of Hobart and Launceston, the rest of the state has remained relatively untouched for the past twenty five years. It exudes tradition, with statues and historic buildings reminiscent of times past. Then there are the waves. In the South East, Port Arthur is surrounded by a diverse landscape and coastline. From Eaglehawk Neck in the east, to Remarkable Caves in the south there are plenty of adventures to be had. Climbing through a cave, at low tide, to a secluded beach on the other side is just one of the many obstacles that face you.

It almost looks warm and inviting, almost. Pic Stroh.

A classic image of Matt Fisher at Eaglehawk Neck

Essentially Tassie has four different coastlines, north, south, east and west, giving surfers an amazing choice. Some hard core locals have been known to surf the southern point breaks, then drive three hours to the points on the east. Riding the same swell, offshore again, under the setting sun.

Most of the state's surfers ride the waves of the south east, as the rugged coastline of the south west is inaccessible to even the keenest adventurers. Only twenty five minutes from the capital there is surf, which most people wouldn't know. The north coast is usually passed by wave seekers, yet it can be fun, but eventually, as on the mainland, you will be drawn west. The coast road, twists and bends around the windswept stretch. Past windswell points and frothy brown tubes, further and further, eventually turning to dust. The dust is just the beginning to your adventure on the west coast. A joyous wave haven in the summer months, transformed in winter to a wet, windy and hard place to be.

If the isolation is too much, Hobart may have your answer. Plenty of nightclubs and general street life. Colourful markets and friendly locals ease the desolate location of this state. Winter though, is not the best time to visit, with summer months the go, unless you are in search of that perfect wave.

Tasmania is the perfect place for the hardy adventures, with plenty of discoveries to be made in a compact area. What it lacks in size, is easily compensated for its hidden treasures.

TAS

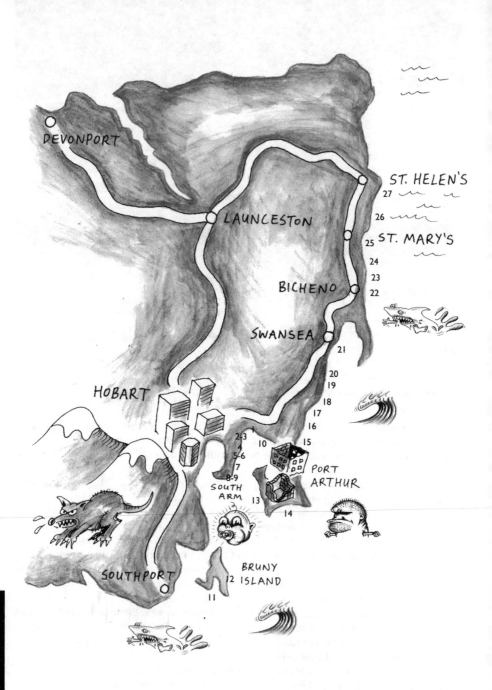

DEVONPORT

ST. HELEN'S
27
26
25 ST. MARY'S
24
23
22

LAUNCESTON

BICHENO

SWANSEA
21
20
19
18
17
16

HOBART

2,3
4
5-6
7
8-9
SOUTH
ARM
10
13
14
15
PORT
ARTHUR

SOUTHPORT
11
12 BRUNY
ISLAND

The Adventure
When you embark upon a trip with waves on the agenda there are no barriers too great.

Tassie surfing legend, Tim Upston at the Wedge.

The South Coast & The East Coast

South
This stretch is as extreme as it is safe. There are areas that are the most populated by surfers to bare isolation and raw ocean power. Cray fisherman are a few of the hardy souls who have ventured to the heart of this goldmine. Stories are scarce, which should give a clue. Its position in the extreme southern latitudes gives rise to extreme weather conditions, but when it's right........

East
The east cost is protected from the full force of the seething ocean. The south east quarter lays dormant for two thirds of the year. When the swells do finally arrive though, they wrap around long grassy points and funnel across the rocks onto empty white beaches. The northern section is often more consistent, rarely gets over four foot but this is often four foot of perfection. There is a dedicated surfing community with a strong boardriders club. It is obvious why so many choose this place to immerse themselves in the waves. With crystal clear waters and few crowds, it is a magic place to be.

TAS

1.
Break Name: Seven Mile Point
Wave Description: Long righthand point, over sand, that can break up to 300 metres.
Best Conditions: Huge SW-S swell, SW-W wind, low-mid tide.
Getting There: Turn left at Lauderdale Primary School and follow the signs.
Dangers: Can get really shallow when its small. Watch your noggin.
Rumours: Some rippable tubes and long walls.
Something Else? It's called seven mile because of the beach, not the point.

2.
Break Name: May's Point
Wave Description: A reeling rock and sand point break, can break up to 200 metres.
Best Conditions: Massive SW swell, SW-W wind, low tide.
Getting There: First left turn past Lauderdale tip.
Dangers: The rocks on the way out and scary locals.
Rumours: If it's below zero degrees and snowing, get there!
Something Else? Ten second barrels, sound good?

3.
Break Name: Lauderdale Point
Wave Description: Long righthand point break, over sand and rock.
Best Conditions: Huge SW-S swell, SW-W wind, all tides.
Getting There: Main break at the namesake.
Dangers: Exposed rocks on low tide.
Rumours: Usually smallest of the surrounding points.
Something Else? Great longboarding wave.

4.
Break Name: Cremorne Point
Wave Description: Fun righthand point break, over sand and rock.

Best Conditions: SW swell, SW-W wind, low tide.
Getting There: Take the Cremorne turnoff off the South Arm Rd.
Dangers: The paddle out over the rivermouth is a little sketchy.
Rumours: Mostly overrun by grommies.
Something Else? Great windsurfing in the lagoon.

5.
Break Name: North Clifton
Wave Description: Punchy right and lefts over sand, with deep gutters for good rip action.
Best Conditions: SW-SE swell, NE-NW wind, mid-high tide.
Getting There: Turn left at the beginning of the residential area.
Dangers: Watch out for 'the twisted ankle in mutton bird holes' scenario. Not good, especially when you almost made it to the surf.
Rumours: Great long rides if the swell is right.
Something Else? The beach is worth a look anyhow, especially for the fishermen amongst us. Try the north end for a bit of dinner.

6.
Break Name: South Clifton
Wave Description: A fairly mellow beachie. On a medium swell, it gets a righthand peak. It's known as the pit.
Best Conditions: 2-3.5m SW-SE swell, NE-W wind, mid-high tide.
Getting There: Turn left off South Arm Road onto the Clifton Beach turnoff.
Dangers: Nup!
Rumours: Good beginners' waves.
Something Else? It's the centre of all the 'action' in summer!

7.
Break Name: Goats
Wave Description: Shifting beach breaks, surrounded by deep channels.
Best Conditions: 1-3m SW swell, NW-NE wind, high tide.

Getting There: Turn left before Rebounds.

Dangers: Thieves. Leave nothing in your car!

Rumours: Check after a big swell.

Something Else? If you walk east to the end of the beach, then over the hill, you will be greeted with a tranquil little bay with a deceivingly punchy left.

8.
Break Name: Rebounds

Wave Description: Fun righthand peak, created from the steep rock face nearby.

Best Conditions: SW swell, NE-NW wind, mid-low tide.

Getting There: Take a left turn just before Betsey Island lookout (the Wedge).

Dangers: Gnarly exposed rock face, next to the takeoff, and some suspect brown debris in the water.

Rumours: It takes some practice to line up the rebound peak, but when you get it....oooohhhhh baby! Can be ridden up to 2 metres. The beachie is also pretty good.

Something Else? Good fishing off the point. For the air freaks, the wave can get a sick ramp.

9.
Break Name: The Wedge

Wave Description: Super sucky right and left peaks, which are formed by swells being split around Betsey Island and then reforming. Pretty crazy stuff.

Best Conditions: Huge SW-SE swell, NE-NW wind, any tide.

Getting There: Go to the Betsey Island lookout, take the track on the right side. If it's on, you won't be alone.

Dangers: Shallow sand banks.

Rumours: It's no rumour that the sand dunes are shrinking due to sand mining.

Something Else? From the lookout you can see a small group of rocks known as 'Black Jack Rocks', which is where a very expensive catamaran was grounded for a month back in '96.

10.
Break Name: Park Beach

Wave Description: A righthand peak, bouncing off a rock face.

Best Conditions: SW swell, W-NE wind, mid-high tide.

Getting There: Forty minutes east of Hobart, take a righthand turn at Dodges Ferry.

Dangers: uhh uhh.

Rumours: Well it all started a long long time ago in a galaxy far f....

Something Else? The Carlton River mouth can get long rides on a big swell.

11.
Break Name: Cloudy Bay / Bruny Island

Wave Description: Beautiful left and right beachies, which can be magic at times.

Best Conditions: SE-SW swell, W-NW wind, all tides.

Getting There: To get to the Island you need to take the ferry from Kettering. If you have a car it will cost $18 on weekdays, and $23 on weekends. You can hop on the mail bus at 9:30am which takes you to most settlements.

Dangers: Not too many to worry about.

Rumours: This place can get some of the best breaks in Tassie.

Something Else? To the west there is a break called 'Lagoons', which produces excellent waves with the right banks. Don't count on this place for waves though.

12.
Break Name: Adventure Bay / Bruny Island

Wave Description: Several breaks, the best being a lefthand point break at the southern end. This can be a scary wave, with a crazy takeoff, then a flatter end section.

Best Conditions: SE-NE swell, most wind, mid tide.

Getting There: Follow the instructions for Cloudy Bay.

Dangers: The bare rock takeoff, and the

TAS

thick kelp can provide some
entertainment.
Rumours: Plenty of other breaks in the
area worth checking out.
Something Else? A great place to visit
regardless of the swell.

13.
Break Name: Roaring Beach / Nubeena
Wave Description: Peaky beach breaks,
with a sucky rebound wave at the south
end.
Best Conditions: S swell, NW-E wind,
mid-high tide.
Getting There: About an hour from
Hobart, on the Tasman Peninsula.
Dangers: Some pretty sketchy tracks
around, and our favourite friend, the
shark, is back,!
Rumours: There can be some solid
waves here, and excellent quality.
Something Else? Take your sandboards
along, as there are some killer dunes.

14.
Break Name: Remarkable Caves
Wave Description: Small sandy bay with
punchy peaks.
Best Conditions: 1-2m S-SW swell, NE-
NW wind, low tide.
Getting There: About a five minute drive
south of Port Arthur, lookout for the sign
to the caves.
Dangers: Getting through the cave at
high tide!
Rumours: Get there at low tide,
otherwise you may be thwarted in your
attempts to get waves.
Something Else? Take the walking track
as there are some cool things to see.

15.
Break Name: Eaglehawk Neck
Wave Description: A super hollow,
lefthand reef break.
Best Conditions: 2-5m N-NE swell, NW-
W wind, any tide, although best on low.
Getting There: Look for the name sake
on the map, on the Tasman Peninsula.
Dangers: The takeoff can be pretty

serious, and then there are the sharks!
Rumours: Two surfers who forgot to
heed the advice of the incoming tide,
were trapped on the reef for four hours.
As if that wasn't bad enough, the boys
said they were circled by a shark,
reportedly in the 20 foot range. Because
of the shallow reef they were spared.
Something Else? Try checking out the
north end of the beach where you'll find
a lefthand reef. There are the Blowholes
and Devil's Kitchen to see as well.

16.
Break Name: Shelly Point
Wave Description: A lefthand point
break over reef, the beachie is often
better though. Good rights and lefts.
Best Conditions: 2-3m NE-N swell (any
other for the beachie), W wind, most
tides.
Getting There: Just south of Orford.
Dangers: Nup, very user friendly.
Rumours: Can hold a very big swell.
Something Else? Check the northern
end, called Freshwater, or some of the
reefs dotted in front of the point, for real
joy.

17.
Break Name: Dark Hollow
Wave Description: A combination of
beach breaks over rock and sand.
Best Conditions: 3-3m NE-SE swell, N-W
wind, most tides.
Getting There: About 15 minutes north
of Shelly Point.
Dangers: Shallow sand banks.
Rumours: There are fun waves at the
northern side of the point, and sometimes
there is a righthand point break when
there is a large swell.
Something Else? Great diving and
fishing.

18.
Break Name: Orford Point
Wave Description: Righthand reef break,
with a left at the river mouth.
Best Conditions: 4-8m SE swell, NW-SW

wind, low tide.
Getting There: Turn right just before the Orford bridge.
Dangers: Watch out for the ledgy take off when the swell gets big.
Rumours: Head to the river mouth if it's big.
Something Else? Try getting over to Maria Island for a bit of wilderness. You can catch a ferry there, (03) 6257 1420. It is worth visiting to see some cool old buildings and hopefully to score waves.

19.
Break Name: Little Swanport
Wave Description: Long lefthand rivermouth, which gets extremely fast and hollow.
Best Conditions: 4-8m SE-NE swell, W wind, low tide.
Getting There: Look out for the sign, about 30 minutes north of Orford.
Dangers: The long paddle takes your strength, and you must always be careful at rivermouths for those Noahs.
Rumours: The surrounding beaches also get very good. Worth a check.
Something Else? Take all available tracks off the road.

20.
Break Name: Buxton Point
Wave Description: Righthand point and reef break.
Best Conditions: 4-8m SE swell, W wind, low tide.
Getting There: Just before Spiky Bridge.
Dangers: Don't get too far inside, as it will thrash you.
Rumours: Umm...Errrr..., well none actually.
Something Else? There is nothing else for this break.

21.
Break Name: Swansea Point (Rubbish Tip)
Wave Description: Righthand point over sand and rock.
Best Conditions: 4-8m SE swell, W wind, low tide.
Getting There: Turn right just before the town centre.
Dangers: Exposed rocks on the takeoff zone.
Rumours: It was once a rubbish tip.
Something Else? This area can get perfect with the right swells.

People do surf in Tassie, east coast. Pic Stroh.

22.
Break Name: Bicheno Beach (Diamond Island)
Wave Description: Weak beach break, with point break off the Island when it gets bigger.
Best Conditions: 2-4m SE swell, W wind, mid tide.
Getting There: Turn right, just out of town.
Dangers: Pretty safe.
Rumours: There are plenty of wave options in the area.
Something Else? If you keep your eyes open you are bound to see more breaks. There is also some great diving around.

23.
Break Name: Little Beach
Wave Description: Punchy beach breaks, with a more consistent left at the north end.
Best Conditions: .5-2.5m NE-SE swell, W wind, mid tide.
Getting There: Thirty minutes north of Bicheno, look out for the turn off.
Dangers: Watch out for the rocks on the end section.
Rumours: Arhhh....Nup.
Something Else? Try the south end of the beach for another reef option, which can have some very intense pits, but watch the bull kelp.

24.
Break Name: Four Mile Point and Beach
Wave Description: A righthand bombie, that works like a point break on reef out the back. The inside banks are formed by a small creek flowing alongside the point, creating magical lefts. The beach is full of waves.
Best Conditions: 2-4m NE swell, W winds, low tide.
Getting There: About 15 minutes north of Little Beach. Look out for the Four Mile sign.
Dangers: The takeoff can be a freefall when it gets bigger.
Rumours: It can get very hollow on the big swells.

Something Else? Halfway along the wave, there is a ledge section that you need to navigate. Try the floater.

25.
Break Name: Cattle Grid
Wave Description: The north end of Four Mile Beach is a lefthand reef point, which holds 2 metres and long rides.
Best Conditions: 2-3.5m NE swell, W wind, mid-low tide.
Getting There: Follow the directions for the previous break.
Dangers: Dodging rocks on the inside can be a little hairy.
Rumours: The name of the break, gives a clear indication to it's whereabouts.
Something Else? Nope.

26.
Break Name: Scamander River Mouth
Wave Description: Punchy left and rights formed by the river, can have excellent banks.
Best Conditions: 2-3m NE-SE swell, W wind, low tide.
Getting There: Directly infront of the Scamander Hotel.
Dangers: Only the standard precautions for a river mouth.
Rumours: Picks up any available swell on the coast.
Something Else? The surf-fishing can be excellent.

27.
Break Name: St Helens Point
Wave Description: Long righthand point break, which can get very hollow.
Best Conditions: NE-SE swell, NW-SW wind, mid tide.
Getting There: Follow the sign from town.
Dangers: Can hold solid swell, which can be brutal at times.
Rumours: There are a heap of breaks in the area, including; Binalong Bay, Perrins Beach and Grants Lagoon which can also turn on waves.
Something Else? Picks up any swell on the coast.

GENERAL INFORMATION

HOBART

Where To Stay:
YHA, Adelphi Court. Ph (03) 6228 4829. There is a variety of accommodation here, with an adjoining guesthouse. Beds from $13. Not quite in the city, about two and half kilometres away.
Central City Backpackers. Ph (03) 6224 2404. Beds from $14. It also has a bar, and a great vibe to it.
Sandy Bay Caravan Park. (03) 6225 1264. Has sights for $12 per double. Very close to the city.

Where To Eat:
The Cornish Mount Tavern, cnr of Barrack and Liverpool St's, serves counter meals for under $5.
Try down in Salamanca Place, where there is a huge variety of eateries.
Try north Hobart for some Asian flavours and a few fancier restaurants.

Where To Party:
Try the Mayfair in Sandy Bay, for a funky pub, that exudes a good vibe. There are several other good pubs in that area as well.

The New Sydney Hotel is an Irish pub and is therefore a frequented venue. Pick up a copy of the 'Mercury' newspaper on Fridays and get the gig guide, which has all the details.

Flat Day Fun:
Salamanca Place, has great markets on Saturday mornings, it also has some great buildings, which hark back to the early 1800's. The Cascade Brewery is definitely a worthwhile visit. Ph (03) 6224 1144, you need to phone first to book a tour, which costs $7.
The Snake Pit is Hobart's skate bowl. It's in north Hobart, and features a 100 metre, grindable half pipe.

BRUNY ISLAND

Where To Stay:
Adventure Bay Caravan Park. Ph (03) 6293 1270. Camp sites for $10.
Lumeah Hostel. Ph (03) 6293 1265. Beds from $13.
You can also camp for free at Jetty Beach and Cloudy Bay.

Where To Eat:
You really need to take your own food, but there are several stores on the Island. The Caravan Park will also organise food

The 360° gone terribly wrong.

if you pre-warn them.
Where To Party:
You came to surf not party! It's pretty much guitars under moonlight here.
Flat Day Fun:
A worth while visit even if the swell isn't running.

BICHENO

Where To Stay:
YHA Bicheno. Ph (03) 6375 1293. Beds from $13, in a great location.
The Bicheno Caravan Park. Ph (03) 6375 1280. $7 per site.
The Silver Sands Resort. Ph (03) 6375 1266. Beds starting from $30.
Where To Eat:
Longboat Tavern for counter meals.
The Silver Sands Resort for the seafood dish.
Rose's Coffee Lounge for your other requirements.
Where To Party:
Basically any pub you see that is open after six.
Flat Day Fun:
There ain't nothing to do other than cruise on the beach, perhaps a spot of fishing or snorkelling.

ST HELENS

Where To Stay:
St Helens Caravan Park. Ph (03) 6376 1290. Camp sites from $12, and on-site vans $30.
St Helens Youth Hostel. Ph (03) 6376 1661. Great location, beds from $12 per night.
Where To Eat:
Try the Bakery or Trimboli's Pizza for the evening meal.
Where To Party:
Ha Ha Ha Ha, ooohhh yeah, that's a good one. Er, not really.
Flat Day Fun:
Take a drive up the Elephant Pass to town.

SECTION INFORMATION

South Coast

Local Shaper
Linden/Stranger - Nick Stranger (Rokeby). Ph (03) 6247 7165. Call in on your way to South Arm.
Best Months
Winter cranks! You'll need your 5mm, hood, booties and gloves. Try December to March for a less intense experience, but still good waves.
Quick Tips
There is so much to see that you need at least a week. You must get to Bruny Island as well.
Getting There
It will cost you about $226 to fly, one way from Melbourne, but look for the deals, as you can get return flights for the same price. Try Rent-a-Bug on (03) 6231 0300 for the best rates.
The local bus service is pretty good. Ph (03) 13 22 01. If you need to get around the state, give YHA a call on (03) 6234 9617. You may be able to tee a lift up or organise buses to get to the breaks.

East Coast

Local Shaper
Nup.
Best Months
The winter months produce bigger swells. Look for the big south east swell that will hit the points south of Swansea.
Quick Tips
You really need big swell for this region, but when it's on, it can produce some of the best waves on the Island.
Getting There
It is about a two hour drive to Bicheno from Hobart. Alternatively Tasmanian Wilderness Travel/Tigerline on 1300 300 520 or (03) 6334 4442 or Redline Coaches 1300 360 000 have services along the coast. Try Hobart Coaches on 1800 030 620.

Mays Point

Dinner

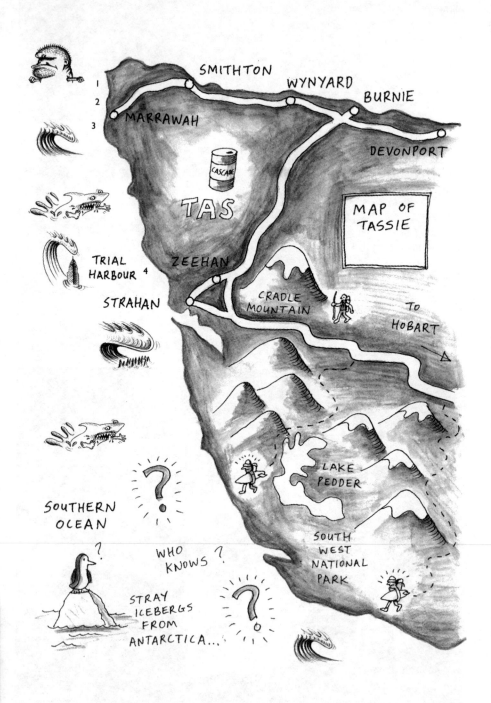

SMITHTON

WYNYARD

BURNIE

MARRAWAH

DEVONPORT

CASCADE

TAS

MAP OF
TASSIE

TRIAL
HARBOUR 4

ZEEHAN

CRADLE
MOUNTAIN

TO
HOBART

STRAHAN

1
2
3

SOUTHERN
OCEAN

LAKE
PEDDER

SOUTH
WEST
NATIONAL
PARK

WHO
KNOWS ?

STRAY
ICEBERGS
FROM
ANTARCTICA...

The North West
Hollow beasts that were only ridden by the lucky or insane.

The north west on a small but perfect day. Pic Glen Saltmarsh.

The West & North Coast

West

This coast is the true wilderness of the Island. It is wild, uninhabited, and extremely fragile with the raw grunt of the southern ocean at the doorstep. There is so much wilderness here, most inaccessible by car or foot. The waves can look magical, but be warned. The sheer power will ingloriously strip you of any pride, or if your lucky, reward you handsomely. The north western tip is the Mecca for soul surfers. There is no hype here, just empty lines and power personified on a rugged coastline.

North

This stretch of coast is very inconsistent when it comes to swell. Most breaks work on windswell and consequently don't provide many options. Of course, on the right day, there are fun waves to be had. Devonport River Mouth can have a great lefthand break when north-west to north-east winds blow swell down from Bass Strait. It is best surfed in north to north-west winds. The best time for this coast is between Spring and Summer. You really just have to be lucky. Always good to keep your eyes open when your heading to the west coast. Check out Rocky Cape National Park on your way west.

1.
Break Name: Mt Cameron
Wave Description: Beach and reef breaks that have an eerie feel, being overlooked by the daunting Mt Cameron.
Best Conditions: 3-4m W swell , E wind, high tide.
Getting There: Drive north of the shop at Marrawah and you will see the mountain, Just follow the dirt track.
Dangers: The rips can get furious when the swell kicks in.
Rumours: Take a look on the other side, if there isn't much swell.
Something Else? Mt Cameron is a historic Aboriginal site. Also the state's surfing titles are held here every year over Easter.

2.
Break Name: Greens Beach (Point)
Wave Description: A lefthand point break over sand and rock. A good beginners' or Mal wave. There are beach breaks when it's smaller.
Best Conditions: 3-8m W swell, E wind, low tide.
Getting There: Follow the Greens Beach turnoff, just south of the Marrawah pub.
Dangers: A pretty mellow place.
Rumours: It does get very good on occasion.
Something Else? Between the lighthouse and Green's, lies a Netly place!

3.
Break Name: Lighthouse
Wave Description: A combination of right and left sand breaks, with the left being the best. There is another bay nearby which holds bigger swells.
Best Conditions: 2-6m W-SW swell, E wind, any tide.
Getting There: Follow the road south of Marrawah. Take the first right when you hit gravel and follow your nose.
Dangers: Physco drivers on the gravel roads, and getting stuck in the kelp on a big day.
Rumours: 4WD's are the go for this area,

as there are many breaks south that are accessible only by rugged vehicles.
Something Else? There are some bombies in front of the point that are pure evil, only for the best.

4.
Break Name: Trial Harbour.
Wave Description: A lefthand rock/kelp point, flanked by a deep bay with a huge right hand bombie on the other side
Best Conditions: SW-W swell, E wind, any tide for right and high for left.
Getting There: Head towards Zeehan on the west coast, which is roughly five hours west of Hobart. Once at Zeehan, take the turn for Remine.
Dangers: This place is one of the best big wave spots on the coast, therefore there are many dangers. Not the least which is the takeoff, and the Bull kelp.
Rumours: This IS the premier big wave spot.
Something Else? Take the track to Granville Harbour from Zeehan, where you will find plenty more waves.

The South West Corner
There are obviously many breaks that are world class in this area but access is near impossible. I say near!

Unnamed location in South West Tassie

GENERAL INFORMATION

Check out the Stanly Nut, it's very bizarre, similar to the mountain in Close Encounters.

ZEEHAN

Where To Stay:
Treasure Island West Coast Caravan Park. Ph (03) 6471 6633. Sites from $12, on-site vans for $35.
Hotel Cecil. Ph (03) 6471 6221. Beds from $40.
Where To Eat:
The Pub.
There isn't too much more information on this small town. Take your tents and food.

MARRAWAH

There really is only one pub and a shop. The counter meals are quite good. There are some beautiful places to camp, with grassy areas to comfort the weary bones. Ask at the shop about shacks near the lighthouse. The only other accommodation is in nearby Arthur River. The holiday units there are quite nice. Ph (03) 6457 1288.
The closest Youth Hostels are at Wynard, Ph (03) 6442 2013 or at Stanley, Ph (03) 6458 1266.
Flat Day Fun:

SECTION INFORMATION

Local Shaper
Milch Surfboards.
Best Months
December through to May is the best time for offshores. As this side rarely gets under four foot, all that is needed is an easterly, and it is very likely to be going off. Be sure to hit it early as often the wind becomes galeforce in the afternoons.
Quick Tips
This coastline is best explored in a 4wd with all your camping gear. Not only will it be suitable for the coast, but the south west wilderness is worth visiting in its own right. Is one of the few true expanses of wilderness's left in the world.
Getting There
The ferry from Melbourne to Devonport is the closest point from the mainland. If you want to take your car it will cost you between $250 and $350 bucks, worthwhile as you will have to rent one otherwise. If you need to rent try Rent-a-Bug on (03) 6427 9034. The Redline and Tasmanian Wilderness Travel coaches will get you most places.

Nowhere is immune to the dreaded drop in, even the NW of Tassie. Pic Glen Saltmarsh.

TAS

311

Roving Reflections

I have known Nick Thomson for years now, we share the same bent perspective on life. He was a perfect roadtripping partner on a long and sometimes tedious, but mosty amazing, adventure. His comic relief is legendary as well as possesing a deep understanding of life. The following prose and sometimes meanderings are from his experiences while on the road.

The Surfer.

It is now that I see him looking back. Enveloped in his true home and comfortable with the elements that reside there. Floating on his back. Gaze skywards. Internal silence as osmotic effect continues to ensure flotation. Ready now for some wave assisted transport. Seeking take off point for maximum height. Briefly disappears, aligning body for submerged propulsion. Breaks through the huge face of the wave. His eyes now zoned on the trim line. Body and soul in perpetual motion. At one with the wave yet blown away by its force.

Walking up the beach now looking back at his home. Dreaming. Everything makes sense and the tame look returns. Hiding the surfers' addiction. The sea providing him with the environment he needs. A place where the spiritual meets the physical. With the sun setting, he heads back from whence he had come. He will be back. He needs to be back. He is a surfer.

Confronting Communal Living

Whilst trekking across the coastline in the pursuit of elusive tubes, many a weary surfer will find lodgings at the various Hostels around the country.

There is nothing better than pulling into the Hostel, generally located only an amble away from the local watering holes, to be greeted by the friendly hosts of Swedish descent, directed to the hot showers and then tucked in for more liquid dreams. However, one must remember that your private surf shack is shared by many fellow travellers, who often share differences in lifestyle and opinion. To make your stay as refreshing and homely as it should be, there are definitive procedures to follow.

On entry and agreement of lodging terms, immediately unload your surfboards and baggage; stroll straight through the communal family room, paying particular attention to the well flamed fire and its often attractive pilgrims. This first procedure shows everyone around you that you are an organised fellow or female who is more than open to a hot chocolate and massage by the fire after braving the elements in dangerous and often unchartered territory.

Always press for a private dormitory, play on your susceptibility to psychotic fits to secure this arrangement. Make your bed as deluxe as possible by doubling up on mattresses, doonas and pillows. Once you are happy that you are indeed the king of your own domain, venture out to the social room. Steer away from travellers who tell life histories. In order not to appear rude (because politeness at all times is your trademark). Simply remind your inquisitive friend that, as much as you have enjoyed chatting, you and your friends have to go and find some barrel relief and must leave him to contemplate why he/she isn't surfing. The managers are your best guides. Uphold the rules and principles at all times and a wealth of knowledge will come your way. With those that you don't want to relate to, practice your ancient Aboriginal dialect to keep everyone guessing.

The Complete Angler

" Teach a man to fish and he will eat for a lifetime. Teach a man to barter and he will eat crayfish out of season in South Australia."

The complete angler is one type of person always welcome on any coastal road trip. How lucky we are to have a myriad of seafood options, so accessible to any man who believes they are worthy of the challenge. The intelligence required to get inside the fish's head and extract it from its ocean bath is alone nigh impossible.

Obviously for one to win over thy great sea beasts, one must have a variety of rods, reels and lines. Also imperative is the oversized tackle box that will be too heavy to lift thereby reducing the chance of losing tour weapons to the wind.

If patience is a virtue then tying your fishing line will have you as virtuous as they come. It is now when the true fisherman will show his colours by calmly rigging his rod, impervious to the hooks stuck in his fingers and his friends snapping their rods before disappearing off to some remote point break.

Push on my friends, for dinner awaits. Saddle up your hooks with the bait you believe will entice your adversary onto your dinner plate. Berley floats provide a massive advantage by slowly releasing an exotic concoction of assorted fish frenzy material. The resulting effect is an excellent visual as the float bobs up and down under the weight of that four kilogram salmon you know is tempting fate.

Nicks reflective mood Pic The lovely Emma Moroney

It is essential to give yourself every opportunity of grabbing a meal by taking into account the rise and fall of the tide, a full moon and time of day. Also look for protected bays or currents of water depositing fish into feeding holes. Be weary of local fishermen, as (like surfers), this crew are renowned for guarding fishing spots.

If all goes to plan then you should have a seafood banquet in your bucket. The unenviable task of gutting or filleting the fish goes to that person with the blood-crazed look in their eye.

If you have neither the desire nor patience, brush up on your negotiating skills. Keep your eyes and ears open to any sources any spare fish and crays from local sea-dogs. If you have something the other party may enjoy, pull it out and smoke it, I mean broker it.

Commit yourself to attaining a fish diet and you will also attain zero cholesterol, zero fat, zero uses of wallet and a maximum sense of survival. Take what you need and release what you don't need and remember; never bleed and clean fish near swimmers and surfers because shark feeding frenzies can often cut short surfing safaris.

The Magic Bus

It was march 1969 when Russell Graham and Gary Mckenzie-Smith (cousin of the famed Terry Fitzgerald) embarked on what was to be an epic roadtrip that spanned over two years. The plans started, as most do, with idealistic visions shared with friends over many amber ales. For these Sydney lads were no different to the thousands of other wave hungry adventurers who have since packed their gear and headed north or south. It was an escape from the routine and a chance to experience whatever unfolded in their travels.

Russ had been working with Midget, learning the art of shaping. This, of course, was coupled with hours of glassing and polishing, but all part of the apprenticeship, which no doubt still lives with Russell to this day. These were times where Keith Paul, Bob Mctavish and others crowded the shaping bay revolutionising the shapes of the day. This was a perfect blooding for Russ and provided invaluable experience for the forthcoming trip. You see Russ had a vision to take custom shaping one step further.

With buddy Gary in tow, the pair purchased a classic Rio/Perkins school bus for $300 which was to be their home for the next two years. Months were spent decking the insides with bunks, propane stoves, sinks and a shaping bay. This was their vision: To take surfboard design where it belonged: at the beach. Russ bought the blanks, necessary material and equipment and they hit the road, with the concept of shaping boards to earn a crust as they went. They could set up practically anywhere, and did. From places like Mouruya, Merimbula and Eden to Victoria's rugged coastline. When they lacked power, they simply hand shaped. Like the boards they shaped at Baldy Point (near Ulladulla.) They shaped boards for stoked locals, who were a little bemused at suddenly having their own personal shapers on hand. These were the days when you could surf the classic point and beach breaks with hardly another soul in site. Russel remembers surfing places like Saltwater (Eden) which were virtually unheard of. They would shape boards under the label "Change" which kinda fitted what their philosophy was all about. During the two years they shaped about one hundred boards for the surfers of the day. The trip wasn't completely focussed on surfing though. Gary and Russell began abalone diving in Eden, when it was the home of the largest fleet of tuna and salmon boats. Even though this was a distraction, it was only temporary, as their passions still lay with the waves. Russel tells of a story of a Mctavish board that he sold to a buddy on a tuna clipper. He recounts how it was such a beautiful board, with majestic lines. The receipiant of this gift, a young 19 year old, unfortunately died of asphixiation as the diesel fumes of the clipper took hold in his sleep while at sea. As a testament to the love of his McTavish they were buried together in the ultimate partnership of man, board and a love of the sea.

Russell lived in Merimbula for a while and scored the elusive and extremely fickle Merimbula bar many times, again virtually alone. Those were the days. Eventually he made the trek to Victoria and the home that he was to make, at Torquay. He fell in love with the coastline and a woman. He met his wife who was sewing the first Rip Curl suits at the time and this sealed his fate. He started out with Rip Curl in 77', glassing all their boards, and became well known at the now famous local breaks of Bells and Winkipop. He continued to glass exclusively for Rip Curl in their factory until about five years ago when he bought his own factory. Still glassing for Rip Curl, but under license, he still finds time to get to Bali and surf his nuts off. Although Russell is nearing 50 he's got the spark of a true adventurer. Gary, unfortunately died about four years ago from cancer but lived the life of a true surfer too. These are the people who were roadtrippin' and surfing before many of us had graduated from the surf mat. Things do change over the years but the spirit of adventure is still alive and strong in Australia, and so it should be. With such an immense coastline and literally thousands of deserted breaks awaiting the brave, there is no excuse to rot our lives away in the confines of our ever increasingly poluted cities. That is not what Australia's heritage was or is. We were explorers from the outset, and Russell and Gary embibed that spirit.

What Happened to that Bus?

Russell and Gary sold the bus to a couple in Queensland where it can still be found, resting in the carpark next to Dreamworld. The guys discovered it about 15 years ago, and could hardly believe it was the old Rio. The bus still carries on the dynasty of roadtripping as it makes an annual trip along the coastline, reminding holiday makers how it used to be.

VICTORIA

NOTES